RACE FOR PROFIT

JUSTICE, POWER, AND POLITICS

COEDITORS | Heather Ann Thompson and Rhonda Y. Williams

EDITORIAL ADVISORY BOARD | Peniel E. Joseph, Daryl Maeda,
Barbara Ransby, Vicki L. Ruiz, and Marc Stein

The Justice, Power, and Politics series publishes new works in history
that explore the myriad struggles for justice, battles for power, and shifts
in politics that have shaped the United States over time. Through the lenses
of justice, power, and politics, the series seeks to broaden scholarly debates
about America's past as well as to inform public discussions about its future.

More information on the series, including a
complete list of books published, is available at
http://justicepowerandpolitics.com/.

RACE *for* PROFIT

HOW BANKS AND THE REAL ESTATE INDUSTRY
UNDERMINED BLACK HOMEOWNERSHIP

Keeanga-Yamahtta Taylor

THE UNIVERSITY OF NORTH CAROLINA PRESS
CHAPEL HILL

This book was published with the assistance of the
John Hope Franklin Fund of the University of North Carolina Press.

Designed by April Leidig
Set in Garamond by Copperline Book Services
Manufactured in the United States of America

The University of North Carolina Press has been a member
of the Green Press Initiative since 2003.

Cover photo: Child on steps of a North Philadelphia row house, August 1973
(photo by Dick Swanson; courtesy U.S. National Archives, photo no. 412-DA-10279)

Library of Congress Cataloging-in-Publication Data
Names: Taylor, Keeanga-Yamahtta, author.
Title: Race for profit : how banks and the real estate industry
undermined black homeownership / by Keeanga-Yamahtta Taylor.
Other titles: Justice, power, and politics.
Description: Chapel Hill : University of North Carolina Press, [2019] |
Series: Justice, power, and politics | Includes bibliographical references and index.
Identifiers: LCCN 2019014012| ISBN 9781469653662 (cloth : alk. paper) |
ISBN 9781469653679 (ebook)
Subjects: LCSH: Discrimination in housing—United States—History—20th
century. | Discrimination in mortgage loans—United States—History—20th century. |
Urban African Americans—Housing—History—20th century. | African American
women—Housing—History—20th century. | Real estate business—United States—
History—20th century. | United States—Race relations—Economic aspects.
Classification: LCC HD7288.76.U6 T89 2019 | DDC 363.5/1—dc23
LC record available at https://lccn.loc.gov/2019014012

For Lauren

CONTENTS

ILLUSTRATIONS

ABBREVIATIONS AND ACRONYMS IN THE TEXT

ADC	Aid to Dependent Children
AFDC	Aid to Families with Dependent Children
AIREA	American Institute of Real Estate Appraisers
FHA	Federal Housing Administration
FNMA	Federal National Mortgage Association
GNMA	Government National Mortgage Association
GS	General Schedule
HCDA	Housing and Community Development Act
HUD	Department of Housing and Urban Development
HUD Act	1968 Housing and Urban Development Act
HUD-FHA	denotes FHA as a subsidiary of HUD
JCUP	Joint Committee on Urban Problems
LIC	land installment contract
MBA	Mortgage Bankers Association
MetLife	Metropolitan Life Insurance Company
NAACP	National Association for the Advancement of Colored People
NAHB	National Association of Home Builders
NAREB	National Association of Real Estate Boards
UBMC	United Brokers Mortgage Company
UMBA	United Mortgage Bankers Association
VA	Veterans Administration
VHMCP	Voluntary Home Mortgage Credit Program

RACE FOR PROFIT

———————

Homeowner's Business

ON SEPTEMBER 18, 1970, Janice Johnson bought her first home in Philadelphia with a mortgage guaranteed by the Federal Housing Administration (FHA). In the now voluminous histories documenting the origins, policies, and practices of the FHA, Janice Johnson stands out as an atypical homebuyer.[1] She was a Black single mother on welfare and living about as far from a "racially homogenous" suburb as one could get. Johnson and her eight-year-old son made their home in a working-class Black neighborhood in Northeast Philadelphia in a decaying apartment in a building that had recently been condemned by city officials. Now facing eviction, Johnson needed to quickly find a new place to live, when her mother told her of an apartment for rent in the same neighborhood. Johnson called the landlord in anticipation, but her hopes were dashed when he told her that she could not rent the apartment because she was a welfare recipient.[2]

All was not lost, however; the landlord suggested that instead of renting, Janice Johnson could buy the house at 2043 West Stella Street. Under the terms of a new program created by the Department of Housing and Urban Development (HUD), low-income and poor people were now able to purchase homes with a small down payment and a low-interest, government-insured mortgage backed by the FHA. Backing from the FHA removed the risk from banks and other lenders who for many decades claimed to avoid lending in areas like Janice Johnson's neighborhood because of the assumption of financial risk in doing so. Lenders could now dispense money freely, as the FHA promised that the federal government would repay all delinquent loans.

Janice Johnson met with the landlord-turned-real-estate-agent, a man recalled as "Mr. Zade," to look at the house, and she liked it. Mr. Zade assured her that she was getting a "good house" because it had been "approved" by the FHA. Zade advised Johnson to contact her welfare caseworker because she would need to complete some paperwork to verify her eligibility for the program. Just weeks before Janice Johnson was to move into her new home, however, Zade called to inform her that the floor of the house had collapsed and she would no longer be able to buy it, but he had another house at 2013 West Stella that was "even better." Johnson was concerned, but by the end of August she was facing eviction proceedings from her condemned apartment. Johnson, with her young son to care for, was desperate. Within two weeks the transaction was complete. Zade had contacted a mortgage banking company called Security Mortgage Services, and the company approved Johnson for an FHA-backed loan in the amount of $5,800.

The widespread access to homeownership across the United States in the aftermath of World War II cemented it as a fundamental feature of the cultural conceptions of citizenship and belonging. This was especially true for African Americans. Indeed, the very first civil rights bill to be enacted in 1866 tethered the right to purchase property to freedom and citizenship: "All persons born in the United States without regard to any previous condition of slavery or involuntary servitude . . . shall have the same right, in every State and Territory in the United States, to make and enforce contracts, to sue, be parties, and give evidence, to inherit, purchase, lease, sell, hold, and convey real and personal property, as is enjoyed by white citizens."[3] This American particularity of property rights as an expression of citizenship was reinforced in the 1948 landmark *Shelley v. Kraemer* decision that affirmed, "Equality in the enjoyment of property rights was regarded . . . as an essential pre-condition to the realization of other basic civil rights and liberties."[4]

Despite the insistence on the rights of property ownership as integral to citizenship, African Americans faced numerous obstacles in their efforts to secure homeownership. But in the ascendant and optimistic rhetoric of the postwar period, Black citizens expected to finally be able to share in those rights "enjoyed by whites." Not only were these expectations shaped by the growing prominence of homeownership as symbolic of the good life in the United States, but they were amplified through the exhortations of U.S. presidents, including Harry S. Truman, who declared a "decent home"[5] as the "goal" of federal policy, and Dwight D. Eisenhower, who described "good housing" as a "major objective of national policy" and stated that it was "necessary for good citizenship and good health among our people."[6] Neither president was referencing homeownership in particular, but certainly by the 1950s, it had become the preferred means of shelter in both public tastes and public policy.

For Janice Johnson, though, homeownership was not the fulfillment of the American dream; it was the beginning of an American nightmare. Within days of moving into her new home, the sewer line broke, spewing wastewater all over the basement floor. The electricity for the house was sporadic and haphazard. There were holes and other irregularities in the foundation of the home. All of the windows in Johnson's new house were nailed shut and inoperable. The floorboards in her dining room were so rotten that she feared her dining room table would collapse through the floor. The compromised structure of the house was not the worst of it. On Halloween night, Johnson's son, Edward, woke up to find a rat in his bed. Janice saw rats throughout her house, including in the kitchen and bathroom. Apparently, the holes in the basement harbored nests of rats that regularly entered the house. She called Zade to complain about the condition of her new house. He sent workmen out on a couple of occasions, and they even patched the failing plaster in her dining room; but soon after, the real estate agent reminded her that the problems in her house were now her own. They were "homeowner's business."

Race for Profit: How Banks and the Real Estate Industry Undermined Black Homeownership examines the critical turn in U.S. housing policy when the FHA, housed within HUD, ended its long practice of redlining, instead turning to new policies that encouraged low-income African Americans to become homeowners in the 1970s. After years during which Black citizens' access to conventional means of financing the purchase of a home had been undermined, the social upheaval and urban rebellions of the 1960s finally forced the federal government to relent. The low-income homeownership programs, the first of their kind, utilized federal subsidies, long amortization periods, and mortgage insurance guarantees to entice the participation of the real estate industry while also making homeownership affordable and accessible to poor and working-class African Americans. These programs generated unprecedented real estate sales in Black urban communities across the country. But the transition from the *exclusionary* policies of HUD and the FHA to *inclusion* into the world of urban real estate sales was fraught with problems.

In *Race for Profit*, I argue that this unprecedented public-private partnership in the production of low-income housing tethered HUD and the FHA to real estate brokers, mortgage bankers, and homebuilders. These partnerships were troubled from their inception because of the real estate industry's long history of racial discrimination against and demonization of African Americans as unfit owners and detrimental to property values. Generous government financial outlays and the near-saturation of white homeownership helped the real estate industry overcome its reluctance to sell and lend to African Americans it believed presented a risk or threat to accruing value within the real estate market. The transformation in FHA policy did not immediately change the practices or the beliefs that motivated the practices within the real estate industry—or among agents working within the FHA. The shift did, however, facilitate the participation of broader networks of real estate operatives and lenders who circulated billions of new dollars throughout the urban housing market.

The declensional framing of "inner cities" and "urban crisis" in urban studies of the 1960s and 1970s belies the dynamic and innovative methods of financing generated to develop the urban housing market. The tendency to view the postriot city as trapped in the stasis of blight, flight, and the inevitability of decay over time misses how the late 1960s and the 1970s were defined by changing political, social, and economic dynamics, and how the inner city was at the nexus of these processes. New financial instruments, such as mortgage-backed securities, produced an intense demand for more homeowners and more money for home financing, while lax oversight and regulation incentivized unscrupulous and predatory targeting of urban communities. Far from being a static site of dilapidation and ruin, the urban core was becoming an attractive place of unparalleled opportunity, a new frontier of economic investment and extraction for the real estate and banking industries. The race for profit in the 1970s transformed decaying urban space into what one U.S. senator described as a "golden ghetto,"[7] where profits for banks and real estate brokers were never ending, while shattered credit and ruined neighborhoods were all that remained for African Americans who lived there.[8]

When historians have written about the big economic shifts that took place in the 1970s, they rarely consider these changes in the real estate market and how they disproportionately impacted African Americans. As interest rates rose sharply in the late 1960s and early 1970s, the slowed pace of housing starts in the conventional housing market made sales in the government-subsidized low-income housing market more attractive than they had ever been. Even while real estate brokers and mortgage lenders were discriminating against women with middle-class jobs and incomes, poor women on welfare, like Janice Johnson, who were also disproportionately heads of their households, were sought out as participants in the low-income homeownership program.⁹

The inclusion of thousands of poor Black women in these low-income homeownership programs subverted both racial and gender norms. Real estate and mortgage bankers valued these women, though, because of the *likelihood* they would fail to keep up their home payments and slip into foreclosure. Black women like Janice Johnson were desired customers *because* they were poor, desperate, and likely to fall behind on their payments. Unlike the programs of old, the HUD-FHA guarantee to pay lenders in full for the mortgage of any home in foreclosure transformed risk from a reason for exclusion into an incentive for inclusion. The struggles of poor Black women provide particular insight into the ways that overlapping patterns of racial and gender discrimination shaped the new inclusive housing market. As historian Rhonda Williams has noted, "Low-income black women['s] ... citizenship struggles draw attention to the issues shaping postwar urban residency as well as the character of the liberal state and U.S. democracy."¹⁰

I describe these and the other new terms on which the real estate industry conducted business within the urban housing market as "predatory inclusion." Predatory inclusion describes how African American homebuyers were granted access to conventional real estate practices and mortgage financing, but on more expensive and comparatively unequal terms. These terms were justified because of the disproportionate conditions of poverty and dilapidation in a scarred urban geography that had been produced by years of public and private institutional neglect. When redlining ended, these conditions of poverty and distress became excuses for granting entry into the conventional market on different and more expensive terms, in comparison with the terms offered to suburban residents. For example, urban-based residents could now use FHA-backed loans, but big depository banks continued to refuse to lend to prospective homeowners in the urban market, opting for higher interest-rate returns on bigger loans and more expensive housing in white suburbs. This relegated most African American urban buyers to the use of unregulated mortgage banks, often subsidiaries of the same depository institutions that refused to lend in Black communities, that were indiscriminate in the dissemination of loans because their profits were based on volume sales. Mortgage bank loans relied on costly origination fees and other costs for the particular services they offered. The differences in physical condition, geography, and location of predominately Black housing became the proxies for race where direct references to race were no longer permissible because of fair housing legislation. These differences, long existent in the urban market, both legitimized the different treatment of Black homeowners and continued to make them vulnerable to predatory real estate practices. Federal fair housing laws had been passed to uproot discrimination in the housing market and held out promises for the unobstructed participation of African Americans in buying and selling homes. But HUD's reluctance to enforce civil rights laws preserved the practice and patterns of segregation that had historically driven up the price of substandard properties in predominately Black enclaves. The failure of HUD to systematically root out the segregative impulses throughout the real estate industry meant that these exploitative practices prevailed even as federal redlining fell out of favor. Historian Nancy Kwak describes how the change in policy from federal redlining to inclusion shifted the priorities of civil rights advocates from "fair access to credit" to "access to fair credit."[11] The continuation of residential segregation after the fall of federal redlining and the passage of federal fair housing created the conditions for predatory inclusion.

Here, I argue that the discriminatory "best practices" of the real estate industry made it resistant to change in adhering to new fair housing legislation. The benignly named "public-private partnership" obscured the ways that the federal government became complicit with private sector practices that promoted residential segregation and racial discrimination. Selling dilapidated homes to poor women who could not afford the repairs, like Janice Johnson, reinforced the idea of unfit Black owners who posed a threat to the quality of a neighborhood. When the federal government guaranteed Johnson's mortgage, it became implicated in the shoddy business practices of private sector agents bent on profiting from the desperation of low-income urban residents. Racially informed real estate practices were not the actions of an industry impervious to change and old in its ways; instead, racial discrimination persisted in the new market because it was good business.

Tethering federal policy to the practices of the private real estate industry complicated the ability of federal agents to regulate the administration of the new homeownership programs. The paucity of oversight in a housing market deeply ingrained with the belief that the Black population needed to be contained or segregated to preserve property values for white homeowners, combined with unprecedented federal dollars and a mandate to produce more units of housing than ever in American history, was a recipe for nefarious business practices. The end of redlining and the introduction of conventional real estate practices into the Black urban market ended one set of predatory practices, like homes for sale on land installment contracts (LICs), without fully resolving the conditions that gave rise to those practices in the first place. The result was the continuation of older predatory practices in combination with the invention of wholly new means of economic exploitation of African Americans in the U.S. housing market. History weighed heavily on the then-contemporary moment. The past could not be so neatly erased from the new world that was created; instead, the past helped to shape how the new policies and practices were implemented.

The 1970s witnessed an enormous shift in how the federal government housed its poor and low-income population. As one writer described it, "A new policy paradigm defined by the free market had emerged to replace that of collective public provision of housing."[12] Moving from public housing to low-income homeownership was not an issue of whether government or the free market was best situated to respond to the ongoing crisis in affordable housing in the country. Instead, housing policy in the 1970s hinged on the *collaborative* relationship between public and private sectors. I argue that as a result of this relationship, the federal government was impaired in its ability to aggressively regulate an industry that had employed racial discrimination in its determined pursuit of insatiable profit as a business principle. Sociologist Christopher Bonastia, one of the few scholars to investigate the HUD-FHA housing crisis, has rightly drawn attention to the "unwieldly" bureaucratic inefficiencies of HUD along with the conflicting political agendas of those at its helm.[13] But this explanation alone does not account for the powerful influence of the real estate industry in shaping the policies and their execution in ways beneficial to the industry and not the public. The continuity of exploitation in the urban real estate market does not suggest that exclusion was preferable. Instead, it compels us to look more closely at the practices of the real estate market and not just inclusion in it. The suggestion that Black equality in the real estate market could be achieved by the formal end to housing discrimination failed to take into account the very ways that racial inequality was structured and embedded within the architecture of the system of buying and selling real estate in the United States. Thus, even when discriminatory policies were formally dismantled, the impulse toward economic exploitation and residential segregation ensued because of the ways that racial discrimination continued to add value to racially exclusive suburbs. The American housing market was an expression of the prevailing racial consciousness of the larger society in which it operated. As social scientist Dalton Conley put it, "White housing is worth more, precisely because it is not Black housing."[14] In general, racial discrimination remained good business for the real estate industry.

The concept of predatory inclusion also captures the failures of racial liberalism and its premise that inclusion into American democracy through the vehicles of citizenship, law, and free market capitalism could finally produce fairness and equality for its Black citizens.[15] African Americans were afforded formal access to those tools of American democracy, but their function and abilities had been *fundamentally* distorted by racism. The enduring obstacles faced by African Americans in pursuit of fair housing defy the narrative of the eventuality of progress over time in the United States. Racism in real estate has remained resilient and ingrained, demonstrating the limits of inclusion as discrimination, exploitation, and predation continued well after the legal hurdles to fair or open housing had been cleared.

The story of the HUD-FHA housing crisis of the 1970s is complex. In order for us to grasp its full impact, there is a set of issues that we must reckon with in the pages that follow. These include the formation of risk, the mechanics of the low-income homeownership program, the role of suburbs in urban housing policy, and the ways that the crisis that erupted within the federally backed low-income homeownership program shaped political discourse, including notions of "urban crisis" and "underclass," by the end of the 1970s.

RISKY BUSINESS

After several decades of refusing to guarantee the mortgages of African Americans, or those who lived in close proximity to them, the FHA charted a new path. With the passage of the 1968 Housing and Urban Development Act (HUD Act), new provisions were made to encourage low-income homeownership. After years of partisan jousting over the creation, placement, and management of public housing programs, President Lyndon Johnson turned to the market to solve the perennial "housing crisis" that had plagued American cities since at least World War II. The private market had largely ignored the regular refrain for more safe, sound, and affordable housing, but the advent of low-interest mortgage loans with the full backing of the federal government piqued the interest of the real estate industry. For decades, the FHA maintained that the deteriorating housing stock and "inharmonious" racial groups within American cities made them too risky for the risk-averse real estate and banking industries. The new legislation induced private sector involvement by removing said risk.

Creating a risk-free environment for business, though, presented new risks to potential low-income homeowners. Advocates proselytized the virtues of ownership, including the creation of stakeholders within otherwise distressed communities. They suggested that the efficiency and speed with which business could produce housing would finally end the perennial scarcity of good urban housing. Private property, then, not only could solve the housing crisis but was presented more broadly as a palliative to an "urban crisis" that had metastasized into annual riots and rebellions throughout the 1960s. The market was championed as a neutral space where capital or credit flattened or eradicated difference. The market was the great equalizer. The consumer experiences of African Americans, however, painted a much different picture.

From the inception of the housing market in the United States, its viability had been structured around a scaffolding of racial knowledge that presumed insight into the speculative elements of "good housing" and "good neighborhoods," which could then be actualized through ascending property values. Transmogrifying real estate into homes and then again into financially accruing assets depended on the alchemy of race, place, and the perceptions of the buying public—or "property values are where culture meets economics."[16] As Frederick M. Babcock, considered an originator of the field of real estate appraisal, wrote in his seminal *The Appraisal of Real Estate*, "It is obvious that there is no absolute iron-clad method of computing real estate values . . . because values are a social phenomenon dependent upon human behavior."[17] The intensely subjective process of determining the value of property or a neighborhood—the pseudoscience of real estate appraisal—was inherently informed by the presence or absence of African Americans.[18] The American Institute of Real Estate Appraisers (AIREA) said as much when its professionalization materials maintained that "the clash of nationalities with dissimilar cultures . . . contribute[s] to the destruction of value. When a new class of people of different race, color, nationality and culture moves into a neighborhood . . . old inhabitants think that the neighborhood is losing desirability."[19]

Segregating African Americans into deteriorating urban neighborhoods and then starving those communities of resources and other investments greatly limited their access to better-paying jobs and well-resourced public schools, while pushing them into substandard housing.[20] Poverty and segregation led to overcrowding in Black housing, thus hastening its deterioration. These conditions were then spun into evidence that African Americans were unfit as potential homeowners and deleterious to property values within the housing market. These were justifications for confining African Americans to Black-only neighborhoods where they could not "infect" the larger housing market. The scarred geography of these developing Black neighborhoods was the physical evidence invoked to legitimize keeping African Americans out of predominately white communities. As Babcock wrote, "There is one difference in people, namely, race, which can result in a very rapid decline. Usually such declines can be partially avoided by segregation and this device has always been in common usage in the South where white and negro [*sic*] populations have been separated."[21]

The racial logic permeating the real estate market was not an invention of the FHA, even if that agency was a willing recipient of the inheritance. Long before the formation of the FHA, real estate brokers had already established rules encouraging the physical isolation of African Americans from white neighborhoods. By 1924, the National Association of Real Estate Boards (NAREB) promised punishment and revocation of membership to any broker who disrupted patterns of racial homogeneity on a given block or neighborhood.[22] These ideas and practices were then codified into policies created by the FHA. Frederick Babcock, as one example, developed his theories of property appraisal during his time as a real estate agent in Chicago in the 1920s. Babcock went on to author the FHA's underwriting criteria that determined coverage within the federal mortgage insurance program. So while it is true, as Richard Rothstein has most recently argued, that the federal government played a critical role in expanding the logic and practices of residential segregation with the invention of its housing policies in the 1930s, government agents did not act in a vacuum, nor did they act alone.[23]

When antipodal objectives of public interest were melded with private enterprise in the American housing market, those policies were bent to satisfy the market demands of real estate. The political and financial influence of private sector actors was outsized compared with the influence of individual homeowners simply trying to secure their housing by obtaining a mortgage. The interests of real estate inevitably meant that the racial practices at the very heart of real estate and mortgage lending practices were then grafted onto public policy. If the real estate industry required segregation to preserve profitability, then what would prevent housing policy from reflecting that same priority?

It was not just the influence of private sector operatives within public agencies that shaped U.S. housing policies, but the public and private collaboration produced tension-filled housing policies strained between meeting a public need while also acting to preserve the economic interests of private enterprise. The tension was born in the conflict between *exchange value* and *use value*, or more intimately, the difference between real estate and a home.[24] If these values are not irreconcilable, they often operate at odds with each other. These contradictory objectives of real estate and home—one a commodity and the other intimating a place of belonging—also reinforced reactionary racial norms and deepened the perception of dual housing markets working at dual purposes. Midcentury narratives of normative whiteness embodied in conceptions of the suburban-based nuclear family shaped the perceptions of *home* as an expression of *use value* within white communities. Conversely, developing narratives concerning perceived domestic dysfunction within Black living spaces—whether nonnormative family structures or poverty or dilapidated living structures— cast Black dwellings as incapable of achieving the status of *home*, thus reducing them to their base *exchange value*. Where white housing was seen as an asset developed through inclusion and the accruable possibilities of its surrounding property, Black housing was marked by its distress and isolation, where value was extracted, not imbued. These racialized narratives of families, communities, and their built environments reinforced and naturalized the segregative practices among real estate brokers, mortgage bankers, and the white public.[25] Indeed, these perceptions of insurmountable difference steeped in the permanence of blood, race, and culture constituted the underwriting criteria that determined who was to be excluded and who should be included.

Racial real estate practices, then, represented the political economy generated out of residential segregation. The real estate industry wielded the magical ability to transform race into profit within the racially bifurcated housing market. The sustenance and spatial integrity of residential segregation, along with its apparent imperviousness to civil rights rules and regulations, stemmed from its profitability in white as well as African American communities—even as dramatically different outcomes were produced. In the strange mathematics of racial real estate, Black people paid more for the inferior condition of their housing. They referred to this costly differential as a "race tax." Real estate operatives confined each group to its own section of a single housing market to preserve the allure of exclusivity for whites, while satisfying the demand of housing for African Americans. This was evidence not of a dual housing market but of a single American housing market that tied race to risk, linking both to the rise and fall of property values and generating profits that grew into the sinew binding it all together. As Arnold Hirsch wrote, "The rise of 'second ghettos' in the postwar era and the suburban boom were . . . organically linked."[26] A "white housing market" would have actually been unintelligible without its Black counterpart; both relied on the other to become legible.

HOMEOWNERSHIP FOR THE POOR

By the end of the 1960s, the National Advisory Commission on Civil Disorders, known as the Kerner Commission, had left no doubt that substandard housing was a recurring factor in the annual bout of riots that roiled American cities. Identifying segregation at the root of raging Black communities, the commission's findings called for a historic change in American housing policy. In the spring and summer of 1968, after the release of the Kerner Commission's final report, federal fair housing was passed, and a landmark Supreme Court decision in *Jones v. Mayer* removed any doubt about the illegality of housing discrimination. Recalling the 1866 Civil Rights Act and the Thirteenth Amendment, the justices held that "when racial discrimination herds men into ghettos and makes their ability to buy property turn on the color of their skin . . . then it . . . is a relic of slavery."[27] The passage of the HUD Act in August 1968 buttressed the antidiscrimination edicts with a mandate to produce 10 million units of new and rehabilitated housing within a decade. Separately these legislations and the judicial decision responded to two significant issues that constrained Black housing opportunities: residential segregation and available housing. The HUD Act was intended to produce record amounts of housing where there had been historic shortages since the World War II era, and federal fair housing was to allow for housing choices beyond segregated ghettos. This program, however, was not considered to be typical of the largesse of the Johnson administration. Instead, the HUD Act represented a new direction in housing poor and low-income people.

For decades, federal officials relied on public housing to shelter poor and low-income people. But by the end of the 1960s, public housing had become politically untenable, with endless jousts over its maintenance, location, and inhabitants. The private real estate industry vacillated between charges of socialism and profligacy in its denunciations of public housing. It opposed a government program that it claimed competed with private enterprise in the housing market. A policy vacuum was created when it came to housing for the poor, which suffered from a mixture of government neglect and shrinking tenancy because of the conditions endured by residents and the constant pressure to exclude anyone other than the poorest tenants. The HUD Act changed this by creating the means for poor and low-income people to purchase their own homes.

With the turn to private property, federal officials were hoping for a cheaper program with smaller outlays and the social stability that, they proselytized, came with property ownership. As with any partnership, the private sector had its own expectations, including the infusion of subsidies and federal mortgage guarantees in a moment of incertitude within the housing market. Private sector actors welcomed the pioneering role of HUD and the FHA in forging a risk-free venture in the new urban housing market. There were other expectations as well.

Placing homeownership at the heart of the nation's low-income housing policies ceded outsized influence and control to the real estate industry over dwellings intended to serve a disproportionate number of African Americans. The implications of this policy shift were that the steep involvement of the real estate industry would make African Americans vulnerable to the practices of an industry whose wealth was largely generated through racial discrimination. The profitability of the real estate industry was contingent on "best practices" that actively encouraged racial segregation, and the public policies that grew from the partnership between property assessors, brokers, bankers, and federal policymakers reflected the logic of the housing market. Even when the policies were in response to prolonged social protest, as was the case in the 1960s, the outcomes still reflected terms that were favorable to private sector actors. Historically, African Americans had called on the federal government to intervene on their behalf in articulating both rights *to* and rights *from* when it came to developing a legal regime in response to unchecked racial discrimination within the private sector. What would it mean for the protection of African Americans from racial discrimination in the private sphere if the state ceded to private entities its responsibility to deliver goods and services, as the homeownership program did?

UNLOCKING THE SUBURBS

A key to Black housing inequality had been how residential segregation circumscribed space, inferred inferiority through spatial isolation, and incentivized substandard maintenance and care from property owners, while driving up the costs relative to the better housing options for white residents. Despite the simultaneity of fair housing legislation and favorable court decisions banning racial discrimination, they were not acted upon, as private sector agents continued to insist on isolating fair housing from the housing production mandate. In other words, while the real estate industry celebrated the passage of the HUD Act, it vociferously denounced "fair housing" as "forced integration." This attitude was certainly not representative of the private sector in its entirety. Homebuilders and mortgage lenders, looking to benefit financially from the housing mandate, became enthusiastic backers of expanding housing choices for African Americans into the suburbs while also capitalizing on the expansion of the urban housing market. But real estate brokers were the first line of encounter for African Americans who hoped to use the homeownership subsidy. And it was real estate brokers who were most adamant in their opposition to fair housing. While a source of vigorous scholarship in social sciences concerning what Gregory Squires, Kevin Fox Gotham, and others describe as "privatism" or "the underlying commitment by government to help the private sector grow and prosper," these conflicts of interest at the heart of this public-private partnership deserve more scrutiny in housing historiography in terms of their consequence for African American consumers and our understanding of the stubborn question of why fair housing has not worked.[28]

Improving the housing opportunities for low-income African Americans was contingent on transforming the practices of the real estate industry. Given the dueling objectives of different sectors within the real estate industry, federal regulators in HUD, newly empowered in this role by the Fair Housing Act (as the Civil Rights Act of 1968 came to be known), would have to take responsibility for implementing the new legislation in fair and equitable ways. By 1968, though, the federal and local governments had a poor record of enforcing the fair housing laws already on the books.

As early as 1960, dozens of fair housing ordinances in cities across the country had already been passed, but none had a perceptible impact on stopping housing discrimination. The 1962 executive order signed by President John F. Kennedy ordered a ban on racial discrimination in any new, federally subsidized housing. The order fulfilled a long-standing campaign promise to wipe out housing discrimination with the "stroke of a pen." Because the order was not retroactive, though, it was limited to a small percentage of the actual housing market. Even within this limited scope, the enforcement mechanisms of the executive order were ineffective, calling only for "public or private hearings for . . . compliance, conciliation and persuasion to cure violations by any person, firm, state or local agency."[29] The 1964 Civil Rights Act banned discrimination in *any* federally subsidized housing with an important exception: homes purchased with an FHA-backed loan. Omitting the FHA from the scrutiny of federal racial regulators exposed not only the suffocating influence of the real estate industry but also the servile reluctance of government officials to seriously confront racism in the housing market. The 1964 Civil Rights Act also included Title VI, allowing federal officials to withdraw federal funds as a form of punishment against municipalities or localities engaging in discrimination. It was another tool that inspired the illusion of progress against discrimination without deploying specific enforcement requirements that would encourage action.

But perhaps the most egregious example of the self-imposed impotence of the federal government regarding discrimination involved not housing but education. The response to the 1954 *Brown v. Board of Education* Supreme Court decision provided ample evidence of federal reluctance when it came to the state enforcing its own laws against discrimination. For years after the *Brown* decision, courts and local officials stood idly by while southern officials established all-white "segregation academies" in a blatant flouting of the Court decision. It was not until 1968 that the Supreme Court ruled in *Green v. County School Board of New Kent County* that states must dismantle segregation "root and branch." If the federal government lacked the will to confront and undo racism within the domain of the public sector, where its authority was overwhelming, what were the chances that it would aggressively confront racist practices in the private sphere of the politically influential and financially connected world of real estate and mortgage lending? The federal government was not suffering from lethargy or even malicious intent, but its delayed response reflected political considerations and deference to market sensibilities that disavowed government intervention in business matters.

Even as federal actors moved at a glacial pace in enforcing their own rules banning discrimination, the formal changes in legislation also indicated the acceptance of the right of African Americans to participate in the conventional housing market. The policy demands against racial discrimination, at least formally, broadened the scope of those who could now expect to participate in the evolving housing market. This opening was created through a combination of upward and downward pressures. From above, federal legislation, judicial decisions, and direct intervention from the executive branch formally excised the language of racial exclusion from the policies of the federal government. Within business, agents of private enterprise who also explored the possibilities of a new market while seeking to minimize their exposure to risk shared this perspective of reform. From below, Black protests targeted the different sectors of the real estate industry to pressure them into allowing Black participation. Activism and other forms of civic pressure from organized African Americans and others demanded inclusion in the "affluent society." The persistence of second-class citizenship evidenced by trenchant housing discrimination, among other badges and indices of inferiority, provoked protests, demonstrations, and eventually urban uprisings. As a result of migration by African Americans from rural areas into American cities, incomes rose and homeownership became a tangible possibility for an unprecedented number of Blacks. Prompted by protests led largely by African Americans, successive political actions produced greater numbers of legal protections against housing discrimination.

The urban turn in homeownership policies reflected the conflicting agendas of government officials and private actors in the housing market. New public policies encouraged homeownership, but there was lax enforcement for the fractious demand of *fair* housing. Indeed, NAREB denounced the Fair Housing Act, but the organization strongly backed the passage of the HUD Act, which came four months after Fair Housing. Real estate agents welcomed the economic opportunities presented by the far-reaching legislation, while still demanding that segregation be preserved as a prerogative of white homeowners. Even as fair housing and the production mandate were passed within months of each other, the legislations operated within different spheres.

The reluctance to leverage the new fair housing legislation against the excitement of the housing production mandate represented shifting political priorities. Even though both of these legislations were created in the twilight of the Johnson administration, they were policies that would ultimately be implemented and administered by the administration of President Richard M. Nixon. Nixon appointed former Michigan governor and noted racial liberal George Romney to be secretary of HUD. But Nixon had run on a campaign that stoked the racial resentments of his white suburban constituency that he cohered into a white "silent majority" on the promise of preserving the racial exclusivity of white suburban communities. The Nixon administration contorted the legislative demands for "fair housing" into charges of "forced integration," while deflecting criticism of the president's position by describing his actions as respecting the *choices* of whites and African Americans in selecting their neighborhoods and communities. Nixon appealed to some African Americans by championing Black capitalism and pledging to finance Black business ventures, which amounted to promises to "gild the ghetto" and not just confine African Americans to it. Nixon had a weak standing in African American communities, but as desegregation seemed less attainable or even desirable among African Americans, his promises amounted to financial incentives aimed at relegitimizing a murky politics of "separate but equal."[30]

PREDATORY INCLUSION

Since the exclusionary practices of the FHA had been such a focal point in explaining the distressed condition of Black communities, the logical solution, then, was *inclusion*. The logic flowed from the ways that the market had created middle-class status for white homeowners. Given the tumult at the center of urban life through the 1960s, the hope was that property ownership could tame the Black rebellion coursing through cities across the country. It was also hoped that opening homeownership possibilities for African Americans in cities would curtail their demands for entry into white suburban communities. In a classic formulation of postwar racial liberalism, exclusion from the normalizing institutions that governed life for white America was situated as the central problem for African Americans. Racial liberalism posited inclusion as the antidote to the crises created by exclusion.[31] The "American dilemma" was how to make the American dream accessible to African Americans as a step toward finally fulfilling the promise of the American creed or American exceptionalism. American exceptionalism was conflated with the free market, and access to both was promoted as the solution to the problems faced by African Americans. The inclusion of African Americans could unlock the market's true potential in creating social stability and middle-class status and facilitating the accumulation of personal wealth. It was what Janice Johnson was banking on when she decided to buy a home when renting was no longer an option.

Inclusion, however, would be conditional, contingent, and tiered. Racism and the economic exploitation of African Americans was the glue that held the American housing market together and would necessarily need to be overcome to fully include Black buyers in the real estate market. But inclusion did not bring an end to predacious practices; it intensified them. Take the end of federal redlining as an example. The FHA stopped its redlining practices even before the passage of the Fair Housing Act, meaning that their cessation was not necessarily linked to the federal government's prohibition on racial discrimination in the housing market. Indeed, FHA redlining was simply dismissed as a problem of location and not of race. The FHA claimed it decided to exclude urban areas from its insurance because of the age and condition of the structures in those areas. FHA officials, of course, failed to take into account their own references to race as part of the underwriting criteria used to determine eligibility for mortgage insurance. It was not the case that African Americans and other unworthy racial and ethnic groups were in the wrong place at the wrong time, but the conditions of distress and dilapidation within those communities were attributed to the race and ethnicity of the people who lived there. In the earliest days of the FHA, theories of eugenics and racial inferiority informed its policymaking with regard to Black people. African Americans were regarded as a pestilence or as a contagion that necessitated containment or quarantine for fear of its ability to destroy value surrounding it.

Coming to terms with the racism embedded in past federal practices was not about redress, restitution, or repair; instead, it was necessary to contextualize the conditions found in African American communities. Identifying racially inscribed policies, such as redlining, from an earlier era was also critical to implementing new policies that aspired to open up and improve Black housing opportunities. Instead, by ignoring race, new practices that were intended to facilitate inclusion reinforced existing patterns of inequality and discrimination. For example, poor housing and neighborhood conditions caused by earlier FHA policies became the basis on which new lenders, in the new era of FHA colorblindness and an end to redlining, could still continue to treat potential Black homeowners differently. African American neighborhoods were given the racially neutral descriptor "subprime." This distinction allowed for certain kinds of lenders while justifying the continued inactivity of other lenders. Though race was apparently no longer a factor, its cumulative effect had already marked Black neighborhoods in such ways that still made them distinguishable and vulnerable to new forms of financial manipulation. Inclusion was possible, but on predatory and exploitative terms.

New FHA backing created a market dominated by mortgage bankers. Mortgage banks were not like ordinary depository banks; instead, they were unregulated institutions that relied on originating and maintenance fees and volume sales to make their profit. Mortgage bankers had no stake or interest in the areas in which they were lending; they just wanted to rack up sales. The FHA's guaranteed mortgage, the subsidized interest rates, and the captured segregated housing market incentivized market actors to speculate that the poverty and desperation of Black urban residents, especially Black women, would drive them toward the low-income homeownership market. In an earlier era, risk had been the pretext for excluding potential Black homeowners; by the late 1960s, risk had made Black buyers attractive. In fact, the riskier the buyer, the better. Janice Johnson was desired as a homeowner because of the likelihood of her failing to keep up with her mortgage payments. With the new FHA-insured home mortgages in

Black neighborhoods, mortgage banks and other lenders were able to parlay fore-closures into profits as the homes went back onto the market and the process was repeated over and over again.

The Federal National Mortgage Association, known as Fannie Mae (FNMA), which was made a private organization as part of the HUD Act, sweetened the deal even more by promising to purchase all FHA loans at face value. The loans that were purchased by FNMA were then packaged and sold to long-term inves-tors, and that money was made available to lenders to continue to ply this devel-oping housing market. There was also the added benefit that poor homeowners such as Johnson could revive "zombie properties," or those dwellings that were economically unviable, into profitable ventures. Johnson's new home should have been condemned; instead, her desperation for housing in combination with her mortgage brought the house back to life. A web of actors benefited from this act of resuscitation. With this series of transactions, including the person from whom Janice Johnson purchased her house, the mortgage lender that extended her a loan, and the service people she called to fix the never-ending defects in her home, the more Johnson poured her meager monies into her dilapidated home, the more *other* people benefited from her investment. Abandoned real estate, cheap mortgage money, drive-by appraisals, quick home sales, defaults, fast foreclosures, and the race for profit all greased the wheels of predatory inclu-sion. Inclusion on predacious terms was not only about banking and real estate, but it raised deeper questions about the progress and triumphalism that pervade the discourses of racial liberalism and uplift so central to the U.S. narrative of progressive change over time.

URBAN CRISES

The federal government's subsidization of homeownership among African American urban residents had a decidedly different outcome compared with the homeownership programs that had been promoted a generation earlier. Instead of creating a bedrock of middle-class prosperity, as the homeowning boom of the 1950s had done for ordinary white people, the urban homeownership programs of the 1960s and 1970s reinforced the optics of urban crisis while simultaneously appearing to confirm the role of African Americans in perpetuating it. The ra-cial liberalism that had animated much of the Johnsonian welfare state, with its insistence on opportunity and inclusion in American prosperity, eventually gave way to the colorblind universalism that became the calling card of the Nixon administration. The conservative-inspired discourse of colorblindness and its erasure of "race talk" did not actually eliminate the invocation of race to make meaning of the shifting social, economic, and political context of the 1970s; it just changed how race was invoked.[32]

"Urban crisis," as a description of infrastructural and complex policy problems in the built environment in the early 1960s, was absorbed into a pattern of coded speech used to describe those who lived in distressed urban communities.[33] Coded speech was, of course, invoked to communicate ideas that could no longer be spoken of freely on their own terms. The new uses of "urban crisis" were a means of articulating the perception of crisis in American cities without using race as its catalyst. Ending race talk was important because the "rights revolution" of the 1960s introduced new rules and regulatory bodies that were statutorily empowered to address explicit acts of discrimination. These new legal tools helped to spur the spate of antidiscrimination litigation throughout the 1970s. Ordinary citizens made sense of the new rights through multiple lawsuits. By shedding reference to race, public and private institutions could shield themselves from the threat of lawsuit. Removing references to race also assisted in tempering the response of civil rights organizations that had become more attuned to the power of litigation than the coercive power of street protests. Indeed, the persistence of racial inequality well into the 1970s dampened the expectation that continued mobilizations and protests were effective means to combat discrimination, compared with lawsuits and deeper involvement in electoral politics. In a similar vein, as the Nixon administration looked for opportunities to fund segregated urban development, naked appeals to racism threatened to put pressure on Black operatives either to reject the overtures of the Republican administration or to publicly back activist responses to public displays of racism. Perhaps of most consequence was how the rhetoric of colorblindness confirmed the critiques of racial liberalism. Colorblind universalism fulfilled the dream of racial liberals in their insistence that removal of racial language was evidence of inclusion. Racial liberals relied on the trace of representation or the physical presence of those who had been previously excluded as proof of change.[34] Thus, it was radicals who coined the phrase "institutional racism" to critique the inadequacy of representation and presence as clear measures of racial equality or racial repair.[35]

The new world of the 1970s was complicated by African Americans armed with new rights and raised expectations, the emergence of electoral conservatism, and the unanticipated and sudden collapse of the postwar economic engine. This contentious environment evidenced by clashing political agendas created even more ideological pressure to explain a rapidly changing economic world. The Republican Party at the helm of the country was bent on undoing the architecture of social welfare that had significantly altered the public expectations of government. It did this in multiple ways, including directing an aggrieved white public to focus their apprehensions about the changing world on the disproportionate number of African Americans who were recipients of federal aid. Republicans were also adept at recasting the insufficiencies, gaps, oversights, and other problems in public programs as the problem of government intervention. This was particularly effective as public cynicism about the role and function of government began to increase with the escalation of the Vietnam War and other evidence of government manipulation and malfeasance.

These relatively new dynamics overlapped with much older, persisting discussions about deserving and undeserving poor people and who, if anyone, was entitled to social welfare.[36] The HUD-FHA low-income homeownership crisis began to unfold in this charged atmosphere. The HUD crisis was wielded to confirm two truths. The first truth was that only the market, as opposed to government, could handle the gargantuan problems rooted in American cities. The Johnson welfare state was declared a failure because, despite the "War on Poverty," poverty still existed. From complaints of red tape, never-ending delays, and numerous other inefficiencies was spun a tale that government was *the* problem. This critique of the state was then mapped onto an evolving, racially motivated cynicism that denounced urban problems as worsening and potentially altogether intractable.

This fatalist discourse of state abnegation was not prompted by the HUD-FHA crisis, but the devolution of the programs aided the narrative. While HUD's homeownership problems were concentrated in a relatively small number of cities, media coverage of the crisis transformed it into a national story of consequence. In an age of investigative journalism, HUD and the FHA provided ample opportunity to uncover local stories of fraud, graft, and corruption. The HUD-FHA crisis was front-page news in publications across the country by the early 1970s, and in 1975 the *Chicago Tribune* won a heralded Pulitzer Prize for its coverage. In the examination of these programs, the role of private enterprise and the potential mismatch of attaching market principles to the crucial effort to provide housing for low-income and poor African Americans were sidelined for the more sensational focus on the program participants and their fitness as homeowners. While race was almost never mentioned, profiles of poor Black women, many of whom were welfare recipients, were highlighted in media coverage.

Political operatives within the Nixon administration seized upon these stories as proof that government was, indeed, the problem. This was explained in the midst of a deepening crisis in American cities. Rising crime rates, an emergent drug crisis, and growing poverty were heralded as proof that Johnson's Great Society had failed, creating an opening for championing market solutions to urban problems. The arguments against perceived social welfare benefits flowing to supposedly undeserving African Americans were not confined to HUD's problems but were part of a generalized attack on the fragile American welfare state. In the realm of housing, this attack culminated in the Nixon administration declaring a moratorium on *all* subsidized housing in 1973. HUD-FHA's homeownership crisis provided a powerful visual component to unending urban crisis as emptied homes, crumbling properties, and abandoned buildings, tens of thousands of which now belonged to HUD, pockmarked Black urban neighborhoods across the country.

In turn, the neglect of cities in the United States added further legitimacy to the stereotype that poor and working-class Black people posed a threat to the property values of white property owners. There was no need to state what seemed so obvious as urban crisis faded into an urban malaise—a prelude to the drug wars of the 1980s. A popular refrain from conservatives in the 1970s and certainly by the 1980s was that antipoverty programs and social welfare created the crisis in the first place. The HUD and FHA homeownership programs were not exactly welfare, even though thousands of people who used the programs were on public assistance.

The critiques of government malfeasance were certainly warranted, but the primary role of the private sector in the HUD-FHA programs has been lost to history. Meanwhile, the promotion of public-private partnerships and, indeed, the regular exhortations on the primacy of the private sector to perform all tasks and provide all services are assumed. In the face of this, the role of poor Black women, many of whom were welfare recipients, in exposing this particular manifestation of fraud and corruption in the low-income homeownership programs deserves to be known and understood.[37] These women braved the indignity of having their personal lives and abilities to maintain a household scrutinized in public hearings, by elected officials, and by other agents of the state, as well as in media outlets that insisted on identifying them as "unsophisticated buyers."

Their willingness to utilize the services of Legal Aid and to endure the stress and uncertainty that surely accompanied the risk of class-action lawsuits uncovers yet another tool that poor and working-class women wielded in their fight for their rights in the 1970s. It would be incorrect to label these struggles as "hidden." More than that, they have been marginalized and forgotten. In some ways, they have been forgotten because of a larger narrative of failure in resolving this country's persisting legacy of housing discrimination. The decades-long search for safe, sound, and affordable housing has been impervious to the country's triumphalism concerning the inevitability of "progress." But over the course of the 1970s, dozens of Black women who were the named plaintiffs in civil lawsuits against HUD, the FHA, and other related agencies represented tens of thousands more women like themselves in asserting their right to a decent home. The particular role of banks and the real estate industry in undermining Black homeownership, which reinforced the racist idea that African Americans lower property values, cannot be understood as clearly without these women. The cheating of Black communities and homeowners continues to skew economic outcomes and shape racist housing policies. These women fought back, and by exposing what happened to them in interviews with journalists, and through lawsuits, their story can now be told.

1

Unfair Housing

Today, in the very eye of the storm of the Negro revolution the
ghetto stands—largely unassailed—as the rock upon which rests [*sic*]
segregated living patterns which pervade and vitiate almost
every phase of Negro life and Negro-white relationships.
—From "A Housing Program for All Americans,"
National Committee Against Discrimination in Housing,
Ten-Year Plan, October 6, 1964

A rat done bit my sister Nell (with Whitey on the moon)
Her face and arms began to swell (and Whitey's on the moon)
I can't pay no doctor bill (but Whitey's on the moon)
Ten years from now I'll be payin' still (while Whitey's on the moon)
The man jus' upped my rent las' night ('cause Whitey's on the moon)
No hot water, no toilets, no lights (but Whitey's on the moon)
I wonder why he's uppin' me? ('cause Whitey's on the moon?)
I was already payin' 'im fifty a week (with Whitey on the moon)
—Gil Scott-Heron, "Whitey on the Moon," 1969

IN AUGUST 1967, nearly two weeks after an uprising in Detroit had prompted the first deployment of federal troops in an American city since the Civil War, dozens of demonstrators burst into the chamber of the House of Representatives chanting, "Rats cause riots!"[1] Just days before, Congress had rejected a two-year, $40-million bill to exterminate rats in the inner city, and in response the protestors sat in the gallery of the hall for twenty minutes, repeating the slogan "We want a rat bill!" at progressively higher volumes. The previous attempt at passing the bill had not been merely voted down but ridiculed in the process. A Virginia Republican made a mockery of the legislation, saying, "Mr. Speaker, I think the 'rat' smart thing for us to do is to vote this rat bill, 'rat' now," while other white representatives filled the Congress with howls of laughter, referring to the rat legislation as "another civil 'rats' bill."[2]

No laughing matter for the people who lived in the inner city, rats were the most visceral example of the unequal living conditions forced onto Black people.[3] In the 1960s, African American media regularly reported on rat attacks on the most vulnerable members of Black urban households—the children. Loraine McTush, a single African American mother, complained to a *Chicago Defender* reporter that she stayed up most nights because of rats—the rats crawling in her bed, which made her nervous, and the rats in her children's beds, which terrified her: "They . . . get into the bunk beds, and so I sit up all night. I am miserable and afraid." McTush received an eviction notice shortly after her story appeared in the newspaper.[4]

Days after Thelma Earl was released from a hospital in Washington, D.C., recovering from rat bites, her landlord served her with an eviction notice as well. Earl, an African American single mother of ten children, had forgone reporting the bites on herself and her children previously for fear the hospital would inform the authorities: "I've been bitten by rats before and so have my babies. But I never reported it because I was afraid an eviction would happen. But you got no choice when you go to the hospital. Now I can't find another place to live and sometimes I think I should have died of rat poison at home."[5]

Popular *Washington Post* columnist Jimmy Breslin went to East Harlem and interviewed a Puerto Rican couple, Ebro and Cathy Marrero, about the condition of their building. During the interview, two rats darted out of the kitchen into the bathroom. Breslin asked why they did not just put poison down. The father explained, "The children. You cannot have traps and poison around the babies." He went on to describe how he and his wife protected their kids from the rats: "Our baby is only three weeks old. We keep him in the bed with us. The other two, we have the crib set up high. No rats come there so far, but you still can't leave the baby alone." Breslin described the sound of rats scratching through the kitchen wall as "the sound you carry with you for the rest of your life. It is something heard by poor people in every poor neighborhood in every city in the nation."[6]

Rosie and R. V. Townes and their two small children were profiled in a five-part *Chicago Defender* series on life in the Chicago slums. Their home at

1321 South Homan Avenue was only a few buildings away from the apartment that Dr. Martin Luther King Jr. would call home when he moved into a tenement on the West Side to dramatize slum conditions in the neighborhood. The Towneses described a life constantly on the move from one apartment to the next in a never-ending effort to find safe lodging for their children. In their first apartment, exposed and faulty wiring that lay outside the plaster of the wall shocked their baby girl. From there, they fled to an apartment where plumes of black smoke from the furnace caused their small son to wheeze and gasp for air throughout the night. The apartment in which they lived at the time of the interview did not have hot water, but it was the daily battle with the rats that kept Rosie on edge. According to R. V., "The rats sit along the banisters like squirrels. You open the garbage pail and they pour out like flies. And there is no heat. We moved to other places . . . and have been without heat and hot water. The way we see it is why should we pay rent?"[7]

In August 1965, in the first few days after the rebellion in the Watts neighborhood of South Central Los Angeles, while the last fires still smoldered, a reporter interviewed two Black teenagers about why the riots had happened. One described where he and his family lived: "We live in a two-bedroom apartment. The rent is too high and rats, they are big. You open the back door and one of them jumps over your foot from the back porch. But we still have to live there."[8]

In 1966, two days before his first birthday, little Andre Adams was "chewed to death" by a rat while sleeping in his crib, a death so shocking that more than a thousand African Americans gathered on Chicago's West Side in protest. One activist recalled the prior summer's deadly riot—"Remember Watts?"—and described in grisly detail the infant's remains: "When he lay in his crib, you could see the holes where the rats had chewed. The little finger of his right hand was tied on with a string."[9] Chicago health officials disagreed, claiming the child died of malnutrition but nevertheless conceding that rats had fed on the baby's corpse. Civil rights leader Dr. Martin Luther King Jr., who spoke at the hastily organized protest, reminded the crowd, "This is why we are fighting the slums in Chicago." Noting the similarities between racism in the South and in urban ghettos in the North, King declared, "This is as much of a civil rights tragedy as the murder of Mrs. [Viola] Liuzzo," a white housewife who had been killed protesting for civil rights in Alabama.[10]

The rat infestation in Black neighborhoods was profound. It was estimated that, by the end of the 1960s, there were more than 90 million rats in the United States, mostly in urban areas. When African American children in a Chicago

neighborhood were given a vocabulary test and asked to identify various familiar objects, more than 60 percent of the children misidentified a rat as a teddy
bear.[11] A report produced about the causes of riots in Philadelphia in the summer of 1964 found that more than half of the housing in the "riot area" had
been determined by the city to be substandard. The report found that "many
of [those] houses have rat infested pools in their basements, rotted and missing
floorboards and exposed wiring." The report also found that children living in
"Negro slums" experienced 80 percent of lead poisoning deaths and 100 percent
of rat bites.[12] The growing presence of rats in Harlem prompted activists to create
a "Rats to Rockefeller" campaign to draw attention to the deteriorating conditions in tenements overwhelmingly populated by Blacks. In New York City as a
whole, more than 41,000 tenements built before the turn of the century housed
over a million people. Ten thousand of those buildings existed in such a corroded
state that they were referred to as "horror houses."[13] The campaign was organized
by housing activist Jesse Gray, who suggested parents keep a baseball bat handy
to ward off rats. He described the urgency of the campaign: "I've seen kids try to
pet them. They don't know what they are. The rats are getting bolder. You can
sit in the living room of some houses and watch them march across the floor."[14]
Three years later, it was Gray who led activists into the chamber of Congress
demanding action on this pressing issue.

The political trope of this urban vermin—most famously deployed by Richard
Wright at the beginning of *Native Son*—came to symbolize the degradation of
Black urban life in the United States.[15] Repeated reports of rat bites in African
American media confirmed the experiences of African Americans living in cities
and pierced mainstream explanations that blamed the housekeeping and hygiene
of individual families for the conditions in slums. President Harry S. Truman
declared that the 1949 Housing Act would provide "a decent home and suitable living environment for every American family," but it was a prediction that
stood in stark contrast to the conditions of Black urban life in the 1960s. Taken
together, multiple stories and reports, carried mostly by the African American
press, wove together a powerful portrait of the exclusion of African Americans
from the full promise of social mobility that was the centerpiece of the concept
of the American dream.

From the 1930s until the late 1960s, U.S. housing policies were caught between innovation and regressive racial attitudes that produced a multitiered approach to public policy: homeownership and development for white residents,
public housing or extractive and predatory tenancy for African Americans in the

wake of urban renewal practices. Along with the racially inspired residential segregation that developed, so too did the economic incentive to keep those policies
in place. The economy generated out of Black isolation helped to ingrain these
practices in such ways that even when housing options began to expand for African Americans, they were constrained within the segregation paradigm. This
not only made Black children vulnerable to dangerous vermin, but the absence of
housing options outside the urban ghetto meant their parents were easily coerced
into paying high prices for the substandard housing. Ironically, these conditions
built over decades finally boiled over and fed the rebellions among Blacks that
forced the federal government to open homeownership opportunities to city-
bound African Americans. This chapter examines these developments in U. S.
housing policy, including how the federal government and the real estate industry's commitment to racial segregation distorted the historic transformations
in public policy that grudgingly made way for more Black homeowners in their
constant quest for better living conditions.

THE FHA AS PIONEER

Fifteen years after World War II, millions of Americans had realized homeownership and achieved general security. By 1960, 60 percent of Americans were
homeowners, and homeownership on a mass scale became a foundation on
which the American economy could grow and flourish. The old business maxim
"What's good for General Motors is good for the U.S." seemed, temporarily, to
hold true, as the process of transforming wood, steel, and oil into cars, washing
machines, and lawnmowers created the commodities that transformed houses
into homes and made the American economy the strongest in the world. But the
bounty that came with expansion of homeownership was not evenly distributed;
the bloom of the suburbs came at the expense of urban development.

   From 1940 until 1970 more than 5 million African Americans left the South
for the urban North, Midwest, and West Coast. A chasm lay between the hope
that fueled African Americans' trek to American cities and the appalling condition of the housing available for them to live in. But the mass movement of Black
people into urban centers transformed their social concerns, such as housing
inequality, into political issues to which elected officials would have to respond.
The continued migration of African Americans out of the rural South into
northern cities augmented what Robert Weaver described as "a growing urban
constituency [that] compelled more systematic attention."[16]

The conditions that millions of African Americans lived in stood in stark contrast to the puffed-up proclamations of the United States as the greatest democracy in the world. By the end of the 1950s, African Americans were 10 percent of the national population but occupied only 8 percent of the housing. The number of nonwhite households living "doubled up," with two or more families to a home, "rose from 274,000 or 13.8 percent in 1940, to 339,000 or 15.1 percent in 1950."[17] As one observer noted, "The simple truth is that the nation's urban whites have resisted giving their cities' new Negro populations as much living space as their money would buy. Only 5.5 percent of the nation's city and rural nonfarm dwellers live in overcrowded conditions, but 18 percent of Negroes do."[18] The housing was not only overcrowded; it was also in desperately poor condition. Twenty-seven percent of Black housing was dilapidated, compared with 5 percent of white housing. The rate of residence in "homes lacking in one or more of piped running water, private flush toilet, private bathtub or shower was twice as high among nonwhites as among whites."[19]

Certainly by midcentury and beyond, the dilapidated condition of urban properties had become synonymous with the African Americans who inhabited them. The segregated housing market inspired little effort from landlords in Black areas. The captive rental market left African Americans few options in choosing their housing. The dearth of housing and a never-ending supply of tenants meant that there was no incentive for landlords to improve their property. Instead of making necessary repairs, landlords schemed to create more dwellings out of existing units. Small apartments were subdivided into even smaller apartments. In Baltimore, this was acted out dramatically when, in the 1950s, more than 45,000 units of housing lacked indoor bathrooms because landlords had converted them into rooms for rent. Instead, they built outhouses in the backyards, known as "crappers."[20] The real estate industry used the conditions of Black communities, born out of a rigid adherence to residential segregation, as evidence to justify the continued exclusion of African Americans from white neighborhoods. These were the conditions of extraction and investment, but not for those who lived there.

This environment was not only a barrier for Black renters; it was also used as "proof" that African Americans lacked fitness as homeowners. Homeownership has long been considered a pathway to political, economic, and cultural citizenship in the United States. Housing advocate and attorney Charles Abrams described homeownership in the United States as "an emotional experience. . . . It bespeaks freedom and security, it is tied up with pride and confidence. . . . The two-bedroom house on 800 square feet of land amid other two-bedroom houses on 800 square feet of land has become the post-frontier symbol of what we call the American way of life."[21] For the aspiring Black middle class, homeownership was complicated and onerous. Despite its centrality to the "American way of life," its availability has been dictated by more than social mobility and financial capability. Racial discrimination has been a determining factor in access to owning one's own home. In the first half of the twentieth century, homeownership among Blacks lagged between 35 and 50 percent lower than what it was for their white peers. Those disparities indicated a mix of poverty, access, and discrimination.

Despite the obstacles to Black homeownership, the number of Black homeowners grew with migration and improved income in the aftermath of World War II. Between 1940 and 1950 the growth of Black homeownership even outpaced that of white homeowners. "In no area of his life has the Negro suffered such stubborn discrimination as in housing. Yet by 1950 one in every three urban Negro families owned their own home. And in the 1940–50 decade, while white home ownership in the cities rose a steep 84 per cent, Negro home ownership in the cities rose 137 per cent," reported *Fortune* magazine in 1956.[22] Even though African Americans had been largely excluded from the FHA's innovative economic tools that made homeownership cheap and easy for millions of Americans, that did not mean that Black people did not buy homes. But racism and exclusion made the costs higher while the quality was lower, and the result rendered homeownership differently for African Americans in comparison with their white peers. Black housing was valued differently from white housing, thus stripping its supposed asset-like quality away. The average value of a single-family home in an urban community was $8,400, but the average value of a Black-owned home in an urban area was $3,700.[23] A quarter of Black homeowners in urban areas believed that their home would not sell for more than $2,000.[24]

These tough conditions in Black housing that helped to catalyze urban uprisings by the 1960s stemmed from policies enacted by the federal government in the 1930s. The exclusionary policies of the FHA have now become widely understood in urban historiography, as well as in mainstream media sources. In 1934, the National Housing Act and the subsequent creation of the FHA set a new era of federal housing policy in motion. The FHA revolutionized homebuying in the United States, primarily by guaranteeing mortgages and amortizing the payments over decades, thereby making monthly mortgage payments more manageable. The FHA's new mortgage insurance program took much of the risk out of lending, translating into lower interest rates and affordable homeownership for ordinary people.[25] Federal policies that encouraged suburban development anchored to suburban homeowners spurred the uneven development of the American metropolis for the next several decades. The essence of this "uneven development" was investment and development for suburbs, compared with extraction and deterioration in urban core communities.[26]

While suburban communities sprang into existence or expanded vibrantly, the urban core that absorbed the heart of the African American migration out of rural and southern outposts strained to support its new, swelling populations. Not only did FHA policies discourage homeownership among African Americans or those living in proximity to them, but these policies even prohibited the disbursement of small home improvement loans available to white homeowners. Investors in urban properties relied on maximum rent extraction with minimal investment in properties to garner the greatest return.[27] Where purchasing property was a possibility for African Americans, it was often on unfair and predatory terms that left little money for maintenance and other repairs that older urban properties were in desperate need of.

The FHA marginalization of urban-bound African Americans reflected the worst of racial pseudoscience, including the presumption of Black inferiority and a consequent detriment to property values.[28] FHA officials, over time, would claim that the exclusion of African Americans from mortgage protections stemmed from their own financial conservatism and not racial discrimination, but the agency's underwriting criteria for mortgage insurance prioritized racial considerations. For example, the FHA's *Underwriting Manual*, which spelled out the terms under which the agency would insure a home mortgage, considered a neighborhood to be "far less stable and undesirable" if white schoolchildren had to attend public schools where "the majority or a considerable number of pupils represent a far lower level of society or an incompatible racial element."[29] While it was certainly true that private enterprise and white homeowners had excluded African Americans in myriad ways from the means to secure homeownership, the role of the federal government in these processes was also undeniable.[30]

The powers of the FHA would not be fully experienced until the postwar housing boom of the 1940s and 1950s. The changes to homeownership implemented by the FHA allowed it to transform millions of working-class and other lower-income renters into homeowners for the first time. The fact that the FHA began as an agency intent on expanding homeownership to lower-income families made its later claims to exclude African Americans for economic reasons ring hollow. Officials within the agency contended that African Americans were too poor to be homeowners. By the 1960s, FHA officials would also claim that the organization's middle-class orientation left them ill equipped to deal with lower-income African Americans when new legislation compelled them to by the end of that decade. But the FHA had not always been averse to backing mortgages for low-income people. FHA underwriter supervisor M. R. Massey wrote in 1940, "There is a direct challenge to private business and the government in the realization that homeownership must be made available on reasonable terms to families of low income. Homeownership on an extensive scale by persons in all income brackets provides a bulwark for our whole economic structure, and the encouragement of ownership by persons of low income is a direct responsibility of business and government."[31] Massey continued, "The low-income groups are just as much entitled to relatively acceptable standards of living as are higher income groups . . . and their purchases of low cost homes need not be confined to slum areas and unprotected or isolated locations."[32] Lenders also agreed with the orientation on lower-income families for homeownership. In 1940, *Insured Mortgage Portfolio*, the trade journal of the FHA, claimed that "almost half" of the 450,000 families purchasing homes under the FHA plan had incomes of less than $2,500 and "expressed the belief that the low-income market could be expanded even further."[33] In the same publication, a mortgage banker wrote that with the aid of FHA-insured mortgages, lenders could reach down into the ranks of the very-low-income population and turn them into homeowners. After pointing out that people making less than $2,000 a year were buying cars and refrigerators, this lender wrote, "It is perfectly clear these families in the $2000-and-under brackets are willing to spend money for the things they want. They represent the potential market for low-cost housing. Once they realize they can acquire new homes of their own at little or no great monthly outlays than for rent, how long will they hesitate?"[34]

In February 1940, "numerous mortgage-lending institutions, builders [and] real estate firms" announced that they were launching a "concerted campaign to promote homeownership among families of modest incomes," followed by an announcement by the FHA that this campaign had its "full support."[35] The new homeownership program was designed to appeal to "families in the lower-income brackets." The FHA's journal described how it would capture this new market: "[With] FHA financing such [low-income] families can acquire attractive, soundly constructed homes with only small initial investments and at monthly payments thereafter approximating the sums they are accustomed to pay[ing] in rent. . . . Its message will be directed to the mass of modest income families and will set forth the terms under which . . . they can eventually own a home on a housing budget of around $25 a month."[36] In California, builders boasted that they sold "thousands" of "small homes" with five rooms with a small down payment of $75 to $100.[37] In another California case, builders built "economy houses" that ranged in price from $2,000 to $3,150. In another article, a different banker wrote of the initial reluctance to finance small homes because of the fear of the ability of lower-income families to afford to keep up with the payments, "yet here were these lower-income families. The FHA stood ready if these families could build or buy houses on terms comparable to the rents they were paying to insure their mortgages."[38] Down payments as low as 5 percent and monthly payments of $25 were expected to dramatically widen the field of homeowners. The FHA continued to liberalize the terms for its insurance, including reducing the size of down payments so ordinary people could qualify for mortgages, to further incentivize bankers to continue to lend.

These "low-income" terms have to be understood within the context of what could be described as typical FHA business. According to historian Gail Radford, the average value of single-family FHA-backed homes was $5,199. She also pointed out that "36 percent of the 2,680 subdivisions analyzed by the FHA Land Planning Department were selling houses for under $4,000, a price well below the average for a new house in the 1920s."[39] The efforts to push further into the ranks of the working class and to pull greater numbers into the ranks of homeownership drove the FHA toward innovations in financing—except, of course, for African Americans. Even critics of the FHA have attempted to explain the hostility of the FHA to Black buyers as a symptom of the agency's purported conservatism.[40] But the FHA's racial politics were neither benign nor marginal to the agency's primary goal of expanding homeownership. Racial concerns shaped the public policies of the FHA from its inception. Because the federal government relied on "experts" from the housing industry to shape its emergent housing policies, it imported the racial common sense of the real estate industry, including the foregone conclusion that Blacks and other nonwhites should be separated from whites to preserve property values.

In 1938, when the FHA released its *Underwriting Manual*, it was imbued with the assumptions about race already rooted in established real estate practices. It read in part, "If a neighborhood is to retain stability, it is necessary that properties shall continue to be occupied by the same social and racial classes. A change in social or racial occupancy generally contributes to instability and a decline in values."[41]

The premise of these underwriting criteria spelled out the rationale for redlining and shaped the practices of the FHA well into the twentieth century. The 1948 Supreme Court decision *Shelley v. Kraemer*, banning states from enforcing racial covenants in the sale of housing, was the first major court decision after World War II with the potential to curb racial discrimination in the housing market. The decision, however, was read narrowly, applied only to restricted covenants, and did not ban housing discrimination against African Americans or other nonwhites, only the state's specific role in implementing or enforcing it. Clarence Mitchell of the National Association for the Advancement of Colored People (NAACP) described the lack of inclusion of antidiscrimination language in the 1949 National Housing Act, which set as a goal "decent" housing for all Americans, as a "cruel and disgusting hoax as far as colored citizens of the United States are concerned."[42]

The FHA and, later, the Veterans Administration (VA) exclusion of African Americans was virtually complete; ten years after the 1949 National Housing Act, less than 2 percent of FHA-insured properties went to nonwhites. The results devastated the ability of African Americans to upgrade their housing. For example, "one-half of Detroit and one-third of Chicago were simply excluded from the [FHA] program by fiat, and after twelve years of operation, there was not a single dwelling unit in Manhattan that had the benefit of FHA coverage. Yet from the mid-1930s until the mid-1970s, FHA managed to provide $119 billion in home mortgages."[43] Even with the ban on racial covenants firmly in place, the FHA remained committed to the practice of residential segregation as a way to preserve the value of property it had insured. These federal policies not only exacerbated the urban housing crisis experienced by African Americans, but they also undergirded the developing racial and popular common sense about Black urban dwellers. With the exclusion of African Americans from the FHA portfolio described as the product of impartial market forces or race-neutral "economic soundness," the condition of the urban ghetto became associated with the behavior, aptitude, and competency of Black citizens. These perceptions, then, legitimized the further exclusion of African Americans, which, as millions of Black people continued to pour into the cities, accelerated the decline of the communities in which they were trapped.

In some ways, the actions of the FHA were contradictory. The agency was quite

FHA materials advertising homeownership program, including a
"low-income" plan for $25 down: a counter card for lending
institutions, a folder, and a poster. (Courtesy FHA)

innovative in its various schemes to pull low-income people into the realm of
homeowners. For example, one of the wilder ideas that never came to fruition
but demonstrated the agency's efforts to push its own boundaries was an FHA-
initiated study to determine the possibility of allowing the FHA to pay for unemployment and health insurance for its mortgagors if they fell on hard times,
so that their monthly mortgage obligations would still be met.[44] These were not
impetuous schemes but reflected what Philip Brownstein, a former director of
the FHA, described as the "apprecia[tion] that the agency works in essentially
opposing directions at all times, for on the one hand it seeks to pioneer and demonstrate in new and untried fields, and on the other hand it seeks to underwrite
mortgages on projects which will succeed financially. That is, it is constantly
seeking the middle ground between overemphasis on pioneering and overcon-
cern for playing it safe."[45]

As the FHA continued to liberalize its underwriting criteria, it allowed for
longer periods of repayment, increasing the loan amortization time from twenty
years to up to forty years. Even as the average cost of homes increased by 52 percent between 1952 and 1965, the down payment for the average buyer decreased by
about $1,800 because the FHA was insuring a larger percentage of the mortgage.[46]
The drive toward lower down payments and higher loan-to-income ratios was
motivated by the desire to continue increasing the number of American homeowners. This was not only motivated by ideological concerns that prioritized

homeownership as the true expression of free market principles, as opposed to public housing or renting in the private market, but the impulse to expand was also driven by the undeniable impact of the homeownership enterprise on the American economy. Housing was directly connected to "a multi-billion dollar market for everything from shingles to bathtubs, plus jobs for more than three million workers."[47] According to one commentator, the gap between the 1.6 million housing starts in 1959 and the lower 1 million starts in 1960 "meant the difference in employment of more than a million workers—enough to account for one-fifth to one-fourth of total unemployment at the time."[48]

The centrality of homeownership to the American economy pushed the FHA to maintain segregation while also expanding opportunities for African Americans to become homeowners. At the same time, the agency's regressive ideas about race retarded its development of the urban housing market among potential Black buyers. There was, however, logic to the contradiction. As African American communities continued to strain under the weight of growing populations with little civic or private investment, their physical separation was further legitimized. The greater the sense of "crisis" in American cities, the greater the perceived value added to exclusive white suburban communities. Conversely, the more exclusive the suburb and, therefore, the more difficult the entry of African Americans, the greater the financial exploitation of urban Black renters and buyers desperate for better housing. The continued disinvestment and marginalization of the urban core helped to sustain suburbanization and all of the financial benefits for business that came along with it. The deterioration of urban neighborhoods was not simply a side effect of suburbanization or an "unintended consequence"; the two were dialectically connected. This connection meant that the proposition of a "dual market" was misleading. Duality suggested distinction and separation, as if the urban and suburban housing markets were not intimately related to each other. Instead, there was a single United States housing market that was defined by its racially discriminatory, tiered access—each tier reinforcing and legitimizing the other.

THE NEW BLACK MARKET

The 1954 *Brown v. Board of Education* Supreme Court decision declared that the framework of "separate but equal" was unworkable within the scope of the U.S. Constitution—at least as it pertained to public education. Even within the narrow scope of the case in terms of its focus on education, it was undeniable that the highest court in the country had delivered a blow to the legality and legitimization of segregation. The decision clearly opened the way for a political challenge to the federal government's involvement in the segregative practices within the real estate and banking industries. For example, at a 1954 gathering of more than forty housing organizations, assembled by the Housing and Home Finance Agency, the right to free and open housing was framed as a basic expression of American democracy: "The role of government in the national economy is to maintain a free and competitive market. To fulfill this function in the field of housing, the government must require that builders, lenders and any others who receive federal aid of any kind for housing programs agree that renters or buyers will not be denied such housing on the basis of race. This condition must apply to all Federal housing activities."[49]

The momentum to open up new housing opportunities for African Americans was not only created by the racial liberalism unleashed by the Cold War and the supposition that the unequal treatment of Black citizens imperiled the new role of the United States as a global superpower, but African Americans were in a stronger financial position because of the migration. These political cracks at the top and bottom of society coincided with the homebuilding boom of the postwar period that created an even greater opportunity for African Americans to partake in the real estate market. In 1939, 3.7 percent of Black families earned between $3,000 and $5,000 a year; in 1950, the number of Black families earning that amount had risen to 17.8 percent.[50] The steady rise in their income helped African Americans integrate into the developing consumer society of the post–World War II period.[51] A study on African American consumerism in 1944 found that Blacks had an annual gross income of $10 billion, of which 62 percent was spent on consumer goods and services. A study on "how Negroes spend their incomes" found that Black people spent $1.7 billion of their income on housing—second only to food expenses. From 1955 to 1960 alone, Black income rose by 15 percent. As one business leader recognized,

> In Houston, Negroes buy at retail annually over $500 million; over $300 million in Atlanta; in New Orleans over $250 million. . . . With that amount of purchasing power Negroes can get banks to treat them civilly; they can get sales people in department stores to want to sell [to] them. Recent data reveal that there are about a million nonwhites on the West Coast, most of them Negros. . . . The income distribution of the nonwhite group is exactly the same as that of the white population in the south. In

Chicago one-third of the Negro families have more income than half of the white families.[52]

Fortune magazine triumphantly declared in 1956, "Not since Emancipation has the Negro known a moment more hopeful.... Signs of the American Negro's economic progress range from the clear to the spectacular."[53]

The housing industry was enticed by the prospect of developing a Black housing market. American cities represented a "new frontier" in development possibilities. The National Association of Home Builders (NAHB) said as much when it declared in a March 1950 memo to its membership that "supplying homes ... for rent and for sale ... for minority groups and families farther and farther down the income scale ... is a challenge to the ingenuity and capacity of industry."[54] Eisenhower insisted that private sector forces must pursue the redevelopment of "good housing." He argued that "programs must be avoided that would make our citizens increasingly dependent upon the federal government to supply their housing needs."[55] Homeownership in the cities became one potential means to resolve this issue.

Even the politically conservative and white supremacist NAREB proclaimed "Negroes as a sound economic risk." A 1944 survey conducted by NAREB's Negro Housing Committee in eighteen cities around the United States found that most of the real estate agents who were asked confirmed that "the Negro homebuyer meets his payments faithfully—often more faithfully than other racial groups in the same economic level."[56] The study also found that African Americans' "tenacity and willingness to sacrifice in order to hold on to their homes" "greatly" exceeded that of whites. When this same group of real estate agents was asked, "Do you know of any reason why the great insurance companies of this country should not freely purchase mortgages upon homes and rented buildings to be occupied by Negroes if such accommodations are *properly located* and managed?" three-quarters of the real estate agents answered "no."[57] Representatives of the real estate association were quick to emphasize that their interest in the survey was to find the "best economic solution," clarifying that they were not interested in "the social, political, or racial issues which are often injected into the discussion of housing for negroes."[58] This framing by NAREB provided insight into how a Black homeownership market with federal backing might be conceptualized. This was a business venture, but its implementation would be tempered by the continuing realities of segregation. The real estate industry communicated that while it was open to Black homeownership, those homes needed to be "properly located." This conveyed a growing reality that African Americans could not be forever kept out of the housing market, but that their participation would be conditional. In this case, it would continue to be on segregated terms.

The real estate industry reflected the contradictory tensions produced in the political moment after World War II. Just the year before NAREB's discovery of African Americans as a worthy market, its 1943 publication *Fundamentals of Real Estate Practice* warned readers that

> the prospective buyer might be a bootlegger who would cause considerable annoyance to his neighbors, a madam who had a number of call girls on her string, a gangster who wants a screen for his activities by living in a better neighborhood, a colored man of means who is giving his children a college education and thought they were entitled to live among whites. . . . No matter what the motive or character of the would-be purchaser, if the deal would institute a form of blight, then certainly the well-meaning broker must work against its consummation.[59]

With African Americans developing into a political constituency and becoming members of the "consumer's republic," combined with the ways that World War II was framed as a battle of "democracy" against fascism, public officials and other reputable institutions outside the South did not wish to be perceived as racist. The real estate industry, however, was pulled between maintaining a discriminatory business practice it believed to be critical to preserving cultural norms that were paramount to maintaining property values and presenting its practice as reflective of racially neutral market imperatives. The industry, cognizant of the changing political culture that eschewed public pronouncements of discrimination, was receptive to the growing possibilities of developing a market for Black homeowners.

Not only did the rise in Black income and consumerism indicate a capacity for homeownership, but postwar urban renewal policies necessitated it. Urban renewal, introduced as a set of public development policies in the 1949 National Housing Act, had been promised as a comprehensive plan to save American cities. It was widely welcomed, given the way that federal policies had perpetuated an "uneven" approach to metropolitan development by prioritizing suburban homeownership. There were multiple components to urban renewal, including plans to raze so-called slum neighborhoods that occupied valuable land throughout the urban districts. These downtrodden neighborhoods were, of course, home to tens of thousands of people, and their removal necessitated the creation of new housing to relocate them. This math necessary to replace demolished homes with new homes did not always add up, because "urban renewal" was never conceptualized as a housing program. Instead, urban renewal was largely viewed as an urban economic revival program that used federal dollars to tear down slum housing that also happened to be in proximity to downtown commercial districts. Private land developers were then supposed to redevelop the heavily subsidized land with affordable housing for those who had been displaced by the clearance program. Instead of rebuilding urban communities and allowing for the return of those who had been displaced by the federal bulldozers, private developers built condominiums and apartments and refurbished shopping districts for a middle-class clientele while ignoring the housing needs of those who had been displaced. One observation about the effects of slum clearance in Chicago showed that "among non-white families earning less than $3,000 a year, median rent rose from 35 per cent of income before relocation to 46 per cent afterward."[60]

In 1959, $2 billion was budgeted for "urban renewal," almost tripling the amount that was originally earmarked for those projects ten years earlier. By 1961, when Kennedy became president on a promise to expand urban renewal even further, its budget doubled again with another $2 billion.[61] The majority of this money was for housing poor and low-income people displaced by slum removal. The expansion of the public housing program had become the relocation housing of last resort for Black renters displaced by urban renewal. As Arnold Hirsch has written, the resurgent use of public housing after World War II was closely linked to urban renewal projects and the displacement of tens of thousands of African Americans from their neighborhoods.[62] By 1957, of people displaced by urban renewal, over a quarter of Black families were relocated to public housing, compared with 10 percent of white families; "urban renewal projects utilized 11,000 units of public housing of which 9700 were occupied by nonwhites, or 88 percent."[63] The survival of public housing was directly tied to its necessity as relocation housing for the tens of thousands of city dwellers forcibly removed from their homes and neighborhoods.

Urban renewal's destruction of cheap housing further aggravated the existing housing shortage in the inner city. The National Commission on Urban Problems was blunt: "Demolitions of housing by public action alone destroyed more units of housing than were built in all federally aided programs."[64] In Detroit, a maximum of 758 low-income housing units had been built with government assistance since 1956, but between 1960 and 1967, approximately 800 low-income units were demolished.[65] In Newark, more than 3,700 publicly assisted low-income housing units had been built since 1959, but during the same period more than 12,000 families were displaced by urban renewal projects, including new highway construction. By 1967, slum clearance polices had allowed for the destruction of 404,000 units of housing, with another 356,000 scheduled for demolition in American cities. There were another 264,000 apartments that had either begun rehabilitation or were scheduled to be repaired. This gives some indication of the scale of devastation to the urban housing market.[66] As one author stated, "Of all the housing activities of government, none has potentially a greater impact upon the housing conditions of minority groups and racial residence patterns than urban renewal."[67]

Ironically, the political concern over the growing usage of public housing and displacement caused by urban renewal opened the small space for the federal government to introduce the first legislation for FHA backing of urban-based home mortgages in "renewal areas." Although tens of thousands of Black families were upended by renewal practices, not all of them qualified for public housing; for some, their income was too high. The growing need for African American housing in cities drove innovative uses of the FHA programs, including "special terms of FHA mortgage insurance . . . authorized to stimulate new housing construction in project areas for displaced families within or outside such areas."[68]

In a small but significant turn, the 1954 Housing Act created an experimental program for homeownership for individuals and families displaced by urban renewal. This was the cumulative outcome of the vocal demands of African American advocates, rising Black incomes, the increasing centrality of homeownership to the American economy, and the need for additional housing created by the rampant destruction and displacement wrought by slum clearance. The new homeownership program created by Section 221(d)(2) of the 1954 Housing Act authorized FHA-backed mortgages for "housing in urban renewal areas and on housing for families displaced by reason of urban renewal programs, [which should] be helpful in enabling many low-income families now living in blighted urban areas to obtain better homes."[69] As whites continued to move out of cities, more homes became available to African Americans to purchase if they could secure financing. If the buyer could find a lender to finance the house, then the FNMA agreed to buy the loan at market value. But the lower fixed-interest rate on FHA-backed loans proved to be an obstacle in sparking interest from conventional banks. The Section 221(d)(2) loans were not lucrative enough for banks to overcome their racial hostility to potential Black buyers in the real estate market. Within a year of the creation of this new urban homeownership program, no home sales were made utilizing Section 221(d)(2).[70]

A representative of the National Association of Mutual Savings Banks was uncertain about the potential of the new legislation to promote new construction within cities: "I doubt very much in and around urban centers because of high land costs."[71] This program was slow to take off, but by the early 1970s, it would become one of the most popular means for inner-city African Americans to purchase homes. In the complex political ferment of the Cold War, small and ineffectual programs like this could be symbols of progress. The programs also demonstrated how progress could be tethered to convention, as the possibility of greater access to homeownership for African Americans was narrowly conceived within existing urban communities and certainly not in white suburban areas, where Blacks were still seen as detrimental to the value of property.

In the 1960 Housing Act, legislators added a Section 235 to further expand the areas eligible for mortgage insurance.[72] This was different from the low-income homeownership legislation created by the 1968 HUD Act but significant as an additional attempt to forge more routes to urban homeownership. The properties in these older neighborhoods were not to be held to the same structural standards as properties covered by the traditional FHA insuring program. Given the age and condition of the properties found in the urban market, the FHA adjusted its standard for insurance from "economic soundness" to "reasonable risk." This change in underwriting criteria for mortgage insurance was amplified by the 1960 Housing Act's authorization of $25 million for the FNMA to buy mortgages in "older neighborhoods."[73]

Given these changes, it would, nevertheless, take time to change the attitudes within the industry. Six years after the 1954 Housing Act, builders had only produced 1,500 houses utilizing all of the new tools for lending and building in dense urban communities. Lenders also continued to express little interest in loans to African Americans, not only because of racial prejudice but because homes sold to white people in suburbs were priced higher and conventional mortgage loans held higher interest rates than the reduced FHA rate. An interview with real estate agents from New Orleans in the 1950s made clear that despite the economic opening for Black homeownership and improved rental units, "there was still a good market for housing for whites, and the building of houses for Negroes must await the saturation of this better market, which may not occur for years." The housing industry preferred the "white market," even when Black buyers were eligible, because of "its stronger and more varied housing demand, fewer difficulties of selling and financing, and greater abundance of good building sites."[74]

Even with the reluctance of lenders, the FHA appeared to signal two things at once. The invention of Section 221(d)(2) was proof that the FHA could get behind Black homeownership, but it was also clear that such ownership would continue to be on the terms of segregation. The FHA made almost no effort to use its considerable authority to convince lenders to break their ban on Black buyers. In this way, the agency's operations demonstrated the limits of postwar racial liberalism. The FHA could remove racist language from its underwriting manuals and orders of operations and even promise to expand homeownership opportunities for African Americans, but the agency's failure to address its deep commitment to racial segregation was to essentially maintain the architecture of discrimination that continued to grossly limit African American housing options. Just as the federal government was jettisoning "separate but equal" in education, the FHA was proposing to institute the same system, in earnest, for housing. Previously, FHA programs offered nothing to African Americans, and now the agency was moving toward a program that would—within limits—insure Black homeownership. It was, nevertheless, a "policy of containment."[75] Hirsch explained how the FHA's shifting policies were to be qualified and that "the real intent of such a program . . . was not to alter racial patterns, but to make the inner city a proper and desirable place to live."[76] Segregation was not the problem; lack of opportunity within the ghetto was the problem to be resolved.

THE VOLUNTARY HOME MORTGAGE CREDIT PROGRAM

In 1954, when motivating the new housing legislation, Republican president Dwight Eisenhower made the observation, "It must be frankly and honestly acknowledged, that many members of minority groups, regardless of their income or economic status, have had the least opportunity of all of our citizens to acquire good homes." Eisenhower went on to insist that "administrative policies . . . must be . . . strengthened and augmented to insure equal opportunity for all our citizens to acquire within their means good and well-located homes . . . and we shall encourage adequate market financing and the construction of new housing for such families."[77]

The fruition of this lofty outline of federal objectives for Black housing was the creation of the Voluntary Home Mortgage Credit Program (VHMCP). This federal program arose in response to the growing African American demand for access to the mortgage market. The new agency was born out of a collaboration that brought together NAREB, the NAHB, and the Life Insurance Association of America.[78] The VHMCP was toothless in that it provided no mortgage money and did not close any loans; instead, its policy was to facilitate the flow of funds for residential mortgages into areas or communities where there may be a shortage of local capital. To qualify for the services of the VHMCP, prospective clients had to have been turned down at least twice by the FHA and the VA before they would be directed to a participating lender.[79] The VHMCP was an underwhelming response to the overwhelming housing needs of African Americans. Even though the program was primarily intended to help minority buyers who could not secure financing, the VHMCP was also utilized to find loans for those in rural areas. To underline the depth of racism within the real estate industry and the FHA, consider that even with a program largely intended to help minority buyers, the VHMCP's overwhelming assistance went to "non-minorities." In almost seven years of existence, it placed only 47,000 loans for $470 million. The highest number of loans processed was 12,000 in 1956, but of those only 2,700 were for "racial minorities."[80]

In comparison with Eisenhower's sharp rhetoric that acknowledged inequality experienced by African Americans, the creation of the VHMCP was a miserable failure. By the VHMCP's own assessment, it was unable to solve the prospective Black homeowner's problem of a lack of adequate access to home financing. Indeed, the inadequate performance of the VHMCP was tied to the historic practices of the FHA and its deleterious impact on housing available to African Americans. An internal VHMCP audit found that "Negroes have generally been restricted to older sections of cities, and many older properties would not quality for VA loan . . . or FHA mortgage insurance." The report concluded that the segregation of African Americans inflated "the price of available properties to a point where FHA . . . financing . . . cannot be used."[81] In effect, the VHMCP only affirmed the discriminatory practices of the FHA; it certainly did not challenge them.

Federal officials insisted that it was the private sector and local government that were responsible for housing in the United States. Albert Cole, the director of the Housing and Home Finance Agency, which housed the FHA, said as much in 1956 when he claimed, "The role of the federal government in the housing programs is to assist, to stimulate, to lead and sometimes to prod, but never to dictate or coerce, and never to stifle the proper exercise of private and local responsibility."[82] Of course, the notion that banks were simply "private" entities beyond the influence of federal or local officials could unravel at the slightest prod. It is true that banks and other thrifts were privately owned, but in the aftermath of the Great Depression, the U.S. government heavily regulated and supported both. Banks and thrifts operating in the United States had their deposits guaranteed by the government—the only way to ensure that people would continue to keep their money there. The Federal Home Loan Bank regulated banks and savings and loan associations across the country. The FNMA purchased billions of dollars' worth of mortgages from banks to maintain a steady flow of money for lending. Far from being independent, private institutions, banks were regulated, insured, and paid for by the federal government. As one report put it, "The federal government is the principal supporter and regulator of the financial institutions that govern the housing market. Its programs of mortgage insurance and mortgage guarantees have been a bulwark to the private housing industry, stimulating the great expansion of that industry and revolutionizing its practices."[83] And it was not only the banks. The entirety of the housing industry also wound through multiple government agencies, relying on subsidies, interest rates set at the federal level, and the secondary market established to maintain liquidity throughout the industry. Perhaps the relationship was best captured by the words of William Levitt, the largest developer in the United States and creator of the 17,000-unit development known as Levittown, who infamously said, "We are 100 percent dependent on the government. Whether this is right or wrong, it is a fact."[84]

Despite the authoritative role of the federal government in the banking industry and, by extension, the housing sector, federal regulators refused to enforce the law, claiming that the market alone could ultimately resolve the housing issues for African Americans. Historian David Freund has pointed out the lengths to which the FHA went to obscure its role as a government agency in facilitating the homeownership boom of the postwar period. Writes Freund, "Federal interventions did more than simply structure opportunity [for whites]; paradoxically they also helped to popularize the idea that government interventions were *not* providing considerable benefits to white people."[85]

Even as the *Brown* decision had clearly declared that segregation, at least in education, was no longer constitutionally defensible, the reluctance of agents of the state to enforce existing and newly developing civil rights law was palpable. The U.S. Commission on Civil Rights in 1961 recommended that the FHA develop a policy to "take immediate steps to withdraw Federal benefits from [accused builders or developers] pending final action by the appropriate state agency or court."[86] The FHA refused. According to FHA commissioner Neal Hardy,

> It is our opinion that enforcement of State [and] local antidiscrimination laws is a local responsibility. FHA should be neither a fact-finding organization nor a policing authority for enforcement of State and local laws. FHA does take the responsibility of refusing to do business with persons who do not comply with such State and local antidiscrimination laws and refuse to correct such noncompliance. . . . No further changes are presently contemplated in FHA policy or practice to impose an open-occupancy requirement in FHA-assisted housing without such a policy directive from either the Congress or the Executive.[87]

When asked whether or not the FHA should create rules requiring banks not to discriminate if they were going to do business with the federal government, the commissioner demurred, "In our opinion, a nondiscrimination requirement for 'approval' could be accomplished without additional legislation, but we do not presently contemplate adopting such a requirement without a policy directive from the Congress or from the Executive. . . . No problems are anticipated. It is probable some mortgagees may reduce their FHA activity or drop out entirely so as to avoid possible controversy."[88] The FHA's refusal to act against discrimination allowed the housing industry and banks to continue excluding urban-based African Americans, even as the agency was loosening its own restrictions on guaranteeing mortgages for African Americans in cities.

The consequences of Black exclusion from conventional lending sources were even more serious than the loss of the economic benefit of FHA programs. The lack of an actual free market in housing created a *captive* market in which Blacks had to pay exorbitant costs for inferior housing. Clarence Mitchell pointed out the hypocrisy of the "free market" in housing during testimony at a federal hearing in 1955:

> The present policy of restriction in the housing field is a startling repudiation of all that the traditional supporters of free enterprise are supposed to stand for. I included this statement about free enterprise because I think in the housing field the free enterprise banner is raised more frequently than in almost any field that I know of. Can anyone imagine the automobile industry restricting its sales to whites only? Can anyone imagine a man

who wants to sell refrigerators ignoring a substantial part of his potential market simply because that market is not white? Yet this is exactly what is happening in the real estate and housing field.[89]

In Cleveland, a real estate broker described the collusion that kept African Americans out of the "decent" housing promised in the National Housing Act as a "gentleman's agreement among the builder, the banker, and the real estate agent in which all have agreed to prevent an open market in housing as far as Negroes are concerned" that "in the final analysis . . . goes back to the bank."[90] But a survey of real estate agents taken in San Francisco in the late 1950s also identified why the arrangement was so difficult to dismantle: "By and large, the vast majority of realtors still believe in residential segregation and believe that to maintain their control of the market for used homes they must find ways to prevent minority prospects from finding housing in all-white neighborhoods."[91]

The Black Tax

When whites fled American cities to move into their new federally subsidized suburban houses, those "used homes" referred to by the real estate agent survey above created new homeownership opportunities for Blacks but on very expensive terms. Although many whites left for the greener pastures of the suburbs voluntarily, others had to be cajoled; the practice of "blockbusting" or "panic peddling" was widespread in the era of mass suburbanization. In a special report on housing in Chicago in 1962, the *Saturday Evening Post* published an exposé on blockbusting featuring a speculator's description of the process:

> I specialize in locating blocks which I consider ripe for racial change. Then I "bust" them by buying properties from the white owners and selling them to Negroes—with the intent of breaking down the rest of the block for colored occupancy. I make my money—and quite a lot of it incidentally—in three ways: 1) by beating down the prices I pay the white owners. . . . 2) by selling to the eager Negroes at inflated prices; and 3) by financing these purchases at what amounts to a very high rate of interest. . . . If anybody who is well established in this business doesn't earn $100,000 a year [they are] loafing.[92]

Blockbusting thrived for two reasons: redlining and the other artificial barriers to Blacks' housing mobility and the growth of a Black population desperate for living spaces. Even with rampant mortgage discrimination, African

Americans still invested in homeownership. There was a small handful of Black mortgage lenders throughout the period of Black migration. Many of the Black lenders organized savings and loan association branches that operated locally among relatively tight-knit groups of people. In 1930, there were seventy-three minority-owned thrifts with assets totaling $6.5 million, but by 1950 this number had dropped to twenty-nine because of the consolidation of smaller thrifts, and their asset holdings swelled to $18 million.[93] Black-owned savings and loans offered some lending options for African Americans, but Black lenders also exploited the inflated costs of the Black housing market and engaged Black customers under predatory terms.[94]

In several cities, however, African Americans in search of mortgages turned to LICs to purchase property. Historian Beryl Satter has written the definitive history on contract buying in home sales. They were akin to "rent-to-own" schemes, in which purchasers paid higher interest rates and higher overall costs as a result.[95] Where African Americans were not able to borrow from conventional lenders, they were forced into financially exploitative relationships.[96] While white homeowners were enjoying small down payments and low interest rates, contract buyers had no such choices. The thousands of additional dollars paid by African Americans for older and inferior housing compared with their suburban peers had long-term detrimental impacts in the many cities where LICs were used. Higher home costs meant less money available to invest in renovations and general maintenance, exacerbating the already deteriorated condition of Black urban properties. The excessive monthly payments incurred by contract buyers also forced residents to bring more people into their households in an attempt to cover their monthly housing costs, producing neighborhood overcrowding that weighed negatively on property values.[97] In 1961, the Urban League estimated that African Americans in Chicago spent more than $157 million over a seven-year period for the added cost of renting and owning homes. The *Atlanta Daily World* calculated that, in part, that money could build and fully equip fifty hospitals with 100 rooms as well as purchase almost 8,000 three-bedroom ranch-style houses with $20,000 mortgages.[98]

The "race tax" in housing was only one way in which the segregation of Blacks created opportunities for economic exploitation. In the September 1968 edition of *Ebony* magazine, Senator Warren G. Magnuson, who was chairman of the Senate Commerce Committee, wrote an article titled "How the Ghetto Gets Gypped."[99] His story was based on multiple reports showing how segregation, overlapped with under-resourced public services such as affordable mass transit, effectively captured the Black consumer market, making it vulnerable to paying higher prices. Magnuson referred specifically to a 1968 study conducted in Washington, D.C., by the Federal Trade Commission that found that ghetto stores charged higher prices than stores in other areas for the same goods. The study found that 92 percent of sales made in urban stores were based on exploitative installment plans, as compared with 27 percent of sales outside ghetto areas. The commission found that urban stores were selling, *on average*, the same merchandise for 50 percent more than other stores. Magnuson described how surveys in "Boston, Philadelphia, Chicago and San Francisco revealed the same pattern: the poor are paying exorbitant prices, usually 75 to 100 percent for goods from stores in low-income areas as compared with those in 'ethical' stores patronized by the middle-class."[100]

When radicals later described Black communities as "internal colonies" within the United States, the color tax supported their rhetoric. In an *Ebony* article describing the political economy of the urban ghetto, Alex Poinsett wrote, "Economic racism? Its effects abound. Ghetto economics are such that black income is half and black unemployment nearly three times the national average. Black dollars buy less, are harder to acquire, and are eaten up faster and in larger bits by usurious and fraudulent practices than white dollars. Markups of 100 to 300 percent are quite common in the ghetto. American colonialism, in short, relegates black people to a subordinate, inferior status, entrapping them in a vicious poverty cycle."[101] Two Black men interviewed in Cleveland after riots broke out there in 1966 described the exploitative dynamic that existed between Black communities and white society. According to one, "The whites know what they are doing. They want us to make the money for them and don't want us to have a damn thing." And in the words of the other, "A major problem in this country is that the white power structure still looks upon the black community as a plantation."[102] A Black youth from Watts connected this exploitation to what became a wave of rebellion when he explained, "Looting and robbing is not the same thing. When you loot a credit store you are just taking back some of the interest that they have been charging you for years on them high-priced installment things they sell you on time—$10 down and $2 a week for 900 years."[103] In Watts, citizens made sure to destroy the records of their debt in department stores before setting the buildings on fire.[104]

Activists Stokely Carmichael and Charles Hamilton described the ghetto as a source of wealth for those who lived outside its boundaries: "Exploiters come into the ghetto, from outside, bleed it dry, and leave it economically dependent on the larger society.... The white power structure has collaborated in the economic serfdom of Negros by its reluctance to give loans and insurance to Negro businesses."[105] They concluded as a result, "The groups which have access to the necessary resources and the ability to effect change benefit politically and economically from the subordinate status of the Black community."[106] Indeed, in a hearing on "financial institutions and the urban crisis," Senator Walter Mondale, a Democrat from Minnesota, gave a description of the exploitation of Black communities that would rival any offered by Black revolutionaries of the day. He testified that "urban ghettos ... share another characteristic with some undeveloped countries—and that is the problem of colonial exploitation. This subcommittee knows only too well the tragic story of the fast-buck operators and unscrupulous lenders who prey upon the undereducated and under informed residents of the ghetto."[107] These crooks were easy to point out. Mondale also described "more subtle forms of colonialism, such as ... savings institutions located in or near ghetto areas ... tapping the savings of the ghetto and reinvesting them in mortgages in white suburbia."[108] Mondale and other reformers used this revelation as an argument for greater "development" of urban areas. But for those suffering the exploitative conditions themselves, the colonial metaphor was the basis of political radicalization and a sharpening critique of capitalism.

Despite the evidence of multiple contributing factors, many of the commissions and studies of the 1960s continued to overemphasize poverty as both the cause of conditions within the inner city and the reason for the persistence of residential segregation. They repeated the theory that Blacks were in ghettos because they could not afford rents beyond the ghetto's borders. Even the Kerner Commission clung to the logic of Black poverty as the impetus of residential segregation: "Many ghetto residents simply cannot pay the rent necessary to support decent housing."[109] It was undoubtedly true that many Black residents were living in extreme poverty in urban neighborhoods, but what Black residents understood to be true and what the researchers completely failed to grasp was that in most cases African Americans were paying as much as, if not more than, whites, but for inferior housing. Civil rights leader Whitney Young described this in a weekly column he wrote for New York's *Amsterdam News*: "Some whites fail to recognize that millions of Negro families are paying more for leasing a Harlem slum than their white counterparts pay for a Hartford townhouse. When Negro leaders assail the 'color tax,' slumlordism, the bigotry of many banks and savings and loan associations and their realtor allies toiling to keep Negroes in the ghetto, these whites look the other way." In an interview with the *Chicago*

Tribune, Martin Luther King Jr. also discussed the "race tax," noting, "My neigh-bors pay more for rents than their neighbors in the white suburbs. In Lawndale, a Negro pays $90 a month for an apartment without utilities and intermittent heat. A white in South Deering, Gage Park or Belmont pays $80 a month for a similar apartment."[110] That African Americans often paid exorbitant prices for housing and a wide range of goods and services makes dubious the claim that Black poverty was the *cause* of exploitative practices in Black communities instead of the outcome of those transactions. It is more likely that exploitative real estate practices *created* or greatly exacerbated poverty. Discrimination and segregation created the conditions where these exploitative practices could take place. A Chicago Urban League report identified the impact of this exploitation in a study of the early 1960s:

> Negroes must pay a color tax of approximately $10 per month more than do whites for comparable housing. The median monthly rent in 1960 was the same for both Negro and white families, i.e., $88, but the quality of housing occupied by the Negro family was more likely to be inferior. . . . It appears that Negroes pay directly an average of $1500 more than whites for com-parable dwellings. In addition, Negro homebuyers generally have to pay higher interest rates on mortgages and/or contract purchases. Although Negro families earned one-third less than did white families in 1960, they spent a higher portion of their take-home pay than did white families for comparable housing.[111]

These patterns of economic exploitation were evidence that it was not just racial hatred that maintained the segregation of African Americans in their urban enclaves. A political economy had emerged and was structured around the cap-tive African American market. Social theorist Noliwe Rooks has identified this phenomenon as "segrenomics," "the business of profiting specifically from high levels of racial and economic segregation," when observing similar dynamics in urban public education.[112] The persistence and perpetual inattention to racial segregation created the conditions for predatory inclusion in the real estate mar-ket when the formal barriers to participation were removed. Black people paid top dollar for substandard housing because their housing choices had been vio-lently curtailed. This economic imperative concerning race structured the hous-ing market and the broader consumer market that inflated prices on the specula-tion that the combination of isolation and immobility would compel Blacks to pay higher prices. Even as the FHA was finally loosening its decades-long practice of excluding African Americans from its unique home financing practices, it was doing so in a market that was primed to exploit Black consumers and extract from their communities. Moreover, the laxity of the FHA and its home office, the Housing and Home Finance Agency, in protecting the rights of African Americans as consumers in the housing market would prove consequential again when the Black housing market began to take shape by the end of the 1960s.

The price of housing was not just high, but its price afforded very little. The combination of poor condition and high price is part of what ignited the urban rebellions. In the weeks after the uprising in Detroit in 1967, a *Washington Post* poll forcefully linked deteriorating conditions in Black communities with the uprisings. Fully 70 percent of Blacks "attributed rioting to housing conditions." Fifty-nine percent of Blacks said they knew someone living in rat-infested housing; 57 percent reported holes in their ceilings; 49 percent said their housing was overcrowded; and 68 percent reported cockroaches in their housing. In the poll, even 39 percent of whites said they believed the condition of Black housing was responsible for the ongoing rioting.[113]

When Los Angeles attorney Caryl Warner was interviewed for a governor's commission investigating the causes of rioting in Watts, he was asked what he thought had contributed to the unrest. He responded simply, "When historians write the story of all of this trouble, they're going to wonder how in the hell such an incendiary element could have been so complacently accepted and overlooked."[114] To what "incendiary element" was he referring? It was the race tax.[115]

In 1967, president of the NAACP Roy Wilkins remarked on the centrality of housing to urban discontent at a 1967 congressional fair housing hearing:

> I might say as sort of a confession that while I have always believed that housing and employment and schools are the inseparable trio that must be dealt with as far as the ghetto living is concerned, I have been a little astonished to discover in recent years the tremendous feeling about housing and even more so than employment. Ordinarily we would say unemployment is No. 1. I personally say schools are [number one] ... but I have been astonished to find the number of people who consider housing. The refusal of housing as a crushing rebuttal of their ... position as human beings, as citizens ... there is nothing more humiliating. ... So in that sense, I guess it is the [number one] consideration.[116]

The rats, disrepair, and financial exploitation that defined Black urban housing throughout the twentieth century were produced in the clash of race, markets, and metropolitan development. The political economy of residential segregation not only hastened the conditions of physical decline in urban areas but forever incentivized their perpetuation. As many by now have noted, the herding of African Americans into ghettos was driven by financial interests that ranged from working-class white homeowners to the real estate brokers, bankers, and others invested in the postwar housing-industrial complex. Those interests were not always discreet. Real estate brokers and bankers became integral to the FHA's massive expansion of homeownership in the 1940s. The partnership between business and government to expand homeownership was as successful in securing homeownership for millions of working-class whites as it was in excluding millions of potential Black homeowners. The race tax was a powerful incentive to maintain the status quo in the field of housing.

The FHA's proclivity for innovation and pioneering in the world of real estate, while guided by conventionally racist ideas about African Americans, would continue to shape the agency's attitude toward potential Black homeowners. The changing politics of the United States, outside the South, in the aftermath of World War II included abandoning explicit acts of racial discrimination by the federal government. The propulsion of the United States into the position of global leader had been complicated by the dubious treatment of its Black citizens. This, along with rising demands by Blacks for greater inclusion and integration into U.S. society, pressured the FHA to shift its hostile policies directed at excluding African Americans. But with little resolution to the persisting racist attitudes within the real estate industry and among bank lenders, along with weak antidiscrimination law and enforcement, it was unclear how these shifting FHA policies would be implemented. It was becoming clear that transforming the law was far different from transforming the attitudes of the federal agents charged with enforcing the new laws or of those within the private agencies where the new policies would be implemented. This was the perplexing climate of uncertainty and anticipation, hope and rage, that shaped the coming federal backing of Black homeownership.

2

The Business of the Urban Housing Crisis

The progress and stability of our free society have been firmly rooted
in a harmonious and creative partnership of public and private actions,
and the constructive cooperation of public and private institutions.
—President Lyndon B. Johnson, speech at Government-Business
Conference on Urban Problems, August 19, 1966

"TODAY, AMERICA'S CITIES are in crisis. This clear and urgent warning rises from the decay of decades—and is amplified by the harsh realities of the present."[1] In February 1968, with this subtle allusion to the rebellions of the prior summer, President Lyndon Johnson began his nationally televised special address to Congress on the crisis in American cities. In the speech, titled "The Crisis of the Cities," Johnson declared poverty and the dilapidated conditions of American cities "the shame of the nation" and vowed to undertake unprecedented action to "change the face of our cities and to end the fear of those—rich and poor alike—who call them home." Even after all of the civil rights legislation he had shepherded through Congress, including the War on Poverty and the creation of the Department of Housing and Urban Development, Johnson observed that "almost 29 million people remain in poverty" and American cities continued to deteriorate. In a proposal Johnson called the Housing and Urban Development Act (HUD Act), he laid out an ambitious legislative program. He described the act as a "charter of renewed hope for the American City,"[2] mapping a new direction in the ongoing battle against urban crisis.

Later in the summer of 1968, this new direction would culminate in the passage of the HUD Act, which called upon Congress to approve legislation to build or rehabilitate 26 million units of housing, including 6 million units of low-income housing, all within ten years. It also approved a program to facilitate low-income and poor people in becoming homeowners. To accomplish these historic goals, the legislation called for unprecedented participation among bankers, real estate brokers, and homebuilders in an urgent effort to avert the spiraling urban crisis. Johnson and other Democrats proclaimed there were limits to what government could accomplish as they summoned what Johnson described as the "genius of private industry" to do what government, thus far, had been unable to achieve. Intended to fulfill ongoing demands for suitable and decent housing for all, the partnership between private enterprise and government agencies was, in some ways, a continuation of public-private partnerships that had always been at the heart of American housing policies.[3] The legacy of the Johnson administration is one of large government-directed programs. The War on Poverty and the Great Society were considered the quintessence of "big government liberalism." These public-private partnerships, so essential to Johnson's formulation of housing policy, complicate the history and popular conceptions of the Great Society as the "era of big government."[4]

Though the Johnson welfare state would become a foil for conservative politicians to run against—and for the Democratic Party to run away from—for Johnson, private industry was central to constructing the Great Society.[5] To create conditions conducive to the success of business while continuing to invest in areas that required a massive infusion of resources and development, state power was needed. This was especially true in cities across the country where banks and the insurance industry had written off the urban core as too "risky," causing the development of urban housing for the poor and working class to stagnate. Subsidies, tax relief, and government guarantees could create the conditions for those institutions to reverse course and help stem the urban crisis. While leveraging state power in this way created pathways for business to capitalize on new ventures, including in housing, the dearth of good, affordable housing was a persistent problem that could easily be described as too big for government alone to solve. This chapter looks at how business came to shape Johnson's housing agenda—specifically, the way that homeownership became the centerpiece of the most important housing legislation of the era.

A "PUBLIC INTEREST PARTNERSHIP"

A 1960 Democratic National Convention report described the challenge of re-building "our cities and cop[ing] with explosive suburban growth."[6] Between 1960 and 1966, the white urban population decreased by 900,000 while the white suburban population increased by 10 million. A report from the National Committee Against Discrimination in Housing showed that, by 1967, two-thirds of Americans were living in metropolitan areas. Within this majority, 57 percent of whites lived in the suburbs, while 75 percent of nonwhites inhabited the "central metropolitan area."[7]

The plight of American cities and the growing visibility of urban poverty complicated the assumption that soaring profit rates in business could determine the well-being of the country as a whole. Urban conditions, particularly for African Americans, stood in contrast to overall claims of American affluence. African Americans had continued their postwar trek to American cities throughout the 1960s and had become a critical component of the Democratic Party's electoral coalition, meaning that the conditions of the places they called home were politicized. Johnson's War on Poverty and Great Society programs were, in part, a response to the intensification of an "urban crisis" and its potential political perils.

Though Johnson would become known for addressing the crisis, he was far from the first to recognize it. Just weeks before the presidential election pitting John F. Kennedy against Richard Nixon in 1960, Kennedy had affirmed a report produced out of a conference held on urban affairs. The report defined the contours of what would become popularly known as the urban crisis: substandard and slum housing, under-resourced schools, inadequate means of transportation, and discriminatory treatment of "minority groups." The heart of the report was focused on poor housing conditions in American cities. It dramatically calculated that more Americans lived in slums than on farms, that 40 million Americans lived in substandard housing, and that 5 million Americans living in cities had inadequate plumbing facilities. According to the report, this housing crisis was caused by the "the inability of the American city, with its limited taxing powers, to finance unaided the massive rebuilding programs and level of municipal services required to prevent decay." African Americans and other "minority groups" suffered, disproportionately, "much worse housing conditions than their fellow citizens." The consequences of these "worse conditions" were "overpricing, overcrowding, and profiteering, and these practices accelerate decay in the neighborhoods in which minorities are forced to live."[8]

By 1972, the Department of Commerce and the National Planning Association calculated that rebuilding the cities would cost $191 billion annually well into the 1970s.[9] As whites continued to move out of cities, the tax base needed to pay the costs of reversing the condition of American cities was dwindling. Complicating matters further was the fierce competition for federal dollars by the mid-1960s, pitting domestic programs against the mushrooming costs of war in Vietnam.[10] These financial tensions created the conditions for unprecedented partnerships. The collaboration between business and the state in the provision of low-income housing was one new result. It was a new partnership that would fundamentally reshape housing policy in the United States.

In the previous three decades, federal policies had notoriously privileged suburban investment and development to the peril of urban America. Indeed, private enterprise had ignored the housing needs of low-income and poor people and led a vociferous fight against policies business leaders believed would compete with their industries. But when urban rebellions threatened to lay waste the core of American cities, urban rehabilitation became a new frontier for the housing industry—with the full backing of the federal government.

For some, the promotion of homeownership and access to credit in neighborhoods and communities that previously had been ignored was appealing as a new means of social control. Desperate federal and local officials believed that greater investment and inclusion in mainstream society would stem the tide of rebellion and property destruction. Herbert Northrup, the director of the Department of Industry at the Wharton business school at the University of Pennsylvania, said in an interview, "A job does wonders. First thing, you know, he's got a mortgaged house and a mortgaged car like the rest of us—he's part of the system—and he's got to stay on the job like all the rest of us to meet the payments."[11]

For other reformers, specifically businessmen, formerly neglected urban markets were oases of new investment opportunities—under certain conditions. Generous subsidies and government guarantees would bring private investment and the extension of credit on widespread, conventional terms into Black urban communities for the first time. In a meeting with corporate leaders, President Johnson described his vision of the *new* partnership with business and government:

> The progress and stability of our free society have been firmly rooted in a harmonious and creative partnership of public and private actions, and the constructive cooperation of public and private institutions. . . . American

business has a large stake in resolving the problems of urbanization. . . . Our cities have been built on a partnership between government and private business in the past. . . . The partnership is, as *Fortune* magazine recently called it, "the new interdependence" and is based on wide areas of mutual interest. The areas must be broadened and deepened if the interdependence is to be of lasting benefit for all Americans.[12]

Johnson's special assistant Joseph Califano believed the accusations against Johnson of facilitating "big government" and federal excess wrongly created the perception of the president as "some kind of Machiavellian sugar daddy—bent on dominating the process of change in American schools, in the cities, and in the life of individual citizens, spending money as fast as it can be printed."[13] A 1965 *Washington Post* article queried how a "liberal, reformist, big spending Democratic president . . . has more conservative supporters than Teddy Roosevelt could ever shake a big stick at."[14] Of course, one answer was that the conservatism-cum-fanaticism of Barry Goldwater drove business into the arms of Johnson. But it was also the case that Johnson kept "the national climate pretty favorable to private enterprise. He doesn't scold business or businessmen. Profit is no longer a naughty word." A second explanation was more significant: "If LBJ ha[d] built a bridge to the business community, it is equally evident that business ha[d] built a bridge to the Administration and to economic policies it used to consider unorthodox and unacceptable."[15]

As Califano explained, the Great Society was a "truly significant [partnership] in our society, [an] alliance between the private sector and the government."[16] The partnership between business and government was not new; over time, the symbiosis between business and the state had become a fact of American life. But during the Johnson administration, Califano described the collaboration as a "creative revolution" born out of a "deepening involvement of the private sector in our public and social problems." By the late 1960s, the United States was entering a period of "Public Interest Partnership" involving the "private sector in the process of shaping the nation's legislative and administrative programs." These partnerships worked because "profits to stockholders coincided with the government's urgent need to fulfill its most basic responsibility to the people it serves: the survival of their society."[17]

These partnerships with government were not just good for business; for some industry leaders they presented new opportunities to rehabilitate the image of corporate America that had come under withering attack over the course of the

1960s. McGraw-Hill, in a 1968 special report addressed to business leaders concerning the urban crisis, described consequences and potential advantages to developing the urban market:

> In the wake of the riots that focus attention on the angry frustrations of American slum dwellers, business faces a choice: Let the anger take its course or act now to relieve it. For rational men that's no choice at all. . . . If you ignore the crisis, slums could siphon off more and more of your profits: slums are a luxury few cities can afford and much of what it costs comes from taxes and business. Costs multiply from police and fire insurance. . . . If you ignore the crisis, you may be overlooking a potential big market: The city has always been a social and economic necessity for businessmen. If today's sick cities can be cured—if ghetto dwellers can be better housed, better educated and above all, better employed—new and profitable markets will open up for business. Even the process of saving the cities creates new business opportunities.[18]

Guns, Butter, and Business

"Time may require further sacrifices," Johnson had acknowledged in his 1966 State of the Union message, "and if it does, then we will make them. But we will not heed those who would wring it from the hopes of the unfortunate here in a land of plenty. I believe that we can continue the Great Society while we fight in Vietnam."[19] By the end, the U.S. government spent almost a trillion dollars on the Vietnam War.

The disparity between domestic spending and war spending became known popularly as the "guns and butter" debate. In 1966, the deficit had been what was considered a manageable $3.7 billion, but by 1967, it had more than doubled to $8.2 billion. Johnson's budget proposal for 1968 was an astonishing $172 billion, the largest in American history. As the urban rebellions surged in intensity, so too did the federal government's spending in response. Between 1963 and 1966, welfare spending had been $14.5 billion, but in 1966 and 1967, it increased rapidly to $35 billion. The costs of the Vietnam War were quickly catching up, reaching $40 billion between 1967 and 1968, and Johnson's advisors feared that number could climb to $72 billion by the end of 1968—a figure not seen since World War II.[20]

The economic and political tensions over budget priorities shaped the context in which proposals for the economic intervention of private enterprise in the cities materialized. Greater participation by the private sector could resolve multiple problems for Johnson. It would allow him to sidestep a Congress reluctant to continue paying for antipoverty legislation. In the 1966 midterm elections, Johnson lost the congressional coalition that had delivered his wish list of antipoverty programming, civil rights legislation, and his historic 1964 tax cut. Ultimately, political strife stoked by persistent demands for civil and economic rights by African Americans, along with deepening fears about the creep of inflation, led to the collapse of the congressional coalition that had produced the historic civil rights legislation of 1964.

Following the 1966 election, Democrats continued to control Congress, but they lost forty-seven seats in the House and three in the Senate. Johnson was no longer the maestro of a sympathetic legislative body. The turn to private enterprise in fulfilling the promises of the Great Society became even more necessary as Johnson's electoral coalition unraveled. But involvement for business was more straightforward. If corporate power could not stem the mounting frustration in the United States, it would be faced with the possibility of growing taxation for the continued build-out of the American welfare state. As one writer put it, business could willingly assist in the effort to rebuild American cities or "business will find itself forced to change in ways far more repulsive . . . than any of the social alternatives."[21]

The strains of Johnson's dual agenda of expanding the war in Vietnam while simultaneously ramping up the War on Poverty were also evident in his plummeting approval rating. The number of his "strong supporters" dipped from 25 percent to 16 percent, and his approval rating hovered beneath 50 percent. His support for a 6 percent income tax hike to generate more revenue was exasperating in a climate of growing inflation that cut into the gains of historically low unemployment and high wages.[22] Senator Robert F. Kennedy captured the dilemma when he told *Life* magazine, "Because of Vietnam there just isn't enough federal money available to do the job. . . . So we must convince the private sector that it is their responsibility too. They can create dignity—not welfare handouts—for the poor."[23] As destructive riots became a seasonal phenomenon, there was tremendous pressure on the federal government to do more. The turn to business seemed necessary because to many, the federal government not only was not doing enough but also seemed incapable of doing more.

African Americans were also disappointed in the performance of government, evidenced by persistent uprisings but also by the turn to business, for some, in search of lasting solutions to the urban crisis. Kenneth Clark testified before the

Kerner Commission that "business and industry are our last hope. They are the most realistic elements of our society. Other areas of our society—government, education, churches, labor—have defaulted in dealing with Negro problems."[24] Even some Black militants welcomed the investment of the private sector in the inner cities. In Detroit, Black militant Frank Ditto organized a meeting between white corporate leaders and neighborhood activists to discuss what business could do for the city. Ditto said to the businessmen, "If you cats can't do it, it's never going to get done."[25]

Not everyone welcomed the role of business in rebuilding American cities. Robert Allen, in his important book *Black Awakening in Capitalist America*, decried "corporate imperialism" as a vehicle to undermine developing Black radicalism in the ghettos. Academic activists Frances Fox Piven and Richard Cloward warned that corporate influence would undermine democracy in rebuilding cities. They argued that "the new corporate role will help to erode the power of municipal government at a time when the black is about to obtain control of the city. . . . Since these new administrative complexes will be largely removed from popular control—the blacks of the ghetto cannot hope to control them."[26]

Over the course of the decade, while a sharper focus on the role of business developed, critiques of capitalism more generally concluded that the economic system was incompatible with attending to the human need that appeared to be everywhere. These critiques were also leeching into the developing student movement and the emergent "New Left" as well. The consciousness of these formations was not only shaped by the Black urban insurgency but also impacted by the widening war in Vietnam and the perception that the war "meant military contracts for the companies that built napalm bombs and the airplanes that strafed the jungles of North Vietnam . . . [and] was a crusade for capitalism devoted to protecting American institutions."[27] As New Left activist Staughton Lynd wrote, "We need to find ways to lay siege to corporations."[28] Meanwhile, a study done by Oklahoma Christian University in 1973 ranked businessmen last for ethical standards. Henry Niles, a former executive of a life insurance company complained, "A lot of young people are disoriented and have lost confidence in the economic and political system."[29]

This deepening disillusionment was most brutally evident when several banks were bombed and set afire in the late 1960s and 1970s, including a Bank of America branch in southern California and Chase Manhattan Bank in New York City. In a fifteen-month span, thirty-five Bank of America branches were bombed or set afire.[30] After the bank bombing in the town of Isla Vista in southern California, Bank of America claimed that it created a $100 million pool for mortgage loans to be made available to prospective African American homebuyers.[31] Bank president Robert Truex conceded, "We don't deny we're part of the establishment," but, he continued, "we have to dispel wrong notions of what we stand for."[32]

By the mid-1960s, business had become a popular target for boycotts and protests.[33] In Philadelphia, Leon Sullivan organized "selective patronage" to punish businesses that refused to hire and promote African Americans despite the fact that Blacks were their regular patrons.[34] In Chicago, civil rights organizers created Operation Breadbasket to pressure businesses to hire African Americans.[35] Northern businesses with segregated outposts in the South were subjected to boycotts, pickets, and other forms of protest. When cities went up in flames, businesses with poor reputations in a given community were targeted for looting—or worse. In the wake of these events, corporate leaders hoped that job training programs or the building of new housing in the inner city would change perceptions of business. One banker explained, "Business must move from the defensive to the offensive and begin pushing the boundary line between the public and private sectors the other way. Both business and society stand to gain from the doctrine of socio-commercial enterprise."[36]

In 1968, Charles Lazarus, president of the American Retail Federation, said in a speech to the National Retail Merchants Association, "Our very profit system is on trial today. We have not been sufficiently sensitive to the cries and shouts for change in our society. We've got to recognize our own shortcomings and do something about them."[37] The decisions of business leaders to engage in what many of them referred to as "socio-commercial enterprise" was intended to recast business as a vehicle for social change.

Investment in the inner city also provided business with an opportunity to remake its image in the public eye while capitalizing on an emerging profit source. Despite the relative impoverishment of African Americans when compared with whites, their move to the cities improved the resources of many Black families, and the mass migration of Blacks into cities and those rising incomes created the conditions for a new market to be developed. The *Pittsburgh Courier* described African Americans as a $24-billion market and posed the question, "Why ignore this market?"[38] This, of course, had been the case for much of the postwar period, but by the late 1960s the urban rebellions had created an urgency for its development. Consequently, many businesses found that engaging African Americans as a community of consumers could improve their balance sheets as well as public perceptions. A pamphlet written by and for businessmen on the turn toward an urban market recognized that "the enormous need for city housing is a staggering problem; to business, that need represents a huge market—but only if some way can be found to make it profitable."[39] The riots compelled them to look harder than they had in the 1950s.

An Urban Coalition

In 1968 Robert Wood, undersecretary of HUD, spoke directly to business leaders about the Johnson vision of the new partnership necessary to resuscitate American cities. Woods said, "Private enterprise must be the actual builder of the renewed city and the new city. . . . Business has a vital stake in the stability of our urban system and its orderly growth. . . . It is in the long range interest of the business community to assist in the rebuilding of our cities to preserve those basic conditions on which business's own growth and profits depend."[40] Many of the country's most successful corporations took up the call for greater involvement in urban affairs and formed the Urban Coalition. Founded in the winter of 1966, "during the off season between summer riots,"[41] the Urban Coalition held an emergency convocation in Washington after the summer of 1967, convening more than 1,200 businesspeople, local officials, labor leaders, heads of antipoverty groups, nonprofit organizations, and a small number of African American civil rights advocates to discuss urban problems.[42] It was co-chaired by the chairman of Time Inc., the media conglomerate, and African American trade union leader A. Philip Randolph. Other participants included the chief executive officer of Litton Industries, a defense industry conglomerate; David Rockefeller, the president of Chase Manhattan Bank; Henry Ford II, the chairman of the Ford automotive corporation; the president of the Aluminum Company of America; and many others. They represented some of the most powerful companies in the nation. The Urban Coalition's mission was clear: "The crisis requires a new dimension of effort in both the public and private sectors, working together to provide jobs, housing, education and other needs in the cities. We believe the private sector of America must vigorously involve itself in the crisis of the cities by a commitment to investment, job training and hiring, and all that is necessary to the full enjoyment of [the] free enterprise system and also to its survival."[43]

The Urban Coalition established committees in major cities all over the country. The centerpiece of its program was a "massive emergency jobs program" of at least 1 million jobs for the "hardcore unemployed" in the inner cities. It also pledged to build at least 1 million units of low-income housing a year. The moralizing undercurrent shaping much of the public discussion on the role of private enterprise obfuscated the more direct conversation about the urban frontier as a new marketplace to conquer. As Henry Ford II put it, "Some may feel it unseemly to mention cost and profit when urgent human needs are involved, but the profit motive is a powerful force."[44] As *Life* pointed out, "With five million substandard homes in US cities, slum rehabilitation represents a potential $50 billion market."[45] At a conference on private enterprise and the urban crisis, the organizers explained, "It remains true that the biggest undeveloped market in the United States today is in the city. It is an economic opportunity of immense proportion."[46] A former commissioner of the Internal Revenue Service compared the process of investing in urban America to the way multinationals looked at investment in developing nations, once again acknowledging the colonial relationship between business and the inner city: "Let us not forget that the government offers businessmen incentives to invest in underdeveloped countries rather than the advanced nations of Western Europe. In fact . . . if the government wants an oil refinery at a particular location, it offers still further incentives to get a businessman to put it up. . . . Isn't a program to direct investment to our urban ghettos essentially a matter of encouraging private capital to gravitate to the underdeveloped areas of our own nation?"[47] The crux of the new partnership in response to the urban crisis rested on the ability of the government to ensure profitability by eliminating risk. Or as a HUD administrator put it, "Frankly we must bribe business into the slums."[48] Capitalists liked to talk about "risk" as a central feature of their economic system, but when it came to the business of urban reform, they wanted no risk, just the profit derived from investing there.

The Joint Committee on Urban Problems (JCUP)

Even before the crisis of the summer of 1967, its arrival was anticipated. Predicting a long summer, executives representing more than 300 insurance companies from across the country began meeting at Columbia University in November 1966 to discuss what could be done to address the crisis in American cities. The meeting included "leaders in the life insurance industry [and] leaders of the intellectual and academic and sociological fields" who came together to consider "the growing difficulties of urban life, urban problems and how they affected the individual in society."[49]

The serious consideration of these issues was not just an intellectual exercise; it was seen as self-preservation. As one executive put it, "This is no corporate do-goodism. It is a long-range attempt to promote a social environment in which business can continue to operate with public consent."[50] In fact, the objective of the meetings was to chart a course for housing rehabilitation projects that the private sector could dictate and direct throughout multiple cities while forestalling the possibility of an additional government program or agency further insinuating itself into urban affairs. James Oates, chairman of the board of Equitable Life Insurance, mobilized the framework of "socio-commercial enterprise" to explain why and how the insurance industry would reverse its long-standing aversion to urban investments in the service of African Americans. According to Oates, "The criteria of sound investment for a life insurance company should include service of the public interest, as well as the security and soundness of the investment."[51] Out of the meetings that began at Columbia, the two largest insurance associations, the American Life Convention and the Life Insurance Association of America, representing 92 percent of life insurance holdings in the United States, formed the Joint Committee on Urban Problems.

Prudential Insurance and Metropolitan Life Insurance Company (MetLife) were the two largest participants, but there were 349 life insurance companies across the United States that agreed to "assume a larger role in seeking solutions to the serious problems that confront our urban areas."[52] On September 13, 1967, Gilbert Fitzhugh, president of MetLife, the nation's largest life insurance company, and new chairman of JCUP, announced the formation of an "urban investment program" with pledges from hundreds of insurance companies totaling $1 billion "for investment in the city core area to improve housing conditions and finance job-creating enterprises."[53] The insurance companies had agreed to divert $1 billion of their normal investments toward this new, socially motivated venture in American cities. Prudential Insurance and MetLife made the largest and most significant pledges of up to $200 million each to create low-income housing and inner-city jobs.

President Johnson was ecstatic about this timely intervention. The money would instantly provide life for the moribund "rent supplement" program. JCUP, after months of meeting with HUD and Johnson, had agreed to finance several rent-supplement buildings that had already been approved by the FHA for sale but which no private investor had been willing to finance.[54] Johnson heartily praised the new endeavor, thanking the insurance executives for "a historic contribution to your country."[55] The parameters of the program, however, were much more expansive than investment in "rent supplement" buildings alone. There were four distinguishing characteristics of the urban investment program. The first was that this program was not going to be mistaken for an additional government program or bureaucracy. JCUP would coordinate its own clearinghouse to independently vet financing inquiries and proposals, and each company, on its own, would decide which projects it would fund. There was no centralized pool of money or a central, decision-making body to allocate funds. This way, each company retained its autonomy and made business decisions based on what was in its own best interest.[56]

Location was also critical in determining which projects to finance. Financing was only available in areas "of blight or near blight" where life insurance investments would not normally have been made. The insurance companies also made clear that no financing would be available at the below-market interest rate of 3 percent, which federal programs had used for years to keep prices low for nonprofit or other developers. But the insurance companies were lenders, not developers, and the higher the interest rate, the better the return. JCUP promised not to raise its rates above the FHA rate of 6 percent in 1967. It considered this a discount rate because of the risk it claimed was inherent to lending in these new locations. The linchpin of the new arrangement, though, was the FHA's guarantee of all of the multifamily and single-family mortgage loans that were to be financed going forward.[57]

The introduction of mortgage insurance into the central cities for single-family homes marked the beginning of the end of federal "redlining" practices that had been encouraged by the FHA since the 1930s. What was perhaps most ironic was that life insurance companies that had played a key role in restricting the flow of mortgage funds and financing more generally to Black communities were now facilitating this historic economic intervention in those very same communities and neighborhoods. A booklet published by life insurance companies touting their urban investment programs described this shift in housing policy in the following way: "Until life insurance companies made their urban commitment, most financial institutions deemed inner city areas too risky for investment.... The Federal Housing Administration, which for 20 years had approved mortgages only in better neighborhoods and suburbs ... modified its approach. Many people of the inner cities ... now became eligible for mortgage loans, insured by the FHA when their homes were financed by the life insurance companies ... and social progress was begun."[58] JCUP spokesperson Kenneth M. Wright insisted that the insurance industry's earlier lending practices were driven by place and not by the race of those who lived in the cities. Wright explained to the Kerner Commission, "I think you can understand this as a necessary fact of financial life, where many investments in or around slum areas would be subject to sufficient hazards of one sort or another."[59] In words that seemed to echo sentiments that ran throughout the finance and banking industries, he described the "inner city" or "ghetto" as an "area which is normally not undertaken because of this high risk. Similarly, on the question of location, I think you will find that private investors typically avoid areas where there is a deterioration of both the values of the property and the maintenance produced abnormal risks in an area that is going downhill for one reason or another."[60] Undoubtedly, there may have been concern about the depreciating value of older and deteriorating urban areas, but the erasure of race as an additional disqualifying factor reinforced the perception that poverty and location were the driving factors for marginalizing Black residents.

During the Kerner Commission, Wright attempted to recast the racially discriminatory practices of the insurance industry as prudent and colorblind business decisions. Ernest Stevens, who was the director of the FHA in Chicago, by the mid-1960s went so far as to say that "no area was ever redlined, as the saying goes. No area was precluded in Chicago." Instead, he credited the business acumen of the life insurance companies for "start[ing]" an expanded program of providing mortgage money for us to insure. This is what led to expanded FHA mortgages in the area."[61]

A HISTORY OF DISCRIMINATION

MetLife, however, had a history that would not be easily forgotten. For more than twenty years, the largest company involved in JCUP had been the subject of pickets, boycotts, and lawsuits because of its hostility to Black renters and buyers. The urban investment program of JCUP was not MetLife's first foray into urban development. In 1943, MetLife entered an agreement with the city of New York to create Stuyvesant Town, "the largest urban redevelopment housing project in the United States."[62] The creation of Stuyvesant Town was a classic public-private venture. Buildings were razed by the city of New York under the pretext of slum clearance, and eventually MetLife received a $53-million tax exemption for twenty-five years as part of its agreement with the city. Despite the enormous number of public resources afforded to build Stuyvesant, MetLife demanded sole control over tenant placement, and that included the right to discriminate against Black tenants. The president of MetLife, Frederick Ecker, insisted that

"Negroes and whites don't mix. . . . If we brought them into the development it would be to the detriment of the city, too, because it would depress all of the surrounding properties."[63]

In the postwar climate of growing demands for Black rights, Stuyvesant Town became a battleground in the national struggle for "justice, fairness and democracy." MetLife fought for the right to discriminate against Black tenants all the way to the Supreme Court. Ultimately, the Supreme Court of the United States did not hear the case, but in 1947, the New York State Supreme Court took MetLife's side and ruled that Stuyvesant Town was a private development and thus could rent to whomever its owners wanted. The essence of the ruling was that "the dollars of Black taxpayers and policyholders would be used to subsidize homes that Black people could not occupy."[64] One year after the battle was ignited over Stuyvesant Town, in 1944 MetLife announced construction of an all-Black development in Harlem called the Riverton Houses. The NAACP opposed the Riverton Houses as "Jim Crow" housing, but the development showed that MetLife did not have a problem with Black tenants; it was just opposed to them living alongside white tenants. Historian Martha Biondi credits the struggle to integrate Stuyvesant Town with helping to "launch the modern fair housing movement [including] the creation of the National Committee Against Discrimination in Housing in 1950 which campaigned for fair housing across the country."[65]

MetLife's reputation for segregation did not end in the 1950s but continued for years after. In the early 1960s, MetLife was the nation's largest landlord, with 34,170 units in East and West Coast housing developments owned by the company.[66] In 1963, New York City college members of the NAACP sent a protest letter to MetLife president Frederick Ecker accusing his company of maintaining a "racially restrictive and discriminatory policy [that] has served effectively to reinforce a pattern of segregated living in certain areas in the city of New York, and has deprived thousands of persons of an opportunity to live in democratic, diversified communities."[67] MetLife vociferously denied that it discriminated against Black tenants, claiming that "with respect specifically to its apartment development . . . no bona fide applicant is denied housing there because of race, creed or color."[68] It was an incredible statement. MetLife's Parkchester housing complex in the Bronx in New York City had 38,000 tenants, but not one Black family or individual was among them. Stuyvesant Town and Peter Cooper Village, which together offered shelter to 11,250 inhabitants, housed only 11 Black families.[69] The students from the NAACP had planned to launch a campaign of pickets and protests at MetLife offices to pressure the organization into renting to Black tenants. In the weeks before the March on Washington, led by Martin Luther King Jr., officials from MetLife met representatives of the NAACP in New York City and offered only a vague response to the housing struggle. The company never admitted to any discriminatory practices even as its housing developments remained lily-white in one of the most racially diverse cities in the country. Instead, officials affirmed that "Metropolitan is fully cognizant of the trend of the times, and in recent months has again been reviewing its operations to further insure that its policy [of nondiscrimination] is being carried out."[70]

In 1965, MetLife housing in New York continued to be dogged by complaints of discrimination, as Black tenants remained few. MetLife also became the focus of a campaign led by Black mortgage bankers in Chicago "to make mortgage money available to Negroes on a nondiscriminatory basis."[71] Dempsey Travis, a pioneer Black mortgage lender in Chicago who led an organization of Black mortgage bankers called the United Mortgage Bankers Association (UMBA), had initially raised concerns about MetLife in 1963 and had attempted to organize a boycott of the insurance giant.[72] Mortgage banking was different from traditional banking. Mortgage bankers were middlemen who made loans to the general public only to then quickly sell them to investors. Prior to the completion of the sale, mortgage bankers serviced the loans and made collections and other adjustments for a fee to the originator. Once the loan was sold, however, the mortgage banker was completely done with the loan and moved on to the next.

Travis complained that even as MetLife continued to be the recipient of tens of millions of dollars from African Americans in the form of insurance premiums, the company still did next to nothing to make financing and mortgage money available in Black communities. Travis and UMBA launched a campaign to target the lending practices of MetLife in the winter of 1965.[73] When media queried why he was targeting the insurance industry instead of banks and savings and loan associations that also notoriously excluded Blacks from home financing capital, Travis explained, "Because we have found that the life insurance companies are the most flagrant violators, and because they have greater assets. This is particularly true of Metropolitan Life Insurance Company, which has more Negro policy holders than all other insurance companies combined including Negro companies."[74]

By late spring, the Chicago NAACP (the largest chapter in the country) along with the Chicago Congress of Racial Equality and the Amalgamated Cutters and Butcher Workmen endorsed the boycott and agreed to participate in pickets of MetLife's Chicago offices.[75] In the tension-filled political atmosphere of the mid-1960s, MetLife was quick to respond to charges of racial discrimination— much quicker than it had been in New York in 1963. Shortly after the announce- ment of the Chicago boycott, president of MetLife Gilbert Fitzhugh convened a press conference in Chicago where he insisted, "We have no policy that would prevent a Negro buying anywhere. Our policy of nondiscrimination has been published and announced and we live up to it." He explained that the company's policy of nondiscrimination had existed "since 1959 in housing, investments and employment." Fitzhugh stridently denied any discrimination and claimed that the company's local correspondent, Great Lakes Mortgage Company, had "many loans on residences owned by Negroes, perhaps the highest percentage of any insurance company, and these loans are in white and Negro neighborhoods."[76] Despite Fitzhugh's insistence, MetLife apparently kept no records of the racial identity of people who borrowed from it. The company held over $5 billion in loans for single- and multifamily homes but could not say what percentage went to African Americans. It did not matter if MetLife had a written policy against discrimination; the proof of nondiscrimination would be borne out in the actual number of mortgages awarded.

The truth about MetLife's reception of African Americans was challenged when the president of Great Lakes Mortgage, Howard Green, was asked by the media to corroborate MetLife's claims that its local affiliate did not discriminate in its lending practices. Green seemed confused and then contradicted Fitzhugh, explaining that Great Lakes, a MetLife subsidiary, had a "few" mortgages in a Black neighborhood on the South Side of Chicago. When asked if Great Lakes had any Black employees, as Fitzhugh had insisted in his press conference, Green responded, "At the present time we have no Negroes on our payroll. . . . I won't hire a Negro just because he is a Negro or turn one down on that account."[77] He went on to confirm that Great Lakes had never hired an African American.

MetLife's defenses withered quickly, as the mood in the spring and sum- mer of 1965 was not as it had been in 1963, when the conflict with the NAACP over MetLife's segregated housing practices in New York had been ended with a watered-down agreement. Within a month of the Watts Rebellion in Los Angeles, MetLife entered into a more substantial settlement with the NAACP, UMBA, and the all-Black National Association of Real Estate Brokers regarding its distribution of home mortgage funds. MetLife and the NAACP released a joint statement that placed into context the significance of their agreement: "Achieve- ment of a free market in housing has been, and remains, one of the most difficult phases of a long struggle for equality of opportunity. Racial prejudice and stubborn myths regarding the alleged results of Negro occupancy underlie the barriers, but the discriminatory policies of many lenders have provided the solid backing which makes them so invulnerable. In no case is this more true than when the Negro wishes to buy residential property in a white neighborhood."[78] The company agreed, for the first time, to place its nondiscrimination policies into its "compliance control" routine to ensure company oversight. MetLife also agreed to a plan to introduce African Americans in the real estate industry to various representatives within the company as a way of developing relationships between the two. By the late 1960s, there were entirely separate networks of Black real estate operatives with their own organizations, agents, and lenders operating in the shadows of the conventional, white real estate world. The UMBA boycott had intended to unite this Black real estate world with white capital. To that end, the effort appeared to be a success. MetLife conceded on the central demand of Travis and UMBA: that the insurance company assign its coveted "correspondent" status to bankers associated with UMBA to "further [enlarge] the placement of mortgage funds in the Negro market."[79]

The agreement marked the end of the Chicago-inspired boycott but also provides some insight into MetLife's motivation to organize the JCUP it helped to initiate two years later with the other attendees of the Columbia meeting. Obviously, a massive, privately financed urban investment program would help repair the reputation of MetLife, in particular, as well as the insurance industry more generally. If ever a business needed to pivot toward "social responsibility" to redefine its image, it was MetLife, a company that for twenty-five years had been embattled over its racially discriminatory practices.

The threats of protests and boycotts in 1963 and again in 1965 had produced inconclusive results, but the longer the protests persisted through the long, hot decade of the 1960s, the greater the potential for more dramatic and, perhaps, costly confrontation. These calculated business interventions were designed with this very thought in mind. But despite MetLife's efforts, the company's racial and housing woes continued right through the formation of JCUP. In May 1968, the New York City Commission on Human Rights, which had formed in the 1940s during the Stuyvesant Town struggle, charged MetLife with practicing discrimination in four large housing developments. The commission asserted that the company engaged in the "deliberate, intentional and systematic" exclusion of Negroes and Puerto Ricans from its New York housing developments.[80] The commission also accused MetLife of treating the Riverton Houses in

Harlem as a "Black building," meaning that African Americans were discouraged from applying to live in MetLife's other, white apartment buildings. Once again, MetLife reaffirmed its official policy of nondiscrimination in an effort to put its best face forward.

But no business entity invests hundreds of millions of dollars just for the sake of good public relations alone. The Chicago campaign against MetLife opened the eyes of its executives—and those of the industry more generally—to the viability of the Black housing market. The still-rising income of African Americans overlapped with the continued out-migration of whites, thereby opening new housing opportunities for an emergent class of Black homebuyers. Dempsey Travis's argument with the big mortgage lender was driven, in part, by the existence of a housing market in the Black neighborhoods of Chicago with precious few mortgage lenders to serve it. Indeed, the Black mortgage lenders of UMBA said they "held or manage[d] about $120 million in one-to-four family home mortgages" in Chicago. Travis estimated that only 3 percent of $194 billion invested in mortgages nationally was invested in "Negro-owned property."[81]

The financial vacuum created by the demand of Black buyers and the dearth of available financing meant that predatory lenders—like the notorious contract sellers—were able to prey upon potential Black homeowners.[82] It was not that the Black housing market in Chicago was "untapped." Instead, exploitative economic transactions made the Black housing market very lucrative for those positioned to extract capital from Black communities. Even for MetLife, Black housing was a desirable investment as long as it was kept separate from white housing.

From Redlining to "Acceptable Risk"

In the summer of 1968, JCUP took out a full-page ad in *Ebony* to call attention to its new attitude toward doing business in the inner city. The ad posed the question, "Why are the life insurance companies so concerned?" and answered, "Unless the problems of our cities can be solved, we are dismayed at the prospect of greater personal tragedy and at the economic consequences."[83] It had been one year since the urban investment program began, and most deemed it a success, with almost the entire billion dollars accounted for and allotted by the end of 1968. Within months, JCUP was lending tens of millions of dollars to cities across the country: California received over $80 million to finance projects; New York received $46 million; Illinois, $56 million; and Texas, $67 million—just to name the recipients of the largest loans early in the program's life.[84] In announcing its second billion-dollar pledge, JCUP insisted that "this is not a welfare program. This is a business response to a business problem, the health and welfare of the cities."[85]

JCUP's $2-billion investments in housing and jobs programs were intended to meet the obligation that Johnson's administration was straining to fulfill. Two billion dollars was not an insignificant sum of money. It dwarfed the $600 million Congress had allocated for the Model Cities program in 1967. In fact, it was twice as much as Congress allocated for the original War on Poverty legislation or the Economic Opportunity Act in 1964. By the spring of 1969, JCUP had claimed responsibility for financing housing developments in 227 cities across four states to the tune of $900 million. Francis Ferguson, president of Northwestern Mutual, provided details showing that within the first year of the program, $631 million had been used to finance 63,000 units of low-income housing, "ranging from sizable rent supplement housing projects to single-family homes for low- and moderate-income families from the inner city."[86]

In 1965 Congress first began to relax the federal government's redlining practices to help the flow of capital into the nation's cities. An internal FHA memo detailed the impact of the redlining policies it had pursued for years:

> In some instances, there has been hesitancy on the part of insuring offices to make FHA programs available in older neighborhoods. An automatic exclusion of neighborhoods merely because they are older can result in the shutting off of capital investments in these neighborhoods. Unavailability of capital, in turn, accelerates decline. . . . Directors should at all times be aware of the characteristics of changing patterns of residential areas within their jurisdiction. They should be alert to situations in which values can be stabilized and property upgraded by an infusion of capital in older residential sections and should help bring this about by seeing that such areas are not denied the benefits of mortgage capital.[87]

This was the same year that legislation had been passed to create HUD, along with the introduction of specific programs intended to increase the participation of private institutions in the government's housing programs. These programs included lowering interest rates to induce private organizations to develop more housing in urban areas, as well as the first-ever plans to promote the sale of public housing units to public housing tenants. In 1966, there was the creation of Section 221(h), designed to facilitate the rehabilitation or sale of existing units to low-income buyers by nonprofit organizations that financed the purchase of the properties at 3 percent interest rates.[88] Johnson hoped that these kinds of partnerships would lure the private sector into playing a role in building out the Great Society.

But the dependence of the state on business to be the main producer of housing distorted the meaning of partnership. Business, in fact, was stepping in to perform the services of government when the state had fallen short, and therefore business had its own rationale for asserting its own agenda. What would happen when the objectives of business and the state clashed? Orville Beale, the president of Prudential, illuminated this conflict when he discussed how JCUP, in dealing with HUD, could make bureaucracy and red tape simply disappear. Beale assured legislators bewildered by the apparent seamlessness of the JCUP operation that "whenever we have encountered procedural problems on FHA lending, we have discussed them with FHA officials [at] the national level and they have cooperated promptly in making a number of regulatory changes."[89] The FHA's default position was to accommodate business by eliminating "red tape" and other perceived obstacles even when they were intended to monitor or regulate the actions of business, and by the late 1960s, the federal government welcomed the resources of private companies and their potential investment into troubled areas with open arms and few questions. Vice President Hubert Humphrey explained how "public need" could be satisfied if it turned into a "profit making venture for private enterprise." Humphrey continued, "We ought to create markets in meeting these needs for which companies can compete just as they do in designing automobiles and television sets."[90]

At a critical moment, when Johnson was in a politically weakened position that limited his ability to secure the necessary funding for a massive housing program, he defused the potentially contentious issue by allowing JCUP to invest its own funds supplemented with federal subsidies and guarantees. JCUP touted the absence of controls or inputs in the distribution of its funding. Beale emphasized that the loans were made "by the individual effort of the participating companies, rather than through a central fund or pool." Beale elaborated further: "Each life insurance company retains full responsibility for the interest rate and other lending terms on the loans it makes. . . . These companies also retain full control over the choice of cities in which their funds shall be invested and the types of urban core loans they choose to make."[91] For all of the program's decentralization, it was also completely reliant on federal protection of its mortgage loans. After years of government abandonment of urban areas and prioritization of suburban development, the state would now use its power and resources to protect the investment of private capital in the inner city. A partnership based on insuring investments in housing would unleash capital into urban areas while not dramatically adding to the deficit. And the federal government would only be on the hook if defaults and foreclosures began to mount. JCUP's urban investment program was a forerunner to the more general approach to low-income housing that would become the standard with the passage of the HUD Act in 1968. The federal government essentially relinquished control of a major part of its low-income housing program, including enforcement of its antidiscrimination regulations, to lure a lender into Black urban communities. This established a dangerous precedent where federal officials were willing to jettison fair housing principles for the expedience of private sector participation.

ENSURING SEGREGATION

Funding and financing were not, however, the only questions of concern regarding housing in the 1960s. A growing chorus had identified the tiered and segregated housing market as the root cause of the deterioration of urban housing. Without opening access to the metropolitan housing market, could the conditions of deterioration be stopped?[92] JCUP's intervention was taking place in the midst of intense debates concerning how cities should be rebuilt. Should the focus be on rehabilitation or new building? Should the rehabilitation of housing be limited to the inner city while new building took place elsewhere? Perhaps the most important question was where African Americans could expect to live.

The debate existed among African Americans as well as white elected officials and residents. For many Black people, the prolonged violence and racism of white people in an effort to keep African Americans out of their neighborhoods dampened enthusiasm for Black movement into white suburban neighborhoods. More importantly, as political opportunities began to open for African Americans in communities where they constituted the majority, some Blacks were reluctant to move to areas where they would return to minority status. The sentiment was reflected in the influential essay from Detroit radicals James and Grace Lee Boggs titled, "The City Is the Black Man's Land."[93] The authors noted that despite the fact that African Americans financed almost everything in American cities where they were a majority, Black people had little control over how the city was governed. This dynamic began to change in the late 1960s and into the 1970s as the out-migration of whites, combined with the continued pace of Black in-migration, led to the election of the first African American mayors.[94] Black urban concentration offered the possibility of Black political control that

many believed would pave the way to greater economic and even social opportunities, if not equality.

The debates within Black communities about whether to integrate or remain
separate were amplified by discussions happening within Congress about where
to focus its funding efforts. White politicians as diverse as Richard Nixon and
Robert Kennedy converged politically on the importance of developing the
urban core, and not only to stem the fury of Black uprisings. If the cities became desirable places to live, then perhaps the "fair housing" discussions, which
threatened to breach the suburban racial barrier, could be stemmed. This was,
of course, paramount to Nixon's backing of "Black capitalism" and his support
of housing options that remained in segregated locales.[95] By encouraging development of Black business, supporting the creation of a Black housing market,
and promoting Black schools, Nixon embraced Black capitalism on segregated
terms. Nixon vigorously supported JCUP precisely because the organization embodied his vision of Black urban development anchored to an aspirant Black
business class. Not only was JCUP financing housing, but it provided financing
for the development of hospitals and medical facilities, grocery stores, nursing
homes, banks, and a host of other Black businesses in urban commercial districts.[96] When JCUP announced it was committing an additional billion dollars
for urban reinvestment, Nixon praised the insurance companies for having an
"effective way to bring more jobs and better housing to many Americans who
need them." Nixon went on to describe "the cooperation" between private enterprise and government as a "creative partnership" and thanked JCUP for its
"farsightedness and sense of responsibility."[97]

Democrats championing this "separate but equal" approach to urban development described their support as an "urgent" response to the urban crisis. They
argued that pressing housing concerns in the cities dwarfed "abstract" debates
concerning integration and Black access to white, suburban communities. In a
hearing on fair housing in 1966, Senator Robert Kennedy argued for a strategy of
rehabilitation of the ghetto as opposed to fair housing and access to the suburbs.
He explained:

> To seek a rebuilding of our urban slums is not to turn our backs on the
> goal of integration. It is only to say that open occupancy laws alone will
> not suffice and that sensitivity must be shown to the aspirations of Negroes
> and other nonwhites who would build their own communities and occupy
> decent housing in the neighborhoods where they now live. And, in the

long run, this willingness to come to grips with the blight of our center cities will lead us toward an open society. For it is comparability of housing and full employment that are the keys to free movement and to the establishment of a society in which each man has a real opportunity to choose whom he will call neighbor.[98]

Kennedy spoke of the "aspirations of Negroes" to "build their own communities" while simultaneously developing housing comparable to that of whites as evidence of the readiness for an "open society." But many African Americans actually desired housing wherever they could find it. For that reason, over the course of the 1960s, African Americans were concerned not only about the condition of urban housing but also about the prevalence of housing discrimination in general. In 1967, *Jet* magazine conducted a survey of 700 Democratic Party leaders in thirty cities.[99] When asked to identify the issue on which the Johnson administration had least satisfied their own and their constituents' expectations, respondents replied that it was housing discrimination. In another survey on housing, this one conducted in Harlem, residents were asked whether they would rather solve their housing issue by leaving Harlem or by remaining there. Only 17 percent of respondents said they would choose to stay in Harlem. A Harris poll conducted in the weeks following the Detroit and Newark uprisings found that 84 percent of Blacks believed that the ghetto should be "torn down."[100]

These polls were not wholly representative of debates about where African Americans should live, but they show that it should not have been assumed that Black people were only interested in remaining in Black, segregated communities. Moreover, conflating the issues of neighborhood choice with segregation obscured reality. When violent opposition to Black rights in the South began to subside, the perceived threat of residential integration in the North inspired new waves of white violence directed at the homes of African Americans. As late as 1966, white racists bombed the homes of three Black families living in Cleveland Heights, a white suburban neighborhood bordering Cleveland. As the local paper reported, the bombings were "believed connected with integration."[101]

When Martin Luther King Jr. campaigned against housing segregation in Chicago, he was met with as much violence as he had ever experienced in any of his southern campaigns. During a march through a segregated, white neighborhood, Gage Park, King and other activists were confronted by hundreds of whites chanting, "White Power," "Up with Slavery," and "Kill Niggers." This white mob attacked the Black activists, and by the end of the rampage forty-four cars had been burned and fifty people were injured.[102] In 1967, the recently purchased home of a Black couple on the mostly white southwest side of Chicago was firebombed.[103] In December of the same year, three Long Island, New York, youths used a crude pipe bomb in an attempt to destroy the home of a Black real estate broker.[104] There had been two other bombings in the New York area, including one of a city pool used by African Americans and one of an "all-Negro apartment building." In the East Flatbush neighborhood of Brooklyn, a Black family "was blasted out of its home in a predominately white area."[105] In the summer of 1967, weeks after rioting in Detroit, whites voted down a fair housing ordinance in Flint, Michigan, fueling racial tensions. These tensions boiled over when three firebombs were detonated in a Black neighborhood after the ordinance was defeated.[106] The means by which residential segregation was maintained had nothing to do with "choice" and everything to do with violence and hatred prompted by the racist views that Blacks kept property values down and were physical markers of inferior status. Maintaining segregation was about the power of white institutions and white residents to combine and dictate where Black residents should live. This was reflected in the length of time it took to secure a law against housing discrimination in the first place. In 1966 and again in 1967, federal bills against housing discrimination were defeated after intense lobbying by the housing industry, especially the real estate establishment, that produced the fear of political reprisal for senators and representatives who voted for such legislation.

The life insurance industry managed to avoid these thorny issues by simply ignoring federal rules against housing discrimination. JCUP was determined to control its investment in urban and Black communities. In the absence of federal oversight, there would be no particular compulsion to adhere to the new rules regarding antidiscriminatory lending practices. It is true that among JCUP lenders, there would be no discrimination against mortgagors—that was the point of the program. But the lenders could limit loans based on their location and the requirement that the homes or buildings to be purchased had to remain in the "city core." Federal housing regulators—led by Robert Weaver, who had spent his entire working life trying to dismantle housing discrimination—showed no special interest in applying those rules to the life insurance industry. JCUP representatives presented racial discrimination and urban redevelopment as parallel discussions, as if the two had no relationship to each other. JCUP representatives made no mention of race as an explanation for why life insurance companies in earlier years had ignored lending in urban—and Black—communities.

Indeed, in announcing its second billion-dollar investment in 1969, JCUP once again turned to *Ebony* with another full-page ad. In this ad the industry touted its accomplishments while exonerating its historical role in the problems of the cities. The text-laden ad lauded the insurance industry's "new and special case of investment." The ad continued, "It went into . . . the inner cities . . . where capital was not readily available on reasonable terms, because of risk and location. Our business felt this commitment was essential. . . . If those cities crumble, people are going to crumble . . . and business is apt to crumble along with them."[107] The new initiative also avoided any discussion of race, only describing the new projects as "housing investments . . . primarily designed for the benefit of low-and-moderate-income families presently residing in city core areas."[108] Erasing the history of racial discrimination as a factor in the industry's own treatment of Black citizens, along with denying the role of race discrimination in the urban condition, undermined the principles of and necessity for "fair housing." If race played no role in the refusal of banks or other lenders to do business with African Americans, then why was fair housing necessary at all?

JCUP did not need to answer this or any other question, because the federal government required nothing from it, except to lend the hundreds of millions of dollars in mortgage funds at its disposal. In doing so, JCUP effectively created a shadow HUD with its own rules but armed with a guarantee that the federal government would protect all of its investments while requiring nothing in return, including adherence to civil rights laws. This put the facts on the ground directly at odds with the federal government's stated intentions. By 1967, HUD was in the process of clarifying existing policies and creating new ones that prohibited racial discrimination in federally sponsored housing programs. In a memo marked "confidential" sent to the assistant secretaries of HUD, Weaver gave them thirty days "to report action taken to conform all programs and operations under their jurisdiction to HUD policy on equal opportunity." The memo was intended to demonstrate unequivocal support for antidiscrimination measures. For example, Weaver clarified that "if unimaginative site selection or bad relocation practices . . . should result in further disadvantaging Negroes or other minorities . . . it can effectively be contended that the locality was using Federal funds to discriminate."[109] Weaver wanted to implement new policies that would "facilitate [HUD's] equal opportunity objectives of inclusive participation

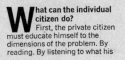

An ad placed in *Ebony* advertising the life insurance investments by the Joint Committee on Urban Problems. (*Ebony*, June 1968; Institute of Life Insurance)

An ad placed in *Ebony* extolling the accomplishments of the life insurance investments after a second billion had been made available by the Joint Committee on Urban Problems. (*Ebony*, August 1969)

patterns in HUD-assisted programs and activity, and thereby afford members of minority groups the opportunity and choice of locating outside the areas of their own minority group concentration."[110] For example, a letter from Weaver's assistant, written during the same time that JCUP was collaborating with HUD on the launch of its new program and sent to the director of the Leadership Conference on Civil Rights, clarified HUD's rules concerning "equal opportunity" in housing, explaining that proposals to "locate housing only in areas of racial concentration will be *prima facie* unacceptable."[111]

It was against HUD's own rules to approve the financing of segregated housing, but the agency turned a blind eye to local housing authorities soliciting financing from JCUP to fund those projects. When HUD would not approve financing for segregated developments, declaring them prima facie unacceptable, some local housing authorities simply went to JCUP directly for financing. Local housing authorities were able to circumvent their legal responsibilities of antidiscrimination as required by the 1964 and 1968 Civil Rights Acts. For example, JCUP touted its support of a project in the "inner city" of New Orleans for "low-income minority families" with $463,000 in financing.[112] There was also a $660,000 loan to finance "100 multifamily units for minority occupants in a blighted area of Winston-Salem." The project was to be leased to the local Winston-Salem housing authority and then sublet to families.[113] JCUP preemptively muted criticism of its segregated life insurance loans by extending relatively large loans to Black lenders and real estate agents. JCUP provided $750,000 for sixty loans to finance single- and multifamily houses in Black neighborhoods in New York City.[114] The loans were originated by a Black savings and loan association, and as part of the agreement, the homes would be owned by members of "the minority group."[115] A $5.5 million loan went to a Black bank on the promise of lending to minority groups in the core areas of Los Angeles.[116] At a meeting in Indianapolis organized by the U.S. Commission on Civil Rights to bring together representatives of the FHA and African American real estate agents to discuss JCUP, the Black agents asked whether the new JCUP program would "promote integration." They were told that while the "programs [were] not specifically designed for this purpose," there could also be "some positive effect."[117] There was no elaboration on how those positive effects could be instituted when the program was going to be implemented *exclusively* in "city core" neighborhoods and their immediate periphery.

JCUP's activities reinforced segregation and demonstrated, once again, the federal government's complicity in discriminatory practices. More than this,

JCUP's dealings helped to establish a troubling precedent that would reappear on a much larger scale in the years that followed. Orville Beale boasted that the FHA removed a stipulation that when a lender foreclosed on a property, it remained the lender's responsibility to maintain that property until it was sold again. This, in fact, was a critical regulation that compelled lenders to help the owner at all costs so as not to have to deal with the added expense of property maintenance. Importantly, it discouraged lenders from foreclosing on properties. When JCUP asked the FHA to drop this requirement, it meant that the "lender no longer [had] to look forward to the possibility that he might have to restore the apartment to good condition in order to qualify" for federal guarantees.[118]

The life insurance industry's financial investments were hailed far and wide, but it is important to take stock of the full implications of this intervention.[119] The insurance industry's investment in urban development was a small price to pay for an industry whose earlier exclusion of the "city core" had contributed to its deterioration. But the blind praise of the insurance companies accepted the logic that there was a choice to be made between the urgency of repairing the cities and opening up housing options for African Americans beyond the city core. This was a false choice contingent on accepting the establishment idea that only one option was available. This false dichotomy ignored how the continuation of racial segregation in the real estate market preserved the potential for exploitative real estate practices targeting African Americans. It also meant keeping African Americans trapped in a real estate market with inferior housing perpetually valued less than the properties found in exclusive white neighborhoods regardless of class. For the multibillion-dollar life insurance industry, the investment was not asset creation for African Americans; it was crisis management.

Combatting racism was never the objective of JCUP, even as that was the formal goal of "fair housing" legislation. JCUP evaded the debates concerning where Black people should live. This reflected a broader trend within socio-commercial business reform that ignored racial discrimination as a driving force in the urban crisis. A *Forbes* editorial in a special edition on business and the urban crisis articulated this perspective directly when it argued that "a good deal of what is commonly thought of as racial prejudice has less to do with race than with class: the animus is directed toward people mainly because of their occupations, grammar and mode of dress."[120] This explanation bordered on the absurd, given that by 1968, when the edition was published, the depth and breadth of racial discrimination experienced by all African Americans, irrespective of class, was well documented in congressional reports as well as in government-commissioned studies of the problem, including the Kerner Commission report. Detroit's Urban Coalition leader, Joseph Hudson, whose family owned a chain of department stores across Michigan, was asked whether or not he should resign his membership from a country club that excluded African Americans. His response showed the continuing contradiction of "solving the urban crisis" without addressing the racial discrimination that was its central feature: "I myself have never met a Negro who asked to become a member of any of these clubs, or who thought it would be significant."[121]

The actions of the International Ladies' Garment Workers' Union in 1965 demonstrated the possibility of a different way. The union pledged $7.65 million for loans to provide low-cost housing for Black families in the South and Midwest. It stipulated that the money "be used solely for construction of one-family homes for Negro families in desegregated neighborhoods."[122] The union's mortgage funds were distributed through Black mortgage bankers, including companies represented in UMBA, to ensure that the money made its way to Black borrowers. Union president David Dubinsky said the primary purpose of the loans was "to foster the development of integrated residential sections, and . . . to avoid the creation of additional Negro ghettos."[123] This endeavor was certainly smaller in scale than JCUP's, but it specifically challenged the notion that one could not both advocate for urban redevelopment and pursue low-income housing in nonsegregated communities.

The billion-dollar project that quickly morphed into a $2-billion project appeared to resolve the long-standing barriers to financing. The quickness with which JCUP was able to allocate money to various projects reinforced the perception that private capital, as opposed to the state, was a more efficient player in urban redevelopment. The supremacy of business was made obvious in other ways as well. Whatever the stated motivations of politicians, it soon became apparent that the end of redlining was intended to create greater penetration and mobility for capital, not people. As Orville Beale explained in a congressional hearing on JCUP, "Ideally, private business would direct its resources and energies to new ventures in the urban core area in the expectation that a reasonable profit could be earned without extraordinary risk of losses." Beale went on to explain that without this clear profit motive bolstered by the federal government, there were "very few inducements for private promoters" to build in the "urban core," as opposed to more profitable "ventures outside of the center city."[124] This was partially borne out in the increasing number of FHA-insured homes in previously uninsured areas. In August 1967, the FHA was insuring up to 200 properties a week in "riot-threatened areas," but by June 1968, it was insuring between 1,600 and 2,000 properties a week in "in blighted areas in central cities."[125] As Brownstein put it, "We have made the task of providing housing for the low income and moderate-income family the primary role of the FHA today."[126]

A Growing Consensus

Meanwhile, homeownership, which was in sync with the trend toward privatization and private ownership, was increasingly prioritized in the nation's housing policies. It was in sync with a greater emphasis on private ownership in low-income housing, away from what had been an earlier emphasis on public housing. Black homeownership in the urban core was also seen as a social palliative against the annual summer rioting. Several politicians spoke in favor of the social benefits of homeownership as much as they described the need for housing. Freshman Republican senator from Illinois Charles Percy repeated a common refrain when he said, "If we can give homeownership to poor people we can cut out the rot that is infecting our cities. . . . A desire to own exists in millions of American families who want to own their own homes. Private enterprise and private money should be put to work through banks and savings and loan associations to bring this problem to a solution."[127]

Over the course of the 1967 legislative season, both Democrats and Republicans had compiled more than thirty-five different pieces of legislation concerning homeownership in the urban core.[128] Percy himself had sponsored the aptly named National Homeownership Foundation Act in the spring of 1967. When he took to the floor of the Senate on April 20, he prefaced his promulgation of the act by describing it as not just another housing bill but, instead, a moral calling. Percy framed homeownership as a vessel to deliver the moral imperatives of "human dignity, self-esteem, the motivation to achieve, a feeling of security and roots, individual and community responsibility . . . [and] participation and leadership in community activities."[129] The act would authorize the creation of a Homeownership Loan Fund as a private foundation to raise money for urban homeownership. The foundation would rely on private funds by issuing debt certificates guaranteed by the Treasury. Despite its lofty language, Percy's bill called for homeownership opportunities on a relatively small scale, facilitated mainly by churches and other smaller nonprofit organizations. St. Louis had attempted a similar pilot program for low-income homeownership on a limited scale in 1966, and even though it secured only 2,000 homes, it was widely considered to be a success.

Percy's bill also called for homeowners' insurance to cover mortgage payments in the event of illness or unemployment. It included a "sweat equity" stipulation allowing homeowners to reduce their costs if they worked to rehabilitate their own property. Finally, the bill included providing nonprofit organizations with the tools to counsel potential homeowners about the rigors of owning their own home. The bill was intended to subsidize homeownership for a relatively modest number of 200,000 homes in a three-year period and with an interest subsidy payment of up to 3 percent of the interest rate, calculated to limit the number of people eligible for the program.[130] There was widespread bipartisan support for Percy's bill, including 39 Senate cosponsors and 112 House sponsors. Percy even vetted the proposal with Andrew Young, a lieutenant of Dr. King in the Southern Christian Leadership Conference. But not everyone was enthusiastic about the new proposal.

HUD secretary Weaver expressed reservations about the supposedly transcendent potential of homeownership for the urban poor. He agreed about the benefits of homeownership but raised concerns about the ability of poor people to handle the financial commitments involved:

> For the ill prepared, the misadvised, and the unsuccessful, participation is a frustrating and disillusioning experience. If a low-income family loses its home when temporary unemployment or serious illness strikes and only a burden of debt remains, its loss is great and its disappointment is severe. Nor will a low-income family's loss or disappointment be less when the breadwinner's job requires that it move to another locality—and the family finds that it owes more on the home than it can get for it on the market. This may be due to the lack of equity in the property or to the rundown condition of the neighborhood. If any substantial numbers of low-income families—led into unstable home ownership by misleading promises of ineffectual government programs—suffer these losses, their bitter disillusionment will be harmful to the country.[131]

Despite Weaver's concerns, Johnson recognized the political popularity of low-income homeownership being advanced by many of his political rivals and outlined his own vision to expand urban homeownership. In Johnson's "Crisis of the Cities" speech, he called for 100,000 low-income families to purchase or rehabilitate their own homes. He described homeownership as "a cherished dream and achievement of most Americans. . . . Owning a home can increase responsibility and stake out a man's place in his community. The man who owns a home has something to be proud of and good reason to protect and preserve it."[132] The Senate Banking and Currency Committee combined the different elements of the varied housing bills and produced a plan for government-subsidized, low-income homeownership that would be incorporated into the HUD Act of 1968.

"The Magna Carta of the Cities"

During an outdoor ceremony on a warm August day in the garden of the new, $20-million HUD building, Johnson signed the HUD Act into law. It was almost four months after passage of the more celebrated Fair Housing Act (as the Civil Rights Act of 1968 came to be known), but Johnson praised his new legislation as a "Magna Carta for the cities." He went on to say of the new bill, "Today we are going to put on the books of American law what I genuinely believe is the most farsighted, the most comprehensive, the most massive housing program in all of American history."[133]

The HUD Act was a watershed event in American housing policy. Johnson described earlier efforts as enlarging "the government's role to bring decent houses into the reach of families with moderate income."[134] The HUD Act was going to be different. Instead of continuing to expand "government's role" in housing low- and moderate-income people, Johnson called for bringing "the talents and energies of private enterprise to the task of housing low-income families through the creation of a federally chartered private, profit-making housing partnership."[135] Johnson described multiple ways to combine the efforts of private institutions with government to resolve the long-standing urban housing crisis. Declaring that "a new partnership between business and government" was needed to end the urban housing crisis, he called on the "homebuilder, the mortgage banker, the contractor, the nonprofit sponsor, the industrialist" to recognize the "new opportunity for American business" in the city.

The centerpiece of the new legislation was a program for homeownership among low-income and poor people: Section 235 of the Housing Act marked a turn in the history of American housing policy. Mortgage insurance in the "city core" opened up the possibility of homeownership through affordable and conventional means to African Americans for the first time. Families making between $3,000 and $7,000 a year could buy homes for as little as $200 down and monthly payments of 20 percent of their income. The federal government paid the additional costs and subsidized interest payments beyond 1 percent.[136] At a time when interest rates regularly topped 6 to 7 percent, the federal government's subsidization of all but 1 percent of the interest for participating homeowners was quite generous. The rock-bottom interest rate subsidy put the program within the reach of hundreds of thousands more participants than the original suggestion of a 3 percent interest subsidy. Families could purchase homes for up to $15,000, unless they were in a high-income area, where the amount increased to $20,000.[137]

More generally, the bill was a true bipartisan collaboration that enjoyed broad congressional support as well as that of industry leaders from the NAHB, who celebrated the bill's emphasis on building new housing developments. The president of the NAHB described the HUD Act as "the first real response to the growing unrest among the poor for better housing and living conditions," an unsurprisingly positive reaction, given the bill's mandate for the construction of millions of new units of housing within the coming decade.[138] Its driving force was the prioritization of "maximum private interest input," exemplified by a reliance on private builders, private real estate agents, and private financing for properties that ultimately were to be owned privately. The legislation called for 26 million units of new housing to be built over the following ten years, including 6 million units of subsidized housing. If successful, this would be a dramatic and unprecedented increase in housing production. In 1966, only 49,000 units of subsidized housing had been built; in 1967, 57,000 units; and in 1968, 128,000 units. Johnson was calling for those numbers to leap to 600,000 new units a year. The projected increase in housing starts reflected a new focus for HUD, one that made production the primary goal.

Across African American communities, the legislation was hailed as a dream come true. The NAACP's official magazine, the *Crisis*, editorialized, "For Negroes the new law means that homeownership can now become a reality instead of a dream for nearly 500,000 families."[139] Black operatives in business and politics saw the passage of the historic legislation not only as a housing bill but also as an opportunity for job creation and business development. The NAACP threw its weight behind organizing a National Housing Producers Association for "Negro builders, architects, brokers, planners, financial agents, insurance men and housing experts" to stimulate "Negro enterprise in the housing field."[140] William R. Morris led this effort. A former developer and real estate broker, Morris became the NAACP's newly designated director of housing after the passage of the HUD Act. His position was to liaise between different sectors of the housing industry in the hope of utilizing the new tools created by the HUD

Act to develop new housing and business opportunities for African Americans. The NAACP established an incorporated housing organization to facilitate these relationships within the organization. Morris explained the NAACP's strategy: "We want a piece of the action.... Far too often housing and other improvements are developed in black communities, and the profits and related economic benefits leave our areas.... We want to reverse that tide and stimulate the flow of money and long range benefits back into our communities."[141] George Romney, soon to be secretary of HUD, affirmed to the press that "black enterprise is essential to achieve this administration's goal of good housing and good job opportunities for everyone."[142] Not only would this particular approach put the NAACP in the literal business of real estate, but it raised potential challenges to the organization's long-standing commitment to integration. It was a dilemma not only for the NAACP but for the entirety of Black organizations faced with building up segregated urban and suburban areas or fighting for access to white suburban enclaves.

The HUD Act also privatized the Federal National Mortgage Association (FNMA) and created the Government National Mortgage Association (GNMA) in its place. The Johnson administration wanted the FNMA's debt off its books, especially as it was preparing to massively expand homeownership to people of low income. Privatizing the FNMA was the culmination of several debates over how to bring the rapidly expanding federal deficit under control. Privatization would make the FNMA debt disappear from the federal budget overnight. The federal government would still influence the FNMA by appointing its board and lending it money from the Treasury to keep its buying capacity as a secondary market intact, but its balances would no longer show up as debt. The GNMA was to play a similar role to that historically performed by the FNMA, except that its funds would be used to purchase low-income FHA mortgages. A secondary market for low-income mortgages would become an important source of revenue, especially considering the regular peril of federal appropriations for housing programs. It would also have a multiplicative effect on monies made available for low-income homeownership. "Mortgage-backed securities" were introduced in the HUD Act as a way to increase the flow of mortgage credit into the newly developing urban housing market. Securitization turned consumer, in this case mortgagor, debt into investor bonds that would then be bought and sold on Wall Street and beyond.[143] Transforming debt into liquid cash ensured the stability of the market from the interests of the builders, brokers, and bankers. There would be no shortage of mortgages; the industry had to produce the houses. As noted by the *Crisis*, "Though the Section 235 program [as the program came to be known] was created in Washington, it was funded on Wall Street."[144]

The contradiction between the goals of profit and public welfare quickly rose to the surface. Real estate brokers had scoffed at the bill's emphasis on new housing but were pleased with its calls for the rehabilitation of 1.7 million homes and apartments over the first three years of the legislation. The California Real Estate Association enthusiastically supported the HUD Act because it called for the creation of more new housing, offering new business opportunities throughout the industry. The association's president said about the new HUD legislation, "We're going to work with city and county government, civic groups, and private enterprise generally... to attack this problem [of low-income housing]." While it welcomed the new real estate business to be drummed up by the HUD Act, the organization also voted to continue its campaign against fair housing in California, claiming, "We have no discrimination problem within our own membership.... Our emphasis has always been on voluntary solution of the equal rights problem."[145]

The HUD Act was poised to amplify the successes that were initially spurred by the life insurance industry's urban investment program. However, while the ban on government redlining indicated a shift in policy, it did not address the residential segregation that had, in fact, been created by the policy in the first place. In fact, moneylenders like JCUP, as well as the mortgage bankers and savings and loan associations that worked in tandem with the FHA, denied that racial discrimination had ever been a factor in their decisions to exclude Black communities from home financing. Now they acted as gatekeepers, with the full backing of the FHA, allowing for the broader real estate industry's penetration into Black communities while still ensuring that Blacks remained locked in ghettos. Allowing capital to move freely while Black people could not helped to fortify the conditions of predatory inclusion as HUD's multiple homeownership programs—Section 221(d)(2), Section 221(h), Section 223(e), and Section 235— began to take hold. The urban investment plan demonstrated the unevenness in the partnership between capital and the federal agencies that were at the heart of the revamped housing policies that culminated in the HUD Act. Just as African Americans had finally secured a guarantee of a right against racial discrimination in the housing market, the government was devolving responsibility for achieving its goal of providing a "decent home" for Americans to the "genius" of private enterprise. Nevertheless, housing integration remained a volatile issue, as evidenced by the continuation of bombings of African American homeowners who violated the racial boundaries that separated Black from white. The offer of business to intervene in the housing crisis was not to undo segregation and expand the housing choices of African Americans. There was no reason why there could not have been new building and rehabilitation of urban housing alongside new building of homes affordable to low-income and working-class Black families in white suburban enclaves. These, along with rigorous enforcement of new federal fair housing rules, could have transformed Black housing conditions. Instead, business used its billions of dollars to keep Blacks locked into cities, but perhaps with their own homes. Chapter 3 explains why using fair housing as a tool to shape urban and suburban development efforts did not take hold.

3

Forced Integration

The federal government will not impose economic integration.
—President Richard M. Nixon, June 11, 1971

THE SPECTER OF the urban crisis loomed large as the backdrop to the presidential race of 1968. Nixon hardly mentioned the omnipresent urban crisis in the long campaign season of 1967 and 1968, despite the fact that the election season had been inaugurated amidst the greatest outbreak of social unrest in the nation's history. In the words of Rick Perlstein, "Race had always been the best-oiled hinge in the strange contraption that was Nixon's ideology," suggesting something about how his positions on race and civil rights managed to remain in flux.[1] Nixon had supported John F. Kennedy's civil rights bill but then decried efforts to enforce it. He supported the 1968 Civil Rights Act, featuring fair housing, only after the assassination of Martin Luther King Jr. made it impossible to oppose. Deep questions still remained over how to end the crisis in the cities—more government programs or more intervention from the private sector? Nixon finally weighed into the debate, sharply, when he secured his party's nomination for president. In a speech at the Republican Party's National Convention in 1968, Nixon targeted the social programs of the previous administration: "For the past five years we have been deluged by government programs for the unemployed; programs for the cities; programs for the poor. And we have reaped from these programs an ugly harvest of frustration, violence and failure across the land. And now our opponents will be offering more of the same—more billions for government jobs, government housing, government welfare. I say it is time to quit pouring billions of dollars into programs that have failed in the United States of America."[2]

But the question remained: beyond the usual acerbic election-year rhetoric, how would the Nixon administration manage the sprawling Johnsonian welfare state given his hostile description of the Great Society as "programs that have failed the United States"? Advocates for low-income housing were especially concerned by rumors that Nixon would get rid of HUD altogether. Only three years old when Nixon became president, HUD continued to resemble a disorganized amalgam of organizations and interests instead of a coherent government agency.

Nixon's nomination of his former political rival Michigan governor George Romney as the new secretary of HUD came as a surprise. Romney was a moderate Republican known for his support of the civil rights movement who, during his tenure as governor, had championed statewide fair housing legislation. If Nixon hoped to keep his domestic policy agenda under control, Romney was a curious choice. For example, Romney appeared to be genuinely affected by the devastation of the Detroit Rebellion; in its aftermath, he toured Black urban communities around the country. His comments during this tour prefigured his approach as HUD secretary. At one stop he said,

> Our best and most extensive efforts in the past have been mere palliatives, not cures. They have treated symptoms, not causes. They have failed to come to grips with the structural deficiencies in American society that are the root of the problems. . . . A strategy for a new America requires us to stop looking at the people of the slums as a drag on our society and see them rather as an untapped asset. There is as much talent and leadership in the slums as there is in the suburbs. Its development will create a new America. We must eliminate restrictions on the availability of capital to start and expand ghetto enterprises. As a rule today, the dollar bounces only once in the ghetto. To achieve a multiplier effect, the financial community must be willing to supply working and risk capital to the ghetto entrepreneur.[3]

Romney's comments resonated not only with the idea that the private sector was pivotal to the transformation of the inner city but also with the findings of the Kerner Commission, which pointed to structural inequality as an urban impediment. In any case, Romney's comments indicated that he could be an activist HUD secretary. That activism would become an underlying theme the first two years of his tenure at the helm of HUD.

Low-income housing policy was deeply impacted by the political transition from Johnson to Nixon and the subsequent transformation of the mission of HUD under Romney. Those political shifts were articulated politically by what Nixon described as "New Federalism," which looked to circumscribe federal powers while ensuring greater local control over the uses and distribution of federal dollars. The biggest challenge to implementing new housing policies, however, was less about funding than about the persisting debate over where the housing would be located. The HUD Act, with new legal tools developed to overcome housing discrimination faced by African Americans with the help of Robert Weaver, was intended to result in new housing in outlying suburban areas. Beyond its political implications, building new housing in the suburbs would keep the construction costs low and the housing affordable.

This chapter examines how, with the tight overlap between race and poverty, policy debates became proxies for discussions about race, class, and housing rights in the aftermath of the civil rights movement. While the pitched political battles in the streets of the United States during the 1960s finally forced Congress to produce a bill banning racial discrimination in housing, the absence of the intensity of those external pressures in combination with a concerted effort to shift the discussion from race to class helped to further muddle the issue. What emerged were politically fraught battles within the Nixon administration, momentarily pitting HUD against the politically calculating executive office. Nixon's objective to hold together a white-majority electoral coalition further undermined HUD's legal mandate to advance an agenda of residential integration. This objective was further subverted as Nixon and his closest aides shifted the discussion from racial and housing equality to focus on the merits of "economic integration." The emergence of this obtuse "colorblind" discourse confused the need for specific housing policies to address the urban housing crisis. Perhaps of even more consequence, the failure to open the suburbs to Black buyers and renters, while simultaneously denying the plausibility of race as a factor, facilitated the thriving conditions of predatory inclusion in the existing, urban market. Faux philosophical debates straining to delineate between "economic integration" and "racial segregation" could not cover the growing reality that Black people would remain locked in the cities. African Americans were hardly passive victims, with many making peace with their urban domiciles as terrorism by white residents in the name of holding onto racial residential boundaries persisted into the 1970s. But the disproportionate power of the state in shaping these discussions was evident as Nixon pledged to withhold the power of the federal government to make local authorities comply with antidiscrimination mandates. The political battle over the placement of low-income housing was the key struggle over American housing policy in the post–Fair Housing Act era.

GEORGE ROMNEY

In the days after his inauguration as the thirty-eighth president of the United States, Richard Nixon introduced himself to his cabinet by saying, "I don't want a cabinet of 'yes-men.'"[4] If Nixon desired conflict, former Michigan governor George Romney seemed certain to deliver exactly that. The *New York Times* described Romney as "unexpected, nervy, and straight from the hip."[5] *Business Week* said Romney's favorite role was that of a "promoter-proselytizer."[6] Romney and Nixon had sparred over a number of issues throughout the Republican primary season, but not the crises in American cities, which for Romney, were unavoidable. Romney had made his initial mark in Michigan politics by championing "fair housing" in his home state, a campaign that earned him an unprecedented 30 percent of the African American vote in his last run for governor.[7] The biography Romney submitted at his nomination hearing highlighted his record on urban issues in Detroit as "noteworthy in strengthening and improving urban government, urban life and the lot of the urban resident."[8]

Romney was a quintessential postwar racial liberal whose support for "equal opportunity" and civil rights predated his long tenure as governor. He had opposed segregation in war housing during World War II as well as in public housing in Detroit. As the president of American Motors, Romney supported the Fair Employment Practices Act. While he opposed segregation in general, Romney was particularly interested in the issue of housing discrimination. In a speech at an open housing conference shortly after he became governor, he declared that "a free and open housing market is a public responsibility and a private goal."[9] In a "state of the state" address, Romney named housing discrimination as Michigan's "most crucial and pressing problem."[10] Romney believed in the promise of the American dream and that it could be unleashed through fairness, equality, and opportunity. Most importantly, he believed that a free market economy was the decisive factor in creating a free society. After all, Romney's rise from marginalized Mormon to the pinnacle of corporate influence and power as a corporate executive was proof of the power of American capitalism. African Americans needed access to the system and the opportunity to make it work.

And if the United States did not live up to its ideals and continued to exclude African Americans from the promise of mainstream society, African Americans would turn to more extreme politics.

By March 1968, Romney had pulled out of the bruising Republican presidential primaries, but he continued touring the country, positioning himself as an expert on urban conditions and as a passionate advocate for fixing the problems ailing American cities. In Romney's view, racial equality had transcended the moral issue of "equal opportunity," and he saw resolving the urban crisis as a matter of survival for the United States. Romney and other officials were genuinely shocked at the urban rebellions whenever they happened. The Detroit Rebellion in particular was unprecedented, on a scale never before experienced within the United States, and the fact that it happened in Detroit was particularly puzzling to the political establishment because good jobs in the auto industry meant Detroit Blacks were substantially better off than Blacks in other communities.

After his urban tour, Romney echoed Gil Scott-Heron's angry song "Whitey on the Moon" when he said, "If the lot of millions of people on earth is more important than putting a man on the moon in this decade, let us invest more in people and even less in space. Let us spend more in Harlem and less in the Sea of Tranquility."[11] He began describing unresolved urban problems in catastrophist terms, for example, weighing the probability of guerilla warfare in American cities and speculating on the likelihood of revolution if the proper policies were not enacted. In one public appearance he said, "The key issue in our cities today is this: can racial justice and human injustice be eliminated by peaceful and orderly changes, or must it be compelled through violence, destruction and bloodshed?"[12] Elsewhere he claimed, "There are citizens organized, trained, and armed for violence, riots. and civil guerilla warfare. They are using the latest methods and means developed in Cuba, China, and Southeast Asia. They are steadily enlisting and securing more recruits."[13]

Romney then went to Washington, D.C., on a mission. Indeed, just weeks after being confirmed as secretary, he was awarded a civil rights honor as the "one member of President Nixon's cabinet most directly concerned with America's ghettos."[14] Not only was he going to Washington with the fight for formal fair housing policies in Michigan fresh in his mind; he was also going with an urgent belief that the United States was on the edge of revolution if it did not resolve its urban issues. Although the Fair Housing Act had been passed by the previous administration, big questions still loomed about low-income housing policies. If Nixon was hoping for a calm transition from the grand ambitions of Johnson's "urgent task" of solving the urban housing crisis to quiet neglect, Romney was not the right man for the job. Romney was committed to doing big things as the secretary of HUD.

THE TRANSITION

By 1968, the Republican Party was also committed to doing big things with an unforeseen opportunity to retake the presidency for the first time since Eisenhower. At the Republican National Convention (far less publicized than the Democratic National Convention) that year, the party introduced a new plank into its platform specifically addressing urban issues. It pledged new efforts to solve everything from housing to mass transit, from unemployment to air and water pollution. It also continued Johnson's quest for partnership between business and government to "solve the crisis of the cities." Liberal Republicans won an amendment to the plank calling for a "just society that would eliminate the causes of violence."[15]

Nixon was not nearly as interested in attending to the domestic policies that were reflected in his party's newly adopted platform, but the threat of violence in the cities kept urban issues at the forefront of American politics. Nixon responded by creating the Council for Urban Affairs, or Urban Council, as his first official act of government.[16] The council was to be the domestic equivalent of the National Security Council, which governed foreign policy. The Urban Council was headed by Democratic Party transplant and Johnson administration holdover Daniel Patrick Moynihan. Moynihan was a well-known figure in domestic politics because of a study he had produced years earlier for the Department of Labor called *The Negro Family: A Call to Action*, popularly known as the Moynihan Report. Although Moynihan was cast as a liberal, Republicans loved him because he relished attacking Black militants and the left.

Rather than sidelining urban issues, the creation of the Urban Council put them at the center of the Nixon agenda.[17] Indeed, the formation of the council involved half of Nixon's cabinet, and in its first year, Nixon personally attended most of its meetings, underlining their importance. In fact, in one of its initial meetings, the council declared that "the poverty and social isolation of minority groups in central cities is the single most serious problem of the American city."[18] In 1969, the problems facing American cities were easy to identify; creating urban policies that could adequately address them, on the other hand, was much more difficult, especially given Nixon's ideological opposition to the increasingly complex web of government agencies, departments, and anti-poverty programs that his administration was now responsible for overseeing. Both Nixon and Romney believed that the constant promise of new programs and more federal spending was raising Black expectations unreasonably high and, thus, was fueling the unrest in the nation's cities. Assessing Johnson's programs, Romney stated, "I think the promises have been big, big, big and far beyond the resources."[19]

Still, Nixon's administration was under political pressure to maintain the programs. On the first anniversary of the urban rebellion that struck Washington, D.C., in the aftermath of King's assassination, Nixon and Romney announced that they were authorizing $200 million to cover urban reconstruction costs in at least twenty cities that had been damaged by riots but lacked the funding to rebuild. Nixon also continued all of Johnson's Great Society programs through the first term of his presidency, even as he began to articulate his vision of more limited government. Nixon used the urban crisis as proof of why New Federalism was the politics of the future. In a small pamphlet to publicize the meaning of New Federalism, he wrote, "We face an urban crisis, a social crisis—and at the same time, a crisis of confidence in the capacity of government to do its job. . . . A third of a century of centralizing power and responsibility in Washington has produced a bureaucratic monstrosity, cumbersome, unresponsive, ineffective. . . . A third of a century of social experiment has left us a legacy of entrenched programs that have outlived their time or outgrown their purpose."[20] New Federalism was described as the flow of "power, funds and responsibility" from "Washington to the States and the people."[21] Despite Nixon's polemics against Johnson, Nixon's New Federalism echoed Johnson's ideological commitment to a market economy as the primary tool to end poverty. Romney agreed with these principles and had commented elsewhere that "government's greatest role should be as a stimulator, clearinghouse and catalyst in helping release the energies of the private, voluntary and independent sectors of the American community. . . . Government should stimulate the people to find answers rather than encourage the people to look to the government for answers."[22]

The fear that American cities would devolve into violence, however, meant that Johnson's programs would not end immediately. Moynihan and Nixon may have shared a hatred of what they called "professional welfarists," but they also understood that dismantling antipoverty programs might reignite the cities.[23] When asked about the possibility of riots recurring under Nixon, Moynihan said, "The fact is the people who live in this part of America, American cities, are entitled to some expectation of a response from Government; that society will try to do something. It hasn't succeeded; we are trying."[24] The New Federalists, led by Nixon, did not believe that there was no role for the state, but that it had to be reconceived after Johnson. HUD's new housing programs presented an opportunity for the government to apply free market principles already in place while experimenting with New Federalist approaches to their execution. To accomplish this, Romney looked to reorganize the department under the doctrines of New Federalism by decentralizing authority away from Washington and directing it toward "local and state authorities without Federal review."

In the early spring of 1969, when the Nixon administration finally took the reins of government, Romney suspended all HUD activity for one month in order to conduct a dramatic and wide-ranging reorganization. By September 1970, Romney had led an effort to increase the number of regional offices, including new posts in Boston, Kansas City, Seattle, and Denver. HUD under Romney also invented the "area office," which was created to exert even greater local control over the decision-making process in the application of housing policy. The number of regional and area offices expanded from seven to thirty-three.[25] The more local of these offices had the most direct hand in implementing HUD policies, including the placement of low-income housing developments. They would also become pivotal to implementing HUD's homeownership programs. Local HUD-FHA staff was responsible for appraising properties and approving applicants where mortgage lenders approved contracts for the Section 235 interest subsidy. The national HUD office was also tasked with implementing and then monitoring the new laws banning discrimination in the sale and leasing of housing. All together, these new responsibilities would have been difficult under the best of circumstances. But HUD was trying to implement historic new programs with a tightened budget and no plans to increase the number of staff even as the number of local offices was dramatically expanded. In Chicago's FHA office, employees complained about the new pressures and constraints created by the new legislation. "We've had a 500 percent increase in our workload in the last eighteen months and only a ten percent increase in our staff," said the director of the HUD in Chicago.[26]

INFLATION AND CRISIS

The political changes happening in HUD were not just the result of the shifting ideological guideposts of Nixon compared with Johnson. They were taking place amid global economic changes that would affect the longevity of the American postwar boom. A credit crunch in 1966 had increased interest rates dramatically and made mortgage money more expensive to borrow, creating havoc in the housing market. Declining mortgage funds produced the most serious housing shortage since the end of World War II. The NAHB described the crisis: "This inflationary situation is being aggravated every day that housing production remains depressed. The annual rate of production is expected to fall to less than 1.1 million units before the end of the year and, unless some relief is provided . . . this will be a disaster for both the housing of our people and for the industry."[27] The growth of inflation in the American economy was linked to the world economy. When World War II began in 1939, the U.S. economy was half the size of that of Europe, Japan, and the Soviet Union combined. At the war's end, the United States was responsible for half of the manufacturing output in the world.[28] In the postwar world, much of the globe depended not only on American products but also on American currency to help purchase them. While the U.S. economy was consumed with Cold War military spending and the hot wars of Korea and Vietnam, countries that had been destroyed in World War II focused on rebuilding their economies. By the end of the 1960s, the United States was not the unassailable economic fortress it had been before the Cold War, and by 1968, it was importing more cars than it exported. Over the course of the 1960s, imports in general expanded at twice the rate of exports.[29]

Meanwhile, even as the United States declined as the dominant economic power, the world's currencies continued to be pegged to the American dollar; the dollar was pegged to gold and considered the most stable currency in the world. For all these reasons, the United States faced the stark reality, according to Nixon, of what it would mean to get its economic house in order: high interest rates, big spending cuts, and budget deficit reductions. Budget deficits were responsible, in part, for the persistence of inflation, as both federal and local governments spent beyond their resources on the books. At the same time, the proliferation of dollars nationally and internationally drove down the currency's value. The only way out of this cycle was either to cut spending or to raise taxes to create more revenue, neither of which would be politically popular.

The Nixon administration made clear the continued privileged position of housing as economic stimulus in the American economy and the lengths to which the federal government would go to maintain it. Romney described the larger economic and political consequences of a weak housing market when he said that "we must be aware of the grave potential economic, social, and political

damage. . . . Fewer housing starts would mean fewer jobs and widespread unemployment . . . [as well as] failure for countless small businesses. Inability to find
decent housing breeds discontent not only in the ghetto but in the suburbs of
Middle America. Frustrated expectations can explode not only in the streets
but at the polls."[30] And the market was weak. As one builder in New Jersey
put it, "The single-family home is moving into the category of a luxury item."[31]
Houses for less than $15,000 were 8 percent of the new single-family housing
market in 1968, where five years earlier they accounted for 29 percent. Seventy
percent of new houses in 1968 were over $20,000, and for the first time, the
median price for existing homes rose above $20,000.[32] According to the Bureau
of Labor Statistics, consumer prices generally rose 6.9 percent between January
1968 and May 1968; housing prices alone increased 7.6 percent. A principal driver
in these expenses was a "spectacular" rise in construction costs, which rose to
9.1 percent when the costs of lumber and wood were factored in. The cost of
lumber increased by 24 percent, and some wood, like plywood, increased in price
by 53 percent. When the building boom subsided, as a result of increased costs in
production, lumber sales and prices sagged along with it.[33]

The escalating price of housing was also inflated by land costs. According to
the National Commission on Urban Problems, land costs had been rising since
the end of World War II. On average, land costs accounted for 20 percent of the
total cost of housing, but in some major metropolitan areas experiencing rapid
growth, the price of "raw land" doubled between 1950 and 1965.[34] Finally, labor
costs were also critical in the growing price of housing. Rising labor costs were
the inspiration for Nixon's Philadelphia Plan, which has been overstated as a
liberal gesture in support of affirmative action. Nixon was less interested in "affirmative action" and Black equality in the workplace than he was in resetting
the wage table for carpenters, who, it was believed, created inflationary pressure on wages overall. In fact, the Philadelphia Plan, which was implemented
through an executive order requiring federal contractors to meet specific goals
in hiring minority employees, was intended to drive down the wages of trades-
people throughout the construction industry, where high wages were connected
to closed shops and the exclusion of Black laborers.[35]

Within the housing market itself, competing interests tried to influence the
direction of federal policy in ways that would benefit their particular sectors. The
"housing industry" was a "very decentralized array of contractors, developers,
landowners, real estate agents, and financing institutions, most of whom [were]
small."[36] For example, while builders championed new construction and even

helped to write the 1968 HUD legislation, real estate brokers opposed the emphasis on housing production, preferring greater utilization of existing housing stock instead. Fred Tucker, president of NAREB, expressed his disappointment with the production emphasis in his testimony to Congress: "We are at a loss to understand why existing housing units cannot be utilized more widely.... The administration apparently views the primary purpose of this program to increase the supply of low cost housing.... We feel that the present limitations in the bill preventing more widespread use of existing dwellings would, unfortunately, delay accomplishment of the program's overriding objective—to provide decent housing for ownership by low income families."[37] The homebuilders had different objectives. Since the 1950s, the NAHB had shifted its political objectives from lobbying against public housing to acting as a vocal advocate for building low-income housing in the cities and the suburbs. The NAHB was one of the first professional housing organizations to vocalize the need for "new homes for the neglected low-income and racial minority markets."[38] The organization collaborated closely with Lyndon Johnson as he steered American housing policy in the direction of new building and away from rehabilitating the inner cities. The NAHB assumed a "shadow cabinet" position in the White House under Johnson, offering lobbying assistance to push different housing legislation, including federal fair housing.

In the transition between the Johnson and Nixon administrations, the NAHB offered President Nixon proposals for action regarding the housing market. Eugene Gulledge was the president of the NAHB and vociferously supported efforts to place controls on credit to ease the growth of interest rates that were choking off housing starts in 1969. Gulledge supported the use of "mortgage-backed securities" to increase the flow of capital necessary to reinvigorate housing sales.[39] And in an effort to make FHA and VA-backed loans competitive with conventional loans, Gulledge supported Nixon's and Romney's efforts to lift the interest rate ceiling on loans offered by the FHA and VA, even if the higher rates would exclude the low-income residents they were intended to assist. Gulledge's objective was to boost home sales, and when he was appointed to be an undersecretary of HUD and the director of the FHA in 1970, these industry goals were absorbed into the federal agency. This was a telling display of the intimacy between the private sector and public officials in the behind-the-scenes debates that ultimately shaped public policies. The selection of Gulledge confirmed that HUD would focus on new housing production.[40]

OPERATION BREAKTHROUGH

Before George Romney became a three-term governor of Michigan, he was heralded for his successful business career in the auto manufacturing sector. Romney's central task as the secretary of HUD was to develop the same mass-production techniques he had innovated in car manufacturing and introduce them into the mass production of houses. Within HUD, questions proliferated over whether or not the housing goals outlined in the HUD Act were achievable. Romney stated the issues clearly: "This administration . . . has a major problem. Congress has established a ten-year national goal of 26 million housing units, six million of them federally assisted. To meet this need we'll have to move rapidly from production levels which have averaged 1.5 million units a year to nearly 2.8 million a year, including a few hundred thousand mobile homes. Production of publicly assisted units will have to go from 200,000 to 600,000 units a year."[41] Romney believed that 200,000 to 300,000 new units of housing could be produced every year using mass production. He gambled that this was the only way to radically increase the number of new housing units in the United States; the limitations of inflation made traditional homebuilding prohibitively expensive. In the spring of 1969, Romney declared a new initiative called Operation Break-through to ramp up production of prefabricated housing.[42] Romney described the program as "a good relationship—a creative partnership—of federal, state and local governments and of industry, labor, the financial community, home-builders and consumers. Why shouldn't we profitably make use of the assembly line system and other mass production techniques to build hundreds of thou-sands of good quality, low-cost housing units all over the country?"[43]

Housing for poor and working-class people had been the subject of federal and local debate and discussion for most of the twentieth century, and yet by the end of the 1960s, when compared with actual need, affordable housing re-mained scarce in cities across the country. It was no coincidence that the new focus on the production of housing along with homeownership coincided with what could be described as a political nadir for public housing. By the late 1960s, public housing developments in Chicago and St. Louis had become very visible markers of the breakdown of the concept. Moreover, the increasing costs of liv-ing in cities pushed affordable housing further from the grasp of the urban dwell-ers who needed it. The introduction of federally backed subsidies was intended to bridge the gap between demand and supply. Indeed, by the late 1960s, builders looked to the federal government to make low-income housing more profitable.[44]

Romney laid out ambitious goals for Operation Breakthrough:

- reduce the cost of housing;
- produce quality homes in volume for persons of all incomes;
- reduce the costs of low- and moderate-income housing;
- reduce urban tension;
- help achieve stable, balanced communities through reversing city-
  suburb migration;
- create a housing industry with year-round employment;
- increase job and enterprise opportunities for minority groups;
- encourage continuing innovation and help the economy.[45]

The challenge was convincing companies to participate in the program. HUD began a competition among developers across the country, challenging them to create a model for cheaply designed houses made with cheap materials that could be mass produced. HUD guaranteed companies that developed successful methods an end to costly delays in processing. This included a promise to undo existing building codes that were considered to be obsolete and that delayed the building process. Many building codes were decades old, differed from one locality to the next, and delayed new construction, sometimes indefinitely. In their desire for expeditious building, however, neither HUD nor the builders considered the potential impact of utilizing new building methods with cheaper materials while simultaneously weakening building codes in place to ensure safety and habitability.

There were many questions surrounding Operation Breakthrough, but there was also interest in participating. The final objective of the program was to find twenty-two companies to design and build "innovative housing prototypes" in ten cities around the country. The winners would share a small ($30 million) budget to turn their "blueprints into buildings" and create 2,000 new units of housing. The big prize in the contest would be publicity through participation in a high-profile government program. Two hundred and thirty-six bidders submitted proposals to join the competition.[46] At a time when the conventional market was struggling with high interest rates and a lull in homebuilding and home purchases, the subsidized-housing market found more interest than had typically been the case. Some of the companies that won were well-known American corporations like General Electric, Republic Steel, and Levitt Brothers.[47]

Operation Breakthrough was celebrated as innovative and groundbreaking in its approach, but it was a small-scale demonstration program with the modest objective of building a few thousand units. This was in sharp contrast to the enormous tally of low-income housing mandated by the housing act as well as the ever-present demand that was growing as housing costs began to swell over the course of the 1970s. Romney believed that the successful production of housing as a result of Operation Breakthrough would legitimize the methods of mass industrial home production. He advocated for his policies with liberal flair: "How much more meaningful our accomplishment would be if we were to carry out completion in the 1970s—our twenty-year goal of a decent home and a suitable living environment for all Americans—rather than content ourselves with setting another priority goal in space on the heels of landing on the moon."[48]

REBUILDING CITIES?

By early 1970, however, there was little progress toward providing either new or rehabilitated housing. Operation Breakthrough was "running six months behind largely because Romney ha[d] trouble firming up contracts for his projects." Some of the delay was typical of complex agreements between the federal government and local authorities, but additional delays were caused by local objections to low-income housing. Operation Breakthrough had trouble breaking through because of the thorny question of where all the newly mass-produced housing was going to be located. This issue was potentially explosive because members of Nixon's white suburban base relished the distance between their new communities and the cities many of them had fled. HUD's focus on dispersal and low-income housing was in total conflict with the president's political calculations and objectives for the coming 1972 electoral season. It was true that elements of Nixon's 1968 presidential campaign were moderate in tone and in policy suggestions; however, Nixon's electoral focus was on the so-called silent majority of white suburbanites who felt they had been driven from the city.[49] Moynihan's ideas concerning the dispersal of African Americans into the suburbs were based, in his view, on the long-term stability of the nation, whereas Nixon had more immediate political considerations. Indeed, the backdrop to the drama of the placement of low-income housing was the shifting demography of the American metropolitan areas. From 1960 to 1970, 2.1 million white people left American cities for the suburbs. Over the same period, 2.6 million African Americans moved into the nation's cities, becoming a disproportionately urban-based population.

It was also true that there would be no large-scale building of new low-income housing in urban communities because of the costs it would incur. An internal HUD memo explained the complications of locating new housing: "The six million units of assisted housing projected for the next ten years simply cannot be built in inner city areas because there is not enough vacant land there even if urban renewal and model cities provides [*sic*] some. The unavailability of reasonably priced suburban land is often cited as an impediment to the construction [of] low and moderate-income housing. Yet the fact remains that vacant outlying land is still far cheaper than inlying land including that attainable only through the renewal process."[50] Not only were the costs of new building becoming more prohibitive with each passing day, but the possibility of continued displacement of Black families by urban renewal seemed likely to catalyze further resistance. Indeed, by the end of the 1960s, more than 51,000 units of housing had been lost because of federal "renewal" policies.[51] It was risky to unveil new demolition plans in cities without a clear idea of what would be built to replace the lost housing stock.

Project Rehab was launched in the winter of 1969 shortly after the confirmation of Romney as secretary of HUD. It was a partial answer to the dilemma that added to the ongoing debate about how to achieve the country's housing goals.[52] It was also a modest plan to rehabilitate 37,000 units of housing in cities around the country, including Philadelphia, Baltimore, Buffalo, El Paso, Seattle, and Pittsburgh, among others.[53] This was the kind of program NAREB had lobbied for because it further developed the existing housing market in cities. Project Rehab allowed for nonprofit organizations and local housing authorities to buy "rundown properties from absentee landlords" and then qualify for government subsidies to pay for rehabilitation.[54] Rehabilitating and rebuilding in the inner city had benefits beyond housing; it also created business opportunities for African Americans in their communities. This dovetailed with Nixon's goals of developing a Black business class with vested political and economic interests in the inner city. Romney had a very expansive view of the program, promising that it would "provide much needed jobs and entrepreneurial opportunities to residents of the affected neighborhoods especially members of the minority races."[55] The projected development of Black commerce was central to wider debates about the placement of Black housing. Rebuilding the urban core—as opposed to dispersing Black housing into white suburban areas—signaled a belief in the necessity of underwriting Black businesses.

Despite these plans to rebuild U.S. cities to stave off the issue of placing low-income housing in suburbs, Project Rehab turned out to be inadequate. An unintended consequence came to light when the program began displacing urban residents. The original project was to rehabilitate abandoned properties, but some developers took advantage of government funds to fix occupied units. The tenants of these properties were displaced and not eligible for relocation funds that typically had been made available to people victimized by urban renewal projects. While creating new units for some, the sloppy execution of the program meant new housing woes for others. A larger problem with Project Rehab that foreshadowed events to come was that HUD's solicitation of "non-profit" developers to buy and rehabilitate dilapidated buildings opened the door for real estate speculators to profit from government subsidies offered to finance the rehabilitation. The news media in Washington, D.C., discovered that a local slumlord with more than 8,000 citations for code violations in his properties received over $9 million from the federal government to pay for the rehabilitation of properties the city had condemned.[56]

This reluctance to relocate low-income housing to the suburbs was further complicated by the changing job market. From 1920 to 1970, the forty largest cities in the United States gained more than 5 million jobs, 85 percent of them in the suburbs.[57] Of the more than 2 million manufacturing jobs included in those numbers, the suburbs gained all but 30,000. As the chief urban specialist within the Nixon administration, Daniel Patrick Moynihan also pointed to the growing number of jobs that had been created outside cities, including those generated when federal agencies moved into the suburbs. This meant that the jobs most available to African Americans were in areas where very few Blacks lived. At the same time, while suburbs across the United States grew tremendously in the postwar era, they remained virtually all white. The census from 1960 and 1970 showed that the Black percentage of the suburban population remained virtually unchanged, rising from 4.2 percent to 4.5 percent. Over the course of the 1960s, 762,000 nonwhites moved to the suburbs, a number that was 42 percent more than in the previous decade but still dwarfed by the influx of 12.5 million whites into the same areas.[58] The movement of almost a million nonwhites into suburban areas did not demonstrate nascent integration; rather, it represented the extension of Black urban communities into new suburban developments. In other words, Black suburbanization occurred at a trickle, created new Black suburbs, and was not indicative of Black absorption into white suburban communities.[59]

As it turned out, these conditions were not always good for business. Suburban-based businesses needed access to the low-wage workforce trapped in the cities. Wage increases significantly affected corporate profits, and employers looked for ways to bring their labor costs down, including hiring low-skilled urban workers. When Blacks were able to get suburban jobs, there were inevitable problems with absenteeism and poor performance connected to the difficulties these workers had in getting to work. A growing number of suburban employers recognized this dynamic and advocated for suburban low-income housing on that basis. In a poll of 210 corporate chief executive officers on their attitudes concerning the availability of low-income housing in the suburbs near their firms, 45 percent said they "regarded a suburb's willingness to provide an adequate range of housing as a factor in plant location." Sixty-four percent also believed "that companies should have a role in securing more housing for employees near their workplace."[60]

Beyond issues of employment and access to the urban workforce, for some political strategists there was a strong belief in dispersing African Americans into white suburbs as a solution to the nation's political maladies. A local HUD director in Detroit commented in a memo in support of dispersal that "dispersal is another way of breaking black power which is located in the inner city."[61] These attitudes did not necessarily translate into the necessary action to break through the building stalemate over the location of low-income housing. But they illustrate the complexity of resolving the housing issue.

Moynihan made such an argument in *Toward a National Urban Policy*, where he said that the concentration of African Americans in cities constituted a crisis: "The poverty and social isolation of minority groups in central cities is the single most serious problem of the American city today.... Efforts to enable the slum population to disperse throughout the metropolitan area [require] the active intervention of government."[62] In another essay, he described the problems of zoning and suburban politics as the main stumbling blocks to building low-income housing in the suburbs. He chastised federal officials for their passivity in the face of suburban opposition to subsidized housing. He wrote, controversially, of the consequences of the federal government's failure to facilitate the movement of African Americans into the suburbs: "There is rarely any punishment for failing.... The federal government should provide market competition for public programs.... Federal aid should be given directly to the consumers of the programs ... providing the most reward to those suppliers who survived the competition.... Housing must not only be open, it must be *available*. The process of filtration out from the dense center city slums can only take place if the housing perimeter ... is sufficiently porous."[63]

Within African American communities, the desire for rebuilding urban Black housing was not an embrace of segregation but an expression of the sheer exhaustion with the multiple obstacles erected to housing opportunities, making "fair housing" seem less possible or even desirable. Out of this frustration emerged debates over political strategy in how to address the persisting urban housing crisis. Emergent questions over whether to "gild the ghetto" by seeking to redevelop urban areas where African Americans were becoming majority populations or to continue to pursue "fair housing" in suburban enclaves ensued. The debate sharpened as suburban officials refused to relent on the entry of low-income housing and the Nixon administration neutered the ability of the federal government to intervene. Organizations like the NAACP and the Urban League operated on both fronts in continuing to pursue legal challenges to housing discrimination against African Americans while simultaneously working to produce urban housing through the respective housing corporations both organizations established after the HUD Act passed.

Among some Black elected officials and African American real estate operatives, "fair housing" and residential integration were portrayed as a luxury that African Americans desperate for housing simply did not have. Black real estate and political operatives often acted as "middlemen" who were especially interested in further developing a Black housing market and the business opportunities expected to follow. Sociologist Mary Pattillo has described these kinds of actors as essentially "brokers" who "emphasize[d] balance compromise, negotiation, and cunning," as they worked to enrich themselves while performing these kinds of functional roles in African American communities. Dempsey Travis, who played a role in early efforts to marshal mortgage money for African Americans, had gone on to own a multimillion-dollar mortgage brokerage firm. He was firmly committed to maintaining the urban housing market and his role in it. This period also represented a moment of political transition when African Americans went from political outsiders to the political stewards of the cities where they were quickly becoming the majority. Building a Black political machine or even just basic political representation would be undermined by dispersal into white suburban communities.[64]

In this climate, as African Americans confronted the political obstacles erected by suburban officials who sought to keep their communities white, while also battling the physical violence and other acts of intimidation by white homeowners, residential integration was portrayed as anachronistic or simply too hard to achieve. Or as one sympathetic publication put it, "Depressing as it may be to white liberals, the truth must be faced: to insist upon racial integration as a *sine qua non* of housing improvement is to consign millions of American families, white and black, to their present slum conditions for years to come."[65] Fair housing seemed unrealistic or even unnecessary while Black urban communities were crumbling and poorly sheltered. Demanding better housing, better services, jobs, and "community control" in existing Black neighborhoods seemed possible and even more desirable than trying to enter neighborhoods where African Americans were clearly unwanted. As the numbers of African Americans swelled city centers across the country, the development of an urban-based Black political and economic class raised the possibility of community autonomy and control. These changes within Black communities looked less like *segregation* imposed from without and more like *community* being forged from within. The social, political, and cultural productions forged in African American communities underpinned the meaning of "Black community."[66] But this community forged in segregation should not be romanticized as superior to other potential living arrangements. Indeed, the hardship of the "ghetto" was borne out in the succession of urban uprisings over the course of the 1960s.

Though challenging residential segregation reflected a moral commitment to integration for some, achieving safe, sound, and affordable housing for African Americans was impossible as long as they were confined to a single section of the housing market. Perhaps if the offers to gild the ghetto had resulted in significant improvements in housing conditions, then this could have been sustained as a viable alternative. Instead, newly developing local Black administrations were faced with shrinking budgets, a declining tax base, and a hardening political discourse affixing blame to African Americans for the distressed condition of their housing. The dilapidation of older used Black urban housing was hastened by residential segregation for a host of reasons. As more employers and jobs shifted to suburban locations, the confinement of Blacks in cities cut them off from more lucrative employment opportunities. Low incomes and poverty had cascading effects in Black life but especially as they pertained to housing. Black residents were more likely to have more people per room to offset the expense of their housing and the higher levels of poverty among African Americans. Black homeowners did not have the discretionary funds necessary for home maintenance, which was likely to be significant, given that their housing was older, used, and in poorer condition compared with the newer housing of the suburbs. When these factors were combined with inconsistent city services, African American communities bore the physical signs of distress that in the eyes of white legislators and homeowners legitimized their continued isolation and reinforced the ascending value of segregated white neighborhoods. Black housing appeared to embody and reflect the deficiencies it had long been accused of harboring. Fair housing and "fair lending" were the keys to unlocking the spatial strangulation that isolated African Americans into old housing, low-paying employment, and poorly resourced public services.[67]

As it had done in the past, the building industry contributed its voice to the side of dispersal and increased production of subsidized housing as the slumping housing market continued to increase the popularity of politically perilous subsidized housing. Perry Prentice, the publisher of *Time* and *House and Home* magazines and a member of the board of the NAHB, thanked the Nixon administration in a speech for having "done far more to help our industry than any other administration has done." He listed the administration's achievements:

> They enabled us to tap the bond market in a great big way for the first time ever. They have diverted more than $16 billion away from corporate exempt and tax exempt bond issues into home mortgages.... Over and above diverting all those $16 billion from the bond market into the mortgages, this administration has already committed the federal government to spending more net dollars for housing subsidies than the Roosevelt administration, plus the Truman administration, plus the Eisenhower administration, plus the Kennedy administration, and plus at least half of the Johnson administration.[68]

Prentice made the important observation that, despite the tensions within the Nixon administration over the placement of subsidized housing, the administration had already committed to an unprecedented amount of federal spending toward its creation. The builders began publicizing their interest in opening up the suburbs as antidiscrimination and recast their support for suburban low-income housing as a civil rights issue, along with a demand for fair housing in the suburbs. In a public hearing before the U.S. Commission on Civil Rights in 1971, the NAHB described the negative impact of zoning ordinances used to stall building low-income housing in the suburbs: "In far too many cases, zoning is being used to protect the narrow self-interest of a particular community without regard to the health, safety, and the welfare of the community and the nation as a whole."[69] Behind closed doors, however, the NAHB was more blunt about its objectives: "Our motivation is pretty straightforward: If a guy can build all types of housing, he can make more dollars."[70]

RACE, CLASS, AND OPEN COMMUNITIES

The President's Task Force on Low Income Housing, created in the fall of 1969, suggested that solving the urban housing crisis included opening American suburbs to low-income housing. The task force urged the federal government "to use the full extent of its influence to overcome racial and economic discrimination as an obstacle . . . to its housing program. And to use eligibility to participate in federal housing assistance and community assistance programs to this end."[71] This had always been Romney's goal, as he argued, "We've got to put an end to the idea of moving to suburban areas and living only among people of the same economic and social class. Black people have got to get to know white people and white people have to know black people in this country. Otherwise, there will be no country."[72] In addition to reflecting his racial liberalism, Romney's stated philosophy seemed to acknowledge the fact that the biggest demand for affordable housing came from African Americans who continued to be trapped in substandard urban housing.

An internal HUD report in 1969 described the organization's mandate as "the promotion of open communities where citizens of all economic and racial groups have the opportunity to secure decent housing in heterogeneous communities."[73] As previously noted, the authority to create "open communities" was contained in the enforcement powers of the 1964 Civil Rights Act and Kennedy's 1962 executive order, both of which authorized the removal of federal assistance and programming as leverage to create compliance with federal mandates banning discrimination.[74] Romney called this continuing attempt to open the suburbs to low-income housing for minorities Open Communities. Urban Council members began outlining the parameters of the policy in the fall of 1969. They described the goals of the program as "providing for those confined to center city ghettos by race or poverty the amenities and opportunities of suburban life: good schools, safe streets, adequate living space, public and private open space, access to wider employment opportunities, housing that enhances positive self-perception because it is like housing chosen by those to whom choices are open."[75] Those within HUD working on Open Communities believed that opening the suburbs would enhance social mobility among "the disadvantaged," giving them a "sense that they are . . . a part of the mainstream of America, moving ahead."[76] Open Communities had the potential to achieve the dual objectives of establishing fair housing policies and achieving the housing goals of the HUD Act. Internally, HUD officials saw their strategy as also rooted in the new legal terrain established by the Fair Housing Act, which included the responsibility to administer the programs in such a way as to pursue residential integration.

There were, however, political and institutional obstacles. Politically, Romney's push to challenge suburban segregation made others in the Nixon administration bristle. When Romney made the strategy publicly known, other Nixon affiliates looked to create distance between it and the president. Harold Finger, an assistant HUD secretary, remarked, "We are not talking about it. We have not settled on what carrots and what pressures to apply." HUD spokesperson George Creel told the press, "Our policy is not to integrate the suburbs."[77]

Suburban municipalities created institutional obstacles that were equally foreboding, using zoning ordinances, subdivision regulations, and other legal tools to reinforce residential segregation and keep out low-income housing and the Blacks who lived in it.[78] The use of zoning ordinances to control the movement of people in and out of cities had been perfected throughout the early twentieth century, before the new federal laws banning discrimination. After the passage of the Fair Housing Act, supposed colorblind zoning practices were even more critical to maintaining the "racial homogeneity" of many suburban communities. Civil rights advocates described "snob zoning" as only the latest method of discrimination in the real estate market. Through local ordinances, "low-income" renters and buyers were excluded on the basis of economic segregation, but that designation enabled the exclusion of Blacks and Latinos as well.[79] Take, for example, a rezoning case in Cicero, Illinois. Cicero, a suburb of Chicago, became internationally known when an open housing protest led by Dr. Martin Luther King Jr. in 1966 almost turned into a riot after angry white protestors confronted nonviolent marchers. Four years later, a nonprofit religious organization applied for a permit to build townhouses that "would be well designed and compatible with the neighborhood. But occupants would be low- and moderate-income families, some of whom were certain to be minority families." The owners of nearby expensive homes opposed the development, but, as usual, they never mentioned race; instead, they emphasized the potential harm to their property values if poor people were allowed to move in.[80] In other suburbs, politicians complained about "density," "astronomical taxes," and unreasonable "burdens" to area schools, traffic, and police and fire services. This is not to say that none of those issues were a real concern, but it was impossible to disentangle race from class. It was no secret that African Americans were overrepresented among the poor and lower-income population relative to whites. The hand-wringing and chatter pondering the exclusion of the poor was a proxy for discussing race.

A Cicero politician pointed out, "Not one of them said anything about black people moving out there. . . . Not one of them said anything about poor people moving out there. But that was the unspoken reason."[81]

For Open Communities to be effective, suburban ordinances would have to be challenged. In one memo, a HUD official bluntly said so: "It is proper for HUD to use its program resources in ways that promote fair housing, and to withhold these resources where their use would promote a continuation of expansion of segregation."[82] In their internal discussions, members of the Urban Council clarified the conditions under which they would withhold resources: "The best test of a community's commitment to fair housing is the extent to which people of all races do in fact reside in the community. If a community is integrated, HUD's initial equal housing opportunity concerns are satisfied. If a community is all-white or segregated, HUD would have some doubt as to whether the community offers equal housing opportunity. . . . HUD should require some demonstration of the community's commitment to fair housing politics."[83] By the early 1970s, it was widely agreed upon in civil rights circles that punishing suburban governments for blocking efforts to build low-income housing was the only way to compel compliance with the nation's civil rights laws. The Presidential Task Force on Urban Renewal was even more direct in its diagnosis of the problem when it declared, "There is perhaps no greater danger to the future of our democracy than the possibility that the cities . . . will be destroyed as affluent and white concentrate more . . . in the suburbs and the central cities are converted into reservations for the black and poor." The prescription for this crisis was clear: "The Task Force urges that federal aids of all sorts be withheld from communities unless they undertake a program to expand low- and moderate-income housing within their boundaries."[84]

The subject of low-income housing laid bare race and class divisions that bisected suburban communities just as intensely as the divisions between suburbs and cities. Suburban enclaves where the rich lived, like Bloomfield Hills, Michigan, where Romney resided, were never under much threat of having to contend with low-income housing or low-income people.[85] HUD targeted working-class suburbs with restrictions on their access to water and sewage grants that were dependent on federal money for improvements as opposed to wealthy suburbs for whom HUD sanctions carried little to no weight. Working-class suburbs were also preferable because the cost of building and the housing in general were cheaper. The whites who made up these suburban communities were recent migrants from the cities themselves, and some were very reluctant, if not hostile, to what they viewed as an invasion of low-income, urban Blacks into their newly constituted communities. Some of this was reflexive anti-Black racism, while some of it was based in fears fueled by economic insecurity. There *were* legitimate concerns about school overcrowding and stresses on public services when no additional federal monies were being offered to support those services.

In a western Michigan suburb called Beecher Township, outside of Flint, African Americans made up 30 percent of the community but had avoided much of the racial violence experienced in Detroit. The situation in Beecher demonstrated how the builders' frenzied approach to subsidized housing could stoke resentment and community turmoil where little had existed before. The profitability of building low-income housing was based on volume; to justify a vigorous production schedule, a builder needed bodies to fill the housing. It was much cheaper to build in Beecher than in Flint proper or Detroit. In Beecher, developers built 716 new units of low-income housing within a five-square-mile area of the township—more than all of Flint's other suburbs combined.[86] Builders opted for larger houses because they were more expensive, and they justified the size of the houses by recruiting African American mothers from Detroit's public housing who were on welfare and had big families.[87] The average number of children in a Section 235 house in Beecher was four, twice the average for families in nonsubsidized housing. Overzealous builders built thirty Section 235 houses on a single block, eight on the next street, and a dozen on the street after. One developer in particular defended the enthusiastic building of the slapdash housing, exclaiming, "These people need houses. They are all red-blooded Americans. The poor are all over. Our [the developers'] deal . . . is this: is there a market?"[88] One local homeowner described the houses as "federally aided ghetto creation."[89] The houses were poorly built with cheap materials. The families moving in were too poor to be able to repair the houses easily. This was not lost on the poor women who lived in these houses. One mother of two small children complained, "Sure this is better than what we had, if only they'd fix up what's wrong and give you the things they promised."[90]

Black community members also expressed concern about overcrowding and deteriorating conditions in the public schools. In the first fall after the new houses were built, Beecher's public school enrollment increased by 16 percent. The percentage of "disadvantaged" students in the school district rose from 8 percent to 28 percent almost overnight. Class sizes jumped from twenty to thirty students per class as the school district contemplated whether or not to begin conducting classes in shifts. Willie Wheaton of the Flint Urban League described the situation in Beecher: "When I first got into this thing, I thought the opposition in Beecher was racial. But it isn't. The fact is that the FHA was running the program for the benefit of builders at the expense of the community."[91] After town protests became public, HUD quietly prevented any more building in the working-class suburb, but the damage had been done.[92] Beecher had survived the racial turmoil of the 1960s, but in the aftermath, because of the careless introduction of the HUD housing, the mass exodus of whites was under way. A comment from the school district's superintendent captured the complexity of the entanglement of demographic shifts and public policy during this period. His insights offer a more complicated understanding of what is described as white flight: "The community had reached a point where the races are living together and it has been that way for three to five years. Overcrowding of the schools is our paramount concern. We do not have a racist angle. We aren't against the 235 housing program or the 236 apartment program. We know the people in the inner city need housing, but we are against the way it has been administered. We had one of the model integrated school systems in Michigan and now it is being ruined."[93] It was not lost on Beecher residents, 70 percent of whom were making an average salary of $8,000 a year, that while hundreds of low-income subsidized units had been built in their community, fewer than six subsidized units were built in a nearby wealthy suburb.[94] As one official said about Beecher, "This is not a rich community."[95]

Beecher demonstrated the web of issues that caused the debates over suburbanization and low-income housing to be fraught with tension.[96] There was no universal white suburban experience. In the early 1970s, white working-class suburbs continued to develop because of flight from the cities. Many of these people had been "block-busted" out of their homes, which certainly stoked the animus of racial resentment. A corollary to this was a distrustful but well-justified conviction that the federal government's policies would devalue white working-class communities further by encouraging low-income housing while offering no additional financial support and by excluding rich suburbs as sites of low-income housing. Rising and falling property values, overtaxed public facilities, and threats of punishment from the federal government for not agreeing to its terms for low-income housing stoked resentment from white residents in these communities. These were more than shibboleths; they had to be understood within the wider context of inflation, emerging economic crisis, the decline of American empire, and the absence of a genuine welfare state. Access to appreciating homeownership determined whether one could afford to send one's children to college, retire, care for aging parents, and more. A house was the most important asset in the lives of ordinary Americans; this fact explains, in part, the extreme reactions of most white homeowners in opposition to low-income housing, especially in white working-class suburbs. It also explains the anxious efforts of African Americans to access this social benefit.

Race was, of course, also a driving factor because it was still a general assumption in the United States as a whole that African Americans had a deleterious effect on property values. This was not only a personal belief of white homeowners but an assumption that continued to prevail throughout the real estate and housing industries. There was no "natural" connection between the presence of African Americans and the automatic decline of property values, but as a result of public policy and private practices within the housing industry over the course of decades, "race and risk" were forever linked in the public consciousness. A focus on the attitudes of white residents or ideological factors, however, should not obscure the political economy of homeownership and housing in general in American society. Economic explanations are not more important than racial attitudes; the two were inextricably bound together in federal housing policies for close to forty years. Nixon was hoping to tap into this resentment.

FORCED INTEGRATION

HUD experienced some initial success with its "carrot and stick" approach and convinced a small number of suburbs to accept its conditions for continued funding. In 1970, as HUD made an effort to implement its new policy, the agency withheld a million-dollar sewer grant from Baltimore County due to its refusal to accept subsidized housing. When the city council of Toledo, Ohio, canceled a contract for three housing projects for 400 tenants, HUD responded by canceling a $15-million grant for urban renewal, open space, sewers, and water.[97] In times of increasing economic distress, especially in state and local government, the "stick" of withholding federal funds could potentially have solved the longtime problem of ineffective federal enforcement of civil rights laws. There were several small, lesser-known successful efforts at compelling small, if not tiny, municipalities to agree to HUD's terms. In Fairborn, Ohio, HUD held up a "clean water" grant until "the city pledged to open up housing for blacks." In Waterloo, Iowa, similar threats of similar denials were made until "open community" steps were taken.[98]

Feeling the momentum of success, Romney targeted a suburb with which he was very familiar. In 1967, in Warren, Michigan, a suburb of Detroit, then-governor Romney had been forced to call the National Guard to restore order after mobs of angry whites rioted and burned crosses on the front lawn of a Black couple who had recently moved to the area. By 1970, tens of thousands of African Americans worked in Warren; but only twenty-eight Black families lived in the suburb, and twenty-two of those families lived on a military base.[99] In the spring of 1970, HUD threatened to cut off Warren's urban renewal funds because of "concern that equal opportunity matters did not appear to be receiving adequate treatment" in the suburb's application for federal funds. The city council had rejected 100 low-income housing units after neighborhood residents protested. HUD suggested many different ways that Warren could have its full funding restored, including reversing its decision not to build the low-income housing and consulting with the NAACP about how to launch an education campaign on the social benefits of fair housing.

According to memos circulated between HUD and Michigan officials, including the governor, there was little disagreement with this approach to the situation in Warren. Within weeks, however, someone leaked an internal HUD memo discussing the Warren strategy to the *Detroit News*.[100] Disaster struck with the July 21, 1970, banner headline, "US Picks Warren as Prime Target in Move to Integrate All Suburbs." The newspaper highlighted choice quotes from the memo, including the following: "Detroit and its suburbs present an unparalleled opportunity for the application of a fair housing strategy. Nowhere else in the . . . country is there the combination of a large central city with a substantial black population, surrounded by predominately white suburbs which use many HUD programs, in which there is extensive black employment, and with a great deal of housing for lower middle economic families (suggesting racial rather than economic exclusion)."[101] In the world of politics, particularly for a Republican administration readying itself for a presidential run, this was bad enough, but the last two sentences of the memo were political dynamite: "We hope to achieve incremental progress in the integration of the metropolitan area. At the least we hope to slow the forces of increasing racial concentration and segregation in and around Detroit."[102]

Once the strategy was public, politicians who had been willing to acquiesce behind the scenes suddenly struck a defiant posture. Ted Bates, the mayor of Warren in 1970, made the incendiary remark that he would not tolerate "Warren being used as a guinea pig for integration experiments." When Romney traveled to Warren to smooth over the controversy, he needed an extra security detail as hundreds mobbed the meeting space; the secretary's safety seemed potentially in peril.[103] Eventually, the citizens of Warren voted to reject $10 million in HUD funding in lieu of allowing the construction of federally subsidized housing.[104]

The writing was on the wall for Romney, who had taken his autonomy in shaping housing policy too far for the Nixon administration. Several members of the administration concluded that Romney had to go. In the fall of 1970, Nixon's chief of staff wrote in his diary, "George won't leave quickly, will have to be fired. So we have to set him up on the integrated housing issue and fire him on that basis to be sure we get the credit."[105] Nixon's attorney and assistant John Ehrlichman warned the president of a "serious Romney problem," noting, "There is no approved program [on suburban integration] as such, nor has the White House approved such a policy. But [Romney] keeps loudly talking about it in spite of our efforts to shut him up." Nixon wrote back, "Stop this one." Shortly after, Nixon suggested, "Romney will go . . . if we can find a good black to replace him."[106]

By November 1970, Romney and HUD were threatening to embroil the Nixon administration in yet another integration controversy. Waiting until after the midterm elections of that year, Romney suggested to the Department of Justice that it initiate an investigation of a small St. Louis suburb called Black Jack. Romney was accusing Black Jack of using racially motivated zoning to prevent the building of a low-income housing development that would house poor Black people from the neighborhood where the controversial Pruitt-Igoe homes were located.[107] Soon after the Warren debacle, Attorney General John N. Mitchell exasperatedly demanded Romney's resignation. Nixon followed up, seeking Romney's resignation with an offer of the ambassadorship to Mexico, the country where his parents had lived in exile from anti-Mormon persecution. Romney refused the position and insisted that if the administration did not like the direction in which he was taking HUD, then it should create its own policy. In Romney's letter to Nixon rejecting the ambassadorship, it was clear that he was having great difficulty obtaining an audience with the president.[108] The lack of collaboration between the White House and HUD, he wrote, had led to "unavoidable variations in administrative decisions," including "publicity difficulties such as occurred in Warren, Michigan." In making his final plea for a real program aimed at developing a national approach to implementing fair housing, he requested an opportunity to "discuss my views with you personally." In the end, Romney emphasized the urgency for the administration to make a decision about implementing fair housing. In his typical hyperbole, he wrote to Nixon, "It is becoming increasingly apparent that the lower, middle-income, and the poor, white, black, and brown family, cannot continue to be isolated in deteriorating core cities without broad scale revolution. This can only be avoided by providing genuine hope for reform based on honest conformance of our constitutional principles and current statutory requirements. Now I do realize we may have different basic views that could lead to a collision."[109] Romney was not going to go quietly, and Nixon did not want political upheaval within his administration during the midterm election season, so he made the decision to marginalize Romney and put Ehrlichman in charge of the Council on Domestic Affairs, which would now include housing policy.

FROM CIVIL RIGHTS TO ECONOMIC DISCRIMINATION

Ehrlichman quickly assembled a team to develop a housing policy more reflective of Nixon's values and political concerns.[110] The entire HUD staff, including Romney, was excluded from this new domestic policy team. Ehrlichman emphasized that federal laws were vague when it came to desegregation and that there should be no hurry to interpret what undefined laws meant. In a paper circulated among members of the Council on Domestic Affairs, Ehrlichman set out a new strategy for HUD that entailed doing as little as possible. He wrote,

> At times, HUD and Justice, not unlike HEW [Department of Health, Education, and Welfare] and Justice in the school [desegregation] cases, are rapidly evolving what they think "ought" to be the law and applying these standards ... in granting federal housing money. ... Nonetheless, choices are still open regarding how narrowly we can construe the law successfully, and how much affirmative action we are willing to allow HUD to undertake in requiring planning or construction of low- and moderate-income housing as a prerequisite to a community's eligibility for any HUD money.[111]

Ehrlichman's approach was consistent with Nixon's overall posture toward domestic issues. Nixon had tried to avoid being pinned to particular domestic programs, choosing to focus most of his attention on foreign policy. While Nixon wanted to strike a noncommittal stance on housing and school desegregation, two of the most pressing civil rights and social issues of the time, a growing number of Black citizens were taking their cases to court in hopes of getting firm decisions in response to their grievances.

Nixon was faced with a choice: either intervene with legislation or risk the courts making the decisions for his administration. Court decisions in the early

1970s had already threatened to establish "open communities" as the law of the land regardless of the intentions of the Nixon administration. In 1970, in Philadelphia, civil rights lawyers sought an injunction to block the local affiliate of HUD from financing a subsidized housing development in the Black enclave of Northeast Philadelphia. Black area residents who joined the lawsuit argued that the addition of the HUD-subsidized building would "have the effect of increasing the already high concentration of low income black residents."[112] In other words, HUD's decision to place low-income Blacks in the neighborhood was likely to deepen the existing segregation in the community.

In January 1971, an appeals court ruled in favor of the plaintiffs. In doing so, the court used the language of the Fair Housing Act to explain that HUD was now required to "affirmatively promote fair housing." In the written decision, the court held that "increase or maintenance of racial concentration is *prima facie* likely to lead to urban blight and is thus *prima facie* at variance with the national housing policy."[113] The Philadelphia case also challenged the argument that African Americans supported separate neighborhoods. This belief underestimated the emergent class tensions among African Americans and the desires of African Americans whose economic situation was improving to see their housing values improve by excluding or marginalizing the presence of low-income and poor Black people. An African American homeowner from Hempstead, Long Island, his home adorned with a painted portrait of Martin Luther King Jr., also made his opposition to a low-income housing development that catered to poor African Americans: "People who rent houses don't keep them up. . . . Maybe what I'm saying would be contrary to what Dr. King would say. But this is my opinion."[114] Historian Robin Kelley has challenged the "presumption of a tightknit, harmonious black community that has existed across time and space." He went on to decry any notion of a "golden age of black community—an age when any elder could beat a misbehaving child, when the black middle class mingled with the poor and offered themselves as 'role models,' when black professionals cared more about their downtrodden race than their bank accounts—as not only disingenuous but a notion that has stood in the place of serious historical research on class relations within African American communities."[115]

On April 26, 1971, the U.S. Supreme Court upheld the constitutionality of a state referendum that allowed voters to block subsidized, low-income housing in their community. California voters had used this referendum law to block construction of almost half of the low-rent housing proposed for the state. The law had been challenged by forty-one families receiving welfare assistance in San

Jose after city voters reversed a decision by the city council in 1968 to approve building 1,000 low-rent apartments.[116] Anita Valtierra and her seven children lived in a small, cramped apartment because of the affordable housing crunch. Valtierra's family "ate, bathed and slept in shifts utilizing a bathroom measuring 10½ by 11½ feet."[117] Nonetheless, San Jose voters voted 68,000 to 58,000 against the housing, even though studies had indicated that the area needed 118,000 more low-income units to meet area housing needs. Justice Hugo Black described the referendum vote as "devotion to democracy, not to bias, discrimination or prejudice."[118] The families had argued that the denial of low-income housing was a violation of the Fourteenth Amendment and the right to equal protection. But the courts essentially ruled that "the poor" were not a protected class and that as long as "race" was not explicitly invoked as a reason for blocking the housing, then the ban was legal. There was no legal precedent asserting the right of the poor to live in communities of their choosing.

In 1971, in a case emanating from Lackawanna, New York, a suburb of Buffalo, city officials were poised to rezone land in a predominately white neighborhood for the creation of a park when it was discovered that the Archdiocese of Buffalo was selling thirty acres of land to an organization that intended to build low-income housing.[119] City officials tried to block the developers by claiming the land was not zoned for residential use because the sewage system could not be expanded. A federal appeals court rejected this explanation and ruled in favor of the low-income housing developers. Even though race was never invoked as an explanation for the emergency zoning decision, the courts understood its intent to prevent the location of low-income housing. Even so, the disparate direction of court decisions regarding discrimination was confusing and did not clarify how racial discrimination in housing would be rooted out.

Federal law had established that HUD could not finance projects or programs where racial discrimination curtailed the access of nonwhites, so excluding subsidized housing on economic terms was soon to be the nexus of the Nixon administration's housing policy. The rapidly developing if contradictory legal precedents established by the courts concerning housing factored into the administration's policy development process. The Council on Domestic Affairs worried that in the absence of a clear executive policy, the courts might harm the right of suburbs to use "traditional economic zoning" to protect property values.[120]

Fortunately for the council, John Ehrlichman and Nixon political advisor Len Garment had a plan. Before Ehrlichman became Nixon's counsel, he had spent eighteen years as a zoning attorney in Seattle. Following the lead of developing case precedents, Ehrlichman and Garment defended the right of suburban communities to exclude on the basis of preserving property values. Garment suggested that the loss of the right to zoning would have "devastating political and social consequences."[121] He rejected the idea that the federal government could "force communities or neighborhoods unwillingly to make provisions for low or moderate income housing by threatening to cut off all of their funding."[122] Instead, Garment suggested a voluntary program based on "incentives and financial assistance," providing the administration with a "politically advantageous housing position." Finally, Garment and the Council on Domestic Affairs rejected what they described as "forcing" integration and other "social engineering" in the demands for low-income housing in the suburbs. Instead, they suggested that the administration distinguish between clear acts of racial discrimination versus "practices that are based on legitimate economic distinctions." Garment suggested that if the administration took legal action to "vigorously attack . . . racially discriminatory zoning," it would be in a much stronger position to "defend the legitimacy of exclusionary zoning addressed to economic, traditional, and other legitimate considerations which have unintended discriminatory effect."[123]

A few weeks before Christmas 1970, Nixon made his first public remarks about Open Communities and the Warren, Michigan, debacle to distance himself from Romney and HUD's policies. In doing so, he also unveiled a reorientation in U.S. housing policies, saying at a press conference, "It is not the policy of this government to use the power of the federal government or federal funds in ways not required by law, for forced integration of the suburbs. . . . I believe that forced integration of the suburbs is not in the national interest."[124] Not only did this statement thwart whatever plans Romney had for HUD and the integration of American suburbs, but it was a shocking retreat from the central premise of civil rights law in the 1960s. The fulfillment of Kennedy's 1962 executive order, the 1964 Civil Rights Act, and the 1968 Fair Housing Act was contingent on the "use [of] the power of the federal government" to force local municipalities or authorities to allow African Americans use of their constitutionally enshrined rights—particularly as they related to housing, education, and employment. This had been especially necessary for protecting the rights of Black people from the tyranny of local officials who regularly ignored federal mandates concerning civil rights. Nixon was advocating an abdication of this federal responsibility and effectively returning African Americans to the racial tyranny of local rule.

The pivot away from federal demands that suburbs comply with the nation's antidiscrimination legislation was cemented in an anticipated policy statement Nixon released to describe his administration's approach to fair and open housing. On June 11, 1971, Nixon released a wide-ranging, 8,000-word statement in which the president acknowledged that the "Federal Government was not blameless in contributing to housing shortages and to the impairment of equal housing opportunity for minority Americans. . . . But despite the efforts and emphasis of recent years, widespread patterns of residential separation by race and of unequal housing opportunity persist."[125] This statement was uncontroversial, but what followed was not.

While acknowledging the reality of "unequal housing," Nixon persisted in describing racial segregation as a reflection of "the free choice of individuals and families in both the majority and minority communities." He described the "choices" individuals make deciding upon neighborhood or community as "essential" to a conception of freedom: "freedom has two essential elements: the right to choose and the ability to choose. . . . Similarly, an 'open' society is one of open choices and one in which the individual has the mobility to take advantage of these choices. An open society does not need to be homogenous, or even fully integrated." In other words, residential segregation and, conversely, integration reflected choice. This segued into the crux of the statement—the distinction between economic and racial exclusion:

> In approaching questions of "fair housing" for low- and moderate-income persons, it is important to remember that we are dealing with a rather imprecise term and with two separate matters. One is the elimination of racial discrimination in housing. On this, the Constitution and the laws are clear and unequivocal: Racial discrimination in housing will not be tolerated. In public discussions of "fair housing" or "open housing," however, another issue has often become confused with that of racial discrimination. This is sometimes referred to as "economic integration." Frequently it arises in debates over whether subsidized low-rent public housing should be placed in the suburbs as a means of moving poor people out of the inner city and, if so, where, to what extent, and by what means.[126]

Nixon went on to claim that opposition to the suburban placement of low-income people was not racist but largely driven by economic concerns. He made this claim by insisting that poverty was not racially based and could afflict anyone:

To equate "poor" with "black" does a disservice to the truth. . . . There are far more poor whites in America than there are poor blacks. Much of the nation's most dismally inadequate housing is occupied by blacks; much of it is occupied by whites. Many of the worst slums are black; many are white. And by the same token, the skilled trades, the businesses, and professions increasingly are populated by affluent blacks whose children go to the best schools and colleges and who themselves have taken their deserved place in the leadership, not simply of inner-city neighborhoods but of urban, suburban, and rural communities all across America.[127]

Nixon then announced his new policy:

What is essential is that all citizens be able to choose among reasonable locational alternatives within their economic means, and that racial non-discrimination be scrupulously and rigorously enforced. *We will not seek to impose economic integration upon an existing local jurisdiction; at the same time, we will not countenance any use of economic measures as a subterfuge for racial discrimination. . . . This Administration will not attempt to impose federally assisted housing upon any community.*[128]

What would this mean for the federal mandate of "affirmative action" in furthering fair housing as a national policy? Nixon wrote, "I interpret the 'affirmative action' mandate of the 1968 Act to mean that the administrator of a housing program open up new, nonsegregated housing opportunities that will contribute to decreasing the effects of past housing discrimination."[129]

Nixon was using a tried-and-true political trick of twisting reality to fulfill his political objectives. For years, the most contentious issue in housing policy was whether African Americans would have access to the whole of the housing market. Discussions concerning the location of and tenant placement within public housing could be interpreted as a "low-income housing" debate, but the predominance of race as a concern was crystal clear. Here, Nixon shifted the policy discussion to one of placement of low-income housing with no apparent regard for race. The problem, of course, was that the whirlwind of housing policies in the spring and summer of 1968 had brought these issues together. By passing fair housing legislation and then the HUD Act, the Johnson administration connected the mandate for the increase in low-income housing with the antidiscrimination mandate prescribed by fair housing. Nixon's expression of concern for "economic integration" was to effectively oppose the central strategy of the HUD Act, which was placing low-income housing into outlying areas. Nixon's attempt to distort the issue could not change what everyone knew to be true: the only controversy over low-income housing was that it was housing for Black and Latino residents.

Nixon's labored efforts to disentangle race from class and poverty lacked credibility. It was certainly true that there were more poor white people than poor Black people, but there was no history or record of angry white mobs protesting housing for poor whites. There was no record of systematic and organized opposition to the presence of poor or low-income white people in white communities. There were white housing projects in working-class white communities, but there was no history of the kind of violence and resistance that the presence of Black people in white residential areas provoked. Invoking vacuous suggestions like "opportunity" and "choice" while only "encouraging" suburbs to allow low-income housing was a recipe for further inaction. Nixon's intervention removed the mandate from the federal government and, instead, put the burden on individuals to break through the wall of residential segregation. Consequently, Nixon's wade into the debate over low-income housing only muddied the waters further. And despite his gestures toward strict enforcement of civil rights law, objective barometers of racial progress suggested otherwise. For all of the insistence that the administration would oppose racial discrimination, Nixon also defended racial or ethnic separation in the name of "cultural diversity":

> An open society does not have to be homogeneous, or even fully integrated. There is room within it for many communities. Especially in a nation like America, it is natural that people with a common heritage retain special ties; it is natural and right that we have Italian or Irish or Negro or Norwegian neighborhoods; it is natural and right that members of those communities feel a sense of group identity and group pride. In terms of an open society, what matters is mobility: the right and the ability of each person to decide for himself where and how he wants to live, whether as part of the ethnic enclave or as part of the larger society—or, as many do, share the life of both.... We are richer for our cultural diversity.[130]

The U.S. Commission on Civil Rights reported that by the time Nixon made his statement on housing, HUD under his leadership had "regressed in the vigor with which they are enforcing civil rights laws."[131] The commission continued in its assessment of HUD: "By April 1971 . . . the Department had retreated from its stance and now states that it is opposed to federal leverage to promote economic integration. The harsh facts of housing economics, however, suggest that *racial* integration cannot be achieved unless *economic* integration is also achieved." It was understated, but the report concluded that Nixon's statement marked the "beginning of the federal government's withdrawal from active participation in the effort to eliminate residential segregation."[132] In a letter to Secretary Romney, the director of the commission wrote, "Unfortunately, your department does not appear to make express provision for refusing to award grants on the grounds that the applicant jurisdiction has acted to exclude low income and minority persons."[133] Within a span of two years, the federal government had turned away from its own history of racial discrimination and segregation to a colorblind posture that left the status quo intact.

Nixon's long-awaited statement inspired a range of reactions. Most civil rights and housing justice advocates rejected Nixon's mixed message. Officials attending the U.S. Conference of Mayors, convened days after the speech, railed against the statement, claiming that it would continue the disproportionate burden on urban localities, compared with the suburbs. Chicago mayor Richard Daley explained the repercussions of Nixon's comments: "What is at issue is whether there is one national policy or two: one for cities and one for the rest of the country. We cannot respond with integrity to two contradictory Federal policies except to ask for one national policy which is equitable to all citizens of our nation. . . . A double standard will be rejected because it seeks to ignore the reality of urbanization."[134] Although he was credited with progressive intentions, Daley, speaking for most big-city mayors, was mostly angry with the suburban resistance to low-income housing because it left the cities alone economically responsible for the urban poor. Cleveland mayor Carl Stokes captured the cynicism of Nixon's new colorblind framing. He said that suburban America "no longer talks about spics, wops, niggers but talks about density, overcrowding of schools to achieve the same purpose."[135]

Nixon deployed many different members of the administration, including Secretary Romney, to combat criticism of his statement. Fielding questions at a press conference, Romney chastised opponents of the statement, saying, "I am totally convinced that those who are enthralled by the idea of sweeping Federal force run the risk of preventing not only what ought to be but what also can be. . . . What we should support now are policies that will achieve all the progress it is possible to achieve at this time."[136] After developing a federal program on withholding federal grants for noncompliance with federal law, Romney now claimed that the federal government had no such authority. Romney assured white suburbanites that the federal government would not "assume the role of omnipotent hero righting all wrongs, knocking down all barriers with a flourish, and redrawing the crazy quilt map of our metropolitan areas." Romney was also pragmatic. His attempts to challenge residential segregation had been thwarted locally and within his own administration. Perhaps leaving these matters to "choice" could produce "what could be" instead of "what ought to be."[137]

In following through with the promise of preemptive action against cases of racial zoning as discussed among the Council on Domestic Affairs before Nixon's statement, the week following the release of Nixon's statement, the Justice Department finally filed a civil rights lawsuit against Black Jack, Missouri, charging the town with exclusionary racial zoning.[138] John Mitchell had sat on the case for months and had used it as an excuse to pressure Romney into resigning, but now in filing the suit, the Nixon Justice Department could prove its willingness to aggressively pursue discrimination. In response to a permit request to build multifamily, low-income housing, the town passed a new zoning ordinance that prevented the exact kind of housing the request had named. The new ordinance would prevent 85 percent of African Americans in St. Louis from being able to move to Black Jack, but race was never mentioned. Neither Romney nor Mitchell could explain why they were pursuing the case in Black Jack as opposed to other cases where racial discrimination was in question despite there being no direct reference to race. This pointed to the arbitrariness of HUD's new direction and its new emphasis on the discretion of how officials perceived alleged transgressions.[139]

The most dramatic challenge to Nixon's new turn in housing policy was delivered the day before his statement was released. The U.S. Commission on Civil Rights released a multicity study examining the effects of the new HUD homeownership programs in promoting fair housing and easing Black housing demands.[140] The HUD homeownership programs had gone into operation in the waning days of the Johnson administration, but they had begun in earnest under the Nixon administration. By the time the commission released its report, the programs had been in operation for two years. The commission's conclusions confounded claims by the administration that it was weeding out racial discrimination in housing. According to the report, not only were the new programs not promoting fair housing, but "the traditional pattern of separate and unequal housing markets for majority and minority families is being repeated in the operation of Section 235."[141] Rather than becoming less of an issue, racial discrimination was persisting, if not proliferating. A congressional report investigating other claims of impropriety in the HUD homeownership programs had been released months earlier; it blamed serious problems in the administration of the program on lax enforcement of civil rights laws—a problem that had been carried through from the Johnson administration. Both reports found in place a weak regime of enforcement procedures to verify compliance with new antidiscrimination laws created by the Fair Housing Act, which meant that the "choices" of Black buyers and renters continued to be constrained by historical patterns.[142] The Nixon emphasis on "choice" diluted the historic and powerful impact that earlier policies and practices had on shaping housing choices made by Black people specifically. Neighborhood demographics in the United States had almost never been solely determined by the individual decisions or choices of buyers and sellers or renters and owners, but the element of choice was significantly restricted when the choosers were Black. As legal scholar Len Rubinowitz explained, "The fact is . . . that [the] continuation of [housing discrimination] stems not merely from choice but also from the perpetuation of processes and perceptions that had their genesis in an earlier period of racial discrimination. Thus, choice is limited because of the existence of this background discrimination."[143] The imposition of a new law banning these practices could not undo the conditions that had helped constitute the market in the first place. As the former mayor of Cleveland Carl Stokes observed, "You cannot separate the pernicious economic discrimination of this nation from the pervasive white racial perversions and problems of our country. The two of them together manage, whether it is white or black, to keep the kind of suburban ring around the central cities."[144]

George Romney's attempt to use water and sewage grants as leverage over newly developed suburbs to prevent their use of racial zoning and other acts of discrimination was short lived and marginally effective. Romney's concerted effort to fulfill his vision of racial liberalism—an unencumbered housing market that allowed African Americans to choose where they wanted to live—disintegrated under the weight of racial realities within the Nixon administration. Nixon had hinged his political career on stoking racial resentments. His deployment of an incendiary phrase like "forced integration" was intended to remind white suburban voters that he was not his predecessor, Lyndon Johnson, willing to use the power of the state to force the "civil rights agenda" on a reluctant white public. Moreover, by framing his opposition to housing equality as opposing "economic integration," Nixon took the awfulness of the old racism out of the equation. But for African Americans, it was a different story, or maybe the same old story told in a new way.

When Nixon publicly pledged not to use the power of the federal government to make local authorities comply with the mandate of the Fair Housing Act that required the federal government to take *affirmative actions* to further fair housing or end housing discrimination, he consigned Black buyers and renters to an inferior status in the housing market. By the early 1970s, multiple reports, studies, and commission releases had affirmed that residential segregation and housing discrimination were at the root of the lack of meaningful housing choices for African Americans. In the absence of good housing choices, African Americans had been locked into inferior and substandard housing, devalued neighborhoods, and under-resourced communities. While the debates over what could constitute "Black power" raged on, the reality was that only an open housing market could guarantee African Americans any opportunity at equity in the market. Without that guarantee, the same dynamics that ruled the pre–Fair Housing Act market—downward pressures on quality and upward pressures on price—would prevail.

The homeownership program that seemed so promising when passed as part of the HUD Act was neutered by the lack of access to the housing market in its entirety. It became difficult to see how it would open new opportunities and not just repeat the discrimination of the past.

4

Let the Buyer Beware

You cannot run a middle-class program in the ghetto.
—Ohio congressman Thomas L. Ashley, 1972

IN PHILADELPHIA IN 1970, an African American mother celebrated her move out of a public housing project and into a "brand-new" home of her own. She, like millions of parents across the country in the postwar period, invested in homeownership and the American dream with the expectation of raising her children in a good neighborhood and sending them to a better school than the ones she had attended in her youth. Her home, though, was not in one of the sprawling bucolic spaces of suburbia, where most of the postwar housing boom had taken place. For $12,000, she purchased a home in the city, one that was riddled with building code violations that included a chronically leaking roof and a flooded basement.[1]

In buying 78 Arch Street in Paterson, New Jersey, an African American mother of eight secured a home with "electrical deficiencies" and "large holes in the plaster" for $17,500.[2] A welfare recipient, she rented out the first floor of her house to another poor family in order to offset the cost of her monthly mortgage. The two families used one "old cooking stove which has all the knobs missing and the oven door hanging on one hinge."[3]

At 471 Graham Avenue in Paterson, a tavern was transformed into a living space even though it had been condemned by the city and boarded up for demolition. One month after it was determined unfit for human habitation, the building was purchased for $1,800 by a real estate speculator who made $450 worth of electrical repairs; four months later, it was sold again for $20,000 to an unsuspecting African American family. An inspection of the house after the family moved in found that "in order to enter . . . the house, one has to go up two steps to the area where tables had been in the tavern. The walls are rough and uneven where fresh paint was placed over old paint without adequate preparation. The bedroom floors are warped and buckling. The front door has been moved from the center to the side of the home and a small bathroom-type window placed where the front door used to be."[4] Eddie Agnew fared no better in Chicago. "A couple of days after we moved in the boiler blew out. It was cold then and my kids were shivering in their bedroom. I had to keep running down in the basement and starting the pilot light again. The boiler just wasn't throwing off any heat . . . [so] my kids were cold," recalled Agnew, the African American owner of a Section 235 house in Chicago.[5] He added that days after the boiler went out, the bathroom caved in completely while his family was watching television. Agnew noticed that the floor joists were charred and later learned that his house, weeks before he purchased it, had been in a fire. He lamented, "I got a raw deal."[6] In Berkeley and Oakland, California, an investigation found that dilapidated homes were sold to low-income families for three and four times more than they were worth. The houses were "largely incapable of passing honest FHA inspection and certainly failed to meet minimum FHA standards."[7]

When federal officials and representatives of the real estate industry spoke of the need to place more emphasis on the "existing" urban housing market, these houses were included. The change to FHA policy in 1967, then buttressed by the HUD Act in the following year, invigorated the real estate market in the urban core of American cities. The debates over the potential placement of low-income housing in the suburbs overshadowed the consequences of this development for those still in a desperate search for safe, sound, and affordable housing. This chapter brings that story out of the shadows as a critical corollary to the history of suburban resistance to poor and working-class Black homeowners and renters in the 1970s. Doing so requires looking at the role of the FHA after it stopped redlining Black urban communities. Almost the entirety of that organization's written history has been based on its first thirty-three years, when its primary role was insuring the mortgages of new suburban properties. But the FHA played a central role in the federal government's programs intended to transform low-income renters into low-income homeowners.

In an effort to comply with the federal mandate to create 600,000 units of low-income housing a year, HUD officials expanded the pool of program participants to include welfare recipients. The contradictions of this transition were laid bare as private actors and institutions, including real estate agents and bankers who had historically championed discriminatory practices as expressions of free choice, market desires, and fiscal responsibility, were abruptly expected to play a pivotal role in the new HUD homeownership programs. But their conversion from arch villains of covert segregation to superheroes of fair housing would be easier said than done. The problems that were to beset HUD's homeownership programs stemmed from the federal government's reliance on a network of private institutions that, in turn, relied on racial discrimination as the guarantor of its bottom line.

A NEW CRUSADE

I am asking... every employee of FHA to enter into a new crusade. This means making our home programs available for the purchase, sale and improvement of properties throughout the inner city. Everyone should carry away from here a sense of urgency which recognizes the importance of the job before us and a determination to take the steps, reach decisions, and make the sacrifices necessary. I have given a number of reasons why I believe FHA must mount a major effort to accelerate and expand use of those of our programs which can serve families of low- and moderate-income and revive and rebuild the inner city. Let me give you one more reason. You should work at this task as though your job depended on it—because it may![8]

So exhorted Philip Brownstein in a speech to the staff and directors of regional and local FHA offices representing seventy-six cities across the United States who were summoned to a meeting in Washington, D.C., in the fall of 1967. HUD was determined to transform the FHA into an agency that paved the way for homeownership in the country's central cities. Deputy Secretary of the FHA Philip Maloney followed Brownstein's sharp comments with his own when it was his turn to address the same group of supervisors. Maloney urged them to "manifest your loyalty and zeal for these causes [equality in housing and employment within the FHA]. . . . The prime thrust of FHA must be in housing for families of low income and in the restoration of the inner cities. The realization of these goals is as of right now the mission of the agency."[9] When Maloney said he would be discussing "equal opportunity in housing and employment in the FHA," he upbraided his audience: "Don't groan."[10] Maloney went on to scold the directors, saying, "I think it's fair to say that you've been measured up and found wanting." Maloney said that the agents of the FHA "belong in the slums, meet-ing with minority groups, groups of the poor, groups of those who can sponsor housing projects for those of the poor and the inner city. You must plow through the dirty streets, the rat-infested housing and apartment buildings. This is where we want you to be. This is where the problems are, where the work is to be done. This is where we want FHA financing to be today."[11]

Maloney pointed to an internal survey of FHA builders as proof of their failure to adhere to the standards of Kennedy's 1962 executive order banning discrimi-nation in the sales of federally financed and backed housing. The survey found that of the hundreds of thousands of houses built since Kennedy's antidiscrimi-nation order, only 3 percent had been sold to African Americans. Since 1962, 410,574 houses with FHA-backed loans had been sold, and of those only 35,000 had been sold to nonwhites. Breaking that down even further, Maloney found that only "13,832 went to Negroes, 12,765 to Spanish, and 8,784 to Orientals and 687 to American Indians."[12] Maloney urged strong enforcement of the govern-ment's antidiscrimination laws as central to solving the housing crisis. This in-cluded Black entry into the suburbs because "we cannot effectively relieve pres-sure in [the inner cities] and restore them unless all other neighborhoods of the metropolitan areas are freely open to all who can and want to live in them."[13]

Maloney further connected the lack of progress toward "equal opportunity" for African Americans to the dearth of Black civil servants within the agency. He argued that the goal of increasing the access of African Americans to the services of the FHA would be facilitated by hiring more Black people. The failure of the FHA to hire African Americans contributed to the failure of the agency to fulfill its legal mandate of nondiscrimination. Overall, 11 percent of FHA em-ployees were African American, but none were in supervisory or other positions of authority. Moreover, there was a lopsided disparity between Black employees in Washington, D.C., and other offices around the country. Thirty percent of FHA headquarters employees were African Americans, compared with only 5 percent in offices around the country. As a remedy, Maloney suggested multiple "affirmative actions" he and Brownstein would undertake to increase employ-ment and encourage greater availability of FHA services for Blacks in the central cities, including a focus on the enforcement of antidiscrimination policies. Ma-loney, like Brownstein, threatened to remove employees who could not get with the new direction of the FHA. Maloney suggested that those not committed to equality should "step aside for men who can provide leadership in these areas."[14]

When Brownstein and Maloney implored the regional directors of the FHA to join the crusade to save America's cities, it was still an independent agency. But as Romney took the reins of the organization in 1969 and began to reorganize it, he turned the FHA into a subsidiary of HUD. The FHA had operated as an independent agency within the federal government, but no longer. Surely, in the eyes of its old guard, the luster of this once-proud and independent agency was changing dramatically. It was being transformed from an organization highly regarded for its role in helping to forge the (white) American middle class into "another" government program for low-income (Black) residents. A striking aspect of the reports assessing the state of the low-income homeownership programs from this period is that they all relay a sense of despair, low morale, and anger among "FHA-HUD personnel, including management, supervisory, and line staff regarding socio-economic aspects of the program."[15]

Many of the multiple federal organizations and agencies connected to housing policy had already been absorbed into HUD, but the FHA had largely been left to continue to operate on its own. The sense of malaise within the organization was not addressed, though, and shifting personnel around did not appear to capture the depth of the problem. Romney persisted with an "order" to end the autonomy of the FHA and make it a subsidiary of HUD. In the words of HUD undersecretary Sherman Unger, noting the tension underlying Romney's directive to the FHA, "We may have to drag it kicking and screaming."[16]

There had been some debate within HUD about maintaining the separation between the FHA, with its upwardly mobile, suburban-bound homeowners, and the growing number of low-income homeownership and rental programs. Given the effectiveness of the FHA in the suburbs, Romney insisted on having all housing programs routed through the FHA despite the vastly different needs of these distinct programs. In the new arrangement, HUD-FHA would maintain the same approach for all of its clientele, though some of the agents within HUD continued to express their concerns: "If we attempt to add to it [the FHA] the responsibility for facilitating the housing of the poor and lower moderate incomed, we can only water down its capacity to deal with the groups with which it has been very successful, while still inhibiting the development of facilitating activity for those less fortunate."[17] In defending his actions, Romney made the important observation that the affluent had benefited from public tax dollars in their housing and the poor and low-income should have the same right. He argued that "the people who have benefited by national housing policy in the main are not even aware that they have had any help from public sources. . . . And thus they tend to resent the idea that . . . their tax money . . . is being used to help the minority groups to meet their housing needs."[18]

Romney was anxious to increase housing production and directed the regional and local affiliates of HUD to go out and make use of the widening array of HUD-FHA housing programs. Rising rates of inflation and interest threatened the housing industry while simultaneously making the new low-income housing programs especially attractive. In particular, Sections 235 and 221(d)(2), which provided for homeownership, made it easy for low-income people to buy their own homes. Section 235 was the relatively new program created by the 1968 HUD Act; Section 221(d)(2) was an older program created by the 1954 Housing Act, but it had been moribund until the end of FHA redlining brought it back to life. Ramping up the use of these programs was beneficial for two reasons. First, they tapped into a new market where the rates of homeownership were low because of previous redlining practices, so there was a thirst for buying homes when other markets had perhaps been saturated. Second, government-backed homeownership programs required low down payments, and, in the case of Section 235, there was a massive interest rate subsidy that dramatically dropped monthly costs for the program participant. Section 221 holders also had a lower monthly mortgage because the program allowed for forty-year loan terms. For those who could borrow mortgage money on conventional terms, costs were becoming prohibitive. In a historic turnabout, low-income Black homeseekers were now attractive and sought-after customers; all that was needed was homes for them to buy.

In the more than thirty years since the United States had first undertaken the challenge of housing the poor, there had never been more than 600,000 units of subsidized housing produced. In 1969, housing production levels rose to an unprecedented 200,000 units of low-income housing. Romney said of his department's successes, "In the 33 years since this nation has had a public housing program, we have only succeeded in providing less than one million subsidized housing units. In a year and a half, we will have increased that supply by about 100 percent."[19] In the first seven months of the program's existence, more than 3,000 homes were purchased with the FHA subsidy, with "firm commitments" for an additional 7,500 units.[20] By the end of 1970, HUD had subsidized low-income mortgages on more than 80,000 homes; by the end of 1971, another 204,000 mortgagors had taken advantage of the subsidized interest rate provided by Section 235.[21] A Committee on Banking and Currency report described Section 235 as "carrying the real estate market" in "many areas of the country."[22] The Mortgage Bankers Association (MBA) also described the importance of the federal programs: "The federal government's assistance to housing through the subsidized programs of Section 235 and Section 236 has been a major sustaining force of the housing industry."[23] One author captured the benefit to the real estate industry: "By 1971 federal subsidy programs were paying the real estate industry $1.4 billion a year and financing one in four new housing units produced."[24] However, even on the attractive terms offered by HUD, the new programs could not maintain the pace necessary to keep up with the national objective of 600,000 units of low-income housing a year. Despite the annual growth in use of the new homeownership subsidy, it seemed as if the programs were barely making a dent. There were many reasons for the shortfall, including insufficient appropriations from Congress, the constant delays involved in navigating the housing bureaucracy, and chronic staffing issues. But perhaps the most significant obstacles to HUD fulfilling its housing obligation were the escalating costs of producing the housing and paying for the land on which it was to be placed.

As HUD liberalized its underwriting criteria at the end of the 1960s, dramatic changes were taking place in the housing market. A study conducted by HUD confirmed that in both new and existing or used housing, there were big increases in cost over the decade. The analysis was based on male buyers in both markets. Over the course of the decade, the income of a consumer purchasing a new home had risen by 49 percent; but the price of his house, by 1969, was also 40 percent more, while the cost of the land it was to sit on had risen by 74 percent.[25] For the buyer of a used house, income had risen by 42 percent, while the cost of the house increased by 27 percent and the land was now 57 percent more expensive. From 1968 to 1969 alone, the cost of new homes jumped by 5 percent, while for existing homes the increase was 4 percent.[26]

The success of the 1968 HUD Act would be determined not only by the sheer amount of housing made available but also by its location. The "existing" portion of low-income housing provided for by the HUD Act was originally to include only 25 percent of the total of subsidized housing, and within two years it was to become less than 10 percent. The focus was to be on producing new housing in suburban areas. But immediate returns from the existing urban market proved too seductive to ignore. In 1970, 30 percent of Section 235 housing was "existing," and by 1971, this had increased to 53 percent.[27] Although 5 percent of HUD's Section 235 budget was dedicated to the rehabilitation of distressed properties, the legislation was never intended to develop a market in old, urban properties.

Three factors helped to undermine its original goals. The first was the urgent demand for more housing in urban areas. The urban rebellions had revealed substandard housing as a fact of Black urban life. Although 1968 was the last year where dozens of riots converged, there was no way for public officials to know that in the early 1970s. The threat of violence maintained the pressure to find an immediate solution to the urban housing crisis. It was widely understood that public housing could not fill the void alone, so urban homeownership became the viable alternative.

The second factor was the continued resistance of suburban officials to the presence of low-income housing in any form, including single-family homes. As discussed in Chapter 3, this hostility manifested itself in zoning ordinances and a proliferation of onerous requirements for building in suburban areas that influenced which materials could be used, the size of lots, and other issues that could drive the price upward. Because the FHA homeownership programs had placed caps on the costs of houses and mortgages, suburbanites' efforts to dissuade the building of low-income housing were largely effective. Finally, and perhaps the most important factor, there was intense lobbying by those within the housing industry for the utilization of existing housing in central cities. In a letter to Romney, the president of NAREB made this very clear: "We believe it was unfortunate to limit the eligibility of existing units for mortgage insurance under this program. The primary objective of Section 235 is to assist low income families to become homeowners, an objective which would be better served if existing structures were eligible for interest subsidies."[28] Even the board of governors of the Federal Reserve weighed in with support for existing housing, noting that "by far the cheapest and most efficient housing available to us is likely to come from the existing stock. I am not clear as to why under Section 235 loans are primarily restricted to new housing. This appears to me part of the neglect of the existing stock."[29]

This drive on the part of powerful players in the industry came to shape the priorities of programs intended to serve the poor, leading to the homeowning disasters that opened this chapter while providing the industry—with the renewed assistance of the federal government—with expanding opportunities for profit.

PROFITOPOLIS[30]

The end of FHA redlining and the introduction of home finance into American cities created a new market for urban housing almost out of thin air. All of a sudden, the old and dilapidated housing structures sitting empty on city lots were for sale and guaranteed by the federal government. Almost immediately, complaints about the condition of this inner-city housing, now being sold via a government program, could be heard from all sides. The complaints were significant enough to warrant a congressional investigation just two years after the passage of the HUD Act. Democrats who led the relevant congressional committees relished the opportunity to launch investigations into the new programs, now being run by a Republican administration. The chairman of the Committee on Banking and Currency, Wisconsin congressman Wright Patman, reviewed many of the complaints about the program and observed that "instead of providing 'decent, safe and sanitary' housing for low- and moderate-income people, many of these homeowners are finding themselves the unhappy possessors of nothing more than slums."[31] Patman's letter was attached to a report filled with details about the terrible quality of the housing and the questionable circumstances under which it had been sold. The FHA was accused of insuring "existing homes that are of such poor quality that there is little or no possibility that they can survive the life of the mortgage or even attempt to maintain any property value."[32] The U.S. Commission on Civil Rights agreed with this assessment, noting that there were common themes to the problems that plagued Section 235 houses: "faulty plumbing, leaky roofs, cracked plaster, faulty and inadequate wiring, rotten wood in the floors, staircases and porches, lack of insulation and faulty heating units." Congressional staffers who led investigations for the commission saw many of the "existing" houses as "instant slums."[33] At 2827 Bailey Street in Northeast Philadelphia, for example, a house was sold with FHA insurance for $6,500. Investigators found its walls caving in and its basement filled with water, while the roof leaked and the gas lines that were intended to fuel the kitchen stove were broken and twisted.[34] Upon publication of the results of the congressional investigation, reporters from the *Philadelphia Inquirer* sought out the residents of the homes listed to get the story behind the disturbing details buried near the end of the report's 200 pages.[35]

Wilhelmina Gause was a twenty-seven-year-old Black single mother of three children. She and her husband had been separated for more than a year, and she received no support from him to help pay bills around her home or to care for their children. Gause had been looking for an apartment to rent when, instead, she was pressured into buying a house. A real estate agent told her that there were no houses for rent, only for sale. Gause insisted that she could not afford a house, but the agent told her, "Something can be done to let you buy it."[36] She needed $500 to move in. This was not a Section 235 house but one being sold under Section 221(d)(2), a low-income homeownership program created by the 1954 Housing Act, but it did not include a subsidy. Gause said, "I scrimped and saved every penny I could. . . . My mother helped me out a bit. And I borrowed the last $100 from a loan shark at work. I still owe him $16."[37]

Her troubles began as soon as she moved into the house. "Rain seeped through the rear wall . . . [and] the drain in the backyard was stopped up. The main drain pipe in the basement leaked, filling the basement with sewage to the depth of one foot."[38] When Gause called the real estate agent who sold her the house about these problems, he said that there was nothing that could be done. She then fell ill with a kidney infection that caused her to miss work and eventually lose her job. Gause retained a pro bono lawyer from a community legal services firm, which is how federal authorities found out about her home and could include its condition in their report. When the real estate agent realized she had a lawyer, he began to send repairmen to her house, but they only seemed to make conditions worse, adding their poorly done work to the pile of disasters. Indeed, Gause told reporters that she did not want any more repairs, saying, "They'll only fix it up some kind of way so that it will break down again in a couple of months and I'll be right back where I am now."[39]

Wilhelmina Gause's deteriorating home raised troubling questions about the federal government's celebrated low-income homeownership program. How could a house that appeared to be falling apart also be appraised by the FHA as having any value and then approved for a mortgage subsidy? Secretary George Romney minimized the significance of the study's findings, insisting that "an analysis of problem cases . . . is not to be confused with an analysis of typical cases."[40] His larger point was that the program was growing and that the highlighted cases in the report were exceptional and not indicative of general problems. Romney defended his agency by suggesting that these were predictable problems to be experienced once HUD decided to move into low-income homeownership. He said, "Until 1964 . . . we had a redline policy and this was . . . of great concern to the Department." Romney continued that in dealing with this new clientele, the department was, perhaps, in over its head, having only previously dealt with persons who had "middle-class incomes and middle-class response to the responsibilities of homeownership."[41]

Romney participated in a congressional hearing called to investigate the mounting problems of the "existing" homes insured by the FHA. In defense of himself and HUD, Romney argued that the scope of the program had been too large for HUD-FHA to handle on its own. He said that the "major reasons for these errors rest squarely on the ambitious objectives which the FHA tried to accommodate through the operation of this program."[42] And yet it was at Romney's insistence that all of HUD's housing programs be routed through the FHA and that unprecedented production rates be maintained. Romney's testimony prefigured a pattern that would develop in response to continual investigations into HUD throughout his tenure. In his pointed statements to the Senate committee investigating Section 235, Romney consistently returned to his perception that the problems of program participants were of bigger concern than the management of the programs. For example, during his testimony, Romney insisted that it was "obvious" that no matter how carefully HUD "inspect[ed] and apprais[ed]" and no matter how much they "screen[ed] and counsel[ed,]" "when we are dealing with low-income buyers we are dealing with fundamental problems of people living at or near subsistence levels."[43]

Although praising the benefits of homeownership was easy, the reality of owning a home was a difficult and unpredictable enterprise for anyone who was not wealthy. The level of difficulty and unpredictability became greater as one's income and the condition of the house deteriorated. This, of course, was particularly true in the market for existing houses, in which the FHA had insured 9,000 properties in "blighted innercity areas" by 1970.[44] This was in part due to the priorities of the program. The poorest people eligible to participate in the FHA homeownership program lived in proximity to housing that was in the lowest, often substandard, condition. Indeed, the HUD Act directed "the Secretary . . . [to] give *preference* in approving mortgage insurance applications . . . to families living in public housing units, especially those families required to leave public housing because their incomes have risen beyond the maximum prescribed income levels . . . and families who have been displaced from federally assisted urban renewal areas."[45]

The people who lived in these homes were either low-income-earning or on fixed incomes provided through public assistance or welfare, but in both cases residents had no discretionary or flexible income that would allow them to attend to problems that regularly arose in their homes, an obvious dilemma that was routinely ignored by legislators. But the greater issue was whether this was the consequence of having an ill-equipped poor person own a home or, rather, a function of the predatory practices of appraisers and real estate agents. Indeed, the case of Wilhelmina Gause and dozens of others in the investigation report demonstrated that there were greater issues than the "fundamental problems" of poor people upon which Romney had hinged his critique.

The poverty of Black homeowners made them especially vulnerable to manipulation by operators within the local real estate industry. Indeed, Patman's original letter to Romney charged that "fast buck speculators" were selling these dilapidated homes at a 1,000 percent markup.[46] Romney decried the accusation as an exaggeration, but it was clear to anyone looking that these formerly "dead" properties were being brought back to life for profit. The fact that Black mothers were choosing housing that was in such a state of dilapidation spoke to the limitations of their housing choices. It is inconceivable that a parent would choose roach- or rat-infested housing if there were other options available. But they could choose only from the housing that was offered. The problem of constrained choice was then exacerbated by the program's reliance on the housing industry, which had so tightly bound its profit margin to racial discrimination that there was not a single moment in its history where racial discrimination had not prevailed as a defining industry practice. The approach was summarized in one of the many reports generated on the progress of the low-income homeownership programs: "All FHA programs, including those aimed at meeting the housing needs of lower-income families, use the facilities of the private housing market—private lenders, private builders and private brokers."[47] A program participant's understanding of the housing market—including HUD-FHA subsidies and insurance—was filtered through real estate brokers.

Under Sections 235 and 221(d)(2), prospective homeowners *never* met or even came into contact with a government employee or staff person; their first contact for the program was either a real estate agent or a mortgage banker. It is true that the entirety of the homeownership program was not especially geared toward city-dwelling residents, but the used, or rehabilitated, housing portion of the program was most certainly aimed at low-income and poor African Americans. The purpose of a government employee mediating between the real estate and banking agents and a poor person buying a home for the first time would, presumably, be to protect the interests of the individual as well as the interests of the government, which was insuring these properties. As one observer put it: "The prospective homeowner cannot rely on the real estate broker whose only interest is a commission, and in the inner city, is more likely than not a speculator."[48] From the HUD Act's inception, poor homeowners were left to fend for themselves.

The definition of "speculator" was the same then as it is today: someone who buys cheap properties with the intention of reselling them very quickly for as much money as possible. Real estate speculators, betting on their ability to turn nothing into something, bought up dozens of cheap properties and flipped them for a quick profit. One speculator summed up his approach to real estate sales as follows: "We don't care if the whites run all the way to Hong Kong as long as they run. . . . I go to where the money is. I'm a money-oriented guy. Its [*sic*] good business for us when they are frightened."[49] Another real estate agent, who was the subject of an undercover investigative journalism series on real estate fraud in Chicago, boasted, "My obligation is to sell. I'm in business to sell. It's not my business to warn people. . . . It's *caveat emptor*. Let the buyer beware."[50] Indeed, Senator Patman's letter to George Romney recognized that "many of these FHA 235 purchasers have been victimized by unconscionable real estate speculators who have made fantastic profits in short periods."[51] In St. Louis, speculators sold 29 percent of houses receiving FHA backing or subsidy, and "in some cases houses that had been rejected by other FHA programs had been approved by the 235 program."[52]

HUD-FHA, having no other model in place, used the same methods it had used in its original, suburb-oriented Section 203 mortgage insurance program, a two-tiered process consisting of property and then buyer approval. A mortgage lender who sought a subsidy for a new or used single-family house had to receive approval based on an FHA appraisal. Transforming a "conditional commitment" into a "firm commitment" from the FHA was then based on the buyer's financial qualifications, as submitted by the mortgage lender. Real estate and mortgage lenders were the "essential participants" in the FHA single-family mortgage insurance programs.[53] By April 1970, the MBA said that Section 235 loans made up three-quarters of the mortgage lending business.[54]

Romney had denounced the congressional investigation headed by Wright Patman as "misleading, irresponsible and incomplete."[55] Weeks later, Romney conceded that the problems uncovered by the Patman investigation "are more prevalent and widespread than had previously been in evidence."[56] Given the controversy, Romney directed HUD to begin its own investigation of the low-income homeownership programs the following year, in 1971. HUD staff directed in-person inspections of 1,281 houses in fifty-two FHA jurisdictions and reviewed 2,000 written complaints.[57] They found deficiencies in one-quarter of the houses they investigated. Eleven percent of the *new* houses were found to have "significant deficiencies" affecting the "safety, health and livability" of about

16,000 new houses subsidized by the FHA.[58] The defects in the *existing* houses were substantially worse: one-quarter were in such poor condition that investigators concluded that they never should have been insured. More than half of the existing houses contained "significant deficiencies affecting safety, health or livability." Eighty-eight percent of the existing housing had significant problems, compared with 43 percent of new subsidized housing with defects.[59] The number of substandard new houses was obviously too high, but in the existing housing market, most of which was located in the inner city, the situation was disastrous.

Poor housing conditions had long been a staple of urban life. The physical condition of much of the housing stock, after all, had prompted the calls for new housing. Had the overwhelming focus on new production exacerbated the problem? HUD's own investigation concluded that "too many . . . used houses . . . were insured which contained deficiencies that should have been corrected prior to final endorsement. . . . We believe this general condition results from a combination of factors including . . . [the fact that] when production goals versus quality appraisals and inspection were at issue, the matter was often resolved on the side of production."[60] The unprecedented production goals demanded by Operation Breakthrough were being met at the expense of quality housing. New Section 235 houses were mass-produced quickly using cheap materials and methods, resulting in faulty suburban housing. Urban properties would need to be rehabilitated, but the inconsistency among FHA appraisers meant that real estate agents were not being held to professional standards. It was true that these new buyers were unfamiliar with the intricacies of buying a home, but it was also the case that when they asked for defects to be remedied, their requests were ignored. An important part of the appraiser's job was to certify that the proper repairs had been done to each house. Making that determination was contingent on close and observant viewing of the property, but the pressure to meet housing goals in order to keep up with the production mandate while maintaining good relationships within the real estate business impaired the vigilance of FHA appraisers. Properties condemned to demolition days and weeks earlier were brought back to life and sold to unsuspecting prospective homeowners. The General Accounting Office conducted a review of HUD programs that overlapped with HUD's internal audit. Looking at ten cities across the country, the accounting office also found that, within the existing housing program, 54 percent of Section 223(e) housing, another HUD Act creation, and 36 percent of Section 235 housing had "serious defects" and should not have been insured.[61]

Far from liberating the nation's cities, as former president Lyndon Johnson had pledged, HUD's low-income homeownership program recycled many of the same problems that gave rise to the housing crisis in the first place. It was still early in the life of the subsidy programs, but for African Americans who remained embedded in the urban housing market, it was difficult to ascertain what was new about the HUD Act. The substandard condition of the housing and the unfair terms on which it was being sold were not new, but the scale on which a segregated housing market—with all the financial manipulation it involved—could flourish had expanded significantly. The introduction of FHA insurance harnessed much larger sources of financing than were ever available under the old system of contract sales for Black homeowners. Previously, contract sellers had been limited by the dollar amount on loans that could be legally tendered by savings and loan associations. Mortgage-backed securities packaged through the GNMA would dramatically multiply the mortgage money that would circulate through the urban market. The mortgage guarantees of the FHA also brought fresh actors into the exploitation of prospective Black homeowners. Real estate agents and speculators familiar with the landscape of the Black housing market were newly partnered with appraisers, mortgage bankers, and, of course, the FHA itself, which was quite inexperienced when it came to Black buyers and the urban housing market. These were the conditions that constituted predatory inclusion, where African Americans were no longer excluded but welcomed into the housing market on terms most favorable to the industry. While this could be a general description of the operations of real estate, the difference in the emerging urban housing market, in comparison with its suburban counterpart, was that the housing was not viewed as an asset but valued for the capacity to extract profit out of it.

VALUE JUDGMENT

The market, however, was only viable if the properties were of value. The role of the real estate industry in the racial stratification and deformation of the American metropolis is widely understood. But the same cannot be said of the impact of the appraisal industry and its role in the social construction of "value" in the housing market. The contrived sciences of real estate brokerage and appraisal were developed in the shadow of a eugenic pseudoscience in which fatalistic assumptions linked biology, race, and ethnicity. This toxic brew was then stirred into "risk" and property values. It was widely accepted that proximity to African Americans, specifically, determined the likelihood of whether one's housing value would rise or fall. The prevailing wisdom that "homogenous neighbor-hoods" were the most valuable persisted over most of the twentieth century and comprised the starting point for value creation. On their own, none of these practices would amount to much, but together they would remake not only houses but also neighborhoods, cities, and residents.

The process of creating value was layered and involved multiple actors across a chain of institutions and individuals, but appraisers played a critical role in affixing value to a home. There was, however, no exact method for deducing this value. As a representative of the Society of Real Estate Appraisers explained, "Value is a function of one's mind," and the job of the appraiser was to "mirror the market.... The market value is all considered through the eyes of the typically informed purchaser in the market."[62] But not just the property was assessed in determining value; so was the buyer: "What kind of individual will this property, most probably, appeal [to]? What are the purchaser's economic, social, and demographic characteristics? These factors must be ascertained before the appraiser can begin to estimate the market value of the subject properly." The obvious issue was how these questions would be shaped in an industry that was "98% white, 98% male and 98% real estate oriented."[63]

The subjective nature of appraising was reflected in a lack of uniform standards and general licensing requirements. There were, of course, guideposts that identified sound structure and building, as well as the potential for value to appreciate. Most of the field, though, was defined by the subjective judgments of appraisers and the belief that they understood what qualified as "good" housing, "good" neighborhoods, and "good" homeowners. Despite the lack of clear standards, appraisers did take courses to learn the inexact "science" of appraising based on industry-created measures of what constituted "good" housing.[64] AIREA functioned in ways similar to those of NAREB, offering training and certification to appraisers around the country. Also, like NAREB, AIREA's training manuals were steeped in racist stereotypes that explicitly linked housing and neighborhood values to their proximity to nonwhite ethnic groups and African Americans. AIREA's earliest appraising standards, published in the 1930s, were as concerned with the supposed connections between race and property value as the FHA was in its underwriting criteria, published one year earlier. AIREA's first text, published in 1937, also warned of the adverse effects on property values of "infiltration of inharmonious racial groups."[65] These concerns continued to appear in the organization's written materials even after such explicit warnings regarding race had been banned by various federal admonishments. For example, in 1967, AIREA textbooks still warned of the consequences of neighborhood "infiltration": "The causes of racial and religious conflicts are not the appraiser's responsibility. However, he must recognize the fact that values change when people who are different from those presently occupying an area advance into and infiltrate a neighborhood."[66] Even after the passage of federal fair housing legislation, a 1973 study guide for AIREA counseled that "ethnological information is also significant to real estate analysis. As a general rule, homogeneity of the population contributes to stability of real estate values." The guide continued, "Information on the percentage of native born whites, foreign whites, and non-white population is important, and the changes in this composition [are] significant. As a general rule, minority groups are found at the bottom of the socio-economic ladder and problems associated with minority group segments of the population can hinder community growth."[67]

These were not just the ideas of anachronistic organizations clinging to real estate's past, but the normative instincts of an industry concerned primarily with creating, legitimizing, and preserving market value through the rigorous defense of residential segregation. Indeed, in the early 1970s even HUD participated in the ingrained logics of racial homogeneity and ascending property value. The organization had commissioned a report on neighborhood change from the Real Estate Research Corporation, an investigative arm of NAREB. The report, titled *The Dynamics of Neighborhood Change*, linked the various stages of neighborhood health to the presence or absence of "minorities." Thus, "healthy" markets were described as having "moderate to upper level incomes" and "ethnic homogeneity." A neighborhood in "incipient decline" shared the characteristics of "aging housing stock" and an "influx of middle-income minorities." And finally, a "decrease in white in-movers" and "more minority children in schools" marked neighborhoods that were "clearly declining."[68] HUD's commissioned report repeated and amplified naturalized theories of neighborhood decline where the movement of Black and white populations served as indicators of the health or lack of health of a given neighborhood. When the federal government's regulatory agency for housing, HUD, issued this kind of "common sense" regarding neighborhood stability, it legitimized residential segregation and the continuing marginalization of African Americans by conventional mortgage lenders. Indeed, as late as 1976, *The Real Estate Study and Guide*, published by the state of California, read in part, "The value of a residential neighborhood is affected primarily by the social characteristics of the people. . . . The lack of homogeneity may affect the neighborhood's present and future desirability."[69]

Appraisers brought these intensely subjective perceptions about housing stock, neighborhoods, and perhaps most importantly, the people living in the neighborhoods to bear as the urban housing market came under the protection of FHA mortgage insurance. And yet, within HUD-FHA, appraising was a lightly regarded entry-level position that received just nine months of training, largely consisting of observing other appraisers on the job.[70] It was a position viewed as a stepping-stone to better prospects within the organization or in the private housing industry. This attitude created three immediate problems. If the perception was that urban housing was already in a natural state of decline, then the vigilance needed to spot defects or perhaps larger structural problems was dulled. These perceptions in combination with minimal standards of training left FHA appraisers ill equipped to properly evaluate the properties they had been charged with determining the value of. HUD-FHA appraisers were not prepared enough, let alone skilled enough, to knowledgeably understand or judge the soundness of inner-city housing.

Many appraisers had incentive to ignore even obvious problems that could lower the price of the home because they were trying to stay in the good graces of the real estate broker or mortgage lender whose commission would be a percentage of the asking price. As entry-level workers, appraisers were on the lookout for better opportunities within a lucrative business, whether as a broker or as an agent for lenders. The low pay associated with the position also created the potential for abuse. More sharply stated, low pay made appraisers susceptible to bribes in a market in which new standards were being determined and value was unclear. It was in an appraiser's interest to make friends, not enemies, in the industry. Complicating matters further, real estate agents and mortgage lenders were regular fixtures in local FHA insuring offices. They did not set up offices within the FHA, but there was regular correspondence among all of them. All three institutional actors worked collaboratively to fulfill the heavy demands of the program while also looking for substantial returns. After all, private enterprise was not involved in the FHA's subsidy programs for altruistic reasons; it was taking advantage of new market opportunities.

The dynamic interplay of race, risk, and determining property value was well under way before a house had even been appraised. The *FHA Appraiser's Manual* defined "value" as "the price which typical buyers would be warranted in paying for the property for long term use if they were well-informed, acting intelligently, voluntarily and without necessity."[71] The FHA had been redlining urban areas for decades, so it was unclear who was a "typical buyer," what was meant by "well-informed," or how the value of a home in a previously redlined area was determined. Even Romney conceded that "FHA values are . . . misleading in that previous prices rather than FHA values are used in comparables."[72] And what were "comparables"? They were similar houses in the same neighborhood that had been sold recently and were used to create a baseline for determining the value of a house. Using comparables was HUD policy, but in a redlined market, the practice was questionable at best.[73] Comparable prices were based on the exploitative and predatory prices set by speculators and contract sellers in the redlining era. Real estate speculation was setting the floor of the urban housing market.

Internally, HUD-FHA officials blamed the inconsistencies in appraisals on the end of redlining and the liberalization of the agency's underwriting criteria.[74] Of course, none of the directives to liberalize FHA underwriting criteria demanded the surrender of structural soundness, but other factors contributed to the ineffectiveness of FHA appraisers. The responsibilities of HUD-FHA had been multiplied while the agency was simultaneously plagued by budget cuts and consequent staffing gaps in the early 1970s. Not only had Romney undertaken an ambitious reorganization effort, but he had done so while managing Nixon's demand for a 5 percent personnel cut in each government agency. When Romney took control of HUD, he had gone to Congress to ask for funding to pay for the addition of 700 new employees, but within a year he changed course. In sync with Nixon's demands to do more with less, Romney offered to cut 7.5 percent of HUD staff, a whopping 1,200 people, even as the problems in HUD-FHA subsidized housing programs continued to bubble to the surface.[75] And this was only the beginning. Indeed, Romney instructed his regional supervisors to "develop three alternative plans whereby your organization can be reduced in employment by 20, 30, and 40 percent."[76] Nixon targeted domestic spending on social welfare as the first place to implement the principles of New Federalism, coming into sharp conflict with the greater amounts of responsibility being heaped on HUD employees. Budget constraints meant still less oversight of this unprecedented program and ultimately a greater reliance on real estate operatives for jobs typically reserved for civil servants. Within HUD, this meant a turn to "fee appraisers."

FEE APPRAISERS

Fee appraisers were part-time appraisers subcontracted by the FHA in an effort
to keep up with demand while balancing staff shortages. Fee appraisers were
typically part-time real estate agents who were familiar with the housing in a particular neighborhood. They were paid per appraisal, and that placed an emphasis
on the volume of appraisals they performed. Fee appraisers were also disproportionately hired to do appraisals in the new urban market. It made little sense to
hire the least-experienced people to do the most difficult job, but it spoke to the
difficulties of management when demand was surging but staff was limited.[77]
Romney's internal audit of HUD found that fee appraisers worked on a quota
system requiring them to produce a certain number of appraisals per day.[78]

In Philadelphia, a newspaper investigation found that the FHA hired fee appraisers who were also real estate agents active in selling houses through the FHA
program. The investigation also found that many of the same agents employed
by the FHA to do fee appraisals had also been employed by real estate firms that
had been disciplined for racial discrimination by the city's Human Rights Commission.[79] Indeed, most fee appraisers were part-time real estate agents picking
up work between home sales. As the Philadelphia case illuminated, hiring fee
appraisers who were active as real estate agents in the market they were appraising created an ethical minefield. At the same time, familiarity with a particular
location was considered an asset for fee appraisers—regardless of how that familiarity had been established.[80]

Because fee appraisers were paid between $25 and $35 per appraisal, they had
an incentive to process as many appraisals as possible. As the demand for HUD's
homeownership programs swelled, some fee appraisers were doing as many as five
appraisals a day, churning them out in fifteen-minute intervals—despite the fact
that industry standards suggested that appraisals should take at least two hours.
In the inner city, however, "windshield inspections" were "more often the rule
than the exception."[81] The fact that many of these appraisers were also real estate
agents trying to sell the same houses during their "day jobs" compounded the
issue of "over appraising" and led to an increase in the value of substandard housing. Even when fee appraisers were not engaged in this kind of activity, there was
the temptation to pump up the value of a home in hopes of getting a kickback.[82]

Not surprisingly, questionable appraisals became a focal point as the problems in the housing programs began to mount. Indeed, in the summer of 1971,
a high-profile newspaper exposé of corruption in the regional office of the FHA

in Philadelphia resulted in HUD's director of the Northeast region, Theodore Robb, suspending all of the 160 FHA fee appraisers, pending the outcome of an investigation.[83] Philadelphia had been the subject of the House committee's original investigation of the subsidy programs. Federal investigators inspected thirteen houses, including Wilhelmina Gause's dilapidated home, for their report. Romney allowed the Philadelphia HUD-FHA office to inspect, again, the same thirteen homes that had been written up in the committee's report. Upon reinspection, local investigators from Philadelphia reported that the thirteen houses were, in fact, in good shape and disavowed the federal investigation.[84] The dispute over the dueling reports spoke to tensions that existed between the national headquarters and the local affiliates of HUD-FHA. Romney wanted to ramp up the use of the subsidies and secure greater appropriations for programs that had run out of funds because of two years of heavy demand. But it was difficult to ask for more money when local papers across the country were filling with stories about junk housing being passed off as habitable with government approval.

MONEY FOR NOTHING

Appraisals were a key link in the chain of transactions that involved purchasing a low-income home with a HUD subsidy, but without a mortgage, the sale could not take place. Redlining could only really end when there were lenders willing to extend credit to people in formerly excluded locations. As previously discussed, the life insurance industry first did this on a large scale in 1967. The use of FHA mortgage insurance, however, was not a guarantee that conventional banks would now extend credit in the formerly redlined areas. FHA insurance was not attractive to all banks; it was an alternative for homebuyers who did not qualify for conventional loans. FHA loans had a lower, fixed-interest rate, compared with conventional mortgages. Conventional mortgages also required higher down payments. The end of federal redlining was intended to bring conventional lenders into urban communities and end the predacious activity of real estate speculators and other grifters. But the cheap terms of lending kept conventional lenders at bay and instead opened new opportunities for mortgage bankers to step into the void.

An integral part of the political economy of the FHA-assisted housing market involved the use of mortgage banks in lieu of conventional lenders. Mortgage banks were not like ordinary banks. They did not accept deposits but instead derived their funds from high-interest-rate loans taken from commercial banks. Mortgage banks were also unregulated by the federal government. Since mortgage banks did not take deposits, the lower interest rate on FHA loans was of no concern. Mortgage banks made part of their money through originating and then servicing the loans. But in the FHA market, mortgage bankers also made money by using "discount points" on the front end of mortgage loans.[85] Because FHA loans held a lower interest rate, FHA regulations allowed lenders to charge the *seller* "points" to essentially allow the banker to recoup the differential between the conventional interest rate and the FHA rate. A single point was 1 percent of the mortgage loan and was intended as an incentive for lenders who would otherwise ignore the urban market in search of higher interest returns elsewhere. But those conventional lenders did, by and large, ignore the urban market. The FHA persisted in allowing additional points, or payments really, to be imposed on the seller. This was a boon to mortgage banks. As one analysis observed, "The points are the largest single payment received at any point in the mortgage process."[86] In addition to points, mortgage banks also received the full value of the loan when it was sold on the secondary market to the GNMA. These were just some of the financial benefits of the FHA loan.

A combination of discount points and the host of other fees also explained why some mortgage lenders calculated that foreclosing a mortgage loan was as beneficial as having extended the loan in the first place. When a loan went into foreclosure, the front-end fees and discount points had already been paid in cash. The real money was in originating loans and cashing in on the closing costs—not in the maturation of the mortgage loan. This phenomenon was known as "fast foreclosure," where banks ignored their obligations to prioritize keeping mortgagors in their homes. Once the house was in foreclosure, the banks were also paid a fee by HUD-FHA to maintain the property until it was sold again. Many mortgage banks collected the fee while ignoring their responsibility to maintain the property, but HUD was so overextended, it could not police its own programs. In the end, the sooner a house went into foreclosure, the more money a mortgage lender could make.

Large profits for mortgage banks also came through their ability to package multiple mortgages and then resell them to investors or to the GNMA. These sales allowed mortgage banks to pay off their original high-interest loans while also freeing up the capital necessary to originate more mortgages. Because the interest was high on their original loans, the mortgage banks did not want to hang on to those loans for very long. More importantly, the loans could only be sold to larger investors on a volume basis. It meant that mortgage bankers had to create packages of loans before they could unload them, generating an incentive to lend indiscriminately. An additional incentive in the FHA market was an agreement with the GNMA that required it to purchase any FHA-insured loan at 100 percent of its face value and "without any assessment of its soundness."[87] These loans were fully guaranteed by the GNMA and the FNMA, meaning that the long-term investors did not have to worry about the foreclosures roiling the urban market.

By 1972, when HUD-FHA's housing problems were cresting, mortgage banks originated 73 percent of all FHA-insured loans. One observer described mortgage banking as the "primary child of the FHA mortgage insurance program."[88] Another dynamic at play was the impact of Section 235 subsidies, which helped to push low-income programs forward even as deeply damaging problems continued to arise in cities across the country. The general rise in interest rates in 1969 and 1970 created the conditions for "tight money," meaning that the high cost of loans made ordinary people reluctant to enter the housing market. The tight money conundrum was exacerbated when in 1970 Romney raised the FHA interest rate to 8.5 percent, a new historic high. Romney wanted to keep FHA loans competitive with conventional bank loans, which were flirting with a 9 percent interest rate. Various interests in the real estate industry condemned the move.[89] FHA-insured mortgages were for buyers on the lower end of the economy who could not afford the typically higher interest rates and down-payment requirements of conventional loans. The new FHA rate made even those loans prohibitive to their intended market—unless, of course, the loan was subsidized. Section 235 homes were subsidized down to 1 percent interest rates, making them a significantly cheaper entry point into the housing market.

Meanwhile, the federal government made a hard pivot to the subsidized market, evidenced by the pumping of hundreds of millions of dollars into the GNMA to further encourage lending to low-income people looking to buy a house. Indeed, the MBA spoke out publicly to pressure HUD into diverting more public money into the "existing housing" portion of the 1968 HUD Act. Mortgage bankers understood that the "urban" or African American market was less likely to be able to make the higher down payments desired by conventional lenders, and they were also well aware that conventional lenders had all but abandoned the central city housing market. Their representatives claimed concern with an unequal distribution of subsidies as their motive for championing the expansion of the use of existing housing. The mortgage bankers wanted the subsidy programs expanded to include an even greater number of people. The MBA complained in hearings that "neighbors of unsubsidized home buyers with comparable or higher income have been able to obtain better housing with federal subsidies."[90]

In 1970, Congress passed the Emergency Home Finance Act, which among many things allocated $1.5 billion to the GNMA, a secondary market created specifically to make more money available for low-income housing.[91] Most of the money was intended to buy the mortgages on multifamily apartment purchases, but $250 million was set aside to buy single-family home mortgages.[92] The billions of dollars invested in low-income homeownership and apartments was paying off. By 1971, there were more than half a million starts for units of low- and moderate-income housing with federal assistance. Richard Van Dusen, the undersecretary of HUD during the Nixon administration, pointed out that "more subsidized housing units were produced under the first three years of the Nixon administration than in the entire previous thirty year history of subsidized housing programs."[93] The deep pockets of the secondary market and the mortgage bankers' corner on the FHA-insured, low-income homeownership market meant that just as questions about housing quality began to arise, mortgage bankers were flush with cash and eager to lend.

BAD ATTITUDES

While the growing popularity of HUD-FHA subsidy plans and chronic staffing issues were certainly problems that affected the quality of the agencies' work, the deeply embedded racist attitudes about African Americans within the HUD-FHA bureaucracy guaranteed a hostile climate for fair housing attempts from the beginning. Some white FHA employees complained openly about the change in their clientele. Other agents looked at Section 235 and other low-income home-owners as "undeserving" and "lucky" to get whatever housing was offered, no matter its condition. As one mortgage broker succinctly stated, "Owning property is a privilege and should remain so. Most 235 buyers are undeserving."[94] A Philadelphia broker also groused, "I've shown properties to 235 buyers who turned them down and then sold the same property the next day to a regular unsubsidized buyer."[95] "Section 235" in the existing housing market in cities across the country had become a code signifying a poor, African American potential buyer. By the early 1970s, there were multiple programs that had been created by the HUD Act that allowed for poor and low-income families to buy an inner-city home. The most popular of those programs were Section 235 and the unsubsidized Section 221(d)(2). These programs were stigmatized, and their participants were treated accordingly. During one interview, an FHA staff member predicted a high rate of foreclosure because of "the type of people participating in the program."[96] Indeed, because there were Section 235 recipients who were on welfare and coming from public housing, many FHA staff members suggested that the condition of the housing did not matter: "As long as the people were getting better housing than they were accustomed [to, then] the goals of the program were being met."[97] A broker in Denver, Colorado, complained that some 235 buyers "think they can buy any house."[98]

These attitudes pervaded the FHA. Romney conceded to Wright Patman in a letter concerning the initial investigation into the programs that "while FHA commendably increased its participation in inner city transactions during the last five years, we have nevertheless discovered certain administrative attitudes which we believe have contributed to the abuses you and others have brought to our attention."[99] Another observer concurred, saying, "Attitude and morale was poor and the lackadaisical attitude toward work was a reflection of the attitude of management within the office."[100] Having determined that the program participants were getting the housing they deserved, supervisors and agents alike acquired a "hands off" approach to their jobs while insisting that "it is the responsibility of every purchaser to determine that the property will meet his needs and that he satisfy himself as to the condition of the property,"[101] thereby mirroring the caveat emptor posture of the real estate agents with whom they collaborated. Regardless of its source, this attitude was a completely unrealistic approach to a program that took as its starting point old and substandard properties. What's more, this underlying resentment led to a complete breakdown of the norms by which the agency was supposed to operate. There were lapses in training and supervision that were particularly unfortunate given the newness and complexity of HUD's urban mission. To some extent, this reflected the lack of direction provided by the management of HUD, including Romney. With production goals and large numbers of participants as the central barometers of success, little attention was paid to how the program was actually being implemented and managed. The lack of direction in HUD as an organization, combined with the deterioration of its routines and consequently its reputation, probably also impacted morale. However, the consequences of both were most devastating for the program participants, particularly those in existing housing, who were forced to weather unimaginable conditions in housing they were assured was "government approved." The deterioration in staff morale and attitude was reinforced by the structural impediments created by the housing stock,

HUD-FHA's evaluation of value, and the process by which program participants were to procure their loans. In combination, they undermined the "new crusade" originally described by former FHA executives Brownstein and Maloney.

The reticence of HUD-FHA staff to assist new clients could also not be separated from the agency's subservient relationship to the real estate industry. FHA mortgage insurance did not benefit or protect the homeowner; it protected the lender. Mortgage insurance had been created to entice bankers into lending again after suffering massive losses during the Depression. The premiums paid by individuals whose mortgages were insured by the federal government were paid into a general fund that served to protect the interests of lenders. In other words, the FHA evaluated property, neighborhoods, and potential buyers from the perspective of the real estate industry, especially bankers, because they were the actual clients in these multiple, transactional relationships. Perhaps predictably, the FHA also assumed the industry's reactionary ideas concerning race, risk, and property.

The directives from Brownstein and Maloney mentioned earlier in this chapter, in combination with the HUD Act, attempted to transform the culture within the FHA without actually transforming the basic rules that informed it. Those rules included treating Section 235 and 221(d)(2) in the same way that the FHA had dealt with new suburban housing—even though the houses and prospective buyers were quite different. Most importantly, however, these rules included working through the same private institutions and actors that were continuing to profit from the pervasive inequality that coursed through the real estate industry.

When the U.S. Civil Rights Commission investigated HUD's progress in implementing antidiscrimination measures in 1970, it found that the organization had "regressed" since the passage of the Fair Housing Act.[102] The commission's investigation was part of a broader effort to assess how the federal government was implementing antidiscrimination policies originated in 1964 and 1968. The conclusions were damning. In a report, the commission described the federal government's progress in this area as a "massive failure."[103] One explanation for the consistent shortcomings in enforcement of fair housing rules was the lack of mechanisms to change discriminatory actions when they were identified. There was no shortage of examples of how racism and discrimination existed throughout the private and public sectors, but short of court action, next to nothing was done to systemically root out discrimination. Though the failure of the government was a general observation, the report saved its harshest critique for HUD.

The commission pointed to Romney's and HUD's abandonment of the touted Open Communities program, noting that the "change in HUD's 'open communities' policy may not only represent a narrowing of that agency's view of its fair housing responsibilities, but also may mark the beginning of the federal government's withdrawal from active participation in the effort to eliminate residential segregation."[104]

Romney is often described as the outermost liberal edge of the Nixon administration because of the short-lived Open Communities program's attempt to make the suburbs accessible to low-income African Americans. But that assessment of Romney must be tempered with HUD's failure to employ any serious effort to combat racism in the dissemination of its programs. A glaring example of this was HUD's persistent unwillingness to collect racial data across its programs. Without a way to know the race or ethnicity of program participants, it was impossible to determine the racial impact of HUD's housing programs— or those of any of the other agencies with which HUD interacted. Even as HUD was demanding such information from mortgage lending institutions and its other private partners, the agency was very slow to implement a plan to collect its own data. In 1970, NAACP leader Samuel Simmons was appointed by Nixon as the first assistant secretary for equal housing opportunity in HUD.[105] Congress then appropriated $6 million for the office to carry out its responsibilities. Though $5 million of that money was intended for staff salaries, the office had a skeletal staff of 120 people, including 19 clerical staff. For 120 people to police antidiscrimination within housing programs nationwide was an impossible task, and HUD was left to rely on "conference, conciliation and persuasion" as its main tools for combatting housing discrimination.[106]

HUD's inability to eradicate racial discrimination in the housing market was not limited to the FHA. The absence of a rigorous routine for rooting out racial discrimination affected all the regulatory agencies throughout the banking and housing industries. Those organizations, like HUD, also hid behind a lack of data collection to claim ignorance on the exact ways that Black consumers were denied constitutionally protected services. In June 1971, the Federal Home Loan Bank Board was strongly urged by the U.S. Commission on Civil Rights to send a survey to lending institutions to determine their lending practices. The survey revealed what was already understood by millions of African Americans: discrimination was rife throughout the banking industry. The survey was not as conclusive as it could have been because thousands of banks refused to participate. Of the 5,000 banks that received the survey, only 74 agreed to return it to HUD.[107] Of those who completed the survey, "some lenders" admitted to using race in determining whether to lend and in establishing the terms of the loan if they did. The survey also found other evidence of discrimination that was less obvious, including the refusal to consider a spouse's income as a factor in the decision to lend. A disproportionate number of wives in Black families worked outside the home, so this policy clearly penalized African American borrowers.[108] Thirty percent of the banks confirmed that they continued to redline Black neighborhoods as risky. These activities had been prohibited by the Civil Rights Act of 1968, but with a lack of mechanisms, staff, or apparent desire to confront the continuation of rank discrimination in housing, changes in the law would have little, if any, resonance in practice.

HUD-FHA'S BLACK EMPLOYEES

The inattention to racism was not only an external problem concerning the organizations that HUD monitored, but internally, Black employees of HUD complained bitterly about racial discrimination. African American HUD-FHA workers charged that "systematic racism" permeated the agency tasked with rebuilding the cities that a majority of African Americans called home. In September 1970, Black employees of HUD were the subject of an article published in the Washington Urban League newsletter *Urban Action*.[109] The article, titled "Systematic Racism Rampant at HUD," listed many of the grievances of Black HUD employees, including the fact that African Americans made up 75 percent of GS1 (General Schedule 1) through GS5 entry-level positions within HUD and only 5 percent of supervisory positions listed as GS14 through GS18.[110] According to one Black worker in the Department of Health, Education, and Welfare, Black government employees earned $3,400 less than white employees each year. The Urban League had been filing complaints on behalf of Black HUD employees since 1968, particularly those who worked within the FHA, which, the league said, "practices racial discrimination of a most pervasive and damaging kind against four hundred black employees."[111] HUD workers also complained about the indignity of training white employees who came into the organization at higher pay and at higher grades even when they had the same education as African American employees. The Urban League investigation, prompted by the request of a Black woman employed by HUD-FHA for twenty-one years, Earline Tibbs, found that Black workers filled 75 percent of GS1 positions, the lowest designation within the federal system.[112] Black workers across the federal government bureaucracy described their overwhelming placement in low-grade jobs as the "basement occupancy."[113]

Eugene Cole was a prime example of the absence of career mobility for Black workers in prized federal jobs. Cole had worked across multiple agencies within the federal government for thirty-eight years, and by 1971, two years before he retired, he was only a GS5 working for HUD and making $10,000 a year. Shortly after the publication of the *Urban Action* article, Cole joined with other Black HUD employees to form the HUD Task Force Against Racism. As its first action, the task force put together a petition with fourteen complaints aimed at increasing job opportunities and advancement within HUD.[114] The task force also had specific complaints against the FHA. It demanded a targeted investigation into the hiring and promotional practices within the FHA department of HUD. The written petition received no response, so on October 13, 1970, 300 African American HUD employees stormed the administrative offices of HUD and demanded to see George Romney.[115] One report described Romney "scampering down ten flights of stairs to escape" the workers' "demands for equal employment."[116] Romney briefly stopped to address the workers and acquiesced: "I will admit there have been grounds for complaints . . . but we have taken steps . . . to see that a true equal opportunity program is established. But we can only do it in an orderly manner."[117] Their petition demanded "an end to institutional racism and discrimination practiced daily in HUD and FHA against blacks and other minority employees." They also demanded to be "treated equally for promotions and training and for consideration of supervisory jobs."[118] Within a few weeks, HUD announced that 42 Black employees were being promoted and that another 200 would be considered for promotion the following month.[119]

When HUD dragged its feet in implementing an affirmative action plan that ensured Black workers equal treatment on the job, they protested again. On May 13, 1971, 300 Black HUD employees walked off the job to demonstrate against their workplace conditions. HUD management retaliated and suspended 156 of those workers for one day and refused to pay them.[120] The charges of racism and discrimination were eventually taken up by the Civil Service Commission. The case came before Julia Cooper, an Equal Employment Opportunity appeals examiner who, after hearing from 88 witnesses, reviewing 110 statements, and viewing 65 pieces of documentary evidence, ruled emphatically in favor of the Black employees.[121] On October 16, 1971, Cooper delivered her decision. In twenty-one-pages, Cooper linked the history of FHA discrimination to a hostile work environment for Black workers. She wrote, "There is no doubt, and it is not seriously disputed, that historically a pattern or practice of racial discrimination existed in the FHA."[122] She found that there was a "systematic pattern of racism at HUD ... [that] held blacks immobile in the lowest grade levels while whites moved ahead." This "pattern" included failing to "provide training and in some cases conceal[ing] knowledge" about the availability of training, permitting racist white supervisors to "remain for many years in positions to help maintain these practices," and penalizing those who complained about discrimination.[123] In illustrating the immobility of the Black workforce within HUD, Cooper highlighted the story of an African American woman who after eighteen years had only advanced to a level of GS4. It would take her another ten years to advance to GS5, but in the interim, she was tasked with training white men who later became her supervisors. Other Black employees made similar complaints. One employee said that after twenty-four years, he "had trained three white supervisors to be my supervisor." It took another Black man twenty years to move from GS2 to GS3. He said, "I stayed a GS2 until 1969. If that is not discrimination, I don't know what is."[124]

Cooper concluded that HUD's practices were "totally out of focus with the trend of current law." It was a historic outcome for HUD's Black workers. The *New York Times* commented that it was "unprecedented to find an entire government agency guilty of discrimination."[125] The Civil Service Commission was used to handling individual complaints of discrimination, but the Task Force Against Racism had compiled the complaints of 500 Black employees when it charged HUD with rampant racial discrimination, forcing the commission to take on the problem on a much wider scale. Romney vehemently disagreed with the conclusions that Cooper had reached, saying that he "found them difficult to understand." Cooper did not blame Romney alone. She pointed out that the "pattern of discrimination" began before the tenure of Robert Weaver or George Romney. She did, however, make the point that Romney had done nothing to change the pattern during the twenty months he had been secretary of the agency.[126]

CONTINUITIES

In the spring of 1971 the U.S. Civil Rights Commission unleashed a new wave of criticisms against an embattled HUD. The commission's assessment of the Section 235 housing program confirmed that the new homeownership programs had not forged a new direction for HUD but were simply replicating the discriminatory patterns that gave rise to the programs in the first place. According to the commission, HUD-FHA had "abdicated its responsibility and, in effect has delegated it to members of the private housing and home finance industry," which continued to have a financial interest in maintaining a segregated housing market, as well as an ingrained antipathy toward Black buyers and renters. In a press conference announcing the publication of the report, Howard Glickstein, staff director of the commission, revealed that the investigation had "found . . . a dual marketing system so pervasive, so entrenched and so commonplace that most real estate brokers described it openly to the Commission staff without any sense of wrongdoing."[127] A pointed example from the commission underlined the dilemma. When an inquiring person contacted, for example, the Philadelphia office of the FHA for information about the Section 235 program, the caller was told, "You should talk to a real estate broker about that. . . . Have you ever seen a plate glass window in your neighborhood with 'Real Estate' written on it? That's right. A real estate man. Just go and ask him and he has all the information. He'll be able to tell you everything you need to know."[128]

The *Washington Post* concluded, "Brokers, developers, bankers and FHA officials themselves . . . discriminate against black 235 buyers directing them into already existing housing in already black areas . . . or into already integrated 'changing neighborhoods' . . . [while] white buyers . . . get the new 235 housing in white suburbs."[129] The commission blamed the leadership of HUD, most pointedly George Romney, for failing to "provide local FHA officials with instructions for affirmative action" in responding to housing discrimination.[130] HUD's reliance on private sector institutions and methods left the agency vulnerable to discriminatory lenses through which the real estate industry viewed its transactions.

In reality, the racism endemic to the practice of real estate was amplified when conjoined with the resources of the federal government. Romney was typically furious with the report, decrying it as "sensational," "largely unfounded," and "out-of-date." And yet Romney largely agreed that Section 235 was being used to perpetuate racial segregation in metropolitan housing markets. He admitted that the federal housing program had failed to change "the dominant pattern of racial separation" because the program "operates within the framework" of the private real estate market. He elaborated, noting that "the FHA has traditionally been structured and administered to respond to the private market. . . . The FHA doesn't by itself control such things as housing-site location, housing consumer preferences, the choice of broker or the willingness of brokers to deal or not to deal in FHA-insured properties."[131]

It was a surprisingly candid description of how ill-equipped the FHA was for the socially oriented role that had been thrust upon the agency by Romney when he forced it both to function within HUD and to take responsibility for the execution of the agency's low-income housing programs. In the days after the release of the commission's findings, Romney announced several new rules geared toward achieving greater compliance with federal antidiscrimination laws. One of the main changes was the requirement of "affirmative marketing" practices, which included a slew of purported changes for the private partners of HUD-FHA. Not only would the various components of the housing industry be compelled to advertise their services to African Americans in a nondiscriminatory way, but they would also be required to advertise properties to African Americans and whites regardless of where the properties were located. Companies would also be obligated to hire African Americans and create displays that announced "equal opportunity," be it in real estate sales, home loans, or new housing starts.

The generation of even more new rules, however, was a misplaced effort. The overwhelming conclusion of the commission involved the lack of enforcement of already existing rules. When Romney was asked at a hearing three days after the publication of the commission findings how he would ensure greater compliance with fair housing rules, he responded, "through spot checking and processing complaints."[132] This mechanism (or lack thereof) was no different than the approach that had resulted in inattention to racial discrimination in the first place. Moreover, processing individual complaints against discrimination was hardly an effective strategy for weeding out the deeply ingrained and institutional nature of housing discrimination. Housing discrimination was not going to end on an individual level. There would have to be fundamental shifts in how the real estate market functioned, how banks were lending money, and how builders conceived of development. Despite his bluster, Romney seemed unwilling to participate in such a radical transformation—or any transformation at all.

Perhaps most indicative of the administration's shallow commitment to addressing the issue was Romney's stance on existing housing. When Glickstein asked Romney whether the new rules for affirmative marketing applied to existing housing—which made up the vast majority of the American housing market—Romney quietly replied that they did not.[133] The proliferation of rules that would be spottily if at all enforced was, apparently, the best that Romney thought could be done. Frankie Muse Freeman took over the questioning of Romney shortly thereafter. Freeman, hailing from St. Louis, had been the first Black woman appointed to the commission in 1964. In trying to unravel the difficulty HUD-FHA was experiencing in shedding its practices of the past, she asked, "With respect to the FHA now—executives or staff of FHA who were formerly members of the real estate industry which is responsible for the exclusion in the first place—are they the same people who were responsible for the exclusion in the past? Are they still with the FHA?" Romney replied, "If you are asking me if all of the FHA personnel changed overnight, no." "People," according to Romney, "change more slowly than almost any other thing on the face of the earth."[134]

5

Unsophisticated Buyers

The problem is that we have been putting families into homes who
have no sense of responsibility of homeownership and that is where
the problem has been, and that is the intrinsic problem in the program.
Is that not true? . . . We found welfare mothers whose sole income was aid
for dependent children, plus other benefits that come from that status in
life, and they were put in housing, presumably as owners and yet, they could
not even fix a faucet washer. Have we concluded there are some people
who should not be put in the status of home purchasers? Can we not
conclude that there are some people who do not have the sense
of responsibility or the economic income to own a home?
—Representative Ben Blackburn (R–GA)

THE TRICKLE OF INFORMATION about poor housing insured by the FHA and HUD slowly swelled into a deluge of troubling news as journalists in Philadelphia and Chicago published exposés of the homeownership programs in their respective cities. Stories of corruption and collusion between the FHA, real estate speculators, and shady bankers became front-page fodder, creating a crescendo of turmoil for HUD. The agency had become the focal point of intense news coverage, but there was a developing subtext. The news was also concerned with the recipients of this government assistance, a disproportionate number of whom were poor and working-class Black women who had bought deteriorating or deeply damaged housing with the backing of the federal government. As the heat of the spotlight intensified, so too did the search for a culprit or responsible party to blame. The media, elected officials, and HUD agency representatives identified a cluster of issues to explain the strife in the urban housing market. Congressional inquiries, tinged by political partisanship, had questioned staffing levels, poor appraising techniques, poor attitudes throughout the FHA, and generally the poor management of the housing programs discussed in Chapter 4.

Within HUD, officials including Romney emphasized a different set of issues. Romney lamented the legislation that had ended redlining and created homeowning opportunities in the nation's cities. He publicly questioned poor women's homemaking skills and described them as "unsophisticated." As the investigations into the housing scandals expanded, it was discovered that the improprieties extended far beyond Section 235 of the Housing Act. There were two additional sections of the Housing Act that allowed for an even broader contingent of potential homeowners. Section 223(e) allowed for FHA insurance to be made available in older sections of cities that had previously been described as "riot prone." Section 237 of the Housing Act was even more far reaching in authorizing mortgage insurance for poor families that did not qualify under regular FHA programs because of poor credit histories or inconsistent income, but whom the secretary of HUD could deem to be a "reasonably satisfactory" credit risk and capable of homeownership with the "assistance of budget, debt management and related counseling provided by the Secretary."[1]

Section 237 opened the doors of homeownership to poor families on welfare, including women receiving Aid to Dependent Children (ADC). Despite the legislative mandate that Section 237 provided, budget and debt management and "related counseling" were never integrated into the services offered by HUD because they never received appropriations from Congress. As investigations began to hone in on availability of counseling as a factor in the crises pervading the homeownership programs, the issues of persisting racial discrimination and the structural inadequacies of the urban housing market were pushed to the margins of the investigations. Moreover, the focus on counseling lent itself to intrusive inquiries into the suitability of families on welfare as homeowners as the behavior and domesticity of Black women became a central issue in the function of the low-income homeownership programs.

While their exact rate of participation is unknown because of HUD-FHA's reluctance to collect racial or gender data for its programs at the time, thousands of Black women who purchased homes through HUD's programs became the focal point of congressional and media inquiries. These women were portrayed as unsophisticated and domestically dysfunctional, evidenced by alleged difficulty with the simple maintenance of their homes. These portrayals of poor and working-class Black women, especially those receiving public assistance, presumed knowledge about their lifestyles and habits. These perceptions or ideas had formed over time and were certainly influenced by the caustic debates concerning the character of Black women receiving welfare that were circulating at the time the legislation was passed. As historian Premilla Nadasen has written, "The political attacks on welfare in the 1950s and early 1960s were framed in racial terms and rooted in stereotypes of black women."[2]

Section 235 and other low-income homeownership programs were not welfare—far from it. Indeed, program participants paid the federal government a monthly insurance premium for the mortgage insurance on their homes. Although these women were able to budget monthly payments for their homes, they lacked disposable income with which to make unplanned payments for the kinds of repairs that are a regular part of owning a house, particularly an old and used house. Because of this "predictable" shortfall, women and others who bought existing houses were described as "ignorant" and "foolish" for buying houses that were in such disrepair. In one interview, a member of the Chicago real estate board admitted that "speculators and real estate men" exploited the market to their benefit and claimed to be "concerned with the way people are dealt with" while also insisting that there was "little" that the board could do because "we cannot protect the people from their own ignorance against real estate men who are not members of this board."[3] These were not just the musings of a single broker in Chicago; they represented the perspective of many widely discussed media accounts of HUD as well.

This chapter shows that the crises in HUD's existing housing market were construed as the problems of program participants who were disproportionately Black, female, and in some cases, receiving various forms of public assistance or welfare. Existing housing constituted a smaller portion of the homeownership programs than new, suburban housing, but the concentration of defaults and foreclosures in HUD's existing housing market gave those program participants an outsized role in the evolving story. None of this is to say that homeownership for the poor made much sense as an antipoverty program. Taking on thousands of dollars of debt for ownership of an old and declining property while also being tied to a community with few prospects for reinvigorating its job market was a tall order under the best of circumstances; for the poor, it exacerbated and deepened one's descent into the ranks of the poor. But since homeownership was firmly situated as a cornerstone of the American dream, the aspiration for inclusion into its ranks went without question. Instead the questions turned to who was capable and responsible enough to assume homeownership. Poor Black families—led overwhelmingly by Black women—were easy targets for blame in this scenario. But they also defied the role of victim. Poor Black women would play an important role in bringing to light the role of racial discrimination in the application of HUD's programs.[4] Their complaints, social activism, and willingness to engage in litigation to make their grievances public opened a gradually widening aperture into the depths of the crisis in HUD and exposed the lie in repeated suggestions that they were nothing more than "unsophisticated buyers."

ANATOMY OF A FAILURE

By 1972, a growing number of foreclosures in the existing housing portion of the program perpetuated the sense of failure within HUD. Nationally, Romney predicted that HUD's inventory of repossessed homes would grow to 36,000 by the end of 1971.[5] Within three years, from 1968 to 1971, FHA foreclosures had risen from 96 a month to 381 a month.[6] This was not even the largest number of homes under the control of the FHA in its history. In 1964, the FHA held 54,000 repossessed homes, the most in its history.[7] Yet by the early 1970s, the *pace* of foreclosures in the low-income homeownership programs had become alarming. After a period of declining foreclosures from 1966 to 1969, they began to rise, and most of those numbers were driven by foreclosures in the low-income homeownership programs. By 1972, the foreclosure rate for the FHA's traditional suburban program was 1.9 percent. By contrast, foreclosures for Section 235 had reached 4.45 percent, and for Section 221(d)(2), 2.54 percent.[8]

The rapid growth of mortgage defaults, the stage of delinquency before foreclosure, also caused great concern. Defaults resulted when a mortgage payment was at least thirty days late and the property was on the verge of becoming a foreclosure. By mid-1972 there were another 244,000 units in default, meaning that they were one or two payments away from falling into foreclosure.[9] The head of the FHA in Detroit, William Whitbeck, warned that "in many cities most, if not all, of the mortgages" developed with funding through the Project Rehab program "will go into default due to the enormous marketing and management problems."[10]

Not only were these numbers proportionally higher, but they also threatened to exhaust the special insurance fund that had been established for the low-income programs.[11] The climate of crisis, so palpable to the media and elected officials, was fueled by the possibility of having to allocate tens of millions of dollars to cover the federally guaranteed mortgage insurance claims. In the midst of the public debates over the deservingness of welfare recipients in the early 1970s, these potential claims ignited a firestorm.

Philadelphia and Detroit became epicenters of HUD's troubles. Detroit already had the highest rate of homeownership in the nation, and in the aftermath of the 1967 rebellion, city and federal officials looked to dramatically increase homeownership among poor and working-class African Americans. The local HUD-FHA affiliate in Detroit had been "honored and applauded" for the rapid pace at which it enrolled people in subsidized and unsubsidized homeownership programs. By April 1972, HUD was in possession of 7,574 properties in Detroit, representing 17 percent of HUD's entire inventory.[12] The General Accounting Office predicted that HUD would soon own 20,000 repossessed homes in Detroit alone, costing the federal government $200 million in FHA insurance payouts.[13] Investigative journalist Brian Boyer of the *Detroit Free Press*, who would go on to document the HUD crisis in his book *Cities Destroyed for Cash* in 1973, considered this a conservative estimate. Boyer said that the General Accounting Office had underestimated the payout of insurance on each foreclosure in Detroit at $10,000, while the local HUD affiliate showed that the actual cost of the mortgage value of each house was $15,000. This would put the total insurance loss at $450 million in the few short years of the life of the program.[14] A staff member of an investigative congressional committee ominously warned, "If what we found in Detroit is true only to a degree elsewhere, the residential areas of a number of large cities are in serious trouble and the FHA insurance fund faces tremendous losses."[15]

In Philadelphia, the decline of the homeownership programs had not received as much attention, but the consequences were just as dire. By 1972, one out of thirteen homes insured by the FHA in Philadelphia was in foreclosure. Between 1968 and 1972, HUD-FHA had more foreclosures on homes it insured than in its previous thirty-year history.[16] The crisis extended far beyond a single program, as it engulfed almost all of the homeownership programs that had been brought to life by the lending that had been unleashed as redlining ended. In Philadelphia and Detroit, defaults and foreclosures for homes purchased through Section 221(d)(2) exceeded those for all other programs.[17] Elsewhere there were forecasts that Section 235 foreclosures could rise by between 20 and 50 percent in the coming months.[18] George Romney described the troubled "existing" housing program as "a failure and I think we ought to recognize it."[19]

As foreclosed properties were returned to HUD, the federal agency was described as the largest "slumlord" in the country.[20] HUD's problems were national news and adorned the front pages of newspapers across the country. Its home-ownership programs were discussed on the news program *60 Minutes*. Even as HUD's problems were unfolding nationally, news coverage in some cities ampli-fied the depth of the local impact. Investigative reporters Donald Barlett and James Steele of the *Philadelphia Inquirer* uncovered fraud and corruption in the local Philadelphia FHA office that inspired the first congressional investigation into the low-income homeownership programs. The Philadelphia reporting, along with special investigations led by the *Chicago Tribune*, examined collu-sion between real estate brokers, speculators, mortgage bank lenders, and FHA agents all working together to enrich themselves at the expense of the program participants. These inquiries became the basis for further investigations into the impact of the housing programs in particular cities, while more general questions were being raised about the role of subsidized housing in the nation as a whole. Newspapers across the country teemed with stories about deceptive tricks used to lure poor people into buying junk property, all with the apparent blessing of the federal government.[21]

The problems dogging HUD's housing programs featured a nefarious group of actors including shady mortgage lenders, appraisers on the take, and deceptive real estate brokers as the starring characters in the drama about the persistent urban housing crisis. But the focus on the chiselers averted investigation into a more systemic understanding of the problems with these low-income homeown-ership programs. These included the persistence of residential segregation and the inability of Black buyers to access the entire market. There was the related issue of promoting homeownership among poor and low-income people in exist-ing homes that were distressed and in need of expensive repair and maintenance. Given the constraints of a fixed income, how could they be expected to manage these costs? These questions were buried beneath the efforts of HUD administra-tors and the elected officials who originally backed the legislation that made low-income homeownership possible to distance themselves from the mounting spectacle of failed public policies.

The first investigations into the federal homeownership programs in 1970 had coincided with Nixon's declaration against "forced integration" and then his statement renouncing the use of federal authority to open white suburban communities to African Americans. Romney was left in virtual isolation within the Nixon administration, especially as Nixon shifted into campaign mode for the 1972 electoral season. Romney struggled to provide an analysis of the fail-ing housing programs, but he eventually identified four persisting problems that dogged the development of effective housing policy. The first was that the "urban housing crisis" could not be separated from the "social, economic, and physical problems" that existed in American cities. The second problem was the "multiplicity of autonomous governments" that prevented the development of comprehensive policies for suburban areas concerning low-income housing. The third was the unwillingness of states to effectively direct local governments to bear responsibility for creating "metropolitan" housing. Finally, Romney blamed the continuation of the "widespread abandonment" by private enterprise of American cities, which contributed to the dearth of capital necessary to revamp American cities.[22] Of course, there were particular problems with the implementation of the programs, but they were happening within a context where "urban renewal" had continued to fail as a strategy for redeveloping cities in ways that matched the economic vibrancy happening in many white suburban enclaves.

Romney and his staff at HUD suggested several reforms to the programs as they related to the existing housing market in cities. These reforms involved everything from demanding stringent vigilance on the part of appraisers to remanding those suspected of wrongdoing to the FBI.[23] There were efforts to rein in the pervasion of real estate speculators and their quest to exploit this portion of the housing market. But while there were certainly illegal practices, most involving fraud and deception in the quest to pump up the value of poor-quality housing, many of the practices within the existing urban housing market were legal. Real estate speculation was, in fact, very legal and the prime impetus for the pursuit of private property. The ability to "buy low and sell high" was a marker of sophistication within the housing market; it certainly was not a crime.

Given this dynamic, along with the central role played by agents and officials within the real estate industry, the inequities were difficult to stamp out. Within the larger constellation of problems identified by Romney, they were next to impossible to address in any serious way by the Nixon administration, especially with an election on the horizon. Nixon had already dismissed Romney's desire for a housing solution that involved the suburbs, thereby undermining any effort of HUD to pursue "fair housing" with any vigor. But the challenge from Black workers within HUD also demonstrated the limits of the organization to attend to its own racial crisis, let alone the multiple crises it faced with regard to housing equity. Conversely, it was easy to draw attention to the supposed "unsophisticated buyers" who were at the heart of the existing market. The focus on individuals fit neatly with the escalating rhetoric within the Republican Party condemning women on welfare, with its unmistakable racial undertones.[24]

There was a great deal at stake in unpacking the blame and responsibility for the scale of problems experienced by HUD-FHA's intervention into the urban housing market. This was especially true as Nixon asserted that he was best suited to continue leading the country.

DIFFERENT CONSUMERS, DIFFERENT VALUES

In a 1972 interview with the *Wall Street Journal*, Assistant Secretary of HUD Norman Watson questioned the concept of providing FHA services in central city neighborhoods and to the people to be served by HUD-FHA within those central cities. Watson said, "We took a program designed for the suburbs where the family had the resources to adapt to mistakes . . . and we pushed it into the inner city where you had *different* consumers with *different* resources and *different* values."[25] The author of the story further elaborated and wondered whether American cities should be altogether excluded from federal aid: "Is federal intervention the way to salvation, or should natural forces be allowed to take their course?" The argument was as old as the housing market itself: the difference in the suburban and urban housing markets was a "natural" phenomenon; in the former, value organically appreciated, while in the latter, it just as spontaneously declined. The article went on to argue that "underlying the dialogue is a simple truth. In contrast to a suburban community that is appreciating in value, federal investment in a deteriorating city neighborhood is bound to suffer because, even though a house or project may be new or rehabilitated, the neighborhood around it continues to decline."[26]

Unlike white working- and middle-class people, some of whom found their American dream in the suburbs, African Americans stuck in cities were confronted by an American nightmare. The consequences of shallow investments and poor infrastructure and public services drained home values for urban homeowners, as did the low quality of housing that was made available to potential Black buyers. The relative poverty of African Americans exacerbated the condition of the housing to which they were relegated. The average median income for Black families in 1971 was $6,279, compared with $10,236 for whites, and 28 percent of African American families were living in poverty, compared with 7 percent of white families.[27] A congresswoman from St. Louis, Leonore Sullivan, described the subsidized homeownership market within the city as having houses that were "60, 70 and 80 years old."[28] The physical characteristics of urban housing made accessible to the Black buying public helped to establish

value in both urban and suburban markets. The physical distance between urban
housing and suburban housing was amplified through developing social conceptions of an idealized "white neighborhood" and a despised "Black ghetto"; a
desire for inclusion in one and avoidance of the other added to or detracted from
the value of a given property.

But even as low-income homeownership programs brought the purchase of a
home within the reach of people who otherwise could not afford it, they made
no allowances for the more unpredictable costs of maintaining a house. This was
an unsustainable model, as it turned out, because costs, such as maintenance,
that went beyond the fixed price of a mortgage were in constant fluctuation,
apt to change wildly on a monthly basis, especially in older and distressed housing. Of even more critical importance was the burden of high property taxes,
which "inflicted a double, mutually reinforcing penalty on black homeowners,
forcing them to shoulder a heavier tax burden (for inferior public services) than
whites . . . reducing the market value of their homes even further."[29]

The failure of even sympathetic officials to attune themselves to the very
real differences between early efforts to create a market for low-income white
homeowners in the 1940s versus the market constructed for low-income African
Americans thirty years later marked the inattention throughout U.S. society to
the details of how race and location shape the outcomes of homeownership. It
also called attention to the limitations of the racial liberalism of people like Romney and other HUD officials who had championed an end to redlining and had
tried to force suburban enclaves to follow the new civil rights laws. The premise
of racial liberalism, and postwar liberalism in general, was that the systems and
institutions of the country were strong enough to bestow the political, economic,
and social riches of American society onto all who were willing to work hard
and commit themselves to a better future. In trying to expand homeownership
to include Black property owners, racial liberals upheld the "market" as a space
impervious to race, where economic fitness, above all, would prevail. Instead,
the supposedly colorblind market continued to produce different experiences
and outcomes for white and Black people. To avert a more systemic engagement
with the multiple problems concerning low-income homeownership, the critics
remained focused on the Black families and, in particular, the Black women who
were a focal point in the urban, existing housing program.

A public discourse was developing with avowed concern about home subsidies and attendant assumptions about the people who used them. Program
critics conflated their comments with broader discussions about poverty and

low-income people that were under way in the United States, but the racial subtext was unmistakable. Take, for example, the commentary of well-known real estate analyst Anthony Downs, who had sat on the Kerner Commission and was a consultant for HUD in the late 1960s and throughout the 1970s. In an interview with the *Chicago Tribune* about the mounting problems in HUD's homeownership program, Downs explained that "the underlying cause of urban slums is that the residents are too poor to pay for adequately maintained housing. Also many of those residents display destructive behavior patterns that raise maintenance costs. . . . The real problem is that our housing standards keep rising and these people don't have the capacity to keep up with the standards."[30] This comment, while never mentioning race, is obviously about African American urban residents. Downs appears to be conflating familiar issues around public housing with the emergent issues of the homeownership program.

By the early 1970s, the wide-ranging discussions concerning the difficulties plaguing the nation's public housing stock began to revolve most closely around the condition of the housing and, in particular, the problem of maintenance. There was a long history of dramatic clashes between public housing tenants and housing authorities over the cost of rent and its relationship to the regular maintenance of buildings.[31] The deteriorating condition of poorly built housing developments and niggardly federal appropriations to arrest their decline brought public housing to the brink in the early 1970s. The demolition of the Pruitt-Igoe development in St. Louis in April 1972 cast a large shadow over the ongoing debates concerning race, place, housing, and federal intervention. Downs cynically disparaged the low-income homeownership program by tapping into existing public disapproval of public housing and speaking about two very distinct programs as if they were interchangeable. Despite their lack of precision, Downs's words appeared to remove all ambiguity concerning who or what was to blame for problems in federally subsidized urban homeownership. Clearly, according to Downs, the lack of "capacity" of Black homeowners to "keep up with the standards" deserved censure. Downs added his voice to a growing chorus that accused Black homeowners with "deficient capabilities" of being at the root of HUD's problems.

The housing choices of African Americans were constrained at best. Their relegation to the segregated urban or suburban housing market continued to exert downward pressure on the quality of that housing, as it had done historically. As one advocate said in a public hearing, "The buyer [has] no choice. . . . Many of the buyers recognized certain deficiencies in homes in Detroit in the 235 program. . . .

[We are] now recognizing there are certain deficiencies, with no other choice, no other place to go; as long as you have got a captive population like that . . . then programs like these are going to be exploited."[32] A counselor in St. Louis came closest to the truth: "Sure, people know they are being cheated. They halfway expect to be cheated and they don't look a gift horse in the mouth. It's all relative anyway, if you've got nothing and you get something—or nearly nothing—for the same price, you take it."[33]

BROKEN PROMISES

Real estate ads in the local Detroit papers appealing to women who received Aid to Families with Dependent Children (AFDC; formerly ADC) screamed, "ADC Mothers—No Money Down," while others advertised "rent to own" as an attractive option. Under the heading "RENT—Option to Buy," ads in a January 1972 edition of the *Detroit Free Press* beckoned the attention of poor women on welfare:

ADC-Buyers / Rent While Buying
ADC Mothers / Steady Workers / Low down payment
ADC-Workers / Why Rent? Low Down Payment moves you in newly
  decorated 2, 3, or 4 bedroom / Credit no problem.[34]

Similar ads could be found in the local papers of other cities as well. A common complaint made by program participants confined to the existing housing market was that many of those who had originally intended to rent were pressured into buying. As the *Philadelphia Inquirer* described it, "For most of these families . . . they really wanted to rent, rather than buy, but they were given limited choices. Most are black or Puerto Rican. Many are women—separated, divorced or widowed—who are raising children alone."[35] Francetta Jenkins, a twenty-six-year-old mother of three from Philadelphia, complained that she was "looking for a house to rent, actually," when instead she ended up buying a house for $4,330. Even though the house was in rough shape, she was assured that it was "FHA approved" and that she "didn't have anything to worry about." Ralph Riviera was also "looking to rent." He explained, "When I went out shopping, I was looking to rent a house. I went to the real estate man thinking he has houses to rent and he said, 'I don't rent, I sell.'"[36]

The allure of space, privacy, and independence, however, compelled poor families to take a chance on homeownership even when they were unsure if they had the wherewithal to maintain a house. This was especially true of single Black mothers receiving public assistance and trying to escape the deteriorating conditions in public housing developments. Nationally, 44 percent of the homes purchased in the existing market through a homeownership program were bought by women, a disproportionate number of whom would have been African American. Fifteen percent of the homeowners in the existing market were receiving welfare assistance.[37] The *Detroit News* reported that "welfare mothers automatically qualif[ied] for FHA insured mortgages under the 221D-2 program and nearly 50,000 have bought homes here [Detroit] under the program."[38]

The possibility of buying a home—the cornerstone of the American dream— represented new opportunities, from living in a better neighborhood to having a long-term investment to having autonomy over one's life outside the scrutinizing and scornful gaze of public housing officials. For many African American women, the HUD-FHA programs seemed to offer an unprecedented opportunity to find what many believed would be decent housing. An AFDC counselor in Philadelphia explained that Section 235 housing was "a way for people to move to a better neighborhood. . . . They were afraid of gangs. They wanted to get out of their old neighborhoods."[39] An attorney with the Legal Aid Society in St. Louis described how women on welfare fleeing the crumbling Pruitt-Igoe housing projects ended up in the Section 235 program: "They were desperate to get out. They would take anything available. And for people like them, renting possibilities just don't exist."[40]

To many, homeownership appeared to offer a potential reprieve from the dangers of socially deteriorating neighborhoods. In 1967, 24 percent of AFDC families had no running water, 30 percent lacked enough beds to accommodate their families, and 46 percent had gone without milk at least once in the previous six months.[41] A 1969 report on housing conditions for Black mothers receiving AFDC explained why so many would rush into just about any new housing opportunity. It was estimated that half of welfare recipients lived in "housing which is deteriorating or dilapidated, unsafe or overcrowded." It was estimated that 60 percent of AFDC families were living in similar conditions; for mothers on welfare in particular, conditions were even worse. An investigation also found "higher proportions of defective housing for ADC families than for the other public assistance categories."

Section 102 of the 1968 HUD Act had been designed specifically to help poor families become homeowners. In April of that same year, HUD-FHA published an internal circular that declared the "income" from AFDC to offer "sufficient stability to be included [as] effective income if the children are young and it is received from a governmental agency under a permanent program."[42] HUD's authorization of mothers on welfare to purchase homes was the green light for speculators and mortgage bankers to target those same mothers for inclusion in the homeownership programs. In St. Louis, one broker sent 12,000 postcards to potential Section 235 buyers.[43] A disproportionate number of the cards were sent to AFDC mothers living in the Pruitt-Igoe towers. Indeed, one-quarter of Section 235 buyers in St. Louis were formerly public housing residents,[44] while half of Section 235 buyers in Philadelphia and St. Louis were receiving welfare, and most of those were recipients of AFDC.[45] Once in the office of the real estate broker, "the buyer was shown pictures of available houses and they were assured that the homes had been renovated and were FHA approved."[46] According to a study of FHA buyers in St. Louis, salesmen would follow up with visits to the projects and "offer assurance of a nice house and FHA approved deal."[47] In its aggressive pursuit of new clients, one real estate company went so far as to employ a social worker from the state division of the Department of Welfare to recruit buyers. The implications were clear: "With ready access to financial information of welfare clients, this [social worker] was able to compile a list of potential buyers who would be eligible for Section 235 assistance. [The social worker] was also able to steer his clients towards his second employer [the real estate company]."[48]

In the wake of the demolition of Pruitt-Igoe and the crumbling of other public housing developments, the possibility of homeownership was a risk worth taking. With a growing emphasis on statistics as proof of HUD activity and success, recruitment of AFDC recipients was inadvertently incentivized by HUD's national office. Indeed, HUD offered an annual George Romney Production Award to the regional office that enrolled the highest number of participants in HUD's new subsidized programs.[49] As one observer described it, "For over three years [HUD] has emphasized its production goals and statistics even to the degree of producing production merit awards with disregard for management responsibilities for its existing housing inventory."[50]

Before the criticisms, however, the Detroit office was heralded for its large tally of people using subsidy programs, numbers that were padded by the heavy recruitment of mothers receiving AFDC. HUD-FHA sold as many as 30,000 subsidized or low-down-payment homes a year in the city. When an ad in Detroit screamed, "Attention ADC Mothers—No Money Down," more than 5,000 women responded. The appeal was particularly "tempting to . . . those who had many children and difficulty renting suitable quarters on welfare income."[51]

Within the first three years, more than 11,000 of these houses were sold to women receiving AFDC in Detroit—women like Alice Mundy.[52] The East Edith Corporation had purchased the "small sagging house" on Detroit's east side for $3,000 before selling it to Mundy one year later for $9,750 with an FHA-approved loan. With her house in appalling condition, including everything from "rat infestation to holes in the ceiling," Mundy called the city to complain. Instead of sanctioning the real estate company, the city fined Mundy because, as the owner of the property, she was responsible for its condition. She would eventually lose her house when she could not afford the fines accrued from violations of the city's housing code.[53]

Mundy was not alone. For Annie Jeminson from Detroit, her old apartment in public housing "smelled bad and it felt bad." Explaining her decision to try homeownership, she said, "I have never had the chance to live in a house in Detroit so when I saw the ad, I decided to call."[54] A real estate broker from Montgomery Real Estate Company showed her one house, insisting that it was the only one available when Jemison asked to see others. Jeminson said, "It looked like a nice house. . . . I don't know nothing about houses but, the walls were nice. They just painted them. He took me down to the basement. The power was off so . . . he lit a match and said the furnace was in a corner. I believed him." Jeminson signed several papers but sought advice from a free legal aid clinic about purchasing the house. The lawyers assured her that the house was fine. Still, she was wary enough of the real estate agent that she asked him to make a list of all of the defects in the house, with a promise that they would be fixed by the time she moved in. The agent, Donald Warren, signed and returned the list but made none of the repairs. Ultimately, Jeminson bought the house for $11,800, only to discover later that the realty company had originally purchased it for $5,000 two months prior. Once she and her three children moved into the house, the real estate company told her the house was now her problem.[55]

Annie Jeminson had sunk all of her savings of $375 into the cost of closing on the house. It had taken her years to raise that money because she was poor. There was no money left over for the major repairs that were necessary to make the house habitable. Despite what Warren had said, the house did not have a furnace, which meant facing the Detroit winter without heat or hot water. Rats lived in multiple dens in her basement. The doors were difficult to open and close, and the windows did not open at all. According to Jeminson, her living room had "one wall . . . [that] was damp and running with moss and water and ice." The conditions in Annie Jeminson's house led to serious health problems for her youngest daughter, three-year old Sandra, requiring her to be hospitalized. Yet despite the condition of the house, the FHA in Detroit approved it for mortgage insurance. After conferring once more with attorneys at a legal aid clinic, Annie Jeminson was advised to stop paying her mortgage in order to force foreclosure proceedings so that she could get out of the house. She and her children moved in October 1972 before the cold weather took hold again. The Jeminsons moved back into a cramped apartment, leaving behind Annie's savings but bringing with them the debt of a foreclosed house. In spite of everything, Jeminson did not view her brief stint as a homeowner as an entirely negative experience. She missed the neighborhood where she had bought her house: "The neighbors were so friendly. It was nice feeling you belonged somewhere. I would have stayed in the house. I would have kept making payments if only it would have had heat and hot water."[56]

Sally Fordham, also of Detroit, saw an ad for the services of Montgomery Real Estate Company in a local newspaper. She decided to take the leap and buy a house. Unlike Annie Jeminson, Sally Fordham was shown three houses within a two-block radius. She chose the smallest of the three, figuring it would be the easiest to maintain. She called it a "beautiful little house, just like a little doll house." Fordham contacted her welfare caseworker, who reminded her to check the house's water pressure before signing any documents. But Fordham was desperate for more living space. She said, "My husband and I separated in 1964 and I had nine kids."[57] As with Annie Jeminson, the real estate agent thrust papers at her, asking for signatures on the spot, and within moments, Sally Fordham was a homeowner.

When she moved in, she quickly discovered that the house had no light switches and that the plumbing was completely defective. There was no pipe connecting the toilet to the sewer, so waste just dropped into the basement. She had paid $12,500 for the house, not knowing that Montgomery Real Estate Company had purchased it hours earlier on the same day for $9,000.[58] Winter came, and she discovered that the oil furnace did not work. It was so old that the parts necessary to repair it were no longer manufactured. Fordham used the gas stove to heat her house until the night it exploded, clogging the house with smoke and black soot. "We are lucky we woke up," she said, relieved. "We would have choked to death for sure." The lack of heat and constant chill meant her two youngest children were often sick, missing days of school at a time. But there was no reprieve in summer. The entire house reeked from the raw sewage settling in the basement. "I bought gallons of Lysol and stuff last summer and poured it down in the basement but nothing seemed to help. We've applied for a place in a public housing project. I don't know what else to do." Just like Annie Jeminson, Fordham was advised by legal aid lawyers to stop making payments on the house. Also like Jeminson, Fordham hadn't asked for much: "All I would like is a good old standard home. Nothing fancy. Just a good home with heat. That's all."[59]

Jemison's and Fordham's stories were not at all unusual. The *Detroit Free Press* found that 41 percent of the 8,000 to 11,000 homes sold to mothers receiving AFDC ended up in default, on their way to foreclosure.[60] This figure was based on a study of only the eleven most active mortgage companies in Detroit; as with most aspects of the FHA's failure, the details are missing.[61] Nevertheless, the concentration of bad loans within the program became a basis upon which Romney would declare poor people no longer eligible for FHA loans. Once again, even though mortgage companies appeared to be targeting mothers on AFDC as likely to fall into foreclosure because of the condition of the housing, it was the mothers who were paying the steepest price. Twenty-one mortgage firms in Detroit held over 1,000 mortgages that were in default. In some firms, more than half of their mortgages were in default.[62] When the *Free Press* conducted an informal survey of ten Detroit houses sold to mothers receiving AFDC under federal subsidy programs, they found results not dissimilar to the findings of the national investigations into the new HUD programs. Real estate speculators were making "handsome profits" by flipping houses and using FHA insurance and the favorable terms of its housing programs.[63] The profit as a percentage of investment was a usurious 59 percent to 69 percent.[64] This was certainly a part of the political economy—and calculation—of the program.

Even when AFDC mothers tried to repair or report the damage to their homes, they were summoned to court for housing code violations after they had called the housing office out of concern for the condition of their property. Women receiving AFDC experienced a 3.5 percent foreclosure rate, which was 150 times higher than the foreclosure rate on conventional mortgages—yet this was still a small percentage of program participants.[65] The percentage of women on welfare who lost their homes to foreclosure in cities was a smaller portion of the overall program, but it received disproportionate news coverage. Media coverage gave the impression that welfare recipients were the primary recipients of HUD help in becoming homeowners. This perception helped to arouse suspicion about the program at a time when welfare usage more generally faced greater scrutiny.[66] Regardless of what the experts insisted, the problems faced by these Black mothers in Detroit had less to do with their lack of sophistication than with the lack of ethics among real estate brokers, mortgage lenders, and FHA appraisers.

THE MILWAUKEE WAY

While HUD-FHA offices in Detroit were being applauded for their heavy use of low-income homeownership programs, Lawrence Katz, who had directed the FHA in Milwaukee, Wisconsin, for nine years, was fired because of his jurisdiction's comparatively slow placement of poor people into FHA-insured homes. Katz said he had predicted the collapse of HUD's low-income homeownership program as early as 1968—as soon as it began. He said, "You are going to have problems. It had to happen. We discussed at a national meeting . . . that no matter how good the condition of a house is when it is bought by a welfare mother, if a repair program is not included, with money coming from the outside, it won't work."[67] Proponents of the program celebrated Katz because he crafted an approach that appeared to be successful. But he did so in overbearing ways that infringed on the freedom of the Black women who were in the program. Perhaps as importantly, for all of the applause that Katz would garner, his resource-laden imprint on homeownership for the poor in Milwaukee also worked to preserve housing segregation instead of challenging it. While it was a short-term solution, strengthening the ghetto would ultimately undermine the housing choices of poor and working-class Black women.

But early on, before his dismissal from HUD in 1971, Katz had led the Wisconsin FHA office beginning in 1962, and in that time, he eventually made the state, especially Milwaukee, a national model for how to tame the problems plaguing the existing housing market. Katz's slow and patient approach had driven the speculators out of the market while atypical collaborations with the state welfare agency had allowed Wisconsin to have the most unique, successful, and underutilized approach to using the Section 235 subsidy in the country—if only on a small scale. Katz began by recognizing the obvious: poor people purchasing homes in a distressed housing market would need additional funds to pay for repairs. Katz was willing to admit and act on the fact that there was no other way that women on very fixed incomes would be able to afford the maintenance necessary to keep up an old house. Indeed, the age of the housing available to African Americans in Milwaukee ranged from forty to seventy years.[68]

HUD-FHA met with officials at the Wisconsin welfare department to inquire into the possibility that the federal agency would guarantee the financial stability of buyers who might have to meet unexpected maintenance expenses. Of thirteen Wisconsin counties, nine agreed to contribute funds to offset the cost of repairs in the homes of AFDC mothers using a homeownership subsidy, earmarking at least $500 per AFDC family as additional annual monies.[69] In Michigan, AFDC mothers received only $5 a month to cover home repairs.[70] The key in Milwaukee, according to Katz, was the assumption that the inner city did not have "prudent buyers."[71] The urban housing market reversed what Katz described as the FHA's "historical assumption" that the "value and price of a home is determined when a prudent buyer and a knowledgeable seller is [sic] present in the inner city."[72] Instead, as Katz asserted, the urban buyer is "frequently uninformed and unskilled."[73]

Perhaps because of this characterization, Katz determined that homeowners on welfare needed more resources to better protect themselves from vultures in the real estate market. Significantly, Wisconsin was also one of the few states to abide by the stipulations within the HUD Act that required debt management training and homeownership counseling for poor people who were utilizing the services of HUD in their quest for homeownership. In doing so, Katz admittedly rejected the FHA's premise of caveat emptor and instead used the bevy of HUD-FHA resources to protect the interests of the homebuyer and HUD. The counseling regimen required for AFDC mothers in Milwaukee was unlike any other. Before buying a house, each prospective homeowner was required to attend classes that explained property taxes, insurance, amortization, and the responsibilities of homeowners, including instructions on making basic home repairs.[74] After they purchased the home, homeowners took more classes on how to varnish floors, repair windowpanes, and replace faucet washers. The women received $106 for attending the classes for eight weeks. They were also provided with funds for childcare and offered free transportation to and from the classes, which were held at the University of Wisconsin. At the end of the classes, the mothers were given $65 worth of tools via government grant.[75]

Once the women finished their homeownership classes and set out to purchase their own homes, a separate set of protocols was followed. Even before the FHA did its appraisal, the state welfare agency sent a team of "housing aides," employed by the Milwaukee County Welfare Department, to inspect the property. A staff of ten housing aides checked "the physical condition of the house . . . to determine that the family [had] adequate living space and basic comforts." Five of the ten housing inspectors were women who had previously received AFDC but had reached greater financial stability. They helped to determine if repairs were needed, and if necessary, they then helped make requests for state welfare funds. The former AFDC recipients were paid $3 an hour for their work, and more importantly, they became a conduit between the AFDC mothers and the welfare agency.[76] The point was to maintain communication and contact with the mothers so that, if problems developed, they would know whom to quickly call. To that end, Katz even reached out to a local Black Power organization called the Commandos, who were the local youth section of the Milwaukee NAACP. In the late 1960s, they, along with a white Catholic priest named Father James Groppi, formed the vanguard of the local open housing movement in Milwaukee.[77] Under Katz, the FHA in Milwaukee called on the Commandos as a social conduit through which to communicate with welfare recipients who remained hostile to the idea that the Department of Welfare would play a continuing role in their lives even after they had become homeowners.[78]

After workers from the welfare department had inspected the house, then and only then would the FHA send its own appraiser to look at the property. Once the house was sold, it would be inspected at least four times a year to monitor its condition, and workers in the employ of the state welfare agency would quickly intervene if repairs were needed. The process of purchasing a home in Milwaukee's version of the FHA's low-income program stood in dramatic contrast to any home-purchasing process, whether subsidized or not. A local church provided the $200 down payment required for Section 235. Once the house had been inspected and the mother was prepared to buy it, a volunteer group of lawyers working for the Office of Economic Opportunity represented the buyer at the closing.[79] Five days prior to the closing, the Wisconsin HUD-FHA required the buyer to examine the house one last time and record any repairs needed. After all of these steps, when the house was finally purchased, the state Department of Welfare agreed to cover the cost of all minor and major repairs necessary to keep the family in the house. When all was said and done, the Office of Economic Opportunity covered 55 percent of the costs of the AFDC homeownership program, 27 percent was covered by the state, and 7.5 percent was covered by the mother, with the help of grants to cover the balance.[80]

Why was Wisconsin, in the midst of national attacks on welfare, willing to invest in homeownership for poor Black mothers receiving AFDC? As it turned out, it cost the state less money to invest in the repairs of old inner-city houses than to pay the constant moving expenses of single mothers. When an AFDC family moved, it cost the state welfare agency $1,000 a day. The average family receiving AFDC moved twice a year, and the state calculated that its total costs were $350,000 annually.[81] Moreover, the Section 235 interest subsidy left the family with a monthly mortgage payment that was cheaper than the typical rent allowance given the average size of the family on welfare. Welfare budgeted $135 as a rent allowance, compared with a $100 monthly mortgage payments for families receiving the Section 235 subsidy.[82]

Despite Katz's obvious success, the Detroit office of HUD had chastised his approach. Said Katz, "We were getting some memos out of the regional office in Chicago indicating that Detroit and some other cities in the country were doing a fine job in volume underwriting of ADC mothers for homeownership.... They said Detroit [was] doing a far greater job than we [were]."[83] In Detroit, the speculators and real estate brokers were providing the down payments to the low-income and poor people to whom they were trying to sell homes, which was illegal. Despite all of the caution of the Wisconsin HUD-FHA and the especially low rate of foreclosure in Milwaukee, Katz was considered "a difficult case."[84] The plodding pace of the program in Milwaukee stood out during the early years of Romney's tenure when production was the main goal. Katz was fired in 1971 as the number of subsidized housing units was soaring and before the HUD-FHA scandals became national news. His fortunes changed one year later when defenders of the homeownership programs rallied to Katz's side and lauded the Milwaukee example as proof that low-income homeownership could work. A *Washington Post* article on an MBA study of the Milwaukee program noted, "Nowhere [is the function of quality counseling] more evident than in the dramatic success of the 235 program in Wisconsin. If [HUD] wants a model program, it would do well to recommend that insuring offices in other states adopt the program of counseling and assistance developed by Wisconsin's former FHA administrator Lawrence Katz."[85]

In congressional hearings, in the newspapers, and among private sector forces defending low-income homeownership, Milwaukee was celebrated as a model for managing homeownership for the poor. Milwaukee, they would say, was proof that the programs could work, but they needed close management, homeowner counseling, and more financial resources. It was obvious, however, when looking at the vast array of services offered by HUD-FHA in Wisconsin, that this was an outlier and not a functional model for cities with the weightiest problems to emulate. The pace was much too slow and the need was too great. In Milwaukee, local officials were offering much more than "counseling"; they required classes, instruction, and the agreement of multiple organizations and public agencies to produce positive outcomes for a small number of people. In Milwaukee, HUD-FHA also provided childcare and paid for the participation of the mothers who had been selected. After this massive expenditure of human and material resources, Katz's success was measured by the effective housing of the families of only 850 women receiving AFDC.

Milwaukee was a city with great need, a deeply segregated housing market, and an urban housing crisis that was a result of poverty and segregation. For all its power to impress, Katz's program accommodated only a drop in the sea of families who needed assistance. By 1972 there were 28,000 families on welfare in Milwaukee, 90 percent of whom were receiving AFDC.[86] The pace at which the HUD-FHA program operated was not enough to efficiently serve the vast numbers of people in desperate need of good housing. It is also doubtful that the program and all of its interlocking components was scalable to Detroit, Philadelphia, or Chicago, where there were even greater numbers of poor families and even more women receiving AFDC.

In Milwaukee, homeownership for poor Black women was the antithesis of what homeownership was for white people. The overbearing nature of the program, including the repeated inspections of the property after closing, resembled public housing tenancy. Instead of independence, security, and investment, homeownership for poor Black women was an invitation to greater state surveillance, continued economic marginality, and the inheritance of a debt burden. There was little question as to whether the homes owned by these women would accrue value and become the foundation of a middle-class lifestyle.

Katz would later say that most of these women would have rather rented; but most rental properties refused large families, and the rent was often too high. In his words, "I am convinced that many of the low-income families currently buying homes in our central cities—if given the alternative—would prefer renting. Many are buying because they have no choice."[87] Pushing these women into homeownership was akin to transferring the housing problems of poor women with children from public housing or the private rental market to the private confines of their own homes, while at the same time saddling them with thousands of dollars of debt over time—hardly an antipoverty program.

Finally, the rehousing of these women within the "Black community" was more proof that the Milwaukee HUD was continuing to operate within, instead of challenging, the segregated housing market. Of course, there was a debate to be had over the urgency of creating housing opportunities within the cities versus allowing open housing opportunities for Black women in the suburbs.

There was existing housing available with the Section 235 subsidy in the suburbs of Milwaukee as well, but those houses did not appear to be on offer. Margaret Lancaster, the chairperson of the Montgomery County Welfare Rights Organization in Maryland, argued, in another setting, that some AFDC mothers would prefer to live in the suburbs, but despite fair housing legislation, that housing was never made available to them. When talking about her own experiences with finding good housing, she said, "When you want to move or you want to move into a better house, you automatically feel that you would like to live somewhere in the suburbs if you have children—that is if you have adequate transportation." Lancaster identified other factors limiting AFDC mothers' access to suburban housing: "If you look for a place out in the suburbs . . . they don't want you because . . . you're black, you're poor and they feel you're going to run the standards of the neighborhood down."[88]

Inattention to the dynamics of race was also evident in the ways that HUD-FHA officials, including Katz, discussed the women at the center of their social experiment. The descriptions of program participants as unknowledgeable reinforced the paternalistic posture of public officials toward poor and working-class African Americans. Katz described Black men and women as almost childlike. When emphasizing the centrality of counseling in his approach to implementing the National Housing Act, he asked, "Where was the black to learn the do-it-yourself skills that we whites take for granted?"[89] Adding insult to injury, the MBA wondered whether the presence of "illegitimate children" in the homes of some AFDC recipients made them "risky," passing on the concerns of insurance companies that were serving as mortgagees for the low-income program.[90] Katz shared their concern but reminded the insurance companies and the mortgage bankers of the bigger issues at stake, arguing,

> If there is serious current promiscuity, the caseworker will so report. This may well be a deterrent to this agency's underwriting. On the other hand, the presence of an illegitimate child in the household will not deter mortgage insurance underwriting and hopefully will be acceptable to the mortgagee. This agency strongly urges the acceptance of this type of mortgagor. Our underwriting and the cooperation of lender and the welfare department will serve as an instrument in encouraging upward mobility, not only for the mother involved, but primarily and significantly for the children growing up in the household—children that within a few years will be young adults of a disadvantaged community. Now is the time for a total community to display its concern by tangible action—not merely talk.[91]

Katz's approach was in step with the "socio-commercial enterprise" of the era, but its paternalism perpetuated racist and sexist depictions of Black women that exacerbated rather than alleviated their condition. The exchange between Katz and the MBA fit comfortably with broader discussions linking welfare and race to the "suitability" of Black homes that were happening at the time. In his part of this discussion, Katz convinced mortgage bankers and insurance executives that the "suspect" behavior and immorality of mothers on welfare could be overcome through counseling.

Katz's dismissal in 1971 ended his innovative approach to counseling, as the Milwaukee FHA ended its precounseling program in general and the Department of Welfare ended its agreement to provide financing for repair services.[92] The upshot of the successful implementation of the Wisconsin program was to turn the national discussion toward counseling as both a cause and a cure for low-income homeownership: the absence of counseling was now seen as the main reason for the failure of the homeownership program, while the use of counseling was offered as a palliative. By the spring of 1972, Romney had named Katz a "special consultant" to HUD's national operations.[93]

GOOD HOUSEKEEPING

Despite the legislative mandate to provide counseling to homebuyers who sought it, between 1968 and 1972, Congress never appropriated funds to make counseling available.[94] Even as Romney identified counseling as important to ending the HUD housing crisis, he did not appear to fight Congress for the money to make it possible. In its budgets for 1969 and 1970, HUD made no appropriations requests for counseling.[95] When HUD finally asked for $3 million for counseling in 1971, Congress rejected the request, and in 1972, HUD once again did not request appropriation for counseling. In 1972, as the crisis was cresting, Congress finally did appropriate over $3 million for counseling, even though HUD had not asked for it.[96] Instead of paying for counseling, however, HUD used the money to conduct a study on the effectiveness of counseling and a training program for counseling agencies.[97] By this time, HUD had already established a thin network of voluntary counseling agencies.

As the number of foreclosures began to increase nationally, and in the wake of Katz's success in Milwaukee, HUD officials raised counseling in a new light: it was presented as a solution—as *the* solution. Even George Romney abruptly declared, "I consider the provision of homeownership counseling services to Section 235 homebuyers of the utmost importance for the successful operation of the program."[98] Counseling, such as that provided in Wisconsin, certainly went a long way toward preparing poor people to move into poor housing, but the turn to counseling as both the explanation for success and the solution to failure continued to elide the bigger issues facing low-income homeownership. Even HUD's own extensive study on the effects of homeownership counseling found that "families who purchased used rather than new housing encountered a larger number of housing condition problems—such as inadequacies in plumbing, heating, and electrical systems—against which FHA administrative safeguards had been ineffective."[99] The emphasis on counseling perpetuated the false idea that a knowledgeable consumer could overcome the institutional or systemic problems within the existing urban housing market. This train of logic crowded out the much more important discussion about the condition of the housing into which poor people were moving. Budgeting skills, housecleaning, and the ability to make small repairs were not unimportant, but they could not overcome many of the structural issues that faced poor families moving into sixty-year-old housing.

In St. Louis, the homes sold to low-income and poor families were full of defects "so fundamental as to suggest that there had been little or no renovation."[100] Of 283 HUD houses that had been foreclosed, 101 "were declared unworthy of repair." That determination was based on simple math: bringing the houses into conformity with FHA standards would cost more than half of "the stated resale price." In the case of Section 221(d)(2) houses, 84 of 259 returned houses were demolished. In 27 of the 84 houses, the homeowner had lived in the house for less than a year before foreclosure and demolition. The rate at which HUD was demolishing foreclosed houses was evidence against the claims of local HUD officials that the poor condition of the homes was a result of poor housekeeping. As the author of the study wrote, "The most startling fact revealed in post-foreclosure files is that HUD decided to demolish more than one-third of the houses it acquired after foreclosure."[101] This was evidence of severe structural deficiencies with the housing as opposed to issues of cleaning or hygiene. As Harry Wilson, the author of the study, put it, "The claim the owners made fictitious allegations about defects in their homes seems ridiculous in view of the condition in which HUD found one-third of these houses. Similarly, the response that ignorance of household skills accounted for the defects is absurd."[102]

Wilson, a former reporter for a major St. Louis daily newspaper, claimed in his notes that he was "frequently" told "off the record" by HUD employees that "those people just don't know how to take care of a home."[103] Wilson said HUD employees who were formerly in the "home building, real estate or mortgage industries" made most of those statements. Indeed, in the very first congressional investigation of Section 235, investigators reported that a "common assertion made by mortgagees, real estate brokers, mortgage bankers, and the FHA" was that Section 235 houses were in good shape, but they were sold to the wrong "type of people"—people who were "so abusive to the property as to render [it] uninhabitable in a short period of time."[104]

Nor was this sentiment confined to the ranks of HUD employees. Senator Henry Reuse, a Democrat from Wisconsin, spoke bluntly in favor of maintenance funds as the "only way to develop homemaking skills in these people."[105] Another congressman proclaimed that he had "observed that the families apparently are too lazy or too indifferent to even pick up a paintbrush and make normal repairs which would be well within their capability of making."[106] These opinions were perfectly in step with comments made by Romney when the first investigations into HUD-FHA low-income homeownership had begun. In a 1970 hearing, Romney had insisted that "in the case of lower income families, you have many . . . who have not had the responsibility of homeownership previously, and therefore . . . [there is a] greater tendency on their part to not undertake the work necessary to maintain the home."[107] The MBA placed the entirety of the blame on the new homeowners' bad habits. "Usable houses are also being abandoned because people do not take care of them—because in many cases they do not know how to take care of them. . . . For many years, the Agriculture Extension Service has successfully aided farm families providing housekeeping and the domestic arts. Institution of the same methods by government or private agencies is a requisite to improving the quality of urban living."[108] Secretary Romney, the congressmen at the hearing, and the men of the MBA did not sound much different from the real estate speculators and bankers who also blamed Black families for the condition of the housing—as they were getting rich from selling them homes. These unscrupulous real estate actors, who, in an effort to distance themselves from scandal, looked to tap into existing ideas that categorically blamed African Americans for the condition of their housing and their neighborhoods, did not have to look far. The idea that Black renters and owners were destructive and careless was so deeply ingrained in the popular consciousness that it was almost effortless to make the charge. HUD even went so far as to produce a fifteen-cent pamphlet, called *Simplified Housekeeping Directions for Homemakers*, for women in subsidized housing on how to clean one's home. The pamphlet included visual instructions on "how to dust furniture" and "how to

SIMPLIFIED HOUSEKEEPING DIRECTIONS

FOR HOMEMAKERS

Housekeeping Job Sheets
for use
With Aspiring Homemakers

Prepared by the Cleanliness Bureau
of the Soap & Detergent Association
with the aid of Extension Service
Home Agents, Home Economists,
and other professionals

Have a Plan to Keep the House Clean

How to Keep a Stove Clean

How to Keep a Refrigerator Clean

How to Clean the Bathroom

How to Clean the Floor

How to Keep Cleaning Tools Clean

How to Dust Furniture

How to Keep Trash Cans Clean

How to Wash Woodwork

How to Be Safe at Home

No, no!

DEPARTMENT OF HOUSING AND URBAN DEVELOPMENT

For sale by the Superintendent of Documents, U.S. Government Printing Office
Washington, D.C. 20402 · Price 15 cents

Simplified Housekeeping Directions for Homemakers. (Urban Archives, Housing Association of Delaware Valley, box 37, Temple University, Philadelphia, Pa.)

keep trash cans clean," among other instructions.[109] But a report from an audit of the Section 235 program refuted this dogma by observing that "no homeowner can be expected to cope with poor construction, cracked foundations, improper wiring, and a general failure of contractors to meet local hiring and maintenance requirements. A welfare mother with four or five children may well have a house

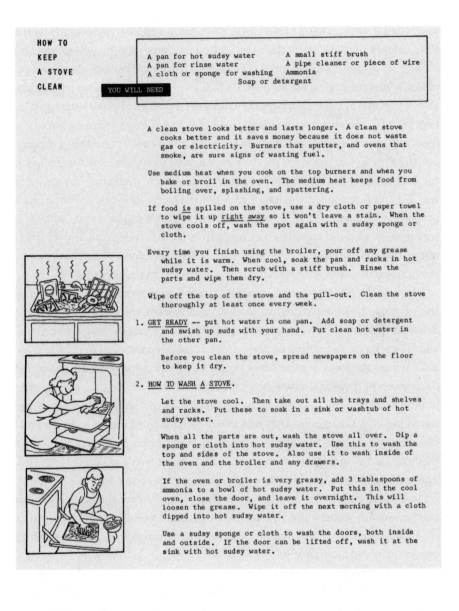

HOW TO
KEEP
A STOVE
CLEAN

A pan for hot sudsy water	A small stiff brush
A pan for rinse water	A pipe cleaner or piece of wire
A cloth or sponge for washing	Ammonia
	Soap or detergent

YOU WILL NEED

A clean stove looks better and lasts longer. A clean stove cooks better and it saves money because it does not waste gas or electricity. Burners that sputter, and ovens that smoke, are sure signs of wasting fuel.

Use medium heat when you cook on the top burners and when you bake or broil in the oven. The medium heat keeps food from boiling over, splashing, and spattering.

If food is spilled on the stove, use a dry cloth or paper towel to wipe it up right away so it won't leave a stain. When the stove cools off, wash the spot again with a sudsy sponge or cloth.

Every time you finish using the broiler, pour off any grease while it is warm. When cool, soak the pan and racks in hot sudsy water. Then scrub with a stiff brush. Rinse the parts and wipe them dry.

Wipe off the top of the stove and the pull-out. Clean the stove thoroughly at least once every week.

1. GET READY -- put hot water in one pan. Add soap or detergent and swish up suds with your hand. Put clean hot water in the other pan.

   Before you clean the stove, spread newspapers on the floor to keep it dry.

2. HOW TO WASH A STOVE.

   Let the stove cool. Then take out all the trays and shelves and racks. Put these to soak in a sink or washtub of hot sudsy water.

   When all the parts are out, wash the stove all over. Dip a sponge or cloth into hot sudsy water. Use this to wash the top and sides of the stove. Also use it to wash inside of the oven and the broiler and any drawers.

   If the oven or broiler is very greasy, add 3 tablespoons of ammonia to a bowl of hot sudsy water. Put this in the cool oven, close the door, and leave it overnight. This will loosen the grease. Wipe it off the next morning with a cloth dipped into hot sudsy water.

   Use a sudsy sponge or cloth to wash the doors, both inside and outside. If the door can be lifted off, wash it at the sink with hot sudsy water.

that is in less than spotless condition, but they cannot be blamed because there is only one electrical outlet in the entire house and no heat or even heating vents in any of the bedrooms on the second floor of the house."[110]

Wilhelmina Gause, the African American mother in Philadelphia whose badly damaged home was the subject of federal investigation because she had purchased it with an FHA-backed loan, was scrutinized more thoroughly by the Philadelphia office of HUD than the real estate agent who pressured her into buying her house. After an initial congressional investigation into the condition of Gause's home in 1971, the local HUD office followed up with its own investigation. In an article that didn't get the same fanfare as the original investigation, Gause and others like her were disparaged. The conditions in Gause's home immediately raised questions as to how the FHA could have insured the property. For the FHA agents involved, the answer appeared to be relatively simple: when the house was sold, it was in good condition, but that changed after Gause moved in: "This property appears to have had very hard recent usage . . . and little or no proper maintenance."[111] The local office's investigation claimed that "while it is very possible that our appraisers occasionally missed an item requiring repair . . . it is our belief that most of the conditions cited by the House Select Committee were caused by inadequate maintenance subsequent to the appraisal."[112]

Blaming the poor served a purpose. HUD officials desperately wanted to keep the narrative from becoming one of federal officials signing off on criminally defective houses—a task made much easier by the fact that the story of negligent and lazy poor people failing to perform basic maintenance was so readily available. Where the story of poor Black people as willful culprits would not fit, the description of them as overwhelmed and ignorant and devoid of common sense in purchasing a home was alternatively pursued. In testimony before a congressional hearing, George Romney was asked about a particular case in Newark, New Jersey, that was like many others in that the buyer had been duped by a shady real estate speculator. Romney cut off the questioner and blurted out, "You know, Mr. Congressman, it is amazing what goes on. Some of these people . . . some of these people that buy homes never go in to inspect the home. . . . I just can't personally understand how people in all aspects of this situation could be doing what they have [been] doing. You wouldn't think of buying a home without going in and looking at it."[113]

It was inconceivable to the white men testifying in congressional hearings or editorializing in the pages of the MBA journal how anyone could buy a house for $12,000 that was riddled with code violations, ranging from a leaking roof to a flooded basement. They could not comprehend what it was like to live in conditions that made *anything* else seem better. They could not understand that *they*—rather than "unsophisticated" low-income Black homeowners—were, in fact, the ones in need of an education. The depth of racial segregation was so complete that white people could not *see* what the Black housing market looked like. And even when they knew it existed, they could count on the fact that the majority of the white voting population—steeped in centuries of racism and looking on from the other side of the divide—could not.

As Philadelphia resident and mother of seven Mary Sims put it, "When I first heard about the FHA-235 program, I thought it was too good to be true. I know the government never gave Blacks anything for nothing, but I had hopes because you can't get a decent apartment anymore."[114] Mary Sims pointed out the dilemma facing Black mothers without partners and other poor women who were overrepresented in the homeownership programs. The desperation for housing in a rental market overwhelmed with damaged and substandard properties made these women vulnerable to the housing scams that pervaded government programs. It was simply wrong to suggest that Black women on welfare had many good options in their search for better housing. A mother of ten, addressing a conference on social welfare in Virginia, talked about the desperate living conditions she faced in her rented apartment. After she and her children moved from her mother's home into a four-room apartment across the street, she noted, "With ten children we were cramped, but that was not the worst problem." She continued: "The water pipes were always breaking, and this meant no water and leaks. The floor around the commode was rotted from the water, it leaked so often . . . the mantle piece fell over into the front room, all in one piece. If my baby had been there it most likely would have killed her. That is when I began to feel that I just had to move. I had asked the rent lady to fix these things, all along. She always said she would, if I gave her the rent, but she never did."[115] These pitiful conditions of housing and the abusive attacks on poor, disproportionately Black women did not go without notice or response. When African American congresswoman Shirley Chisholm addressed 1,000 people at an NAACP event in Andover, Massachusetts, she delivered a blistering assessment of the federal agency:

> The FHA [is] marked by a legacy of racism and profiteering in the administration of previous housing programs and has knowingly tolerated the development of federally financed slums, the perpetuation and acceleration of segregated housing patterns and the gouging of the poor by speculators, builders and bankers who all pocket federal dollars for violating federal laws. FHA has turned an official back to the victims of blockbusting and profiteering and it has tolerated corruption in its own ranks and it has sanctioned a policy of "separate and unequal" in its administration of

subsidized programs. These are strong words and the facts stand behind them. The FHA is both industry oriented and industry controlled.[116]

In a position paper presented at a conference, an unknown representative from the recently formed Congressional Black Caucus described how "subsidized housing for poor families is being deceptively presented to the American public as a sociological and financial disaster attributable to the character of the occupants themselves." The paper linked these attacks to a larger political agenda looking to upend public support for housing subsides more generally. The author quoted an article from *Fortune* magazine that essentially criticized housing subsidies as a form of social welfare. The critic described the former head of HUD Robert Weaver as having "turned the main emphasis of federal housing policy away from reinforcing the private market and toward subsidies for the expanding list of people."[117] It was an assertion that lacked legitimacy, considering that the overwhelming beneficiaries of subsidies were the private sector forces that were being paid in multiple ways to participate in the urban market. It was also true that the greatest number of foreclosures were happening in the unsubsidized housing programs like Section 221(d)(2). As the Congressional Black Caucus recognized, "Subsidy has become a dirty word with connotations of race and class."[118]

In hindsight, the focus on maintenance, counseling, and the morality of poor mothers consciously deflected attention away from the larger and systemic problem of the FHA's relationship with its private partners in the real estate and banking industries. As John Herbers of the *New York Times* argued, "The Federal Housing Administration has been permissive with the private interests involved, permitting them to take advantage of consumers in many instances. . . . Charges are beginning to be heard that the housing industry is becoming like the defense industry, dependent on government support and thus less efficient than industries in private competition."[119]

CRIME WAVE

Federal investigations and criminal indictments implicating federal officials, real estate operatives, and members of the banking and finance industry made curious the suggestion that AFDC mothers and other poor people should have been a focal point of HUD's existing housing crisis. Between 1971 and the fall of 1972, the Inspector General's Office, the FBI, and the Justice Department initiated more than 4,000 investigations into charges made by FHA-assisted low-income homeowners.[120]

These cases involved not only low-ranking FHA staff but also high-ranking officials. There were allegations of fraud surrounding the directors in Miami, St. Louis, and New Orleans as well. In New Orleans and Miami, the directors received thirty-day suspensions without pay because they accepted preferential loan terms on their own residences.[121] There were even rumors that 300 pending indictments were being held until after the 1972 presidential election.[122] By the end of 1972, forty-eight people had been imprisoned and another eighty-four individuals were on probation for crimes committed in connection with the homeownership programs. These numbers did not reflect the depth of the problem. Federal investigators from the "office of audit reports" also exposed how regional and local offices did not always refer cases that were in need of criminal investigation. One report noted, "Our reviews in Washington, D.C., Richmond, Virginia, Pittsburgh and Philadelphia, Pennsylvania, revealed that 85 subjects involved in 48 insured transactions deserved investigatory follow up." These cases were to be remanded to the FBI, but after three months had passed, the audit office found that the "operating officials had not referred any of the subjects to investigatory action."[123] The criminal indictments from around the country demonstrated that housing speculation and profiteering at the expense of poor people could not be dismissed as lowbrow crime carried out by con artists and "fast-buck" thieves; rather, it involved sophisticated networks of actors, including "lowly appraisers and prominent FHA chiefs, rich realtors and middle-level bureaucrats."[124]

In describing the scandal plaguing HUD-FHA, the *Washington Post* noted that "the Justice Department . . . investigations of FHA frauds [were] underway in twenty cities, making this one of the biggest white-collar prosecutions in history."[125] At the end of 1973, 180 indictments involving 317 persons "engaged in inner city programs of HUD" had been handed down by grand juries. By 1974, the directors of three metropolitan FHA insurance offices had been indicted, including in Philadelphia; Hempstead, New York, on Long Island; and Coral Gables, Florida. In Philadelphia, the top FHA official went to prison.[126]

Perhaps the first indication that HUD's issues with real estate speculation and fraud went far beyond local hustlers and "suede shoe" swindlers came with federal charges against the powerful Dun & Bradstreet credit agency in New York City. In 1972, the agency was charged with twenty-four counts of bribery, fraud, and conspiracy. Dun & Bradstreet played a critical role in an expansive plot to sell "depressed-area homes by real estate speculators to low-income blacks and Puerto Ricans," with the hope that they would default on their loans quickly.[127] After a few months, when a homeowner fell into foreclosure, it was not uncommon for the same house to be quickly resold under the same dubious terms to another unsuspecting family. In total, forty individuals, including seven FHA employees; a public official; and ten corporations were indicted for bribery and fraud involving home foreclosures of 2,500 homes that cost the FHA insurance fund $200 million.

The Dun & Bradstreet scheme worked in a fashion similar to housing fraud scams in other cities: in order to secure a large loan for purchase of a property with an inflated price, a speculator convinced a prospective homeowner to sign a blank credit report, which was then taken to a mortgage bank. A mortgage banker in on the conspiracy would take the blank report to the people at Dun & Bradstreet, who would give the homeowner a favorable credit report that allowed for an even larger loan. The mortgage company would then pay off an FHA employee to inflate the value of a property for sale and confirm its good condition. If a house were to be found in obvious disrepair, a crooked contractor would sign false papers claiming repairs had been made on the house.[128] The intricacy of the fraud resulted in a 500-count indictment against multiple parties across the New York housing industry. As a result, HUD suspended the eighty-seven offices of Dun & Bradstreet from doing any further business with the agency for an undisclosed period of time. Federal prosecutor Anthony Accetta understood the long-term effects of this fraud: "I don't see how anyone who is Black or Puerto Rican could have faith in the white system after being shaken down like this and then losing his house two months later."[129]

In Philadelphia, mortgage companies rewarded speculators who brought in new clients, no matter the unscrupulous methods used. One company, the United Brokers Mortgage Company (UBMC), took real estate speculators who met mortgage-bank-determined quotas for recruiting unsuspecting poor homeowners on all-expenses-paid cruises.[130] The UBMC had real estate agents compete with one another for a spot on a cruise based on achieving a predetermined number of sales. A letter sent to brokers by the UBMC reminded them, "The contest is now almost over for the trip to Barbados. Get on the bandwagon and make that last effort to join us on this vacation."[131]

On one of these excursions, Delores Tucker, an African American woman who managed the Pennsylvania state office that investigated complaints about real estate brokers, accompanied forty real estate speculators and officials with the UBMC on an eight-day cruise in the Caribbean.[132] In addition to Tucker's role as a regulator, she was also a licensed real estate broker and a stockholder in the UBMC. Not surprisingly, the UBMC was notorious in Philadelphia. The UBMC was accused of having "processed more mortgages on defective inner-city houses than any other Philadelphia lending institution—all insured by the FHA or the Veterans Administration."[133] Indeed, Tucker's husband, William Tucker, was a well-connected real estate speculator who had sold enough properties with UBMC mortgages that he was invited to participate in the cruise. In the months prior to the cruise, the *Inquirer* disclosed that in North Philadelphia the Tucker real estate agency had sold a home in which the entire back wall had collapsed just six months later. Though riddled with violations, the house was nevertheless purchased with a mortgage insured by the FHA.[134]

In Philadelphia, the corruption was so well integrated into the normal workings of the FHA that even an elected official, William Wilcox, the secretary of community affairs for the state of Pennsylvania, complained that it "seem[ed] as though the forces of government were arrayed in an alliance with the speculators . . . to victimize the poor."[135] Wilcox contrasted the treatment of poor African Americans in Philadelphia to that of wealthy white people and the public developments in their neighborhoods. He noted that in Washington Square, an affluent neighborhood in Philadelphia, a consultant was hired by the city to make sure each house being rehabilitated was up to standard. Conversely, "in most cases, poor black men and women [were] given [no] real protection against fraud and abuse."[136] By the summer of 1972, 133 individuals had been indicted, including 80 real estate brokers; 12 FHA employees, including the regional director of the FHA; and 11 contractors. Several of the real estate speculators indicted worked for the UBMC and had been invited on earlier cruises.

In Detroit, a grand jury indicted more than 100 government officials, real estate speculators, and repair contractors. One real estate speculator, who became a witness for the government, said that he had paid the FHA's "chief deputy appraiser" in Detroit more than $100,000 in bribes over a three-year period.[137] In response to corruption in Detroit, the federal government indicted four officials working with HUD-FHA. The four were "responsible for more than half of all appraisals made by the Detroit Federal Housing Administration office."[138] Indicted along with them were the real estate speculators they had colluded with in the conspiracy to defraud poor Black buyers. After a three-month investigation into the activities of the HUD Detroit office, officials there banned twenty-five housing repair firms from doing work with the city.[139] In order for HUD to more quickly process demands for housing, it had waived the requirement that FHA appraisers do an in-person inspection to confirm that the repairs had been completed. Astoundingly, given the context, HUD-FHA had chosen to use the honor system, based on the affirmative statements of contractors. Investigators found that at least twenty-five firms accepted payments for work that was never performed.[140] The twenty-five firms identified handled 20 percent of FHA work orders, amounting to $8 million worth of work over twelve months. Emmitt Newell, who was deputy chief of the FHA appraisal office, was accused of "inflat[ing] prices on buildings sold to Detroit's poor." He was also accused of thirty-six counts of accepting bribes.[141]

The strain of scrutiny on Romney motivated him to send a memo to the staff and agents of HUD-FHA declaring, "I am sick and tired of the cases being brought to my attention by the press, the Congress, the Justice Department, and our office of inspector general, which show that some of our employees are accepting favors in the form of meals, gifts, entertainment, preferential treatment in business dealings and other gratuities from those who participate in our programs. There is no excuse for this kind of petty chiseling and in some cases outright bribery."[142]

Of course, not just HUD-FHA employees were taking advantage of the situation. Even a U.S. senator, Edward Gurney, a Republican from Florida, was indicted for conspiracy, fraud, and making false statements to the grand jury that ultimately charged him.[143] He was a stalwart Nixon supporter who sat on the Senate Watergate committee, so his legal troubles intersected with the president's. Gurney was the first sitting senator in fifty years to be indicted for a crime. He was charged with depositing bribes, upward of $233,000, from builders and developers into a slush fund used to finance his reelection campaign and pay for other personal expenses. Developers and builders eager to secure contracts for subsidized Section 235 housing paid a kickback to Gurney to jump the line of those waiting for the opportunity to build the subsidized developments. He was eventually acquitted of five of seven charges, and a jury deadlocked on the additional two charges. Nevertheless, Gurney was forced to resign in 1974 after bowing out of his reelection campaign. In the end, he blamed his assistant and claimed his only crime was being "careless, unobservant, and too trusting."[144]

To the chagrin of Nixon's political team, the constant turmoil over housing issues was a major distraction in the midst of an election year. Chatter about scandal, fraud, and indictments posed an unexpected nuisance that Nixon's closest aides wanted to shut down permanently. Although the HUD housing scandal rarely emerged as an election issue, when it did, it exposed a potential political threat. In a rare statement on the issue, George McGovern, running as the Democratic Party presidential nominee, aptly skewered the Nixon administration: "For four years, the FHA programs passed by Congress to make it possible for middle income and poor families to purchase homes . . . have served as engines of destruction in Detroit, Chicago, St. Louis . . . and New York. Manned by political hacks and favor-seekers, FHA has become a sewer of bribery and fraud, infested by corrupt officials, real estate speculators, and shady mortgage sharpshooters. Greedy middlemen have picked the FHA clean, leaving urban America with a vast array of abandoned houses and a vast army of homeless families."[145]

HOMEOWNER'S RIGHTS

On August 4, 1970, Liza Mae Perry, Ida Mae Foster, Ada Coleman, and Sandra Fox of Seattle, Washington, had their lawyer write a letter of complaint to the FHA.[146] They had all purchased homes in Seattle using the Section 235 subsidy, but instead of basking in the pride of new homeownership, they had found, as their lawyer wrote, that "the 235 program was not all it had been held up to be. For instead of the peaceful security of a decent and sanitary home, they found themselves beset with a nightmare of leaking and stopped up plumbing, sparking electrical switches, flooded basements and innumerable other defects."[147]

Perry, Foster, Coleman, and Fox had contacted the Legal Services offices to find recourse for the damaged homes they had purchased. As would be the case in several lawsuits against HUD because of Section 221(d)(2) and Section 235, these women were the lead defendants in a class-action lawsuit demanding reimbursement for money spent to repair their homes as well as attempting to force HUD to change its approach to its existing housing program. All four women were AFDC recipients who "were happy and excited about finally getting a home of their own."[148] All were told that the homes had been "FHA approved," but after they moved in, the houses quickly began to fall apart.

The basis of their lawsuit was simple. This was not a tough-luck case of caveat emptor; indeed, Congress had made the provision that for "existing" housing sold with the Section 235 subsidy, the property "*shall* . . . meet the requirements of all state laws, or local ordinances or regulations relating to the public health or safety, zoning or otherwise which may be applicable thereto."[149] In other words, selling these deeply damaged homes was a violation of the law as it was written.

This partly explained why HUD and other officials connected to the program were so invested in blaming the program participants. The suit raised other questions about how properties in such disrepair could be sold with a positive FHA appraisal. All four homes in question in the Seattle class-action lawsuit had been inspected by the city of Seattle within weeks of purchase, whereupon they were declared unfit to live in and subsequently condemned.[150]

Of course, these were not the only legally documented cases of women who were targeted by real estate speculators and sold faulty houses. In Denver, Carol Currie, Carol Barber, Barbara Brown, Virginia Roberts, and Joyce Richardson told similar stories of buying "FHA-approved" homes that shortly thereafter had fallen into deep disrepair.[151] Letters from Legal Aid attorneys were pouring in from around the country: Seattle, Spokane, and Everett, Washington; St. Louis, Missouri; Denver, Colorado; Philadelphia, Pennsylvania; Paterson, New Jersey; St. Paul, Minnesota, and elsewhere. In Kansas City, Thelma Herring, Lenora Richards, Queen Thompson, Maddie Trotter, and Enola Vaughn were poor Section 235 homeowners receiving welfare.[152] They, too, were threatening to sue HUD-FHA, with the help of Legal Aid, because of the dismal condition of their homes.

Mounting complaints made their way into local newspapers and eventually to the desks of various representatives within a short year of the 1968 HUD Act being set in motion. George Gould, an attorney representing a group of poor women from Philadelphia, was invited to address a subcommittee of the House of Representatives about the HUD homeownership programs. His words described the torment of many: "Thousands of families in Philadelphia are now living in FHA insured houses, which the Philadelphia Department of Licenses and Inspection aptly describes as, 'unfit for human habitation.' . . . The inspection[s] of these properties by the FHA were atrocious. Conflicts of interest prevailed at every level. Although the purchasers were ignored, FHA made sure that the economic interests of the speculator and mortgage companies were all protected."[153] As a result of the pressure created by the threat of litigation, HUD was forced to acknowledge that it had helped facilitate the sale of faulty properties in its existing housing program. In the 1970 Housing Act, Congress included a new provision, listed as Section 518(b), which allowed Section 235 subsidized homeowners to be reimbursed for damages in the amounts that they had paid to have repairs done in their homes.[154] This was a victory for the thousands of poor women, many of whom were welfare recipients, who had been coerced into buying damaged homes out of desperation for better housing.

Homeowners had until the end of the year, December 1972, to make a claim for reimbursement for repairs made or payment for rehabilitation of their homes. Given the time constraints, HUD made little effort to let Section 235 homeowners know that this new program existed. Instead, HUD called on mortgage companies that had supplied loans to program participants to inform their clients that money for home repair was available.[155] Given the role of a significant number of mortgage companies in facilitating the sale of faulty properties to poor homeowners, relying on them to inform homeowners of their new rights undermined the reparative nature of the legislation. As a result of this lackluster effort, by October 1971, with only months left on the hard deadline for filing a claim, HUD had spent only $51,000 nationally for either reimbursing homeowners or providing grants for home repair.[156]

The process by which claims were evaluated also influenced this low number. In Philadelphia, for example, by October 1971, 159 families had filed claims under Section 518(b), but all had been denied because the director of the Philadelphia FHA rejected the premise of the program.[157] A Philadelphia representative of the FHA inflamed poor homeowners further when he said that he was "sick and tired" of street demonstrations after Section 235 homeowners set up pickets in front of the Philadelphia FHA office.[158] The lethargic pace and bad attitude with which HUD-FHA approached its new legal responsibility to Section 235 homeowners inspired grassroots activism and renewed legal action.

Section 235 homeowners formed the Concerned Section 235 Homeowners. The organization met in the Community Legal Services office of attorney George Gould, which was funded by the Office of Economic Opportunity. The group formed with an eye toward litigation against HUD-FHA for reimbursement, to make permanent Section 518(b), and to include Section 221(d)(2) homeowners within an expanded law. Section 518(b) only addressed defects in Section 235 homes. It left wholly untouched the Section 221(d)(2) program, which made up the bulk of homes sold to poor people by way of government support in Philadelphia. Philadelphia was second only to Detroit in the number of homes repossessed as a result of foreclosure in the low-income homeownership programs. In 1968, HUD-FHA had no houses in its Philadelphia inventory, but by 1974 it held 4,176.[159] Thousands of these homes had been purchased under the Section 221(d)(2) program, but their owners had been left with no legal remedy.

Sarah Porcher, a mother of four and co-chair of Concerned Section 235 Homeowners, summed up the feelings of many when she spoke at a rally in front of the FHA offices in Philadelphia: "The abuses of FHA have been exposed time and time again. . . . By law we are entitled to have our homes repaired, but how many of our homes have been repaired? How many of us live in the 'decent homes' we were promised? Hundreds of us 235 homeowners still live in run down shacks that get shoddy repairs at best."[160] Porcher's home had twenty-seven defects, which had cost her $1,000 to repair before she found out about Section 518(b). In an open letter to HUD published in the *Philadelphia Tribune*, the city's main Black daily, Concerned Section 235 Homeowners articulated the frustrations of thousands of other poor homeowners across Philadelphia:

> The lower people in the bureaucracy of HUD . . . have failed to meet the housing repair needs of 235 homeowners. . . . They have broken many promises with regard to getting the work moving and reimbursing the homeowners. There is never any explanation of what is going on, merely a blanket promise that everything will go better and "they will take care of it." People cannot live in these intolerable situations. To date, HUD has done almost nothing to correct the abuses of the Section 235 program. It is the stand of the Concerned 235 Homeowners that further action must be taken in whatever form we see necessary.[161]

In 1972, Carmel McCrudden, along with hundreds of other Section 221(d)(2) homeowners, formed the Concerned 221(d)(2) Homeowners and eventually the Concerned City-Wide Homeowners, which included both Section 221 and Section 235 homeowners.[162] McCrudden's public statements in response to the demeaning queries concerning why these families would buy such a poorly conditioned home helped to articulate the experiences of many Section 221 and Section 235 buyers. McCrudden had purchased her home for $9,000 shortly after the passage of the HUD Act. She noted that when she went to look at the house, a family was still living in it, and the carpet and furniture covered holes and other major defects inside. But McCrudden also noted that she was not a licensed electrician, plumber, or carpenter, and the expectation that she or any other layperson could identify major structural issues within a house was unrealistic. Still, McCrudden and her husband complained about the condition of the house, and the real estate broker assured them that repairs would be made prior to their moving in. Later, the broker went so far as to produce notices certifying that the work they had requested had been performed. Momentarily satisfied, the McCruddens moved in—only to realize that none of the work promised had been completed. By then, it was too late.[163] When McCrudden was asked to

speak before a congressional hearing on criminal activity in government housing, she spoke passionately on behalf of the poor Black women who had become
the face of the issues in the existing housing program. McCrudden said, "A year
later, the homeowner wonders if it was all worth it. She's tired of living in a half-
built, torn apart house. Sometimes she feels she would have been better off with
what she started with. . . . As the concerned 221(d)(2) and 235 homeowners of
Philadelphia, we don't want to go backwards, back to the projects, back to slum
apartments. We want to make homeownership work for low- and moderate-
income families."[164]

Homeowner organizing and protest began to coalesce around another class-
action lawsuit. For months, Section 235 and Section 221(d)(2) homeowners
across Philadelphia had been lodging complaints about their homes with George
Gould, a staff attorney at Community Legal Services. Gould was one of the attorneys who contacted congressional investigators, so Philadelphia was included
in their inaugural report. When that report was subsequently leaked to *Philadelphia Inquirer* reporters Donald Barlett and James Steele, their investigation
eventually helped to produce dozens of indictments of Philadelphia businessmen, bankers, and FHA employees.[165]

Months after the 1970 congressional investigation was completed, Gould filed
a class-action lawsuit on behalf of Rubylee Davis, Janie Barnes, Maria Figueroa,
Janice Johnson, and Maxine Lewis. The Philadelphia lawsuit involved the same
issues as the Seattle lawsuit filed by Perry, Foster, Coleman, and Fox and added to
a growing demand for accountability from the FHA locally. Several months after
the Philadelphia filing, federal FHA officials issued new regulations regarding
subsidized and unsubsidized low-income homeowners that were applicable only
in "eastern Pennsylvania." The mounting pressure from grassroots homeowner
activists, the relentless coverage from city newspapers, and the lawsuit filed by
Community Legal Services forced HUD-FHA to adjust—if only locally. The new
FHA rules for Philadelphia made mortgage companies financially responsible for
defective houses sold with FHA mortgage insurance.[166] If a mortgage company
signed off on a mortgage for a defective house, then the company, not the FHA,
would be responsible for reimbursing the homeowner or providing a grant to pay
for the repair. The point was for the mortgage company to verify the completion
of repairs that were certified by contractors. The new rules required that all properties be thoroughly inspected for defects prior to purchase, which meant that
mortgage companies assumed responsibility for correcting legitimate complaints

TROUBLED — Mrs. Gladys Harris, who still has contractor's paraphernalia in her living room, says of her $8,000 job: "My daddy was a contractor and a builder but I never seen my father do this botched-up work. I never seen nothing like this done before in my life."

Mrs. Gladys Harris holds her head in frustration with the condition of her home. (*Philadelphia Inquirer*, March 5, 1972. Photo by Michael Viola. Used with permission of *Philadelphia Inquirer* Copyright© 2019. All rights reserved.)

and assuring that contractors completed the work for which they were responsible. In addition, the seller was responsible for explaining and documenting how each defect in a house had been repaired before settlement.

George Gould of Community Legal Services liked the direction the new rules were heading but had some reservations: "It does show FHA is finding the strength and guts to stand up to the mortgage companies . . . but I don't think it is the answer." He explained further, "This fails to put the FHA in line. The whole problem is to get good inspection. I think the FHA has to be held responsible for that. I don't think it's fair to put it all on the mortgage companies." For Gould, the FHA was still shirking its responsibilities as a public agency by clinging to its hands-off approach. He said, "This is typical of the FHA in not recognizing that they are responsible for some of these things."[167]

Among the most courageous of the women who went public was Johnnie D. Brown. Brown was a mother of six receiving AFDC when she was struck with an illness that landed her in the hospital for a week. The illness, in combination with a late welfare check, meant that she missed a mortgage payment. Brown spent several months sending in partial payments until she believed that she had caught up with her debt, only to be charged a $625 legal fee that she then refused to pay. At that point, her mortgage lender initiated a foreclosure.[168] Brown went to a local attorney to complain, and they filed a class-action lawsuit on behalf of her and hundreds of other homeowners. The basis of the lawsuit was that the "fast foreclosures" of the mortgage companies were a violation of HUD's own policies that stipulated, as a requirement of banks accepting the Section 235 subsidy, that foreclosure could only be a last resort, not a first option. But Brown's attorneys also argued that the actions of HUD and the mortgage lenders were a violation of the Fourteenth Amendment's equal protection clause, because subsidized homeowners were being treated differently from other homeowners when rapid foreclosure processes were initiated on their properties. FHA lenders were looking to cash in on the extra points paid on the closing costs. These were monies that could be recouped in addition to the full mortgage at the end of a foreclosure proceeding. For homeowners receiving conventional loans, there were no added points and so there was no incentive for a "fast foreclosure."

HUD immediately tried to have the case dismissed on the basis that no legitimate claims were being made, but a federal judge disagreed. Judge Hubert Will delivered a blistering ruling in which he allowed the lawsuit to continue because "the situation is made further suspect by the plaintiffs' contention that HUD has constructed these programs so that it is financially advantageous for mortgagees to move for an early foreclosure."[169] He continued in his ruling: "HUD has apparently preferred to become the largest owner of abandoned slum buildings in the Chicago area rather than monitor these mortgages or take steps to assist mortgagers with bona fide economic crisis.... HUD has forced foreclosures rather than taking action to prevent them. If HUD had deliberately set out to frustrate the Congressional purpose and sabotage the program, it could have hardly done so more effectively.... [HUD] caters to mortgage companies."[170] This case caused an uproar because it challenged the deference of HUD to the mortgage banks and threatened to disrupt the lucrative relationship between the two. The judge chastised HUD for apparently believing "its commitment [was] limited to assisting poor families in acquiring a mortgage but that the commitment somehow evaporates thereafter."[171] Indeed, HUD-FHA included in its guidelines that banks do all in their power to keep homeowners in their homes, including allowing late payments and creating agreements to allow repayment over time. But mortgage bankers ignored the guidelines, claiming that they were not requirements or the law. As a result of the ruling in the Brown case, there was a push to transform the guidelines into regulations bound by law. The success of the Brown lawsuit would remove the financial incentives for mortgage banks to remain engaged in the FHA market to the extent they had been. As one banker responded, "We have an obligation to be fair to them and to be reasonable when they have problems. But we don't have a social welfare obligation to do everything possible to keep them in the house."[172]

BY 1974, THE EXPERIENCES of the four women from Seattle had been multiplied thousands of times as complaints and legal action against HUD-FHA mounted. The stories of low-income homeowners, predominately women, from across the country were critical for multiple reasons. Foremost was the willingness of Perry, Foster, Coleman, and Fox and many others like them to make their deplorable housing situations publicly known acted as a catalyst in exposing the malfeasance, corruption, and fraud pervasive in HUD-FHA's transactions in its subsidized and unsubsidized, existing and new housing programs. The public proclamations of these disproportionately African American and almost always poor women offered a counternarrative to the popular argument of HUD and George Romney that these homeowners were ultimately responsible for the poor condition of their homes. As historian Rhonda Williams has written, "In response to the 'ghetto' conditions of postindustrial capitalism, the flowering of vociferous struggles, and social disrepute, low-income black women waged their own battles for citizenship based on achieving empowerment, human dignity, and other basic necessities of human existence."[173] The demands of the disproportionate number of poor and Black women who were willing to file lawsuits and fight for their rights as homeowners threatened to upend the preconceived notions of these women as undeserving, unprepared, and unsophisticated. Their situation was typical for the women who were preyed on in HUD's homeownership programs. There was an expectation that HUD-FHA as a federal agency would take some responsibility to protect its own interests and the interests of the public. But the attacks on housing subsidies as an undeserved form of welfare were part of a revanchist strategy that sought to sunder public programs and services from the obligation of government.[174] This strategy was rationalized by depicting poor and working-class African Americans not just as undeserving but also as domestically dysfunctional, violent, and criminal. With the threat of collective urban violence drifting further into the background, the actors most hostile to the Johnson welfare state went on the offensive.

6

The Urban Crisis Is Over— Long Live the Urban Crisis!

Blacks and the poor in America have travelled through the
New Deal, Fair Deal, New Frontier and the Great Society only
to find themselves with no deal.—Amiri Baraka, 1973

IN MARCH 1973, nearly four months after Richard Nixon soundly defeated
Democrat George McGovern and began his second term as chief executive of
the United States, the president declared an end to the "urban crisis." Taking
to the airwaves, Nixon cited numerous statistics charting a decline in crime,
cleaner air, and record numbers of low-income housing units having been built
during his first term. These all indicated that, in his words, "today, America is no
longer coming apart.... The hour of crisis has passed. The ship of state is back
on an even keel, and we can put behind us the fear of capsizing."[1] Among the
barometers Nixon deployed, perhaps the most telling was that "civil disorders
[had] also declined." When Nixon ran for president in 1968, he ran against the
Great Society and the notion that the government should play a significant role
in social support and the distribution of social welfare. Yet once he won, his administration was thrust—by the centrifugal force of urban rebellion—into the
role of managing the Great Society instead of euthanizing it.

It was fear of the easily combustible American city that kept Nixon at bay.
Of course, the Democratic Party still controlled Congress, but the five years of
violent upheaval that ended the 1960s had exerted a kind of discipline on elected
officials of both parties, who looked to perform surgery, as opposed to amputa-
tion, on domestic spending that had grown with each spasm of rebellion. By the

early 1970s, the threat of violence had been replaced by campaigns for political office in Black communities across the country. Even Bobby Seale of the Black Panther Party turned his energies toward running for mayor of Oakland. Newark, site of one of largest rebellions in the country in 1967, elected its first Black mayor in 1970. The small yet palpable growth of Black political representation made it seem that African Americans were no longer on the outside looking in.[2] It did not mean that Black communities were quiescent—as evidenced by the growing organization among Black tenants and homeowners—but it did mean that the period of major upheaval and mass uprisings had passed.

For more than the previous two decades, urban life and varying notions of "urban crisis" had animated the political landscape and dominated domestic politics in the United States.[3] The apex of this political and legislative focus had come with the War on Poverty and Great Society programs of the 1960s. Of course, those programs addressed wide swaths of the American public, including people living in previously ignored and abandoned rural areas, but with the outbreak of urban rebellions and uprisings that dominated most of the 1960s, the fate of the cities became a political obsession. Nixon interpreted his decisive victory over McGovern and his consolidation of the white suburban voting bloc as a mandate to turn away from urban governance.

Nevertheless, Nixon allowed for a long rollout after his reelection before ceremoniously declaring the urban crisis to be over. It had been a tumultuous four months. George Romney tendered his resignation from HUD immediately after Nixon's reelection in November 1972. In a letter of resignation that was released to the public, Romney cited the lack of integrity and honesty in political contests as a reason for leaving public life. He complained that "inherent limitations in those political processes make the achievement of fundamental reform too dependent upon a crisis."[4] There was no doubt that he was referring to his inability to shift the administration or, in his mind, the country toward his understanding of the need for a solution that involved cities and suburbs to solve the urban housing crisis in the United States. Indeed, Romney's political relationships within the Nixon administration had never recovered from the initial fallout over his advocacy of "open communities" and the strategy of using political leverage and the threat of municipal punishment to get (some) suburbs to open their communities to housing for poor and working-class Black families. This strained relationship continued despite the fact that, after the conflict over the placement of low-income housing, Romney became the loyal party man who thereafter vouched for every detail of Nixon's approach to housing.

In the weeks after Romney tendered his resignation, a new batch of rumors that HUD was going to declare a moratorium on all subsidized low-income housing for the coming year began to gather steam. When it became clear that, yes, the Nixon administration was preparing to take a historic and drastic step by issuing a moratorium, the regional offices of HUD began frantically processing as many new building requests as possible. On January 8, 1973, in one of his final acts as secretary, Romney announced that HUD was suspending all funding and construction of low-income housing across the country, effective immediately. Builders who had been lucky enough to receive warning that the moratorium was coming were able to submit their proposals for new building projects. There was at least one report that "HUD field offices worked all of New Years' weekend processing applications ahead of the moratorium deadline."[5] But for everyone else, it was too late.

It was fitting that Romney made the announcement at a national gathering of the NAHB.[6] The moratorium's timeline was described as "indefinite," and it included not only the programs created by the HUD Act but also public housing regimes that had long preceded it. And this was only the beginning. The Nixon administration also called for the elimination of community development programs, including "water and sewer improvements, open space preservation, and new town projects."[7] As if that were not enough, it was announced that as of July 1, 1973, the urban renewal and Model Cities programs would end. Although Romney was a Republican and a loyal one at that, his departure represented the beginning of the end of the Great Society.

Nixon's decisive victory over McGovern provided a political mandate to move away from federal involvement in cities. Nixon also interpreted the win as an opportunity to align domestic governance with the principles of New Federalism. It was time to deconcentrate and disperse federal authority to the state and local levels. Nixon's actions were aimed at coercing Congress into passing his "revenue-sharing" plan, which included bypassing federal authorizations for state-level decision-making on the distribution of federal funds for housing and community development projects. To achieve this end, Nixon had consolidated the so-called silent majority of white suburban voters by stoking perceptions of urban dysfunction and exploiting racist fears about African Americans. The continued focus on the crisis within HUD's urban-based, low-income homeownership programs not only appeared to justify the housing moratorium but was used by figures within the Nixon administration—particularly George Romney in the months and weeks before he left office—to define a "new" urban crisis that was impervious to the welfare state. Romney described the "emergent" problem succinctly: "We don't have a housing problem. . . . We have a people problem. Government may be able to provide a decent home, but that doesn't guarantee a suitable living environment."[8]

This was nothing less than the same urban crisis under a new name. The same old story of undeserving low-income people was now redeployed to blame the persistence of urban problems on the people who lived in urban environments. This attitude helped to justify a return to redlining practices and the retreat of the federal government from low-income homeownership and the housing question more generally. Indeed, characterization of the housing problem as stemming from a combination of dysfunctional city residents and incompetent government bureaucrats was consistent with New Federalism and paved the road of retreat from most of the civil rights commitments embodied in federal fair housing legislation. There was a new focus that went beyond blaming people in the cities, but the notion of incompetent government became a central theme in Nixon's attack on the fragile system of social welfare and the programs that were perceived to be welfare. It had been five years since the passage of the HUD Act— what President Lyndon Johnson had triumphantly referred to as the "Magna Carta of the cities"—and even longer since the federal government had set as a goal "a decent home for every American." But the movement away from the promise they represented was about to accelerate as seismic events that were to occur early in the second Nixon term cast a pall over the future of housing equality for ordinary African Americans living in American cities.

MORATORIUM

In a 1973 *New York Times* opinion piece, columnist John Herbers described to his readers what would have seemed unfathomable in 1968 when the HUD Act was considered the long-awaited solution to the nation's housing woes. Herbers wrote, "Tens of thousands of foreclosures, tens of thousands of mortgages in default, and a rising tide of abandoned houses dotted communities across the nation: were the federal policies originally crafted to quell the crises in the inner city actually hastening their demise?"[9] Within the span of five short years, the promise of the HUD Act had turned into doubt about the survival of its most widely known programs.

Underpinning those doubts were misgivings about the viability of HUD as an agency capable of leading development efforts in American metropolitan areas.

In the month prior to Romney's resignation as secretary of HUD, he called for a major overhaul of the agency, suggesting that the federal government get out of housing altogether: "The first alternative is the termination of a direct federal role in housing. . . . We would end subsidy programs, privatize FHA, move to a combination of housing allowance income subsidy for the poor and end operating subsidies for public housing. . . . We can no longer afford $100 billion mistakes," he concluded.[10]

In late December 1972, Romney had leaked to a gathering of the National Housing Conference, a low-income housing nonprofit organization, that the Nixon administration was going forward with an eighteen-month moratorium on housing subsidies beginning in 1973.[11] Behind the scenes, Romney was engaged in a high-stakes negotiation to try to minimize the cuts. In a letter to Nixon written one week prior to the announcement of the moratorium, Romney explained that he did not object to a "substantial cutback in these programs" but did oppose a sweeping moratorium: "The actions proposed will only be taken by the American people—and especially those in the central city—as further evidence of a hardheaded, cold-hearted indifference to the poor and racial minorities. This, in my opinion, could inflame the central cities and could contribute to eventually bringing Belfast to the streets of our cities."[12] Romney's letter indicated the gulf that had grown between him and the administration. Romney, whose resignation had already been tendered, was reduced to making announcements on behalf of the administration.

In an effort to temper the severity of the moratorium, Romney described it as a series of minor revisions based on careful assessment that would ultimately lead to program improvements: "The time has come," Romney assured his audience, "to pause, to re-evaluate, and to seek out better ways."[13] Nixon's people, however, were planning something much more drastic, a kind of shock therapy. On January 8, 1973, in one of his final acts as secretary, Romney made the announcement during a speech to the NAHB in which he said that HUD was suspending all funding and construction of low-income housing across the country, effective immediately.

The moratorium's timeline was described as "indefinite." As of January 5, the federal government would no longer accept applications for Section 235 and 236; it would freeze payment for the rent supplement program, Section 23 leased housing, and all public housing. In its daily newsletter, *Urban Affairs*, HUD tersely reported that while Romney described the Nixon directive as a "temporary holding action," it was more accurate to use the terms "suspended" and "terminated."[14] These programs were not just being put on hold; many of them were being eliminated altogether. Programs connected with community development, including "open space land" programs that provided funds to create parks in empty lots, water and sewer facilities, the urban renewal program, urban rehabilitation loans, public facility loans, and grants for new communities, were completely eliminated. In total, the Nixon administration effectively removed $16 billion in appropriations that had already been agreed upon by Congress for these programs. This included the $48 million appropriated for rent supplements, $500 million for Model Cities, $1.2 billion for urban renewal, $70 million for housing rehabilitation loans, and $40 million for grants for neighborhood facilities.[15]

HUD's subsidized homeownership, public housing, and rental assistance programs were spared immediate elimination; instead they were put on hold indefinitely, pending a study on how to improve them. Affected agencies included the Farmers Home Administration, which helped to make homeownership affordable for poor people living in rural areas. The Farmers Home Administration estimated that the moratorium would cancel plans to approve 30,000 additional single-family housing loans to low-income rural families by the end of the summer of 1973.[16] It was no surprise that these policies were predicted to have a disproportionate impact on rural Black families.[17] Farmers Home Administration officials estimated that 117,000 people would lose their loans as a result of the moratorium, eventually totaling nearly $2 billion; 70,000 of these loans were directed at poor people with incomes under $7,000 a year.[18] But the moratorium was going to have a much greater impact on Section 235 homeowners. The number of subsidized home loans issued was already decreasing because of the increasingly complex web of new rules HUD had created to uproot fraud and corruption in its program. The *Wall Street Journal* referred to the increased oversight of FHA programs as "harsh regulations" that had resulted in "mortgage lenders [cutting back] sharply their writing of FHA-insured home loans, while others have abandoned the market entirely."[19] One of the supposedly draconian regulations included the requirement that lenders prove "the accuracy of all statements made to FHA appraisers."[20]

For the real estate industry at this point, Section 235 was creating more headaches than profits and was nearing the end of its usefulness. In 1972, HUD-FHA had authorized 157,000 subsidized Section 235 home loans, but that number was expected to drop to 40,000 in 1973 because even before the moratorium was announced, Congress had decided to appropriate less money as a form of punishment.[21] As a result of the moratorium, it was predicted that by 1975, the number of subsidized housing units would drop to 550,000 from a projected need of 2.25 million. The moratorium would result in a 77 percent cut to housing subsidies.[22]

The impact was swift and was felt across the country. In Baltimore, city officials lamented the loss of 10,000 units of low-income housing. In New York City, tens of thousands of units were going to be lost. But the freeze on building new units was only one problem. New building projects were being stopped in the middle of construction as money was cut off by the immediate suspension, adding silhouettes of unfinished buildings that contributed to the optics of crisis and deterioration in Black urban neighborhoods.[23] In a memo, the staff of a HUD undersecretary strained to lend legitimacy to this unprecedented display of executive power by casting aspersions on the FHA-assisted homeownership programs. In an attempt to explain the moratorium, they wrote, "The [FHA-backed loan] program tends to destroy homeownership responsibility. Because Section 235 homebuyers are responsible only for a small portion of their total monthly mortgage payment and are not obligated to repay the subsidy, they tend to feel little sense of ownership responsibility for their housing and in periods of unexpected economic difficulty are prone to abandon the property rather than remain in ownership."[24] For all of the note's brevity, it captured the well-trod refrain that situated blame for the problems in HUD's subsidized housing programs on the program participant, though it lacked the specifics necessary to justify the unprecedented denial of access to federal money for housing.

As part of its overhaul, HUD now refused to back any mortgage that was above the "prevailing value" of other houses in a neighborhood. This served to punish homeowners in communities that HUD's own policies and practices had diminished in the first place. Take the Jefferson Chalmers neighborhood in Detroit as an example. In this neighborhood, which existed on the periphery of the exclusive and white Grosse Point suburb of Detroit, there were 4,500 units of housing. By 1973, 296 of those units had fallen into foreclosure and were returned to HUD.[25] As the units sat empty, vandals stripped them of usable materials and then destroyed much of the remaining property. As a result, HUD demolished 93 of the properties and put another 120 on the list awaiting demolition. By the end of 1974, the federal government was spending more than $460,000 a day to maintain its stock of 78,000 repossessed homes.[26] The housing reserves were being buoyed by the recession and the poor quality of the houses that made them nearly impossible to sell. It would stand to reason that this would have a debilitating impact on the property values of the homes in the surrounding neighborhood. But according to HUD's new policy, homeowners would not be able to sell their homes above a prevailing value that was inevitably diminished by HUD's practices elsewhere in the neighborhood.

The impact of the suspension was measured not only in the loss of housing but also by the loss of employment. In Georgia, elected officials predicted a loss of $383,000 in housing assistance and an additional loss of 44,000 jobs.[27] The NAHB projected that the loss of subsidies would mean a loss of one million man-years of employment and $16 billion in the gross national product over a twelve-month period.[28] The impact on employment would also be felt in the rollback of federal agencies themselves. According to social scientist Virginia Parks, the most pronounced growth in Black public employment occurred during the 1960s and 1970s. During this period, employment of Blacks in the public sector increased at twice the rate of whites. By the mid-1970s, 25 percent of all Black men and 34 percent of all Black women were employed in the public sector, compared with 16 percent of all white men and 24 percent of all white women.[29] Gutting government programs and ordering layoffs in public sector work would have a disproportionate impact in Black communities that were already reeling from the housing crisis. The efforts to downsize HUD spoke directly to this phenomenon. HUD was one of the largest employers of African Americans in Washington, D.C. In crafting a budget for the following year, HUD officials requested barely half of what they had requested in appropriations a year earlier, from $4.2 billion to $2.6 billion for fiscal year 1974. In line with the directive from the White House, HUD projected 1,900 layoffs of full-time employees and additional staff cuts, bringing HUD's workforce down to 13,000 employees. While the racial makeup of the layoffs was unknown, African American civil servants lacked the seniority and skilled positions necessary to avoid the brunt of the cuts.[30]

Staff layoffs were only one way that Black workers were negatively impacted. Section 3 of the HUD Act mandated "that when employment or contracting opportunities are generated because a covered project or activity necessitates the employment of additional persons or the awarding of contracts for work, preference must be given to low- and very low-income persons or business concerns residing in the community where the project is located."[31] So, for example, in 1969, the Office of Economic Opportunity had used Black contractors for 7.4 percent of its construction work, but by 1971, this number had grown to 34 percent.[32] According to one report, "ninety-one metropolitan areas [had] begun plans requiring contractors on federally financed projects of $500,000 or more to establish hiring goals" for Black workers. Almost 1,000 different housing agencies had formed "to handle government developmental programs" created by the HUD Act.[33] Because of the moratorium, these brief openings of opportunity for Black employment would once again be closed.

The HUD Act had also opened up new opportunities for Black developers and builders. Nixon had cynically used affirmative action in the building trades and the threat of Black employment to bring down rapidly escalating labor costs in construction as part of his drive toward "wage controls." This initiative, known as the Philadelphia Plan, was never fully implemented, but the increase in building projects in urban areas had created more construction jobs for Black workers.[34] All of these projects were coming to an abrupt end. When speaking of the moratorium's impact on jobs, Black mortgage banker Dempsey Travis said, "The first impact of this cutback will affect jobs. . . . I've talked to many mortgage banks and construction companies . . . and they've told me that they are going to cutback about twenty percent of their employees. . . . This is going to snowball into everything . . . that goes into a house."[35] NAACP president Roy Wilkins said that the cuts showed that the Black community was "under siege" and was "being pinned down by the mortar fire of discrimination in shelter."[36] Black nationalist and playwright Amiri Baraka lashed out at the Nixon administration when it was discovered that the moratorium would freeze funds that had been promised for the construction of public housing units in Newark, New Jersey. He described the federal reneging as "the hypocrisy of the free enterprise system and the hypocrisy of the government supporting the free enterprise system."[37] The president of the NAHB declared the moratorium a "disaster and a catastrophe."[38] Senator William Proxmire fumed, "President Nixon has decided to spend billions more in bombing Asia, and to spend several billion dollars less for housing. The effect is to increase the housing shortage both in Asia and the United States. That is reorganizing priorities with a vengeance."[39]

Community activists had vociferous critiques of HUD's programs, but they wanted reform, not termination. As Gail Cincotta aptly observed, "Every once in a while here in Chicago we have a scandal in the police department. No one has ever even entertained the idea that abolishing the police department would solve the problem."[40] Carmel McCrudden, the housing activist from Philadelphia, even after enumerating all of the ways that HUD programs had burdened her and other women in her community, still insisted on reform instead of dissolution. She made the observation, "Past legislative reforms have opened the doors to the possibility of better housing for low- and moderate-income people.

We are tired of promises that are never kept. We look to you, as our elected representatives, to work with us—not passively against us—in our struggle to save our decaying inner city."[41] Attorney George Gould, while testifying at a congressional hearing on the impact of the moratorium, stressed the mismanagement of the programs to better argue that they could be fixed. Gould called for the "revision and expansion" of the federal commitment to housing so that the "goal of a decent home and suitable living environment" could become "more than just a promise or a slogan. The problems before us are immense but our goal must be not to retreat from the inner city but instead to work toward and demand a competent and lawful administration of these housing programs."[42] These advocates were less interested in theoretical debates concerning the advisability of homeownership for poor and low-income people. They were, instead, weighing the meager options that had been left to poor people to secure their housing. In their view, they were on the verge of losing another housing program, with no serious proposal for its replacement.

Nixon did not formally address the moratorium until March 4, 1973, when he mentioned it in the midst of a speech announcing the end of the urban crisis. "A few years ago, we constantly heard that urban America was on the brink of collapse," he began. He continued, "It was one minute to midnight, we were told, and the bells of doom were beginning to toll."[43] And with that, Nixon declared the crisis in the cities to be over. Pivoting quickly to policy, he announced wholesale changes to the country's housing policies because "some of the methods which have been tried in the past . . . are not appropriate to the 1970s." Nixon was disavowing the idea that the resources of government should be leveraged to respond to social problems confronting a society. It was an odd juxtaposition; Nixon announced that the hour of crisis in the United States had passed while simultaneously castigating the social programs whose creation had been inspired by that crisis as wasteful and ineffective. Of course, Nixon offered no data to demonstrate how he determined that the urban crisis had come to an end, just a simple declaration.

In charting a new course for the 1970s, Nixon persisted in concern over urban development that apparently no longer constituted a "crisis" but still required attention. He said, "One serious error of the past was the belief that the Federal Government should take the lead in developing local communities. America is still recovering from years of extravagant, hastily passed measures, designed by centralized planners and costing billions of dollars, but producing few results."[44] Nixon's comments suggested that rather than cultivating "community development," federal programs had undermined them, and thus his actions were intended to return decision-making about community issues back to the local level and free it from federal "impediments." He referenced the subsidized FHA-assisted homeownership programs as examples of an "extravagant" failure when he described the federal government as the country's largest "slumlord." "Some of our programs to help people buy or improve housing are also back-firing. Too many of the owners fail to meet their payments, and the taxpayer gets stuck with the bill. He also gets stuck with the house and the added expense of looking out for it," Nixon declared. In a deft rhetorical move to absolve his own administration of any responsibility, while simultaneously foreclosing the pos-sibility of reform, he argued, "This does not mean that the people in charge of these programs were dishonest or incompetent. What it does mean is that they are human, and that no human being, accountable only to an office in Washing-ton, can successfully plan and manage the development of communities which are often hundreds or thousands of miles away."[45] It was a bold statement to make, considering that twenty-eight HUD officials had been indicted for crimes related to the housing scandal and that there were another 1,930 active investiga-tions for fraud being conducted by the FBI.[46]

This was not an overstatement by the president. Instead, Nixon was cynically using the spectacle of crisis within HUD-FHA to remake the federal government's entire approach to housing and urban development policies. Despite the venom directed at the Johnson administration and the accusations of big and intrusive government, Nixon's actions were completing the shift that Johnson and Ken-nedy had initiated in their turn to the market to resolve the lack of safe and sound affordable housing in cities. After all, the Kaiser Commission that had formed and created the parameters for the HUD Act was composed almost en-tirely of businessmen and industry heads. Driven by urban uprisings and market possibilities, Johnson had envisioned a partnership between government and the real estate industry to produce low-income housing on an unprecedented scale. But that vision was only possible by building new housing for poor and working-class African Americans in the same suburbs that white families had frantically escaped to. Nixon had torpedoed that course of action with his declaration of "no forced integration" and the preservation of the residential status quo. Nixon, instead, would emphasize the partnership with business while rejecting the idea that integrating the suburbs was the key to opening up housing opportunities for African Americans.

The "new" turn announced by Nixon would fortify racial segregation and certainly not challenge it. With the threat of urban rebellion no longer influencing the trajectory of domestic policies, the Nixon administration embraced residential segregation with its renewed emphasis on existing housing and a housing allowance for low-income and poor residents and a de-emphasis on new building in suburbs. Six months after his initial comments on the urban crisis, Nixon announced a more developed shift in policy that fall. Nixon described his new "community development" initiatives as the Better Communities Act.[47] The Better Communities Act was Nixon's first attempt at revenue sharing in the form of block grants, but it never developed into legislation because of vociferous opposition from the Democrat-controlled Congress.[48]

Despite the failure of that legislation, the shifts in Nixon's housing policies were still dramatic. Nixon proposed that the FHA raise its interest rate to that of conventional lenders. He also proposed raising the down payment for an FHA-insured loan to 5 percent as opposed to 3 percent or, in the case of the Section 235 program, 1 percent. The combination of these two measures was enough to make homeownership prohibitive for those who had qualified after the HUD Act, especially African Americans. Inflation was wildly driving up the cost of housing over the course of the 1970s. It was predicted that by 1974, the average cost of a single-family home would be over $33,000, a significant increase from $25,000 in 1971.[49] With the interest rate hovering between 9 and 10 percent, the price of owning a home would be even higher. To account for this, Nixon proposed that the Federal Home Loan Bank Board adopt flexible measures for repayment to avert foreclosures. To ensure that money for mortgages on the lower end of the market continued to flow, Nixon pledged $3 billion for the GNMA to purchase mortgages on *new* homes. GNMA purchases of low-income mortgages had fueled the urban housing market when the GNMA was created by the HUD Act, but shifting its purchasing power to new housing essentially ended its participation in the urban and used housing market.[50]

After all, a 1971 study of the U.S. Commission on Civil Rights confirmed that there was a dearth of new housing in cities. Conversely, 70 percent of existing housing sold with the Section 235 subsidy was found in the mostly Black central cities.[51] In that vein, Nixon insisted that low-income housing programs had "ignore[d] the potential for using good existing housing" in putting too much emphasis on building new housing in outlying areas. Nixon counseled that new construction should be used "sparingly."[52] He made "housing allowances" or vouchers a priority for low-income housing while placing homeownership beyond the reach of many working-class African Americans. Taken in unison, Nixon's new policies were a return to the past; they threatened to marginalize African Americans in segregated cities and suburbs with crumbling infrastructure while continuing to prime the pump for even more building and development of white suburban enclaves. Nixon was apt to strengthen the role of government in gilding the housing market while leaving poor and working-class African Americans to fend for themselves with housing vouchers. The transition that Nixon was mapping out was not conjured in a vacuum; it was rolled out with a developing narrative about an urban dysfunction that transcended public policies and spoke to something deeper and more unsettling.

INVENTING THE UNDERCLASS

Given the expectations of and investments in federal housing, the programs were difficult to just walk away from. But that was certainly made easier by the argument that these programs were inconsequential in addressing the urban problems they were created to alleviate. For Romney, there was the added bonus that if HUD's problems were ascribed to the magnitude of the problems facing American cities, then he could be exonerated for his lack of management skills. In the months before Romney resigned his position and as the daily newspapers filled with stories of scandal and crisis concerning HUD's FHA-assisted homeownership programs, he was called on to assess and explain these problems. He tried to expand the scope of the discussion beyond the issue of housing to include the deteriorating condition of the cities. At one point he stated to an investigative committee of Congress, "We will not solve these problems, if we pretend that housing is the cause. FHA housing programs did not start blockbusting. Housing didn't take the jobs away. Housing didn't reduce the population. Housing didn't reduce the public services. Housing didn't destroy the quality of public education in the schools. Housing didn't bring the drug addiction in. Deep social changes are at work that have little, if anything, to do with housing. Yet too often the result is accused of being the cause."[53] But this was a bit of a historical sleight of hand. The earlier decisions of the FHA to marginalize urban communities from mortgage insurance played a deeply consequential role in the uneven development of Black urban communities and their white suburban counterparts. Those decisions certainly contributed to the out-migration of white taxpayers and businesses that abandoned the city for lower taxes and land on which to conduct business on cheaper terms. By the early 1970s, it was much too late to deny the culpability of federal policies in the devolution of Black urban communities. And yet, this is exactly what was being argued.

For the first time, Romney began to project a fatalistic perspective that questioned the possibility of ever resolving the problem of urban housing. He said, "I believe that it is time we face the real dimensions of our problem. I do not believe that any useful purpose can be served by holding out the false hope that we have the programs on the books, or the appropriations necessary, and all that we need to do is clean up the administration of our housing program."[54] Romney went on to describe what he believed to be a more pervasive problem. He agreed that "mistakes had been made"; however, "if we had been able to avoid all of the mistakes that have occurred, we would still be up against the larger tragedy— the growing critical mass of people with problems in our cities."[55] In earlier testimony Romney had elaborated on the greater context within which the "people with problems" were operating. He counseled that "housing programs will not solve the housing problems of the inner city. We need to find cures for other social conditions—chiefly poverty, and also crime, drug addiction, lagging education, poor health facilities, and inadequate public services . . . and disproportionate inner-city unemployment. . . . The unemployment is worst among teenage blacks, who are committing most of the crimes—teenage blacks."[56]

Romney's comments gave the impression that HUD's activities in cities had been peripheral at best, perhaps even inconsequential, to the disintegration of urban life he was now describing. Few, if any, analysts argued that housing "alone" was responsible for poor conditions in American cities. It was, however, undeniable that the dearth of housing choices available to African Americans outside racially segregated cities or suburbs put them at great disadvantage in terms of access to good jobs, the best schools, and the opportunities available to white people in the United States. The corruption, graft, and fleecing of urban African Americans in the FHA-assisted housing programs certainly contributed to the poverty and desperation that existed in cities where the programs flourished. Consider the wrecked credit of Black mothers in the aftermath of foreclosure or the precious savings wasted on a dilapidated, FHA-approved house. Consider what sociologist Matthew Desmond has written about the impact of evictions on the lives of poor and working-class renters in contemporary U.S. society, a disproportionate number of whom were Black women. It is instructive in how we can understand the impact on low-income Black women of foreclosures from their homes in the 1970s: "Losing your home and possessions and often your job; being stamped with an eviction and being denied government housing assistance; relocating to housing in poor and dangerous neighborhoods; and suffering from increased material hardship, homelessness, depression, and illness.... Eviction does not simply drop poor families into a dark valley, a trying yet relatively brief detour on life's journey. It fundamentally redirects their way, casting them onto a different, and much more difficult, path. Eviction is a *cause*, not just condition, of poverty."[57]

HUD's problems were exacerbated by its failure to consistently enforce and pursue "fair housing." By 1973, the U.S. Civil Rights Commission found repeatedly, and in multiple forums, that HUD had no consistent regimen for enforcing civil rights laws prohibiting housing discrimination. Quite the opposite: HUD's practices were known to be deepening residential segregation.[58] This was driven by factors that were, if not controlled, then certainly dictated by HUD. Romney's voracious pursuit of housing production goals fueled the entire process. Amid Romney's searching explanations for HUD-FHA's failures, he was also claiming credit for HUD's robust housing numbers. As he proudly announced to a gathering of the NAHB in 1972, "We are now one-half million units ahead of the pace for meeting the 1978 housing goals. And we did all this at a time when we were implementing new programs, organizing and decentralizing the Department, and formulating and implementing fair housing policies."[59] In other settings, it was apparent that the pace of implementing Romney's policies along with "decentralization" amplified the built-in problems of the HUD programs.

There were, however, problems with the housing market that did not originate with HUD but that the agency's inaction contributed to. More specifically, HUD did not cause the crisis of abandonment that pockmarked Black, urban communities throughout the 1970s, but the department's practices exacerbated the phenomenon. Existing HUD houses often sat, abandoned, in real estate limbo. Because the houses had been overvalued as a result of fraudulent appraisals, they were difficult to resell. As per HUD's own policies, when foreclosure procedures were initiated, the homeowner was required to vacate the property, thus leaving the house empty until, ultimately, it was resold—*if* it was resold.[60] Even as more urban housing was made available as whites moved out, the jobs and employment crisis and growing poverty experienced in American cities meant that it was difficult to sell those houses. Moreover, by the mid-1970s, escalating interest rates made the rehabilitation and resettling of deserted working-class neighborhoods less likely. One report observed that "entire neighborhoods housing hundreds of thousands of city-dwellers were on the way to a state similar to that caused by war—utter desolation."[61] There were over 100,000 abandoned units in New York City by the mid-1970s; 36,000 in Philadelphia; 15,000 in Detroit; 10,000 in St. Louis; and 5,000 in Baltimore.[62]

The apparent failure of homeownership in these communities as evidenced by the growing number of home foreclosures and subsequent abandonment, while leading to activism and reform in some places, also renewed discussions about the wisdom of having ended redlining. "Are we to prohibit the use of our programs in the core of urban areas because they are not considered 'reasonably viable'?" Romney asked rhetorically. He concluded, "If you had to ask me today to certify whether or not in inner-city areas many of our metropolitan areas are reasonably viable in areas of acceptable risk ... considering the social circumstances, the total environment, more than the physical aspect of the property ... I would have to say no.... In good conscience it confronts me with a horrible decision, and I mean a horrible decision, to cut off entire areas and to say they are not reasonably viable and they are not areas of acceptable risk."[63] But the end of government redlining meant that ordinary *white* homeowners could now sell their homes and move to the suburbs, while African Americans were still restricted in their movements, unless they were moving to segregated suburbs. The resurrection of the viability of redlining was made possible by highlighting the perceptions of urban dysfunction. The more intense the problems in American cities, the more legitimacy was lent to the boundaries that limited the spatial movement of the people who lived in those cities. When defending the previous regime of redlining, officials had claimed that race was not a motivating factor and, instead, the exclusion was based on location and the lack of viability of places. The emerging discussion concerning the urban place focused on the people who lived there.

If, in the calculations of Romney, government was only part of the problem, then the "people with problems" certainly constituted the rest of the equation. In a draft copy of a speech he was to deliver to the Economic Club of Detroit in April 1972, Romney painted a much more negative portrait of that population than he had when testifying before Congress. It's unclear whether he delivered the speech as it was written, but the crossed-out passages give some insight into his thinking. In the draft, Romney described the growing issue of drug abuse and crime in dystopic ways that cast a pall over urban life. He wrote, "There are an estimated 30,000 drug addicts in Detroit paying over $300 million annually for their habit, with major impacts on crime rates and the personal security of

Detroit residents."[64] These addicts, according to Romney, personified the "pathologies of the cities." Romney linked this change to the loss of manufacturing jobs, but he also connected it to the exit of white citizens and the influx of African Americans. As Romney wrote, "The white population of Detroit . . . declined by . . . 29 percent. But the black population grew by . . . 37 percent."[65] Romney spun a combination of these factors into a wide-ranging explanation for urban decline while simultaneously downplaying the particular role of public policy or private enterprise. In the actual speech he delivered, he said,

> The decline in economic function and population, and rising levels of crime and violence, and insecurity and heroin addiction has had the effect of introducing a deep and pervasive fear in present Central City, low- and moderate-income neighborhoods, and has attached a stereotype of social menace to low-income groups, particularly minority groups. When we preoccupy ourselves with abandonment and mortgage failures we are dealing with a facet of the problem but we are missing Detroit's real problem, the confined concentration of people with problems in our central cities.[66]

In a separate speech at the National Housing Conference in March 1972, Romney merged his critiques of the FHA-assisted homeownership programs with a critical assessment of public housing. Romney lamented the transition from the supposed golden age of public housing in the 1930s, when, he said, the tenants were a "predominantly white, upwardly mobile, normal two-parent working-class population," to the 1960s, with a "predominantly non-white, poverty-affected, non-mobile lower-class population."[67] He linked this transformation to the deterioration of public housing, blaming it for everything from vandalism to rent strikes. There *were* significant issues in public housing projects across the United States, but they ran much deeper than the supposed non-normativity of the families living in them.[68] Public housing, like the existing housing of the FHA-assisted homeownership programs, was affected by residential segregation, poverty, unemployment, and public policies meant to protect the interest of private enterprise. The most well-known public housing projects during this time were the Pruitt-Igoe projects in St. Louis. Upon its inception, Pruitt-Igoe had been heralded as an expression of modern architectural genius. The development stretched over fifty-seven acres with thirty-three concrete buildings jutting eleven stories high out of the flat plains. By the late 1960s, however, Pruitt-Igoe had become notorious.[69] One government report on the state of public housing described the development as "a scene of such social disorder and physical squalor that a sociologist said its name had become a household term for the worst in ghetto living."[70]

In the summer of 1972, two of the thirty-three buildings were demolished before a television audience, further confirming the descriptions of Pruitt-Igoe residents and public housing as beyond repair and hope. At the time of their demolition, the Pruitt-Igoe projects were the largest public housing development in the United States, but their size outstripped the budget allocated to maintain the buildings. The budget for maintenance expenses in public housing was based on rent payments made by tenants. But the housing development never reached its maximum capacity in tenancy, creating a discrepancy between what the local housing authority could collect from tenants and the costs of repairing the massive yet underpopulated structure. As the costs of maintaining the buildings exceeded the rents collected, the buildings quickly fell into disrepair. But as was so often the case, the structural issues, including poor public policy decisions, were shrouded behind a wall of blame laid on African Americans.[71]

Indeed, Pruitt-Igoe residents were cast as the culprits in the devolution of the housing complex from the start. Ira Lowry, a researcher for the Rand Corporation, wrote, in 1973, an assessment of low-income housing for a congressional committee in which he blamed residents for the condition of Pruitt-Igoe. In an essay promoting more use of existing housing as opposed to new construction in Black urban communities, he wrote, "Unless provision is made to ensure that the new dwellings get better care than their predecessors, another cycle of decay immediately begins. Well-built new housing can be reduced to ruin in an astonishingly short time as evidenced by the Pruitt-Igoe public housing project in Saint Louis."[72] The crisis in Pruitt-Igoe and public housing more generally was interpreted not only as the result of tenant misbehavior but also as evidence that government social welfare promoted dependency and disregard for private property.[73]

When Romney, in his National Housing Conference talk, claimed, "The combination of poverty, crime and anti-social behavior has now raised the most serious question as to where the poor can be housed," he effectively tied public housing and the low-income homeownership program together in a dismal assessment of subsidized housing. As Romney stated, "We are now experiencing the full force of the disappointment and the actual counter-productive affects [sic] of this program."[74] Romney's bleak assessment was not only about the programs but about the populations they were attempting to serve. He reached back to older debates about the deserving and undeserving poor when he described the existence of "two classes of poor people." The first class, which he identified as the "working poor," included those who "maintain a stable life pattern and who are not a danger to society." Then there was a second class, which he referred to as the "welfare poor," "a much smaller group who have become the victims of social disorder, entering into the heroin subculture and . . . participating in crime and vandalism on a large scale. The second population is a threat to the larger group of the poor around them and to the general population."[75]

For Romney, the welfare poor were a central catalyst in the deterioration of American cities. He situated his analysis among a growing conservative chorus that not only questioned antipoverty programs but did so by denigrating the poor. For example, Romney in his housing speech positively referenced an editorial written by *Newsweek* magazine columnist Stewart Alsop that referred to urban neighborhoods as "diseased." In a column titled "Road to Hell," Alsop described social welfare as the core of the problem in American cities, writing, "Well-intentioned and liberal-minded people (including this writer) have assumed that [social welfare is] the way to cure conditions like those in the South Bronx and other New York slums." Alsop assailed the idea, claiming that spending had made the city "worse—and worse and worse."[76] Alsop went from criticizing social spending to attacking the recipients of social welfare. In a sentence that preceded a section subtitled "Bad People," Alsop wrote, "If the disease is to be controlled, it is first necessary to jettison the notion that poor people are good people, especially if they are black. Some poor, black people are evil people either because they were born that way, or much more often because their heroin addiction forces them to be evil."[77]

In Romney's address, he continued this theme while quoting from another unnamed publication. He connected the "diseased" city to the real estate market. He said, "The junkies, with an assist from drunks, criminals, and the naturally violence prone, make a neighborhood unlivable. The Mom and Pop stores at the bottom of an apartment building have been 'hit' too often. There have been many muggings in the lobby. The stores are boarded up: the apartments are deserted, one by one. The owner cannot sell the store at any price, and the bank and other mortgagees refuse to take possession, so the owner abandons the property."[78] In this passage HUD, the FHA, "the bank," and "other mortgagees" are subtly transformed from institutions with power and influence to innocent victims at the hands of the "junkies," "drunks, criminals, and the naturally violence prone." Romney also included himself and President Nixon in his list of new victims when he declared, "We will not solve the problem by hiding be-hind scapegoats—whether Secretary Romney, HUD, the Nixon administration or other available targets."[79] These were not just gratuitous attacks on the poor, but they exemplified a larger ideological, economic, and political shift under way. Romney embodied the trajectory from postwar liberalism to questioning whether government had any role in ending poverty. In a retreat from his earlier embrace of "big government," Romney said, "We have been throwing billions of dollars into these problem areas without making a dent upon them. It is now foolish to say that if we will only spend a little more money, we will resolve these difficult issues."[80]

Social geographer Neil Smith coined the concept of the revanchist city to de-scribe the combative right-wing attack on the liberalism of the 1960s and 1970s in order to reconfigure urban space without the urban poor in the 1980s and 1990s.[81] For Smith, this was primarily a project of gentrification, but the po-litical attacks against the poor prepared the wider public for the reorganization of the city. Smith made these observations within urban politics in New York City but was able to generalize them as a more common method of urban gov-ernance. Social theorist Jordan Camp has observed more recently in a historical rendering of social movements and politics of the 1960s and 1970s that "revan-chism is reproduced through the common-sense notions of race, gender, and sexuality underpinning neoliberalization, and through the depiction of labor, civil rights, feminist, and socialist movements as the enemies of the nation.... It has thwarted the class anger unleashed by capital's abandonment of the social wage in U.S. cities through moral panics about race and crime. It has done so by defining the behavior of the purported 'underclass' as a source of violence and disorder."[82] Indeed, Romney's speech and Alsop's editorial were composite sketches of an emergent concept of "underclass" that urban decline would soon be pinned on.

The notion of an underclass as a category of the poor was not new. The late so-cial scientist Michael Katz explained, "Commentaries on the underclass revived the oldest tropes in the literature on poverty. They echoed the nineteenth cen-tury behavioral and cultural descriptions of the undeserving poor and picked up on the culture of poverty theme."[83] Throughout the 1960s, the same people later described as the underclass were referred to as the hard-core unemployed, and they were a target population of War on Poverty and Great Society programs. They were considered a part of the "social dynamite" of the inner city that was too explosive to ignore.[84]

Edward Banfield, a Harvard political scientist who was appointed to direct a task force assessing the Model Cities program, wrote a reactionary book titled *The Unheavenly City* in 1970. Banfield claimed that there was no such thing as the "urban crisis." Instead, he argued that there were no bad cities, just bad people: "The lower-class individual lives in the slum and sees little or no reason to complain. He does not care how dirty and dilapidated the housing is, either inside or out; nor does he mind the inadequacy of such public facilities as schools, parks and libraries. Indeed, where such things exist he destroys them by acts of vandalism if he can. Features that make the slum repellent to others actually please him."[85] Banfield's claims about complacent slum dwellers were not far from the description of urban dwellers in Romney's speeches. By the summer of 1977, *Time* magazine officially introduced the term "underclass" to a broad popular audience, but by then the description was familiar:

> Hopelessness is at home in a fetid ghetto flat, where children make morbid sport of chasing cockroaches or dodging rats. There may never be hot water for bathing or a working bathtub to put it in—or any other functioning plumbing. Under these conditions, afflictions such as lead poisoning (from eating flaking paint) and severe influenza are common. Siblings often sleep together in the same bed, separated by a thin wall or a blanket from parents (though frequently there is no man around). Streets are unsafe to walk at night—and, often, so are halls. Nobody starves, but many people are malnourished on a diet of hot dogs, Twinkies, Fritos, soda pop and, in rare cases, whatever can be fished out of the garbage can. Alcoholism abounds; heroin is a favorite route of escape. Another road to fantasy is the TV set. On it dance the images of the good life in middle-class America, visions that inspire envy and frustration.[86]

This horrid description collapses adults and children living in poverty with the conditions of their housing and environment. The lack of distinction between people and place renders both as permanent, underlying the hopelessness and misery of the observation.

The concept of revanchism describes the punitive turn away from the social welfare and consumption-side Keynesianism that underpinned the twentieth-century concept of the social contract.[87] The struggles during the 1960s had been fought, in part, to include African Americans under the protection of this social contract. Revanchism, then, is closely connected to a strategy that used race to undo the social contract, not just for African Americans but for all who reaped its benefits. The term is also tightly connected to a broader understanding of the neoliberal turn in the United States in the early 1970s.[88] Neoliberalism has been misunderstood as only "privatization" or the removal of state support. Of course, there are elements of privatization in the application of neoliberalism, but privatization does not encapsulate the full meaning of neoliberalism. Many tributaries have fed the concept, but above all, neoliberalism is a political, social, and economic rejection of the social welfare state and the social contract more generally. It is a strategic effort aimed at restoring the profitability of business and capital by undermining the social obstacles that had destabilized its primacy.

The regressive politics of conservativism and the project of neoliberal restructuring were not the same, but in the United States each was able to influence the development of the other. The Black struggles of the 1960s had legitimized the buildup of the social welfare state to combat the disproportionate poverty experienced by African Americans. These were expensive realizations that came with demands for social welfare, fair and equitable housing, and above all, good jobs with benefits. Indeed, the business turn to "socio-commercial capitalism" reflected the investment of capital into stabilizing tumultuous American cities. But that process had been fueled by the anger and violence of the urban rebellions. As that motor began to quiet, the desire to restore social order on the terms of business presented itself. This would happen not only through rollbacks of aspects of the welfare state but also by attacks on unions, especially public sector unions made up of Black and Brown workers. Romney, in his National Housing speech, not only stigmatized poor Black people, but he also attacked public sector workers and their demands for higher wages. He said that "the growing fiscal crisis for the central city" was a critical factor. He explained that municipal workers were "becoming more organized and more able to pressure annual wage increases," and this was part of the "challenge that is facing our society in the urban centers."[89] It was certainly a contradictory position to hold. Romney and other Republicans lamented the poverty they blamed for destroying the city, and at the same time they decried the mobilizations of public sector workers in their efforts to secure high wages and strong benefits. Access to those well-paying municipal jobs was the real key to ending the unwieldy urban crisis that Romney was describing.[90] As historian Thomas Sugrue pointed out, "No institution played a greater role than government in breaking the grip of poverty and creating a Black middle class."[91]

Neoliberalism and neoconservativism converged around the demonization of working-class and poor Black people in cities to undermine the legitimacy of a welfare state perceived to be prioritizing the care of "undeserving" African Americans. But the struggles of Black people throughout the 1960s had legitimized the idea of social welfare and depicted them as deserving of it. Because of this, a virulent ideological campaign that rarely mentioned race worked to undermine the idea that the state should fight poverty or create a "great society."[92] The movements of the 1960s undermined the assumptions of African American inferiority in ways that made open displays of racial prejudice unacceptable. This shift in political sensibilities rendered open appeals to racism socially and politically untenable. This, of course, did not mean that racism ceased to exist, but these dynamics changed how it was expressed. Instead, racial claims were now couched in ostensibly neutral language. The emergence of post–civil rights colorblind discourses found expression through narrow readings of the law and legislation with no apparent appeals to race. This shift was manifested not only in approaches to politics but most profoundly in legal decisions that indicated that the absence of clearly defined racial intent was tantamount to the absence of racial harm. The turn to colorblindness also invited a kind of judicial and political amnesia or, more simply, willful ignorance, facilitating a "refusal to acknowledge the causes and consequences of enduring racial stratification."[93]

A discourse of colorblindness and meritocracy that included references to culture, family structure, and subjective frameworks like "personal responsibility" replaced the naked race-baiting that had been a regular feature of earlier attacks on welfare and perceived Black indolence. The absence of race talk did not, however, mean the absence of coded racial incitement. "Low-income," "urban," and "poor" all stood in for Black people. Republican strategist Lee Atwater explained this transformation as follows:

> You start out in 1954 by saying, "Nigger, nigger, nigger." By 1968 you can't say "nigger"—that hurts you, backfires. So you say stuff like, uh, forced busing, states' rights, and all that stuff, and you're getting so abstract. Now, you're talking about cutting taxes, and all these things you're talking about are totally economic things and a byproduct of them is, blacks get hurt worse than whites. . . . "We want to cut this," is much more abstract than even the busing thing, uh, and a hell of a lot more abstract than "Nigger, nigger."[94]

The subtext of neoliberal ideology was pervasive individualism as an ingredient for success as well as failure. Removing race from the law and public discourse did not, of course, remove the reality of racial difference and inequality. African Americans continued to lag behind whites in the social and structural barometers that measured success in American society. But the structural impediments to Black social mobility that had been so clearly articulated in the 1960s by the various iterations of social movements were subsumed beneath an avalanche of "dysfunction discourse" that assigned blame for urban decline to individuals and not systems.

This fit with the larger objectives of neoliberal restructuring, which did not necessarily prioritize identifying undeserving individuals as previous attacks on the welfare state had done. Its objective was undoing social welfare altogether, but the attack on perceived undeserving individuals opened the door to a larger questioning of social welfare more generally. This is why Nixon officials focused as much on individuals as they did on the state itself as a source of the problem. The federal government and its derisively named "bureaucrats," as Nixon termed them, were just as much the villain as the inept welfare recipient. As the HUD-FHA crisis appeared to be deepening, the "shock" of tens of millions of dollars in FHA insurance payouts created the opportunity to redo the relationship between the state and its role in the distribution of low-income housing.[95] Milton Friedman, an economic advisor to Nixon and a theoretical architect of neoliberalism, chimed in with a response to Alsop's article on urban decline. Friedman's essay was titled "What Is Killing the City?" He wrote, "Government spending is the problem, not the solution. We do not need new government programs. We need to abolish the old programs and let people spend their own money in accordance with their own values. The city would then get better—and better and better."[96] Elsewhere Friedman wrote about the use of crises to advance a political agenda: "Only a crisis—actual or perceived—produces real change. When a crisis occurs, the actions that are taken depend on the ideas that are lying around. That I believe is our basic function: develop alternatives to existing policies . . . until the politically impossible becomes politically inevitable."[97]

The pivot from liberalism to neoliberalism could be charted through the political arc of George Romney and the generation of Cold War and racial liberals he represented. Their liberalism had been rooted in the idea that Black equality could be achieved through greater access to or inclusion in U.S. democracy and its governing institutions. But the durability of political and social crises exposed the fragility of the supposed democratic institutions of the United States. Eunduring crises pointed to *systemic* inequality. For many Cold War liberals, the persistence of inequality did not lead them to question the governing structures and institutions; it compelled them to question the abilities and aptitude of (some of) the recipients of government subsidies and social welfare. Romney was conflicted, as he did not completely disavow a role for the state in the distribution of social welfare, a disavowal that many within the Nixon administration were sympathetic to. But Romney's equating the "welfare poor" to criminals and drug addicts was vicious and based in the worst and most racist stereotypes. It was, however, the logical conclusion for someone who believed in the promise of American capitalism, even as its luster dulled in the face of looming economic crisis.

Neoliberalism foreclosed the promise of the American dream for African Americans. The country was entering a period of retrenchment regarding anti-poverty programs, even as robust spending on an emergent regime of repression was to ensue. The neoliberal project did not require the absence of state programs, as the massive expansion of spending on police, prisons, and the military in the 1970s demonstrated. There was a concerted attack on the programs that were easy to assail politically, but even more intense was the attack on the idea of social welfare and persons believed to be its recipients. The perceptions of crisis in the FHA-assisted existing housing program, along with the growing price tag on HUD's swelling inventory, contributed to an environment of recrimination and resentment about the program and social welfare programs more generally. Nixon's postelection budget for 1974 proposed terminating over 100 programs with roots in the War on Poverty and the Great Society, including ending the controversial Office of Economic Opportunity, the same office that had supported the lawsuits of the low-income Black women activists in Seattle, Philadelphia, and Chicago. Not only did Nixon's electoral landslide bury McGovern, but it buried the Great Society and discredited the notion that government had a responsibility to the poor.

Black journalist Samuel Yette described a postelection meeting between representatives of the new Nixon administration and publishers of more than 100 newspapers. Yette recalled that when a similar assembly of journalists had convened nine years earlier when Johnson was elected president, he had told them off the record the following day that he would announce an "unconditional war on poverty." The meeting in 1973 was very different. When Black journalists asked about Black unemployment, poverty, and the availability of government programs to young African Americans, Herbert Stein, Nixon's chief economic advisor, tersely responded, "The government is not the solution to the problem." Yette opined further about the subtext of Stein's declaration: "What he was saying was that they [journalists] had failed to recognize something truly different about the *nature* of the new injury and its implications for the future. It wasn't that government didn't understand; it didn't care. That . . . [is] the message to Black America contained in the Nixon-'74 budget."[98]

Public debates on federal spending had moved in a conservative direction during the presidential election of 1972. Nixon had couched the election in terms of the "welfare ethic versus the work ethic" as he tried to appeal to white voters in the orbit of George McGovern while still distinguishing his campaign from that of independent and former arch segregationist George Wallace.[99] Governor Ronald Reagan of California, who was vociferously opposed to welfare as a social entitlement, put Nixon on the defensive as a political challenger to his right. Nixon initially backed a proposal called the Family Assistance Plan, which would provide a "national income" of $1,600 for all citizens as a replacement for individual welfare payments. It was a plan supported by Friedman, but it stoked suspicion among other political conservatives. Reagan recast Nixon's plan as even more welfare and came out aggressively against it while simultaneously leading a campaign to criminalize fraud in California's welfare system.[100] In the ensuing debates over Nixon's Family Assistance Plan versus Reagan's efforts to overhaul welfare as an entitlement, the discussions centered on who deserved benefits but was not getting them versus the undeserving recipients who were cannily cashing in.

The political volleys in the debates between conservative and liberal elected officials over the meaning of social welfare in the United States cynically tapped into growing public concerns with inflation and growing tax commitments. As Nixon said in his Labor Day speech, two months before Election Day, "The work ethic tells us that there is really no such thing as 'something for nothing,' and that everything valuable in life requires some striving and some sacrifice."[101] Republican officials almost never groused about the extraordinary costs of the Vietnam War, but only about programs that had been created to address issues of social welfare. These included programs that were not "welfare" at all but nevertheless were perceived as such, like HUD's homeownership subsidies. The never-ending news coverage of HUD's urban housing scandals always made reference to tax dollars lost through FHA insurance payouts. One editorial described "taxpayers [as] the real losers."[102] The demonization of social welfare recipients also had the ancillary consequence of rationalizing the continuation of racial segregation. The negative portrayal of American cities and, most importantly, the Black people living in them legitimized the efforts of suburbanites to continue to exclude low-income city dwellers from their communities. Thus the HUD-FHA crisis of the 1970s should also be understood for its contribution to the discourse of urban decline and the emergence of the underclass, a useful political tool in the efforts to reestablish a particular kind of order in American life.

A NEW CRISIS—AGAIN

The attacks on the welfare state were not driven by ideology and rhetoric alone. By the early 1970s, a number of interlocking events also worked to erode support for the social programs of the 1960s. Even as the War on Poverty was credited with a decrease in the number of people who were officially designated as poor, Republicans and conservatives more generally blamed the expansion of Johnson's social welfare programs for the rising rate of inflation in the 1970s. By 1973, inflation in the United States had reached its highest rate since the Civil War and was ravaging the lives of ordinary people. The rate of inflation was pegged at 8.7 percent in the consumer price index, a doubling of the 1972 rate.[103] Despite the vitriol from the Nixon administration against "big government" and "federal centralization," Nixon imposed price controls, trying—and failing—to stem the tide of inflation. The spike in fuel prices combined with crop shortages caused by weather resulted in increases in food costs, which rose by 30 percent in 1973, something experienced acutely by ordinary people. Wholesale grain prices had increased by 21 percent in a single month, which had a cascading effect on all food costs. For the first three-quarters of 1973, food prices spiked by 24 percent. Three months after Nixon had been inaugurated as president, federal officials reported that the consumer price index "for February had risen at a rate unseen since 1951."[104] Living standards for ordinary people were devastated again when meat prices rose by 75 percent in the spring of 1973. The cost of meat and food more generally prompted a weeklong meat boycott in April of that year.[105] By May, food costs continued to spiral out of control as the price of soybeans rose by 45 percent, wheat by 22 percent, and corn by 30 percent.[106]

When prices began to climb in 1971, Nixon imposed what was referred to as the Phase II freeze, which was applied to prices with the exception of raw agricultural products but did not apply to wages, which infuriated business. The freeze had little impact because it did not roll prices back; it only froze them at their grossly inflated rate.[107] Perhaps the most graphic demonstration of the crisis of inflation occurred when workers at a Texas hatchery drowned 43,000 baby chicks in barrels on the evening news. The company owners had decided it was more cost-effective to kill the baby chicks, since the price of their feed was rising but the cost of chicken was frozen, or as the owner said, "It's cheaper to drown 'em than to put 'em down and raise 'em."[108]

By the fall, prices had begun to come back down, but the shock of inflation was lasting.[109] A Gallup poll in September found that 89 percent of those asked said "the high cost of living" was the main problem facing the country.[110] Just as the food prices were easing after a record-setting harvest in the fall of 1973, an energy crisis would produce new economic shocks. Oil shortages prompted by domestic production issues overlapped with an international crunch in oil production and distribution. An embargo staged by oil-producing Middle Eastern countries helped to drive up the price of oil in the United States. Perhaps the most lasting memories of the oil shock of 1973–74 were of hours-long lines for gasoline and heating oil, with queues of cars circling city blocks.

The shock of inflation combined with the oil embargo brought the long postwar boom to a stunning end. There were sharp debates over the causes of inflation, but most economists seemed to vacillate between the postwar rise in wages, high employment, and the welfare state versus food and oil shortages. The rising rates of inflation and other cost-of-living expenses were exacerbated by the new erosion in employment. By January 1974, the Black unemployment rate ticked up to 9.6 percent, with forecasts that it would rise further through the end of the year.[111] It was the first rise in Black unemployment in six years. In the spring of 1975, at the height of the postwar recession, Black unemployment swelled to 14.2 percent.[112] By 1976, according to the Urban League, Black unemployment would reach an astonishing 25.4 percent, and for Black teenagers it would leap to 64 percent. An indication of the spiraling economic situation for African Americans was borne out in the statistic that showed 39 percent of Black children lived with their mothers in the households of other relatives.[113]

Republicans, led by businessmen, seized on the argument that blamed the Keynesian social contract for economic woes and used it as the basis to reset social expectations in order to restore profitability to the corporate bottom line. As *Business Week* editorialized, "Some people will obviously have to do with less. . . . Yet it will be a hard pill to swallow—the idea of doing with less so that big business can have more."[114] A former Federal Reserve official was even more direct when he blamed inflationary pressures on "the almost universal commitment to the objective of full employment . . . and the welfare-state idea which holds that government out to have a continuing active concerns with the poor, the sick, the aged, and the chronically unemployed."[115] Writer Sharon Smith

described this process as the "employers' offensive":[116] a period of business organizing aggressively to roll back the gains of the 1930s and 1960s in an effort
to restore its profitability while smashing the expectations of ordinary workers.
A part of the process of restoration was an attack on the welfare state and the
people who received its benefits. It was truly a sin of omission to speak feverishly
about the ways that social spending and rising wages were to blame for inflation
while saying nothing about the almost $1 trillion spent on the Vietnam War.
This was just one indication that the concern of business was not just reining in
spending but, more importantly, disciplining labor and turning back the ideas
that underpinned the social contract.

A NEW REALITY

The attacks on the subsidized homeownership programs prompted an assessment
of HUD's work, leading to some unexpected conclusions. The original legislation
had set out the ambitious goal of 26 million units of housing within ten years.
By 1973, HUD had reached the halfway mark for that goal. By some measures, the
federally backed, subsidized housing movement was a historic success. Between
1934 and 1968, there had been roughly 1 million units of subsidized housing
built in the United States. But between 1969 and 1972, the numbers accelerated
dramatically. Production of low-income housing jumped from 226,000 units in
1970 to 472,000 in 1971 and back to 380,000 in 1972.[117] Of course, these numbers were lower than the ambitious goal of 600,000 units a year established by
Congress in 1968, but they were higher than at any other point in U.S. history. In
the five years of the HUD Act, 995,000 new units of public housing were scheduled to be built, but only 386,400 had been produced. Within the homeownership programs specifically, Section 235 had been projected to provide 695,000
single-family homes, and of those, 400,883 were ultimately produced. The HUD
Act had also vested the FHA with the authority to extend rehabilitation loans
in urban areas in anticipation of rehabilitation projects. The original legislation
had predicted 135,000 rehabilitation loans and had financed 53,885 of them.[118]

When George Romney's replacement, James T. Lynn, a corporate lawyer and
a former undersecretary of the Commerce Department, was asked to explain the
relationship between the federal government and subsidized housing, he insisted
that the market, not federal intervention, was responsible for HUD's rapid production of housing. Following his own logic, he argued that a "marketplace phenomenon," not state intervention, would develop more housing opportunities

for the low-income and poor. He explained, "The principal cause of families living in substandard housing is—plainly and simply—lack of income to afford standard units either newly constructed or existing."[119] Norman Waterson, a HUD assistant undersecretary, further distanced the federal government from any particular responsibility to housing when he said, "The additional social benefits of housing the poor aren't known. How many kids who had a warm bed, a light to study by, and now have moved into the system, just isn't available."[120]

Lynn's and Waterson's statements skirted the substantive discussion concerning location, affordability, and access to housing that was even more critical because of the worsening financial situation in the country. There was even less discussion among the new leadership within HUD about pressing issues of housing discrimination. Where George Romney had championed open housing and civil rights for Black people as governor of Michigan, Lynn had no such background and no experience in the field of housing. When he was pressed on these issues, Lynn promised that new housing legislation intended to replace the suspended programs would include "very tough provisions on equal opportunity."

In an interview with *Black Enterprise* magazine, Lynn was asked if the new programs would increase residential integration. In a cautious reply, Lynn echoed Nixon from 1971 when he said, "We've set clear racial goals . . . to undo, to the extent that we can, the effects of discrimination in the past, to afford every opportunity we can for people to have freedom of choice as to where they live."[121] He went on to say, "Does he [the African American] have a choice? That's the important thing."[122] Gloria E. A. Toote, an African American woman and the assistant secretary for equal opportunity in HUD under Nixon and Ford, claimed that HUD's use of experimental "housing allowances," soon to be housing vouchers, would end residential segregation.[123] The disbursement of housing allowances was an experimental program that gave low-income residents lump sums of money to supplement their income, ostensibly allowing them to pay more for rent. This was part of a broader strategy to abandon programs that involved HUD-managed or -owned buildings or that required vigilant enforcement of the bans of housing discrimination.

The new method would include supplementing the earnings of low-income people as the main way to create choice in the private market. The housing allowance was also pitched as a way to facilitate the "dispersal" of poor people. No longer would housing be confined to certain buildings or neighborhoods; the allowance would allow people to look wherever they chose. Toote said that the end of subsidized housing and the introduction of "housing allowances" would "allow minorities to totally integrate throughout the country."[124] She did temper her enthusiasm by adding, "provided [HUD] ha[s] the staffing to properly effectuate its job."[125] William Morris, who headed the NAACP's division of housing, proposed counseling, as discussed earlier, as a way to overcome residential segregation from the perspective of Black renters. Without counseling, according to Morris, African Americans "tend to congregate among themselves, compounding the problems they already have. With proper counseling they would become more aware of the full range of housing, jobs, and school opportunities available to them."[126] Morris was placing the onus for racial segregation on African Americans apparently unaware of housing opportunities outside all-Black enclaves. More generally, the hard times of the mid-1970s were quickly removing the varnish from the big expectations of "Black capitalism." The escalating rates of Black unemployment undermined the purchasing power of the constituency of the Black capitalists. A Black research think tank showed that 18 percent of Black-owned businesses failed in 1974. Rising interest rates also meant that banks were becoming stingy in their loans to underwrite Black capitalist ventures.[127] The crumbling facade of Black capitalism belied the tenuousness and fragility of arguments in support of supposed gilded separation.

Morris's comments were further confirmation that ending residential segregation was not viewed as an important pursuit of the federal government.[128] In Lynn's HUD, outside of responding to explicit acts of racism, the federal government would ignore the mandate to affirmatively pursue residential integration. The Nixon administration's desire to shift responsibilities for HUD's programming to the states and cities would further diminish federal oversight of those programs, in some cases fatally. The promise of a return to "local control" was an affront to the concerted efforts behind the decades-long demand of African American citizens that federal officials enforce the nation's laws when local and state governments refused to do so. Indeed, the heart of the civil rights struggles of the 1960s was the rejection of "states' rights" and the localism where Jim Crow thrived. Black people demanded the oversight and regulation of the federal government as a check on unrestrained racism that thrived on the local level. This reality exposed the exaggerated and often false distinction between de jure and de facto discrimination, as if identifiable actors were implicated in the former and no one was responsible for the latter. In fact, local architects of racial discrimination were often the targets of political and litigious action from ordinary individuals and local activists—*they* knew where the discrimination was coming from.

Federal officials were already reluctant partners in enforcing the nation's antidiscrimination laws, while local and city officials could be downright hostile, as demonstrated in Chapter 3. For that reason, Nixon's proposed return to "states' rights," "municipalities' rights," or "individual choice" would almost inevitably fatally compromise the promise of equal access and open housing—including the end of racial discrimination in the housing market. Walter Hundley of the Seattle Model Cities program made the point: "I am convinced that the only real salvation for the disadvantaged, and for poor blacks in particular, is the direct intervention of the federal government. Local political pressures militate against giving to blacks any priority for public monies, as the federal special impact programs do now. That's why local government is not ready for the burdens which Nixon wants to give it."[129] Nonetheless, the nation's memory was deceptively short. The cry for states' rights and local control had been the mantra of those who rejected federal civil rights protections and deplored the federal government's intervention in local matters. This was not only a matter for the South, but a critical matter for the North as well. These tensions, impervious to regional distinction, had been laid bare in the ongoing struggle over school desegregation, as bitter in Boston as it was in Little Rock. Nixon injected the racial antipathy surrounding debates involving school desegregation directly into the debates over suburban desegregation with his statement decrying "forced integration" over "freedom of choice" in housing.[130]

In the aftermath of *Brown v. Board of Education*, southern schools were mandated to end segregation. In response, southern segregationists in government sought a compromise between segregation and school integration by suggesting "freedom of choice" schools that allowed both white and Black parents to "choose" where to send their children.[131] The fiasco illuminated the charade of choice as white parents chose segregated schools and Black parents risked their personal livelihood if they chose incorrectly by attempting to send their children to white schools. The courts began to react to these attempts by the South to preserve segregation during the Nixon administration. The landmark case of *Green v. Kent County* in 1968 declared that "freedom of choice" schools had maintained a "dual school system" and were an affront to *Brown*'s affirmative mandate for school desegregation. Beyond the significance of the ruling, the sclerotic pace of change in school desegregation across the South and the fierce battles it would provoke in the North exemplified the problem of "local control." In 1971, the Supreme Court upheld a lower court ruling in the *Swann v. Charlotte-Mecklenburg Board of Education* case that busing was an appropriate corrective to school segregation. The continuing crisis over school integration in the 1970s was inextricably linked to issues of residential segregation.[132]

Whether in education or housing, "choice" was a shibboleth intended to divert discussions about compliance with federal law into a separate discussion concerning "personal freedom" and "individual liberty." In schools, as in housing, it was easy to see that the "rights" and "choices" of some carried more weight than those of others. Underlining the political nature of almost all budget choices, while Nixon was in the midst of compiling his austerity budget for 1974, in part by impounding and cutting HUD's budget, he suggested a tax credit totaling $600 million for parents who chose to send their children to parochial schools instead of public schools.[133] The political discourse of passive discrimination, colorblindness, and choice was reinforced in the Supreme Court case of *Milliken v. Bradley* in 1974. This was another case involving school segregation, this time in Detroit. Multiple lower court rulings had agreed with the city of Detroit that a metropolitan-wide plan was necessary to desegregate public schools.

Lower courts had agreed that public policies encouraging and enacting residential segregation were responsible for segregated schools. But in 1974, a Supreme Court packed with four Nixon appointees disagreed and ruled 5–4 that Detroit suburbs did not have to be included in plans to desegregate the public schools. The Supreme Court gave an explanation that defied the common sense well established by the mid-1970s. The justices claimed, "No record has been made in this case showing that the racial composition of the Detroit school population or that residential patterns within Detroit and in the surrounding areas were in any significant measure caused by governmental activity," and that the "predominantly Negro school population in Detroit [was] caused by unknown and perhaps unknowable factors such as in-migration, birth rates, economic changes, or cumulative acts of private racial fears."[134]

It was a startling turnabout for the Supreme Court. Only six years earlier the Court had ruled definitively against housing discrimination in *Jones v. Mayer*. In six short years, public accounts of the roots of racial segregation went from "racial discrimination herd[ing] men into ghettos"[135] to "unknowable factors" creating a Black "core" of the city. There were other cases dealing specifically with the placement of low-income housing that made clear that the absence of any language that could be construed as "racist" meant that the intent of proposed legislation could not possibly be determined. The demands for racial specificity as evidence of racial harm created an impossible standard in a period where public displays of racism were no longer permissible. The political discussions concerning busing and housing integration as led by the Nixon administration reinforced each other in ways that promoted a "colorblind politics of minimal compliance with the law, one that framed residential population distributions as the outcome of individual choice and race neutral economic forces."[136]

A NEW APPROACH TO HOUSING

Thirteen days into his presidency, Gerald Ford signed the Housing and Community Development Act (HCDA) into law on August 22, 1974, almost six years to the day from the signing of the HUD Act.[137] Even though Nixon had been ousted, the HCDA was a hallmark of New Federalist principles. It was drafted with the intention of undoing many aspects of the HUD Act. Ford triumphantly claimed during the signing ceremony, "This bill . . . marks a complete and welcome reversal in the way America tries to solve the problems of our urban communities."[138] In the HUD Act, Johnson had intended to power public-private partnerships with federal subsidies and unprecedented access to mortgage insurance as a way of inducing private sector participation in producing housing for low-income and poor people. Whereas the 1968 bill was debated with American cities burning as a backdrop, the HCDA was being contemplated in the midst of record-high inflation, growing unemployment, and a conservative backlash already under way.

The new bill redirected the resources of government away from the continued expansion represented by the massive HUD Act. The size of the legislation crafted by the Ford administration was still quite large, but its key features limited federal power while acceding to local power. Nixon's Republican Party was not opposed to all government; indeed, it privileged the supposed intuitive power of local governance. Ford continued, "In a very real sense, this bill will help to return power from the banks of the Potomac to people in their own communities. Decisions will be made at the local level. Action will come at the local level. And responsibility for results will be placed squarely where it belongs—at the local level."[139] In 1972, when Nixon first introduced "revenue sharing" into government, he described it as a process whereby "local officials responding to local conditions and local constituencies . . . decide what should happen and not some distant bureaucrat in Washington, D.C." He promised that the revenues to be shared would not be subject to the oversight of federal agencies: "When we say no strings . . . we mean no strings."[140] The centerpiece of Ford's housing legislation featured "no strings attached" revenue sharing and block grants that were touted as new, innovative tools that would transform "urban renewal" into "community development."

Prior to the HCDA, localities received federal funding in the form of categorical grants for all of the programs that had been "categorically" ended with Nixon's moratorium. Those programs included urban renewal, water and sewage grants, rehabilitation loans, and restoration and beautification grants. Funding these projects would no longer be obligatory; instead, it would be discretionary. The money previously appropriated for these projects was now to be rolled into a lump sum and sent to the cities and states that qualified for it. Other programs were designated as "special grants," which required funding. These included appropriations for education, law enforcement, environmental protections, and fire safety. There were written requirements as to how such funds were to be used, but ultimately, those decisions were left to local government. With the HCDA, complex funding formulas were put into place to determine the amount and location of funding for block grants. Numerous factors went into the calculation, but almost all of them were based on census counts, including the local population and the number of people officially in poverty. There was some concern, though, about the ability of the census to accurately capture population demographics and thus ensure the proper allocation of resources. For example, the 1970 census undercounted African Americans by 7.7 percent, but it undercounted whites by 1 percent.[141] These convoluted formulas also relied on old information. The data used to determine block grants for 1977 relied on 1973 population studies and 1970 poverty and housing statistics, failing to take into account population shifts or rises in poverty from 1970 to 1977. This resulted in "the shift of funds from poor central city areas to wealthier suburban areas."[142]

The expanded criteria for funding meant that more cities were eligible for block grants even though the amount of money to be shared did not increase. Congress set the amount that would be appropriated for the block grants for five years into the future. For 1975, $2.5 billion was made available, and the amount increased to $2.95 billion in 1976 and 1977. A "hold harmless" stipulation required that no city lose any funding for the first three years of the HCDA, but cuts could take place in the fourth year.[143] This poison pill was eliminated in 1977 to stave off disaster. If funding formulas had not been readjusted, New England cities would have lost 37 percent of their community development funds, while Sunbelt cities in the West, also Republican strongholds, would have seen their funds increase by 203 percent.[144] The changes in formula and the introduction of block grants ultimately meant a reduction in the overall amount of funds made available for critical community development programs. Efforts to stave off the punitive potential of the HCDA, however, did not fundamentally change the fact that many of the poorest citizens were being written out of housing assistance.

In the newly revamped Section 235, legislators removed the previous require-ment that the "lowest practicable income" take priority. Section 235 was essen-tially changed into a middle-income-oriented program. There would be a new 3 percent down payment on mortgages of up to $25,000 and 5 percent on any mortgage in excess of that figure. The purchaser would be required to pay closing costs, something that did not exist in the program before. The federal govern-ment would now only subsidize the interest rates down to 5 percent, as opposed to the old floor of 1 percent.[145] The income eligibility level was also changed from 135 percent of the median-area income to 80 percent. Given the rapidly rising cost of single-family houses, this immediately put homeownership beyond the means of poor people for whom the program had once made a way. Similarly, in public housing, the requirement that "the dwelling in low-rent housing shall be available solely for families of low income" was removed as a stipulation.[146] The HCDA included a requirement that housing assistance be organized regionally and that, in the absence of a regional plan for low-income housing, the housing funds would be forfeited. As one observer said, "This is an enforcement device HUD has never in the past either implemented or *advocated*, [but] the failure of communities to consider the regional plan could certainly result in the loss of development funds."[147] Once again, this requirement made funding decisions contingent on urban and suburban collaboration in the fulfillment of a "regional plan." Of course, this type of alliance had never succeeded in the past, and there was no reason to believe it would be successful going forward.

This dynamic was best exemplified by the creation of Section 8 housing as-sistance.[148] Section 8 grew out of two previous policy strains. The first was a housing program that began during the Johnson administration called Section 23. It had allowed local housing authorities to lease privately owned units to rent to public housing recipients. It was seen favorably because it kept the govern-ment out of owning buildings and made use of privately owned, existing housing stock. The legislation that eventually became Section 8 was also influenced by a multiyear study on the use of housing allowances that began in 1970. The HUD study had been commissioned as part of the New Federalist effort to search out alternatives to government oversight and involvement. Of course, an allowance would still call for some involvement by state agencies, but it was a program that would largely exist within the private housing market.

There was bipartisan support for Section 8. For conservatives, it fulfilled much of the desire to end the prospect of new construction in white suburbs as well as minimized the imprint of the federal government. For liberals, by relying on existing housing, Section 8 satisfied the long-standing demand that housing be made immediately available. Construction was deemphasized in the original HCDA legislation even as provision was made for the construction of new Section 8 buildings where tenants would be able to use their vouchers for reduced rents. But Section 8 was mostly a program fueled by the use of housing vouchers. The amount of the subsidy paid by HUD was the difference between what tenants paid (25 percent of their income) and the cost of the rent. As a way of preventing landlords from charging Section 8 tenants any random amount, HUD created a rent ceiling based on what it found to be the "fair market rent."[149] It was up to the discretion of HUD to create a formula for deciding on the fair market rent, which was based on the average amount of rent paid in a region. Because HUD cast its net regionally, the value of the rent vouchers was depressed. Given the growing costs of homeownership, many would-be buyers had been pushed into the rental market, which, in turn, reduced the number of apartments available and drove up the rent. The end result was that the Section 8 vouchers were too small to help their users move out of the poor neighborhoods they lived in. As one study concluded, "Structural and administrative flaws in [fair market rent] calculations . . . inhibited the operation of the program."[150]

Within neighborhoods where the voucher was viable, there was another dynamic. Initial studies showed that while rents across neighborhoods did not rise, landlords participating in the program raised their rents to the highest point of the rent ceiling established by the fair market value formula. Even tenants who stayed in the same apartment but began using a Section 8 subsidy saw their rents increase by 28 percent.[151] Liberals supported Section 8, believing that it would give tenants more flexibility and, most importantly, that it would result in the dispersal of the poor and racial minorities. This was, of course, naive, given that there were no requirements that landlords accept Section 8 payments or that the vouchers would provide enough in rent to cover the expense of moving into white neighborhoods.[152] The right of landlords to refuse the subsidy in combination with the inflexibility of the fair market rent raised the likelihood that Section 8 would have little impact on dispersing low-income minorities from their segregated neighborhoods. As Andrea Gill suggested more generally about the HCDA, "The effect of the 1974 Housing Act was to devolve responsibility for desegregation onto local governments, private developers and low-income families themselves, leaving increased economic and racial integration largely as a matter of housing choice."[153]

Fair housing had ceased to be a priority for HUD for many years. Indeed, the structuring of the HCDA, and more specifically Section 8, rendered fair housing a mere afterthought. Of course, there were the obligatory nods to its importance, as exemplified by Gerald Ford when he signed the legislation and assured the public that local government would make the final decisions on "the way the taxpayers' money is used" while still carefully monitoring compliance with civil rights laws.[154] But this was lip service; the entire thrust of the legislation was toward the preservation of residential segregation. The shift in emphasis from new construction to rehabilitation of existing housing would not create any new pressure to build low-income housing in suburban areas. If this were unclear, Ford's statements during the 1976 presidential campaign on the placement of low-income housing in predominately white neighborhoods were to the point. He said, "Ethnic heritage is a great treasure of this country, and I don't think federal action should be used to destroy that treasure."[155]

HUD now argued that the massive wave of housing abandonment had opened up more housing in the cities that people in search of affordable housing should be utilizing. The momentum was toward maintaining the status quo and certainly not pursuing residential integration as a way to open up access to more resources for the urban poor and low-income. Not only had the far-reaching efforts of the HUD Act been reversed, but the logic of the Fair Housing Act had also been subverted because of the perception that the city and those who lived in it would destroy white communities. As one author wrote, "The cloud of Watergate has tended to obscure Nixon's tremendous achievements. He had as much impact on the logic, politics, and distribution of federal urban development program grants as any Great Society liberal. Over seven years, Richard Nixon largely undid their work, killing or severely restricting most of the new agencies the Great Society created."[156]

IN THE SHORT SPAN from the passage of the Fair Housing Act and the HUD Act in 1968 to the passage of the HCDA in 1974, the political atmosphere had changed radically. For the right, the onset of economic crisis in 1973–74 and the absence of urban rebellions created an opportunity to abandon the notion of the social contract and social welfare and its most recent embodiment in the Johnson welfare state. This included what had been bipartisan efforts to create low-income homeownership in American cities. By its tumultuous end, HUD's mission to pursue low-income homeownership had devolved into charges and indictments for fraud and corruption involving hundreds of public officials and private actors connected to the real estate industry. Not only did the spectacle of crime cast a shadow over the program itself, but it was skillfully wielded by the right to cast doubt further on social welfare as a concept. The Nixonian description of U.S. society as one divided between those who embraced a "work ethic" versus those who lazed at the threshold of the "welfare ethic" deflected a deeper engagement with the massive social and racial inequality that constrained the development of Black urban communities. Meanwhile, the lightly regulated relationship between the housing industry and the federal government was allowed to proceed on its own terms, and thus a new crisis in housing unfolded in cities across the country. Racist assumptions about Black communities, Black housing, and Black people appeared to be confirmed in the public's imagination about what went wrong. Perhaps of equal consequence was that the role of the bankers, brokers, and builders in the program's devolution was lost, while the focus became tightly trained on perceptions of a failed government program and the failed recipients of its services.

The question of government competence was closely bound to racial assumptions about the assumed beneficiaries of these programs. The demonization of African American recipients of public assistance had been demonstrated through queries concerning whether they deserved such benefits ever since their movement into cities outside the South had made them eligible to receive these benefits. By the 1970s, these questions were raised within a new context. The onset of economic decline made for an easy political attack on the fragile remnants of the Johnson welfare state, including the programs of the HUD Act. With Black women affixed as the face of the scandals swirling about the HUD programs, there was an easy connection made between the perception of problems within the HUD homeownership programs and welfare or public aid more generally. The demonization of Black women on welfare or as residents of public housing informed the political atmosphere in which housing subsidies were being scrutinized. The language of "underclass" only helped to underscore that there were particular problems attributable to particular people. It was definitive proof that a political shift was well under way.

The Nixon administration tapped the deepening resentments in a new period of economic recession and escalating interest rates. Nixon's focus on the expense of these housing programs over the life of subsidies as well as the costs of the insurance payouts for houses that fell into default ignited the passions of resentful white homeowners who chafed at the idea that African Americans were recipients of special privileges. Welfare rates were rising, as were crime and other features of social turmoil, but no one said the obvious truth that these conditions were exacerbated, not alleviated, by the obstacles erected by suburban municipalities to keep African Americans out of their communities. Instead, the HCDA and the adoption of Section 8 housing were concessions to the political shift to the right and the economic demands of important sectors of the housing industry. The turn to housing vouchers preserved the private sector as the preferred alternative to house working-class and poor people. The federal government subsidized the construction of buildings to be used for Section 8 housing in addition to the use of vouchers, but those buildings were to be privately owned and managed. That the cost of the voucher was based on the average rent in the entire metropolitan area ostensibly would create maximum flexibility for tenants to move wherever they chose. As was the case with much of HUD housing, though, in the absence of a mandate that landlords be required to accept Section 8 and with no real commitment or budget to enforce fair housing laws, the newest invention in the ongoing "housing crisis" was bound to reproduce the same issues that had been recurring for decades: segregation and inequality.

The HUD-FHA homeownership programs were only the latest programs to fail miserably in their claims of "urban renewal." Representatives of the Nixon administration, including George Romney, portrayed the collapse of FHA-assisted low-income homeownership as an indictment of "big government." These observations were hardly benign; they were spun into a larger campaign intended to undermine the system of urban social welfare that had been built up over the course of the 1960s as a result of the convergence of the civil rights and Black insurgent movements.

This campaign was not just an attack on Black working-class families; it was part of a larger effort to undermine the central premise of twentieth-century governance: the social contract. The expectation that the federal government had a responsibility to create a floor through which no citizen could fall was forged through mass protests in the 1930s and again in the 1960s. In the absence of that pressure and of the postwar economic expansion that made it possible, the ruling elite repositioned itself to restore lower expectations and lower living standards.

The Nixon rhetoric to justify this retreat was seductive in a perplexing moment of record-high inflation that expressed itself through astronomical food and fuel prices, persistent war in Vietnam, and an unraveling of the good life for millions of white workers who had come of age amid post–World War II prosperity. The physical decline of urban areas overlay deepening economic and social crises that had been underwritten by years of institutional neglect and official malfeasance. Together, they provided an easily accessible visual to make sense of the terrible turn of fortunes. It was a turn that pivoted on the nasty portrayal of cities in the grip of socially, economically, and morally impoverished African Americans. These portrayals were not innocent observations, but they implicitly justified the hardening objections of suburban officials to allow for the construction of low-income housing in their communities. They legitimized the federal government's return to policies that encouraged residential segregation and the further isolation of poor and working-class urban neighborhoods.

Predatory Inclusion

WHEN RONALD REAGAN became president in 1980, he called for HUD to convene a special commission on housing policy in 1982. For more than thirty years after pledging to provide decent homes for its citizens, the federal government and its department of housing had continued to fail to achieve its goal. The latest housing commission impaneled by Reagan called its report "To House a Nation," and it began with a criticism of the HUD Act. The HUD Act had left as its legacy "a belief in the potency of government programs." Reagan's Commission on Housing promised the opposite: "The genius of the market economy, freed from the distortions forced by government housing policies and regulations that swung erratically from loving to hostile, can provide for housing far better than Federal programs."[1] It was a conclusion that could only be reached by ignoring the actual origins of the HUD Act and the reasons behind its demise. Lyndon Johnson had promised the "genius of private industry" as the key to unlocking the mystery of perpetual housing crises. But lackadaisical management, erratic regulations, and trenchant racial discrimination combined with the end of redlining and the predacious inclusion of formerly excluded Black urbanites allowed the real estate industry to bleed inner cities dry.

It was not government intrusion that sank the FHA-assisted low-income homeownership programs; it was government negligence. But this malfeasance was not just an issue of poorly motivated personnel; it was the outcome of mismatched objectives and impossible tasks. When public policies are guided by the objectives of private enterprise, as the HUD homeownership programs undoubtedly were, they are clinched in a dance of conflict. As magnanimous as the life insurance industry and other titans of business who argued for "socio-commercial enterprise" in the 1960s tried to present themselves, in the end, the objective of profit-making outpaced the necessity for safe and sound housing. One glaring reason for this spoke to the heart of the conflict: real estate profits were rooted in residential segregation.

In this book I have tried to mark the pivot in U.S. policy and political history at the end of the 1960s to draw attention to how statutory changes alone are rarely, if ever, enough to undo deeply ingrained cultural, social, economic, and political assumptions that shape our society. The reality of a racialized political economy challenged the idea that inclusion in the financial and public services that for so long had excluded African Americans was enough to overcome the physical and economic devastation of Black urban communities. Indeed, I have argued that inclusion in those processes while ignoring the larger dynamics created by residential segregation laid the basis for even greater exploitative and predatory practices—or predatory inclusion—in transactions involving the urban housing market. As new as the use of mortgage-backed securities and the privatization of the FNMA were, the value of housing was still based on a very old calculus. Housing value in the United States continued to be scaled according to the proximity of African Americans. The turn to inclusion was only allowable by maintaining other forms of exclusion. Credit inclusion became possible by holding the line on neighborhood exclusion.

This inclusion/exclusion mismatch had two impacts in the urban housing market. First, all of the newly available financial resources created value in substandard and distressed urban housing where previously the property had little to no value. In city after city, real estate operatives were able to bring those properties back to life with Section 235 and Section 221(d)(2) by selling them to vulnerable Black homemakers in search of shelter. But, second, this ability to resuscitate these otherwise dead properties was also made possible when real estate brokers embraced their role as gatekeepers and continued to exclude poor and working-class African Americans from white suburban communities.

Propping up the value of these and other habitable but still substandard properties then required that the community members be able to afford them. Cultivating customers included making credit available for people to buy the houses that had now been made marketable by the various programs of HUD. But there was a dramatic shortage of housing choices available to poor and working-class urban residents. The physical decline of public housing developments in combination with the ever-decreasing income requirements for an apartment in public housing transformed it into the "housing of last resort," and it became unavailable to most of the poor who needed housing. Most importantly, urban renewal policies, continued until 1974, had prioritized destruction over construction, thereby limiting the availability of good housing in urban areas. Finally, the limits on building safe, sound, and affordable housing in white suburban areas had foreclosed the possibility of expanding the availability of housing, which also helped to constitute an urban market filled with dilapidated housing. These factors made HUD's homeownership programs an attractive alternative even when the housing stock was in suspect condition.

Inclusion, in this case, created the conditions for continued extraction as opposed to development and actual renewal. This, of course, was not an argument for the continuation of redlining and other exclusive practices, but racial and residential segregation could not be partially ended in one part of the market while it was accepted in the other. Ending federal redlining while maintaining a cavalier, if not voluntarist, approach to the enforcement of federal fair housing and civil rights laws in housing rendered both ineffective.

The fundamental failure of the federal government to affirmatively pursue fair and open housing for African Americans was not a failure of bureaucracy, organizational mismanagement, or malfeasance alone. Indeed, to reduce the deep problems of HUD-FHA's homeownership program to institutional misconduct or mismanagement elided the systemic conflicts of interest at the heart of the program, including the central role of private institutions that remained vested in a racially segmented housing and mortgage market. Indeed, real estate agents, in particular, vociferously opposed fair housing while enthusiastically backing the HUD Act because of its potential to develop an urban housing market and draw in unprecedented resources.

When federal management and ownership of public housing became increasingly politically unpalatable, the state became dependent on private sector forces to produce, manage, and own the nation's housing stock. This division of labor made it virtually impossible for the federal agents to properly and vigorously enforce civil rights laws in housing. As the production, buying, and selling of homes became indispensable to the U.S. national economy, the more influential the various sectors of the housing industry became in housing policy. Their strategic role complicated the ability of federal officials to regulate these industries and inevitably resulted in ever-shrinking amounts of federal dollars dedicated to enforcement and investigations. Even where investigations proved fruitful, such as with the HUD-FHA scandals that resulted in indictments for fraud, these situations were portrayed as isolated bouts of individual greed.

This emphasis on institutional pressures to maintain the status quo in the housing market was not intended to diminish the desires of Black residents. African Americans wanted to be homeowners, and they wanted access to the entire housing market when making their choices of where to live. The repeated acts of hostility of white residents along with the persistent racial discrimination of public and private institutions created a Sisyphean dilemma for Black residents. But even as African Americans endeavored to create community and meaning within their segregated living spaces, residential segregation was a condition imposed through action and deliberate inaction of the state. The reality is that many African Americans wanted to live in neighborhoods that were integrated, and not because of a particular affinity for white neighbors. White neighborhoods had access to greater resources, including housing, schools, and jobs. These, of course, were the attributes that made the exclusive white neighborhood the most expensive in the country.

RETREAT

The retreat from postwar racial liberalism was not just partisan politics. It represented a wholesale turn in all of American politics. The 1970s economic crisis required the mobilization of massive human and financial resources to resolve it, but in the midst of generalized economic crisis and political polarization, there was no party to make the demand. The political thrashing the Democrats received in the 1972 election made the party reluctant to continue embracing a liberal identity. This became even clearer with the ascent of Jimmy Carter as the leader of the Democratic Party. And as the social movements and protests of an earlier period began to recede into the background, the pressure that had been propelling the Democratic Party into its historic role in the 1960s ceased to exist. Indeed, by 1976, Carter as a candidate for president sought to clarify his position on housing policy. Parroting Nixon's strained delineation between racial and economic segregation, Carter explained, "To build a high rise, very low-cost housing unit in a suburban neighborhood or other neighborhoods with relatively expensive homes, I think, would not be in the best interest of the people who live in the high rise or the suburbs. . . . I'm not going to use the federal government's authority deliberately to circumvent the natural inclination of people to live in ethnically homogenous neighborhoods."[2] When pressed by reporters to clarify his statement, Carter continued, "The government ought not take as a major purpose the intrusion of alien groups into a neighborhood, simply to establish that intrusion."

Even as access to credit liberalized during the 1970s, it was happening through the acceptance of racially tiered housing markets. The Equal Credit Opportunity Act of 1974 finally made discrimination in the distribution of credit on the basis of race, gender, or marital status a crime. The Home Mortgage Disclosure Act of 1975 was intended to force banks to publicly disclose where they provided mortgage loans. The legislation was designed to pressure deposit institutions into providing mortgages in urban areas where they had previously allowed mortgage banks to play that role. Finally, the Community Reinvestment Act was the product of grassroots organizing that aimed to force commercial and other depository banking institutions to lend in the communities they accepted deposits from. All of these legislative accomplishments were created in part by the pressure and campaigning of local community activists and homeowners who recognized how the dearth of credit availability starved their neighborhoods of desperately needed resources. These resources became even more important as the federal government's allocations to municipalities went into sharp decline. But without a commensurate commitment to enforcing fair housing and civil rights laws, these legislative efforts allowed for the influx of funds but without the requirement of the free movement of their recipients. This was not just a matter of "gilding the ghetto," but as the market became cloistered because of the declining economic fortunes of ordinary African Americans in the late 1970s and into the early 1980s, along with a feeble commitment to residential integration, Black entry into these credit markets was not on an equal basis. The disproportionate poverty and underemployment in Black communities combined with their historic exclusion from public and private initiatives in development and residential rehabilitation efforts meant that urban Black communities were in poorer condition. These conditions created by racism and exclusion were, once again, articulated as risk. The reemergence of the discourse of risk within the housing industry legitimized new stringent regimes of fees, fines, higher interest rates, and other modes of extraction.

AGAINST HOMEOWNERSHIP

Even as the federal government turned away from homeownership for the poor to avoid the political land mine of residential integration, the role of homeownership for low-income households was not fully resolved. Of course, some analysts insisted that the failure of HUD's homeownership programs was proof positive that poor people were ill equipped for the responsibilities of homeownership. When extrapolated further, the implications were more specific to low-income African Americans not being capable homeowners. Others pointed to HUD's obvious mismanagement of its programs as the real culprit in their demise. But the lessons from HUD's experiment were muddled by other economic sensibilities, including the commitment to private property and the centrality of homeownership to the American economy.

Today, homeownership, even for low-income and poor people, is reflexively advised as a way to emerge from poverty, develop assets, and build wealth more generally. The historic levels of wealth inequality that continue to distinguish African Americans from whites are powerful reminders of how the exclusion of Blacks from this asset has generationally impaired Black families in comparison with their white peers. Owning a home as a way to build wealth is touted as an advantage over public or government-sponsored housing. It informs the assumption that it is better to own than rent. And the greatest assumption of all is that homeownership is the superior way to live in the United States. This, of course, is tied to another indelible truth: that homeownership is a central cog in the U.S. economy. Its pivotal role as an economic barometer and motor means that there are endless attempts to make it more accessible to ever-wider groups of people. While these are certainly statements of fact, they should not be seen as statements on the advisability of suturing economic well-being to a privately owned asset in a society where the value of that asset will be weighed by the race or ethnicity of whoever possesses it.

The assumption that a mere reversal of exclusion to inclusion would upend decades of institutional discrimination underestimated the investments in an economy organized around race and property. The concept of race and especially racial inferiority helped to establish the "economic floor" in the housing market. One's proximity to African Americans individually, as well as to their communities, helped to determine the value of one's property. This revealed another reality. Markets, as in the means by which the exchange of commodities is facilitated, do not exist in vacuums, nor do abstract notions of "supply and demand" dictate their function. Markets are conceived and constituted by desire, imagination, and social aspirations, among other malleable factors. This does not mean that markets are not real, but that they are shaped by political, social, economic, and in the case of housing, racial concerns, certainly not need alone. And in the United States, these market conditions were shaped and stoked by economic actors that stood to gain by curtailing access to one portion of the market while then flooding another with credit, capital, and indiscriminate access to distressed and substandard homes.

HUD's crisis in its homeownership programs in the 1970s reveal deeper and more systemic problems with the pursuit of homeownership as a way to improve the quality of one's life. It is undeniable that homeownership in the United States has been "one of the important ways in which Americans have traditionally acquired financial capital, . . . tax advantages, the accumulation of equity, and the increased value of real estate property [to] enable homeowners to build economic assets. . . . These assets can be used to educate one's children, to take advantage of business opportunities, to meet financial emergencies, and to provide for retirement."[3] Investment in homeownership and its role in the process of the personal accumulation of capital have been fundamental to the good life in the United States.

The benefits of owning a home, however, have been experienced unevenly. The diminished access of African Americans to homeownership has been identified as a significant "consequence" of Black inequality. A national report on housing said as much: "The majority of nonwhite families are deprived of [these] advantage[s]."[4] The disparity is clear when 70 percent of whites own a home, compared with 43 percent of African Americans. But the source of inequality is not just in the difference between the numbers of African Americans and whites who own homes. Even when African Americans do own their own homes, they experience the supposed benefits differently in comparison with white homeowners.

The conflation of race and risk to property value has been fully absorbed into the popular culture and real estate acumen of the United States. Enduring racist assumptions about Black hygiene and moral fitness overlapped with the obsession of white property owners in protecting their investments. Their defense of private property, including the cultural cues that came along with it, inspired the maniacal reaction to the possibility of Black neighbors. When NAREB established career-ending penalties for violating the organization's commitment to racial segregation as early as 1924, the symbiosis of racial prerogative and value

and its diffusion through the real estate market was legitimized and then rep-
licated. The implications of this practice were hardly abstract; the property of
Blacks and the communities their property was clustered in assumed a permanently subordinate position. As a result, to this present moment, homes owned
by African Americans are worth less than homes owned by white people. Black-
majority neighborhoods are *still* viewed less favorably than white-majority neighborhoods. Indeed, the distance from Black communities continues to factor into
the superior value of white neighborhoods. Segregating African Americans into
deteriorating urban neighborhoods while simultaneously denying those communities access to resources that could be used toward development created an
economic disadvantage for Black people that has been impossible to overcome.

The assumption of property risk and the threat to value was turned into reality by the distressed conditions of Black neighborhoods that had been caused
by decades of policy neglect, real estate exploitation, job erosion, and the out-
flux of industry and tax dollars. Residential segregation and lower incomes have
meant that African Americans rely disproportionately on older, used housing.
As a consequence, their homes are not always appreciating assets. Even when
values rise, their properties do not appreciate at the same pace as those of white
families in exclusive white neighborhoods. Higher rates of unemployment, underemployment, and poverty among African Americans curtailed access to the
housing market while simultaneously increasing their vulnerability to losing
their homes through either eviction or foreclosure. Thus African Americans experience homeownership in ways that rarely produce the financial benefits typically enjoyed by middle-class white Americans.

Discriminatory differentials were embedded in the U.S. housing market
based on a combination of historical and continuing practices within the real
estate, housing, and banking industries—abetted by the failure of the federal
government, in any historical period, to enact rigorous regulatory compliance
with civil rights laws. The dictates of the market have been impossible to sur-
mount when housing is a commodity and thus malleable to the social desires
and expectations of a public molded by racial consciousness. This reality is even
more pronounced when the industries connected to housing have consistently
made race a factor in market imperatives. Racial difference and antipathy are not
unintended consequences of the market; they helped to constitute it.

Under these conditions, how could saddling poor and working-class African
Americans with thousands of dollars of debt in the form of mortgages while they
were still confined to the old and used portion of the housing market realistically

be seen as a means of getting out of poverty? Not only would these houses not accrue in value, but they eventually, and in some cases very quickly, became a burden of debt that worked to extract, instead of increase, value among their owners. Even when the terms were created to make homeownership possible for poor and working-class Black people, this did not change the fact that those homes and the neighborhoods Black people resided in were valued differently. These differentials in value are inherent in a housing market fully actualized by racial discrimination.

The quality of life in U.S. society depends on the personal accumulation of wealth, and homeownership is the single largest investment that most families make to accrue this wealth. But when the housing market is fully formed by racial discrimination, there is deep, abiding inequality. There has not been an instance in the last 100 years when the housing market has operated fairly, without racial discrimination. From racial zoning to restricted covenants to LICs to FHA-backed mortgages to the subprime mortgage loan, the U.S. housing industry has sought to exploit and financially benefit from the public perceptions of racial difference. This has meant that even when no discernable discrimination is detected, the fact that Black communities and neighborhoods are perceived as inferior means that African Americans must rely on an inherently devalued "asset" for maintenance of their quality of life. This has created a permanent disadvantage. And when homeownership is promoted as a key to economic freedom and advancement, this economic inequality is reinforced, legitimized, and ultimately accepted.

The regular promotion of homeownership as a means to overcome poverty or as a method of building wealth in our society has been built on a mistaken assumption that all people enter the housing market on an equal basis or that the housing market itself is a neutral arbiter of value. The promotion of homeownership by the state is not only an acceptance of these market dynamics; it is also an abdication of responsibility for the equitable provision of resources that attend to the racial deficit created by the inequality embedded in homeownership. This may seem like a political impossibility in an ongoing atmosphere where public services and institutions are undermined, but it is no more impossible than the magical belief that homeownership will ever be a cornerstone of political, social, and economic freedom for African Americans.

After all, even if there had been no nefarious acts, including preying upon those desperate for shelter, the racial infrastructure of the housing market still placed African Americans at a disadvantage. These disadvantages continue to play themselves out in the contemporary moment, as Black and white wealth disparities remain entrenched because of their deep roots in a systemically racist and unequal housing market. Even if there is no scandal or controversy, white homes are consistently valued more than Black homes. The Brookings Institution produced a study in 2018 showing that homes in neighborhoods that are at least 50 percent Black are valued at approximately half the price of homes in neighborhoods with no Black people.[5] White neighborhoods are seen as desirable destinations in ways that African American communities are almost never viewed. The historic disinvestment in and physical scarring of Black communities as a result continue to provide the pretexts necessary to finance Black homes differently, including charging higher rates of interest and more fees for lending in those communities. The partnering of public institutions in these private practices that are contingent on racial practices is a recipe for continued inequality, compromised inclusion, and unfair outcomes.

For more than fifty years now, the private sector has been viewed as most capable of ending the persistent urban housing crises. And yet those crises have become even starker over time, creating even greater degrees of housing precariousness. This is especially true in the realm of homeownership. The acceleration of subprime lending in the atmosphere of deregulation in the late 1990s and the early 2000s resulted in unprecedented home losses for African Americans. The practice of subprime lending was contingent on racial practices and assumptions across the housing industry and among the general public. The cascade of foreclosures and mortgage defaults further eroded the value of properties in Black communities, once again hollowing out the notion of homes as assets for African Americans. The net loss of more than 240,000 homes for African Americans has created the pretext for mortgage lenders to, once again, engage in exclusionary practices that marginalize potential Black homeowners.[6] But this is only one aspect of the crisis. The recurring perception of "risky" Black buyers has opened pathways for the reemergence of naked, predatory practices in the real estate market. None of this suggests that Black people should be consigned to the rental market; rather, it is intended to question a social order that makes the quality of one's life and the substance of one's citizenship contingent on the possession of private property. From rent-to-own schemes to the reappearance of LICs in lieu of conventional mortgages, real estate continues to swindle African Americans in search of their American dream in the housing market. It is not history repeating itself. It is the predictable outcome when the home is a commodity and it continues to be promoted as the fulfilment and meaning of citizenship.

ACKNOWLEDGMENTS

WHEN I WAS IN GRADUATE SCHOOL, a (not so old) sage in my department, the late Richard Iton, told me to be selective when considering what I would undertake as the focus of my graduate research because I would have to live with the topic for the next ten years. He was right. This book began as a seminar paper in the spring of 2008, and after a little more than ten years, it wound its way into book form.

As more than one person has observed, writing a book is an isolating and often painstaking process, but it is impossible to write it alone. I am indebted to so many friends, colleagues, and mentors that it is impossible to name them all, but there are some whom I must acknowledge.

The book's long journey was certainly influenced by the guidance and wisdom of my advisor then and my good friend now, Martha Biondi. Martha encouraged me to think and write in my own way while still teaching me how to anchor my work in historical methods. Her influence has been instrumental in my development as a writer and scholar. I am forever grateful for her mentorship, encouragement, and generosity. Martha has spent the last ten years always being available, always making time to meet and talk through ideas, and always advocating on my behalf. I owe special thanks to Mary Pattillo as well. Mary has always made the time to meet, to talk, and most importantly, to challenge me intellectually. There are no easy answers with Mary, only more questions and more prodding. I am grateful for her intellectual tenacity and her extraordinary generosity of time, perspective, and encouragement. Finally, before Leonard Rubinowitz became a noted legal scholar, he worked for HUD during the time period this book covers. His insights into the functioning of the agency and the officials within it helped to clear up so much confusion. Len spent hours meeting, talking, and unearthing materials, and I have benefited so much from his patient explanation, insight, and expertise. His critical writings on this period have been foundational to my understanding of the intricacies of race and housing policy.

I feel especially honored and grateful to be included in the Justice, Power, and Politics series of the University of North Carolina Press, edited by Heather Ann

Thompson and Rhonda Williams. Thompson and Williams embody all that is important to me in the academy: integrity, intellect, and a searching passion for truth and justice. They are role models for so many of us. Brandon Proia has been a revelation. On a humid evening at a conference in Jacksonville, Florida, in September 2013, Wayne State historian and good friend David Goldberg introduced me to Brandon and suggested he go to my panel the next morning. Brandon showed up, and we have been talking ever since. Brandon has read draft after draft of this book in manuscript, and he has always had something new and helpful to add. I am most appreciative of his patience, encouragement, and perennial good spirits. A special thanks to the anonymous readers of the manuscript who provided detailed comments and sharp analysis and critiques, in an incredibly timely manner, that ultimately resulted in a much stronger manuscript and now book. I want to especially thank Stephanie Ladniak Wenzel for her timely and meticulous copyediting. I also wish to thank the tireless work of the entire editorial staff at the Press who have worked so hard in production to bring this book into existence.

As a historian I have relied on untold librarians and archivists to bring this story to life. Thanks to the archivists at the National Archives and Record Administration in College Park, Maryland; the Lyndon Johnson Presidential Library; the Richard Nixon Presidential Library; the Hoover Institute; the Gerald Ford Presidential Library; the Bentley Historical Library; and the Urban Archives at Temple University. I have also relied on the financial generosity of multiple organizations that have helped to fund my research. A special thanks to the Gerald Ford Presidential Library, the Ford Foundation, Northwestern University, and the Lannan Foundation for their financial contributions to my research and writing. A special thanks to Princeton University for providing a sabbatical that allowed precious time I needed to complete revisions to the draft manuscript.

This book has benefited from my relationships with an astonishing group of friends and scholars who have engaged with this book in various forms over the last several years. My friends and colleagues in the Department of African American Studies at Princeton University have amazed me with their selflessness, extraordinary generosity, and crucial feedback. The insights of Imani Perry and Naomi Murakawa pushed me to further develop and refine my understandings of race and housing that led me to the concept of predatory inclusion that was so critical to this book. Princeton graduate student Mike Glass generously invited me to participate in a workshop where I received valuable feedback, including very detailed feedback from Princeton scholar and architect Mitch McEwan. A special thanks to Dov Weinryb Grohsgal from Princeton's history department for his enthusiasm for my research and willingness to always read the work. My colleagues in Princeton's Mellon Initiative in Architecture, Urbanism and the Humanities have organized multiple forums where I have been invited to discuss my research and, in turn, benefited from the extraordinary collection of scholars brought together in this program. A special thanks to Aaron Shkuda and Allison Isenberg for their encouragement and support. More generally, the warmth, support, and enthusiasm for my work while at Princeton has made the process of writing this book significantly easier. I wish to thank my colleagues in African American Studies for their friendship and support throughout this process, including Anna Arabindan-Kesson, Wallace Best, Wendy Belcher, Eddie Glaude, Tera Hunter, Kinohi Nishikawa, Reena Goldthree, Ruha Benjamin, Chika Okeke-Agulu, Josh Guild, and Autumn Womack. A special thanks to the incredible staff—past and present—in our department whose work has made this process easier for me, including Allison Bland, Dionne Worthy, April Peters, Jana Johnson, and Elio Lleo. I want to also thank Columbia University scholar Lynne Sagalyn for providing materials about Chicago real estate practices very early on in my research of this issue.

Thomas Sugrue and Chris Bonastia read the manuscript closely and provided invaluable insights and criticisms that have made the book stronger. Bonastia's willingness to challenge some of my arguments helped me to rework and ultimately strengthen the text. A special thanks to Nathan Connolly and Matthew Lasner for their participation in a workshop at New York University where they made important comments on portions of the manuscript that were still in progress. Very late in the writing process, I met Calvin Bradford in person after having read his analysis on race and housing for years. He is a kind soul and sharp as a razor, and I feel so fortunate to have finally connected. I have learned so much from Calvin, and this book will be better as a result. I owe a special thanks to friend and fellow writer Elizabeth Terzakis, who read the manuscript and rigorously edited every sentence on each page, and whose hard work has been indispensable to the final draft. Any errors in the text are mine alone.

I have also benefited from my engagement with a much broader group of colleagues, friends, and comrades with whom a range of conversations have helped me to clarify the ideas that underpin the book. I wish to thank Amna Akbar, Michelle Alexander, Simon Balto, Jonah Birch, Jennifer Brier, Jordan Camp, Andy Clarno, Cathy Cohen, Michael Dawson, Dan Denvir, Rory Fanning, Lilia

Fernandez, Megan Ming Francis, Zinga Fraser, David Freund, Maggie Garb, Alex Gourse, Saida Grundy, D'weston Haywood, Christina Heatherton, Jeff Hegelson, Paul Heideman, Elizabeth Hinton, Destin Jenkins, Tim Johnson, Robin D. G. Kelley, Naomi Klein, Holly Krig, Kevin Kruse, LaTasha Levy, Toussaint Losier, Nancy MacLean, Jack Macnamara, Manissa M. Maharawa, Emmanuel Martinez, Kate Masur, Dwight McBride, Mike McCarthy, Khalil Gibran Muhammad, Bill Mullen, Donna Murch, Rosemary Ndubuizu, Alice O'Connor, Jorge Ortiz, Tiana Paschel, Courtney Patterson, Kesha-Khan Perry, Dylan Penningroth, Chris Poulos, Leigh Raiford, Barbara Ransby, Leah Wright Rigeur, Noliwe Rooks, Nitasha Sharma, Brandon Terry, Micah Uetricht, Alexander Von Hoffman, Celeste Watkins-Hayes, and Alex Weheliye. I have learned from all of you in ways that have influenced my approach to writing this book.

A very special thanks to my sister-friend Elizabeth Todd-Breland, who has always been a sounding board, full of advice and insight, and a very good friend to me. We began writing our books around the same time, and as Elizabeth pulled ahead of me, she also inspired me to keep working. I have learned so much from Rebecca Marchiel, with whom I share a wonky passion for housing policy, real estate, and banking in the 1970s. She has always been a great friend to me, and this book is such a reflection of the conversations, emails, and texts we have shared over the years. Jayne Kinsman has always and unconditionally been in my corner. I can say that this book would not have been possible without her. A special thanks to my ace friend Anthony Arnove for his professional advice and guidance that helped to make actually writing the book the easy part.

I come from a family of writers and people who have always been thinkers, talkers, and smart about the world. Somehow my dad, Henry Louis Taylor Jr., and I ended up on the same path, curious about cities and suburbs that Black people call home. I learned from him early on about the systems of racism and inequality, but even more importantly about justice and struggle. My father has always encouraged me to do things my own way, and I have tried to live my life in that way. If you know me, then you will see that in this book. My only regret, if I have any, is that my mother is not here to read this labor of love. My mom, Doris Taylor, died unexpectedly more than twenty years ago. It is an absence that you never get over but only hope to learn how to live with. I think she would be proud of me. Finally, to my wife and best friend, Lauren Fleer, this book has traversed the wild swings of our lives, from hustling in Chicago to make ends meet to raising Ellison Turner, our collective happy spot, in Philadelphia. Lauren's patience for the impossibility and unpredictability of the academy has made it possible for me to do well. I am so appreciative and grateful for our amazing relationship. This book is for you for many reasons, the most obvious being that I could never have begun or finished this book without your support and love. I couldn't imagine doing any of this without you. Thank you.

NOTES

INTRODUCTION

1. Jackson, *Crabgrass Frontier*; Rothstein, *Color of Law* (2017); Satter, *Family Properties*; Hirsch, *Making the Second Ghetto*; Freund, *Colored Property*; Gotham, *Race, Real Estate, and Uneven Development* (2002); Baradaran, *Color of Money*; Pietila, *Not in My Neighborhood*; Quadagno, *Color of Welfare*; Connolly, *World More Concrete*; Massey and Denton, *American Apartheid*; Sugrue, *Sweet Land of Liberty*.

2. "Davis v. Romney, 355 F. Supp. 29 (E.D. Pa. 1973)."

3. "Civil Rights Bill of 1866."

4. "Shelley v. Kraemer, 334 U.S. 1, 68 S. Ct. 836, 92 L. Ed. 2d 1161, 1948 U.S. LEXIS 2764—CourtListener.Com": "It cannot be doubted that among the civil rights intended to be protected from discriminatory state action by the Fourteenth Amendment are the rights to acquire, enjoy, own and dispose of property. Equality in the enjoyment of property rights was regarded by the framers of that Amendment as an essential pre-condition to the realization of other basic civil rights and liberties which the Amendment was intended to guarantee."

5. "Harry S. Truman."

6. "Dwight D. Eisenhower."

7. See the testimony of Walter Mondale, in U.S. Congress, Senate, Committee on Banking and Currency, Subcommittee on Housing and Urban Affairs, *Fair Housing Act of 1967*, 222.

8. Quinn, "Government Policy, Housing, and the Origins of Securitization"; Krippner, *Capitalizing on Crisis*; Hyman, *Borrow*; Hyman, "House That George Romney Built"; von Hoffman, "Calling upon the Genius of Private Enterprise."

9. See Thurston, *At the Boundaries of Homeownership*, for a fuller discussion on FHA discrimination against middle-class Black and white women.

10. Rhonda Y. Williams, "Something's Wrong Down Here: Poor Black Women and Urban Struggles for Democracy," in Kusmer and Trotter, *African American Urban History since World War II*, 316.

11. Kwak, *World of Homeowners*, 176.

12. Jones, *Masters of the Universe*, 278.

13. Bonastia, *Knocking on the Door* (2006), 12–24.

14. Conley, *Being Black, Living in the Red*, 38.

15. For more discussion on "racial liberalism," see Biondi, *To Stand and Fight*; Singh, *Black Is a Country*; Sugrue, *Sweet Land of Liberty*; Myrdal, *American Dilemma*; and Duneier, *Ghetto*.

16. Conley, *Being Black, Living in the Red*, 16.

17. Babcock, *Appraisal of Real Estate*, 2–3.

18. Jackson, "Race, Ethnicity, and Real Estate Appraisal." See Looker, *Nation of Neighborhoods*, 77–78, and Babcock, *Appraisal of Real Estate*.

19. Helper, *Racial Policies and Practices of Real Estate Brokers*, 201.

20. Massey and Denton, *American Apartheid*.

21. Quoted in Helper, *Racial Policies and Practices of Real Estate Brokers*, 201.

22. Helper, *Racial Policies and Practices of Real Estate Brokers*. The Realtors Code of Ethics, Article 34, states: "A Realtor should never be instrumental in introducing into a neighborhood a character of property or occupancy, members of any race or nationality, or any individuals whose presence will clearly be detrimental to property values in that neighborhood."

23. Rothstein, *Color of Law* (2017), 59–76.

24. Logan and Molotch, *Urban Fortunes*, 20–23.

25. See Hayward, *How Americans Make Race*, chap. 2, "Black Places," and Harris, "Whiteness as Property," 1716: "The origins of property rights in the United States are rooted in racial domination. Even in the early years of the country, it was not the concept of race alone that operated to oppress Blacks and Indians; rather, it was the interaction between conceptions of race and property that played a critical role in establishing and maintaining racial and economic subordination."

26. Kruse, *New Suburban History*, 35.

27. "Jones v. Alfred H. Mayer Co., 392 U.S. 409 (1968)."

28. This, of course, does not mean that there has been no discussion of the HUD Act and its consequences for the urban communities it was most utilized in. Studies coming from multiple disciplinary perspectives discuss various aspects of the HUD Act and its impact. This book builds substantially on this existing scholarship. See Boyer, *Cities Destroyed for Cash*; Gotham, *Race, Real Estate, and Uneven Development* (2014); Bonastia, *Knocking on the Door* (2006); Satter, *Family Properties*; Hays, *Federal Government and Urban Housing* (2012); von Hoffman, "Calling upon the Genius of Private Enterprise"; Biles, *Fate of Cities*; and Squires, *Unequal Partnerships*.

29. Kennedy, Executive Order 11063.

30. Baradaran, *Color of Money*, 194–267; Hill and Rabig, *Business of Black Power*; Orren, *Corporate Power and Social Change*; Kotlowski, *Nixon's Civil Rights*; Wright Rigueur, *Loneliness of the Black Republican*, 134–77; Allen, *Black Awakening in Capitalist America*; Taylor, *From #BlackLivesMatter to Black Liberation*.

31. For more on Cold War liberalism or racial liberalism, see Dudziak, *Cold War Civil Rights*; Von Eschen, *Race against Empire*; Singh, *Black Is a Country*; Biondi, *To Stand and Fight*; Sugrue, *Sweet Land of Liberty*; Myrdal, *American Dilemma*; and Ferguson, *Top Down*.

32. For more discussion about the politics of "colorblindness," see Taylor, *From #BlackLives Matter to Black Liberation*; Bonilla-Silva, *Racism without Racists*; MacLean, *Freedom Is Not Enough*; Lassiter, *Silent Majority*; Kruse, *White Flight*; and Alexander, *New Jim Crow*.

33. Pritchett, "Which Urban Crisis?"; O'Connor, "The Privatized City, the Manhattan Institute, the Urban Crisis, and the Conservative Counterrevolution in New York"; U.S. Congress, Senate, Committee on Government Operations, Subcommittee on Executive Reorganization, *Urban Crisis in America*; Taylor and Hill, *Historical Roots of the Urban Crisis*; Matlin, *On the Corner*; Sugrue, *Origins of the Urban Crisis*; Weaver, *Urban Complex*; Pritchett, *Robert Clifton Weaver and the American City*.

34. Bonilla-Silva, *Racism without Racists*, 17–60; MacLean, *Freedom Is Not Enough*, 234–38; Lassiter, *Silent Majority*, 1–2, 220–22; Taylor, *From #BlackLivesMatter to Black Liberation*; Ferguson, *Top Down*.

35. Carmichael and Hamilton, *Black Power*.

36. See, for more background, Katz, *Undeserving Poor*; Quadagno, *Color of Welfare*; and O'Connor, *Poverty Knowledge*.

37. Kohler-Hausmann, *Getting Tough*; Quadagno, *Color of Welfare*; Chappell, *War on Welfare*; Neubeck and Cazenave, *Welfare Racism*; Nadasen, *Welfare Warriors*; Williams, *Politics of Public Housing*; Theoharis and Woodard, *Groundwork*.

CHAPTER 1

1. Glass, "75 Invade Capitol Hill for Rat Bill."
2. "By Lyndon B. Johnson."
3. Jackson, "Harlem's Rent Strike and Rat War"; McLaughlin, "Pied Piper of the Ghetto."
4. "Can't Sleep in 'Rat-Infested Slum.'"
5. Filson, "Woman, Children Face Loss of Rat-Ridden Home."
6. Breslin, "Rats Come Every Night."
7. Washington, "Every Morning, a War on Rats."
8. Wilson, "Why We Did It."
9. "Charge Rats Killed Baby Disputed."
10. "Slum Rats Chew Out Baby's Eye."
11. "Women Are Poverty War Force."
12. "Scientists Analyze Philly Riot."
13. "New York Slumlords Told to Fix Tenements."
14. "Rent Strike in Harlem"; Jackson, "Harlem's Rent Strike and Rat War."
15. Wright, *Native Son*.
16. "Robert Weaver, Unpublished Narrative History."
17. Quoted in Woods, "Federal Home Loan Bank Board," 1048–49.
18. Woods, "Federal Home Loan Bank Board," 1048.
19. Woods, "Federal Home Loan Bank Board," 1048–50.
20. Pietila, *Not in My Neighborhood*, 97.
21. Abrams, *Forbidden Neighbors*, 138.
22. Hughes, "Negro's New Economic Life," 128.
23. Tuskegee Institute, Dept. of Records and Research, *Negro Year Book*, 173.
24. Tuskegee Institute, Dept. of Records and Research, *Negro Year Book*, 172.
25. "FHA Developments in Analysis of Risk."
26. Gotham, *Race, Real Estate, and Uneven Development* (2014); Squires, *Unequal Partnerships*; Squires, *Capital and Communities in Black and White*.
27. See Connolly, *World More Concrete*.
28. See Pietila, *Not in My Neighborhood*, 63–64, and Lovett, *Conceiving the Future*, 157–58.
29. U.S. Federal Housing Administration, *Underwriting Manual*, sec. 950–952, "Quality and Accessibility of School."
30. Rothstein, *Color of Law* (2018).
31. Abrams, *Home Ownership for the Poor*, 196; U.S. Federal Housing Administration, "New Small-Home Ownership Program," 15.
32. U.S. Federal Housing Administration, "New Small-Home Ownership Program," 19.
33. U.S. Federal Housing Administration, "New Small-Home Ownership Program," 3.
34. Roth, "Lender Looks at Title I Homes," 13.

35. U.S. Federal Housing Administration, "New Small-Home Ownership Program," 3.

36. U.S. Federal Housing Administration, "New Small-Home Ownership Program," 3.

37. Leimert, "Teamwork Solves the Small-Home Puzzle," 5.

38. Leimert, "Teamwork Solves the Small-Home Puzzle," 25.

39. Radford, *Modern Housing for America*, 193–94.

40. Hays, *Federal Government and Urban Housing* (2012), 89: "Thus, the FHA was, in a very critical sense, a conservative program as this term has been here defined"; Philpot, *Conservative but Not Republican*, 78: "Because the FHA insured loans from default for lenders, it took a conservative approach by only insuring mortgages in low risk neighborhoods"; Leighninger, *Building Louisiana*, 111–12: "Those doing residential construction were also constrained by the conservative tastes of mortgage bankers, echoed by the newly created Federal Housing Administration"; Jackson, *Crabgrass Frontier*, 213.

41. U.S. Federal Housing Administration, *Underwriting Manual*, 936–39.

42. U.S. Congress, House, Committee on the Judiciary, *Civil Rights*, 426.

43. Hirsch and Mohl, *Urban Policy*, 86.

44. U.S. Congress, Senate, Committee on Banking and Currency, Subcommittee on Housing and Urban Affairs, *FHA Mortgage Foreclosures*, 18: "On unemployment insurance, we are aiming at the same general result from amendments dealing with forbearance that are included in the President's housing bill. FHA has underway a study of the inclusion of unemployment and health insurance in its program. We devised a general format for unemployment insurance and concluded that it would not be undertaken without an increase in the insurance premium which we are reluctant to make at this time."

45. U.S. Congress, Senate, Committee on Banking and Currency, Subcommittee on Housing and Urban Affairs, *FHA Mortgage Foreclosures*, 24.

46. National Commission on Urban Problems, *Building the American City*, 96.

47. Dickinson, "Changing Housing Climate."

48. Dickinson, "Changing Housing Climate."

49. U.S. Congress, House, Committee on the Judiciary, *Civil Rights*, 430.

50. Woods, "Federal Home Loan Bank Board."

51. For more on early Black consumer culture, see Cohen, *Consumers' Republic*, 41–51.

52. Ginzberg, *Negro Challenge to the Business Community*, 11.

53. Hughes, "Negro's New Economic Life," 126–27.

54. Tuskegee Institute, Dept. of Records and Research, *Negro Year Book*, 186. Quoted from the NAHB Correlator, March 1950, Memorandum to the Members of the National Association of Home Builders from Frank Cortright, President.

55. "Dwight D. Eisenhower."

56. "NAREB Encourages Negro Housing."

57. "NAREB Encourages Negro Housing," 2 (emphasis added).

58. "Negro House Need Told by NAREB."

59. "Real Estate Boards Urged . . . Improve Negro Housing."

60. Gans, "Failure of Urban Renewal."

61. Dickinson, "Urban Renewal Under Fire."

62. Hirsch, *Making the Second Ghetto*, 100–134; "Renewing Inequality: Family Displacements through Urban Renewal, 1950–1966," http://dsl.richmond.edu/panorama/renewal/#view=0/0 /1&viz=cartogram (accessed June 3, 2019).

63. McEntire, *Residence and Race*, 333–37.

64. Quoted in National Commission on Urban Problems, *Building the American City*, 14.

65. National Commission on Urban Problems, *Building the American City*, 14.

66. National Commission on Urban Problems, *Building the American City*, 64–87.

67. McEntire, *Residence and Race*, 333.

68. McEntire, *Residence and Race*, 334; Kwak, *World of Homeowners*, 173–74.

69. "Insured Financing for Low-Cost Homes," 14; United States, *Recommendations on Government Housing Policies and Programs*, 44–47. See also DiPentima, "Abuses in the Low Income Homeownership Programs," 466–67.

70. For more on the shortcomings of initial FHA-backed homeownership, see Gelfand, *Nation of Cities*, 219–20. For more on the failure of "FHA-assisted private housing," see Hirsch, "Searching for a 'Sound Negro Policy,'" 429.

71. Quoted from "Discrimination against Minorities in the Federal Housing Programs," 515.

72. U.S. Congress, House, Committee on Banking and Currency, Subcommittee on Housing, *Housing Act of 1960*, 5: "This section would add a new section 235 to the National Housing Act authorizing FHA mortgage insurance on property in older neighborhoods."

73. U.S. Congress, House, Committee on Banking and Currency, Subcommittee on Housing, *Housing Act of 1960*: "All of the provisions of the regular section 203 program would apply except that the property need represent only a 'reasonable risk' instead of meeting the regular 'economic soundness' provision, if the Commissioner finds that this is necessary giving consideration to the need for maintaining adequate housing in older urban neighborhoods and to the inability of persons desiring to purchase or construct homes in such neighborhoods to obtain mortgage financing otherwise."

74. Glazer and McEntire, *Studies in Housing and Minority Groups*, 121.

75. Arnold R. Hirsch, "Less Than *Plessy*: The Inner City, Suburbs, and State-Sanctioned Residential Segregation in the Age of *Brown*," in Kruse, *New Suburban History*, 35–36.

76. Hirsch, "'Last and Most Difficult Barrier.'"

77. Eisenhower speech quoted in McEntire, *Residence and Race*, 294.

78. Voluntary Home Mortgage Credit Program, "First Annual Report, " 2.

79. Meyer, *As Long as They Don't Move Next Door*, 157; Voluntary Home Mortgage Credit Program, "First Annual Report," 5.

80. U.S. Commission on Civil Rights, *Housing*; Smith, *Racial Democracy and the Black Metropolis*, 260–64.

81. Administrator of HHFA, "Assistance to Members of Minority Groups," 30.

82. Cole quoted in McEntire, *Residence and Race*, 294.

83. U.S. Commission on Civil Rights, *Housing*, 4.

84. U.S. Commission on Civil Rights, *Housing*, 31.

85. Freund, *Colored Property*, 9.

86. U.S. Commission on Civil Rights, *Housing*, 65.

87. U.S. Commission on Civil Rights, *Housing*, 65.

88. U.S. Commission on Civil Rights, *Housing*, 67.

89. U.S. Congress, House, Committee on the Judiciary, *Civil Rights*, 427.

90. U.S. Commission on Civil Rights, *Housing*, 51.

91. Yinger, "Analysis of Discrimination by Real Estate Brokers," 16–17.

92. Alfred Balk, "Confessions of a Block-Buster," *Saturday Evening Post*, July 14, 1962, 18; Seligman, *Block by Block*, 151–53.

93. Mason, *From Building and Loans to Bail-Outs*, 166–67.

94. Smith, *Racial Democracy and the Black Metropolis*, 255–88; Connolly, *World More Concrete*, 12–14.

95. Danielson, "Installment Land Contracts"; Henson, "Installment Land Contracts in Illinois"; Nelson and Whitman, "Installment Land Contract"; Mixon, "Installment Land Contracts"; Sagalyn, "Mortgage Lending in Older Urban Neighborhoods"; Hirsch, *Making the Second Ghetto*, 29–33; Sugrue, *Origins of the Urban Crisis*, 39–47; Satter, *Family Properties*. The practice of contract buying was largely unregulated because in contract sales the title of the house did not change hands until the final contract payment was made. Thus, there are very few official records documenting the extent of contract sales. Because of this limited paper trail, there has been no academic study of the impact of contract sales on African American communities, even though they were widely used in cities like Philadelphia, Houston, Cincinnati, Albany, Portland, Rochester, Detroit, and Baltimore. Chicago is an exception. The combination of activism and litigation against the use of LICs in Chicago at the end of the 1960s created an enormous archive detailing both the mechanics of the contract-buying system and the grassroots efforts to undo it. Moreover, the movement was covered widely in the local media from 1968 through 1970, creating the kind of documentation that is missing from other cities. Some scholars have alluded to these contracts in general discussions about exploitative conditions created by residential segregation, but none have explored the collusive relationship between housing speculators, real estate moguls, and local savings and loan associations, and their collective effort to keep Blacks locked out of the wider white housing market while using the LICs to keep them trapped in poor neighborhoods and laden with debt.

96. Pietila, *Not in My Neighborhood*.

97. Satter, *Family Properties*. Satter discusses all of these conditions in detail as they related to Chicago in the 1950s and 1960s.

98. Waters, "Urban League Says Chicagoans Paid Huge 'Color Tax.'"

99. Magnuson, "How the Ghetto Gets Gypped"; U.S. Federal Trade Commission, *Economic Report on Installment Credit*, xi.

100. Magnuson, "How the Ghetto Gets Gypped," 113.

101. Poinsett, "Economics of Liberation."

102. Scott, "Nation's Ghettoes Teeming with Discontent."

103. Magnuson, "How the Ghetto Gets Gypped," 121.

104. Horne, *Fire This Time*.

105. Carmichael and Hamilton, *Black Power*, 17.

106. Carmichael and Hamilton, *Black Power*, 17.

107. U.S. Congress, Senate, Committee on Banking and Currency, Subcommittee on Financial Institutions, *Financial Institutions and the Urban Crisis*, 3–4.

108. U.S. Congress, Senate, Committee on Banking and Currency, Subcommittee on Financial Institutions, *Financial Institutions and the Urban Crisis*, 9–10.

109. U.S. National Advisory Commission on Civil Disorders, *Report of the National Advisory Commission on Civil Disorders*, 13.

110. Warden, "Negroes Pay Color Tax—King."

111. League of Women Voters of Illinois, "Minority Group Housing."

112. Rooks, *Cutting School*, 2017.

113. Louis Harris, "Races Agree on Ghetto Abolition and Need for WPA-Type Projects," *Washington Post, Times Herald*, August 14, 1967.

114. Magnuson, "How the Ghetto Gets Gypped," 121.

115. See also Tabb, *Political Economy of the Black Ghetto*; Satter, *Family Properties*; Mendenhall, "Political Economy of Black Housing"; Conley, *Being Black, Living in the Red*; and Allen, *Black Awakening in Capitalist America*.

116. U.S. Congress, Senate, Committee on Banking and Currency, Subcommittee on Housing and Urban Affairs, *Fair Housing Act of 1967*, 119–20.

CHAPTER 2

1. "Special Message to the Congress on Urban Problems."

2. "Special Message to the Congress on Urban Problems."

3. Freund, *Colored Property*, 75, 100–103.

4. Freund, *Colored Property*; von Hoffman, "Calling upon the Genius of Private Enterprise"; von Hoffman, "High Ambitions"; Humphrey, *Private Enterprise and the City*; O'Connor, *Poverty Knowledge*; "Lyndon B. Johnson: Remarks to the Members of the U.S. Chamber of Commerce"; Johnson, "Beyond Retrenchment."

5. Milkis, *Great Society and the High Tide of Liberalism*, 240.

6. "John F. Kennedy: News Release on Conference on Urban Affairs."

7. U.S. Congress, Senate, Committee on Banking and Currency, Subcommittee on Housing and Urban Affairs, *Fair Housing Act of 1967*, 216–17.

8. "John F. Kennedy: News Release on Conference on Urban Affairs."

9. Fusfeld, "Rise of the Corporate State in America," 10–11.

10. Milkis, *Great Society and the High Tide of Liberalism*; Zelizer, *Fierce Urgency of Now*; Brauer, "Kennedy, Johnson, and the War on Poverty."

11. Northrup quoted in Allen, *Guide to Black Power in America*, 196.

12. "Lyndon B. Johnson: Remarks to the Members of the U.S. Chamber of Commerce."

13. Califano, "Public Interest Partnership," 10.

14. Drummond, "Standard Doctrine."

15. Drummond, "Standard Doctrine."

16. Califano, "Public Interest Partnership," 11–12.

17. Califano, "Public Interest Partnership," 12.

18. *Business and the Urban Crisis*.

19. "Annual Message to the Congress on the State of the Union."

20. Zelizer, *Fierce Urgency of Now*, 263–67.

21. Reuschling, "Business Institution."

22. Zelizer, *Fierce Urgency of Now*, 268.

23. Newfield, "Kennedy's Search for a New Target."

24. Quoted from the testimony of Dr. Kenneth B. Clark, in U.S. National Advisory Commission on Civil Disorders, *Report of the National Advisory Commission on Civil Disorders*, 313.

25. "The City."

26. Cloward and Piven, *Ghetto Redevelopment*, 365–66.

27. Phillips-Fein, *Invisible Hands*, 151.

28. Phillips-Fein, *Invisible Hands*, 151.

29. Phillips-Fein, *Invisible Hands*, 154.

30. "Bank of America Hit for 35th Time"; "Bombs Found in 8 U.S. Banks."

31. Wood, "B of A Acts to Show Students 'The Establishment' Also Cares."

32. Wood, "B of A Acts to Show Students 'The Establishment' Also Cares."

33. Countryman, *Up South*.

34. U.S. Congress, Senate, Committee on Government Operations, Subcommittee on Executive Reorganization, *Urban Crisis in America*, 147; Countryman, *Up South*, 83–119.

35. Deppe, *Operation Breadbasket*. This interfaith economic justice program transformed into Jesse Jackson's Operation PUSH (now the Rainbow PUSH Coalition). Begun by Martin Luther King Jr. during the 1966 Chicago Freedom Movement, Breadbasket was directed by Jackson.

36. Goldston, "New Prospects for American Business," 109.

37. "Businessman's Call to Action in the Cities."

38. "Why Ignore a Market Worth $24 Billion?," *Pittsburgh Courier*, February 20, 1965, 10.

39. *Business and the Urban Crisis*.

40. "Private Enterprise Called Key for Cities."

41. Sanders, "Industry Gives New Hope to the Negro."

42. Pilisuk, *How We Lost the War on Poverty*; Cloward and Piven, *Ghetto Redevelopment*; von Hoffman, "Calling upon the Genius of Private Enterprise"; McGuire, *Changing Nature of Business Responsibilities*.

43. Reston, "Gardner Will Head Private Campaign on Urban Poverty."

44. "Crisis in the Cities," 33.

45. "Out of Slums into Instant Homes in 48 Hours."

46. Davis, Kendall, and Stans, "Private Enterprise and the Urban Crisis."

47. "Crisis in the Cities," 34.

48. Roberts, "Slum Role Seen for Private Enterprise."

49. "Transcript of Kenneth M. Wright Testimony before Kerner Commission."

50. "Insurance Firms Continue Programs to Help Inner Cities."

51. "Lessons of Leadership Investing in People's Future."

52. "Transcript of Kenneth M. Wright Testimony before Kerner Commission."

53. "Insurance Firms Will Aid Ghettos."

54. Moeller, "Economic Implications of the Life Insurance Industry's Investment Program in the Central Cities," 101.

55. "Lyndon B. Johnson: Excerpts from Remarks"; "Billion-Dollar Slum Fund Hailed by LBJ."

56. "Transcript of Kenneth M. Wright Testimony before Kerner Commission," 6; Rankin, "Insurance Firms' Aid To Ghetto," 43; Orren, *Corporate Power and Social Change*, 173–75.

57. U.S. Congress, Senate, Committee on Banking and Currency, Subcommittee on Financial Institutions, *Financial Institutions and the Urban Crisis*, 154–57, 160; McKnight, "Possible Agenda Items for the Meeting with Officers of the National Association of Real Estate Brokers"; "Statement to the President, Francis Ferguson."

58. "Response to the Urban Crisis."

59. "Transcript of Kenneth M. Wright Testimony before Kerner Commission," 2673.

60. "Transcript of Kenneth M. Wright Testimony before Kerner Commission," 2688.

61. "FHA Policy Aids Minority Buyers—and Panic Sellers."

62. Biondi, *To Stand and Fight*, 121.

63. Biondi, *To Stand and Fight*, 122.

64. Biondi, *To Stand and Fight*, 123–36.

65. Biondi, *To Stand and Fight*, 133.

66. "Metropolitan Life Housing Open to Non-White Tenants."

67. "Letter from Youth and College Council Members of the NAACP."

68. "Release by National Association for the Advancement of Colored People."

69. Dim, "Metropolitan Agrees to Rent to Nonwhites."

70. "Release by National Association for the Advancement of Colored People."

71. Gilbert, "Insurance Boycott Ready."

72. Satter, *Family Properties*, 141–42.

73. "Chi NAACP to Picket Metropolitan Life"; Lyons, "As New Rights Tactic, Negroes Wouldn't Pay Insurance Premiums," 5.

74. Nuccio, "Insurers Facing a Negro Boycott."

75. Gilbert, "Insurance Boycott Ready," 6.

76. "Metropolitan Life Denies Bias on Loans"; Calhoun, "Metropolitan Prexy Denies NAACP Charges."

77. Calhoun, "Metropolitan Prexy Denies NAACP Charges."

78. "NAACP and Metropolitan Life Insurance Company Agree on Mortgage Loan Policy."

79. "NAACP and Metropolitan Life Insurance Company Agree on Mortgage Loan Policy."

80. Fried, "City Charges Bias at Three Projects."

81. Lyons, "As New Rights Tactic, Negroes Wouldn't Pay Insurance Premiums," 4.

82. Satter, *Family Properties*; Coates, "Case for Reparations."

83. Institute of Life Insurance, "Institute of Life Insurance."

84. U.S. Congress, Senate, Committee on Banking and Currency, Subcommittee on Financial Institutions, *Financial Institutions and the Urban Crisis*, 171; Moeller, "Economic Implications of the Life Insurance Industry's Investment Program in the Central Cities," 100–101.

85. "Statement to the President, Francis Ferguson."

86. "Statement to the President, Francis Ferguson"; "Response to the Urban Crisis"; Clearinghouse on Corporate Social Responsibility (U.S.) and Life Insurance Joint Committee on Urban Problems, *Report on the $2 Billion Urban Investment Program*.

87. Quoted from the memo from Director of FHA, Philip Brownstein, to Insuring Office Directors, "Federal Housing Administration, Commissioner Letter Number 38, November 8, 1965," in U.S. Congress, House, Committee on Banking and Currency, Subcommittee on Housing, *Real Estate Settlement Costs*, 270–71.

88. Abrams, *Home Ownership for the Poor*, 200.

89. U.S. Congress, Senate, Committee on Banking and Currency, Subcommittee on Financial Institutions, *Financial Institutions and the Urban Crisis*.

90. Humphrey, *Private Enterprise and the City*, 14.

91. U.S. Congress, Senate, Committee on Banking and Currency, Subcommittee on Financial Institutions, *Financial Institutions and the Urban Crisis*, 156.

92. Danielson, *Politics of Exclusion*.

93. Boggs and Boggs, "City Is the Black Man's Land."

94. Most of this history is covered in the chapter "Black Faces in High Places" in Taylor, *From #BlackLivesMatter to Black Liberation*, 86.

95. Taylor, "Back Story to the Neoliberal Moment." In this article, I discuss Nixon's support of

the Contract Buyers League federal lawsuit against HUD and the FHA. The Nixon administration signed an amicus brief in support of the contract buyers.

96. U.S. Congress, Senate, Committee on Banking and Currency, Subcommittee on Financial Institutions, *Financial Institutions and the Urban Crisis*, 169–70.

97. "Richard Nixon: Statement on the Life Insurance Industry's Pledge."

98. Kennedy quote from U.S. Commission on Civil Rights, *Sheltered Crisis*, 206.

99. U.S. Congress, Senate, Committee on Banking and Currency, Subcommittee on Housing and Urban Affairs, *Fair Housing Act of 1967*, 242.

100. U.S. Congress, Senate, Committee on Banking and Currency, Subcommittee on Housing and Urban Affairs, *Fair Housing Act of 1967*, 243.

101. Williams, "Seek Hate Combine in Heights Bombing."

102. Schanber, "Police in Chicago Clash with Whites after 3 Marches."

103. "Negro's Home Is Bombed in White Chicago Area," *Jet*, December 14, 1967, 9.

104. Haintze and Smith, "Nab 3 in Bombing of LI Negro's Home."

105. Haintze and Smith, "Nab 3 in Bombing of LI Negro's Home."

106. "Romney Urges Law Support at Flint Rally."

107. Institute of Life Insurance, "When You Invest a Billion Dollars to Help the Cities, You Learn Some Things."

108. "City core," according to JCUP, is "defined as an area or district within a city which is in serious need of revitalization. It may or may not be designated as an urban renewal area but the ingredient of blight or near blight condition should be present. It should be an area where life insurance investments would not normally be made. In the case of a metropolitan area, it could be located outside the corporate limits of the city if the above criteria apply" ("Statement to the President, Francis Ferguson," 3).

109. Weaver, "Departmental Policy Governing Equal Opportunity."

110. Weaver, "Departmental Policy Governing Equal Opportunity."

111. "Letter from B. T. McGraw."

112. American Life Convention and Life Insurance Association of America, "$1 Billion Urban Investment Program," 4.

113. American Life Convention and Life Insurance Association of America, "$1 Billion Urban Investment Program," 5.

114. American Life Convention and Life Insurance Association of America, "$1 Billion Urban Investment Program," 5.

115. American Life Convention and Life Insurance Association of America, "$1 Billion Urban Investment Program," 5.

116. American Life Convention and Life Insurance Association of America, "$1 Billion Urban Investment Program," 5.

117. "Minutes."

118. U.S. Congress, Senate, Committee on Banking and Currency, Subcommittee on Financial Institutions, *Financial Institutions and the Urban Crisis*, 162.

119. "Richard Nixon: Statement on the Life Insurance Industry's Pledge"; Max Frankel, "Insurance Groups to Invest Billions: Most of First Funds Will Be Directed toward Housing in the High-Risk Areas," *New York Times*, September 14, 1967, 1; "Insurance Firms Will Aid Ghettos."

120. *Negro and the City*, 64.

121. Hudson, *Urban Crisis*, 17.

122. "Union Loans Negroes Over \$7½ Million."

123. "Union Loans Negroes Over \$7½ Million." Also see Travis, *Autobiography of Black Chicago*.

124. U.S. Congress, Senate, Committee on Banking and Currency, Subcommittee on Financial Institutions, *Financial Institutions and the Urban Crisis*, 157–58.

125. Brownstein Interview, 16.

126. Brownstein Interview, 16.

127. Pritchett, *Robert Clifton Weaver and the American City*, 306–8.

128. Henderson, *Housing and the Democratic Ideal*, 207–11; Pritchett, *Robert Clifton Weaver and the American City*, 307–11.

129. "Testimony of Secretary of the Department of Housing and Urban Development."

130. Percy, "New Dawn for Our Cities."

131. "Robert Weaver, Secretary of HUD, UPI Interview Program."

132. "Special Message to the Congress on Urban Problems."

133. Hoffman, "Johnson Signs Housing Bill."

134. President's Committee on Urban Housing, *Decent Home*, 1.

135. President's Committee on Urban Housing, *Decent Home*, 1.

136. Hoffman, "Johnson Signs Housing Bill"; von Hoffman, "Calling upon the Genius of Private Enterprise"; Hays, *Federal Government and Urban Housing* (2012); U.S. Congress, House, Committee on Banking and Currency, *Housing and Urban Development Act of 1969*; U.S. Department of Housing and Urban Development, *Homeownership for Lower Income Families (Section 235)*.

137. DiPentima, "Abuses in the Low Income Homeownership Programs."

138. Turpin, "Housing Act 'Not Cure-All.'"

139. "Ghetto Housing Program Announced," 252; "Lyndon B. Johnson: Statement by the President."

140. "Form Housing Unit to Spur Black Enterprise in Field"; "Negro Men Get Housing Lift"; Vale and Freemark, "From Public Housing to Public-Private Housing"; President's Committee on Urban Housing, *Decent Home*, 1.

141. Robbins, "Negro Housing Producers Seek to Widen Market Share."

142. Robbins, "Negro Housing Producers Seek to Widen Market Share."

143. Hyman, *Borrow*; Quinn, "Government Policy, Housing, and the Origins of Securitization."

144. "Ghetto Housing Program Announced," 252–53.

145. Henry Sutherland, "Real Estate Group Launches Own Plan for Urban Renewal," *Los Angeles Times*, April 2, 1967, G1.

CHAPTER 3

1. Perlstein, *Nixonland*, 117.

2. "Richard Nixon: Address Accepting the Presidential Nomination."

3. Quoted from Romney confirmation hearing, in U.S. Congress, Senate, Committee on Banking and Currency, *Nomination of George W. Romney*, 4.

4. Perlstein, *Nixonland*, 359.

5. Donnell, "Can Romney's Approach' Work at HUD?"

6. "Is a Breakthrough Near in Housing?," 94.

7. "Different Kind of Choice."

8. U.S. Congress, Senate, Committee on Banking and Currency, *Nomination of George W. Romney*, 5–6.

9. Angel, *Romney*, 230–35.

10. Fine, *Expanding the Frontiers of Civil Rights*, 97.

11. "Romney Bids U.S. Put Housing First," 1.

12. Foley, "Romney Asks Attack on Problems of the Cities."

13. Foley, "Romney Asks Attack on Problems of the Cities."

14. "Romney Suspends All Housing Action," 14.

15. Finney, "G.O.P. Urban Plank Asks Industry Aid in 'Crisis of Slums.'"

16. Hanson, *Evolution of National Urban Policy*, 9.

17. Nolan, "Urban Council Sets Course."

18. "Interview with George Romney," 79.

19. Welles, "Romney Appoints 2 Negroes to Fill Major Positions."

20. Nixon, *New Federalism*.

21. "White House Press Conference with Daniel Patrick Moynihan."

22. "Let Others Join Romney in Seeking Urban Answers."

23. Perlstein, *Nixonland*, 395.

24. "White House Press Conference with Daniel Patrick Moynihan."

25. Reichley, "George Romney Is Running Hard at HUD"; "HUD Decentralized to 23 Area Cities."

26. "FHA Policy Aids Minority Buyers—and Panic Sellers."

27. "National Association of Home Builders Report."

28. Meyer, "Slum Properties Eyed for Housing Renewal."

29. McNally, *Global Slump*, 89–91: "The ratio of dollars in foreign capitals to gold in Fort Knox is the worst in the modern era. In the last eight years fully 40 percent of American gold has been carted off by foreign bankers. Three times in the final year of Johnson's term, the international monetary system was seized by something approaching a panic—and as Richard Nixon took office the future of the American dollar and gold exchange remained question marks in the commercial capitals of the world."

30. Romney, "Memo to President Richard M. Nixon."

31. "Single House Becomes More Elusive in U.S."

32. Gimlin, "Private Housing Squeeze."

33. Gimlin, "Private Housing Squeeze."

34. Gimlin, "Private Housing Squeeze."

35. See Goldberg and Griffey, *Black Power at Work*, 134–57, and Leiken, "Preferential Treatment in the Skilled Building Trades."

36. Danielson, *Politics of Exclusion*, 135–40.

37. Fred Tucker's testimony quoted in U.S. Congress, Senate, Committee on Banking and Currency, Subcommittee on Housing and Urban Affairs, *Housing and Urban Development Legislation of 1968*, pt. 1, 453.

38. Von Hoffman, *Enter the Housing Industry*, 31; von Hoffman, *Let Us Continue*.

39. Edito, "Builders Urge Credit Controls."

40. Pynoos, Schafer, and Hartman, *Housing Urban America*, 36.

41. "Memo on Housing Production."

42. Fowler, "Operation Breakthrough Passes a Milestone."

43. "Interview with George Romney."

44. Burstein, "Lawyer's View of Operation Breakthrough," 137–38.

45. "Romney Opens $20 Million Test Program."

46. "Progress Report on Federal Housing and Urban Development Programs," 4–5.

47. "Winners Assembled for Breakthrough."

48. "Romney Bids U.S. Put Housing First," 23.

49. Lassiter, *Silent Majority*, 4–5.

50. Ehrlichman, "Strategy for Metropolitan Open Communities."

51. Danielson, *Politics of Exclusion*, 205.

52. "'Project Rehab' to Rebuild Slums on Large Scale"; Driscoll, "HUD Outlines Conditions for Federal Assistance"; "HUD Discloses Plan for the Renovation of Rundown Housing."

53. Finger, *HUD, Space, and Science Appropriations for 1972*, 1012.

54. "Slum Rehabilitation Put into Operation."

55. "'Project Rehab' to Rebuild Slums on Large Scale."

56. Meyer, "Slum Properties Eyed for Housing Renewal."

57. Lawson, *Above Property Rights*, 1.

58. Lawson, *Above Property Rights*, 5–7.

59. Lacy, *Blue-Chip Black*; Wiese, *Places of Their Own*; Taylor, *Race and the City*.

60. Lawson, *Above Property Rights*, 10.

61. Romney, "Memo to All Regional Administrators."

62. Moynihan, *Toward a National Urban Policy*, 10.

63. Ehrlichman, "Strategy for Metropolitan Open Communities."

64. Pattillo, *Black on the Block*, 120; for more on Dempsey Travis, see Satter, *Family Properties*.

65. Hartman, "Politics of Housing."

66. Hunter, Pattillo, Robinson, and Taylor, "Black Placemaking."

67. Lineberry and Welch, "Who Gets What."

68. "Big Questions We Should Have Asked before Spending So Many Billions."

69. Danielson, *Politics of Exclusion*, 132.

70. Danielson, *Politics of Exclusion*, 132.

71. U.S. President's Task Force on Low Income Housing, *Toward Better Housing for Low Income Families*, 4–5.

72. Herbers, "Romney Making His Greatest Impact outside Government."

73. Ehrlichman, "Strategy for Metropolitan Open Communities."

74. U.S. Commission on Civil Rights, *Federal Civil Rights Enforcement Effort* (1971), 829, 457–58, 509–10.

75. Ehrlichman, "Strategy for Metropolitan Open Communities."

76. Ehrlichman, "Strategy for Metropolitan Open Communities."

77. Braestrup, "'Open Communities' Is Goal of HUD."

78. Danielson, *Politics of Exclusion*, 50–79; Herbers, "Romney Asks Ban on Rules Curbing Housing for Poor"; Thomas and Ritzdorf, *Urban Planning and the African American Community*, 23–43; Highsmith, *Demolition Means Progress*, 121–40.

79. "Slums, Suburbs, and 'Snob-Zoning'"; Harvey, "Court Says State Can Overrule 'Snob

Zoning' Laws in Suburbs"; "Government Moves to End Suburban 'Snob-Zoning'"; Robbins, "Manpower Held Housing Problem"; Clifton, "'Freedom Town' Snob Zoning Snubs Moderate-Income People"; Herbers, "Suburbs Accept Poor in Ohio Housing Plan."

80. Lawson, *Above Property Rights*, 13.

81. Lawson, *Above Property Rights*, 13.

82. "Memo from Francis Fisher to Edward Levin."

83. "Memo from Francis Fisher to Edward Levin."

84. *Clearinghouse Review*, 244; Braestrup, "'Open Communities' Is Goal of HUD"; Isaacs, "Romney."

85. Highsmith, *Demolition Means Progress*, 214–15.

86. Braestrup, "HUD Halts Building at Mich. Site."

87. Braestrup, "HUD's Biggest Housing Effort Runs into Trouble in Michigan."

88. Braestrup, "HUD's Biggest Housing Effort Runs into Trouble in Michigan."

89. Braestrup, "HUD's Biggest Housing Effort Runs into Trouble in Michigan."

90. Braestrup, "HUD's Biggest Housing Effort Runs into Trouble in Michigan."

91. Braestrup, "HUD's Biggest Housing Effort Runs into Trouble in Michigan."

92. Braestrup, "HUD Halts Building at Mich. Site."

93. Braestrup, "HUD's Biggest Housing Effort Runs into Trouble in Michigan."

94. U.S. Congress, House, Committee on Government Operations, *Operations of the Federal Housing Administration*, 91–92; Braestrup, "HUD's Biggest Housing Effort Runs into Trouble in Michigan"; Riddle, "Race and Reaction in Warren, Michigan."

95. Braestrup, "HUD's Biggest Housing Effort Runs into Trouble in Michigan."

96. Highsmith, *Demolition Means Progress*, 200–219. Highsmith has one of the few historical accounts of the "suburban crisis" created by the saturation of low-income housing in this area. The failure of this project would resonate loudly in ongoing debates about the placement of low-income housing.

97. Danielson, *Politics of Exclusion*, 223; "HUD Pressuring Suburbs to House Poor Families."

98. Braestrup, "'Open Communities' Is Goal of HUD."

99. Bonastia, "Low-Hanging Fruit," 562–64; Bonastia, *Knocking on the Door* (2006), 105; Mossberg, "Blue-Collar Town Fears Urban Renewal Perils Its Way of Life," A1; Riddle, "Race and Reaction in Warren, Michigan."

100. Bonastia, "Low-Hanging Fruit," 562–66.

101. "Memo from Francis Fisher to Edward Levin."

102. "Memo from Francis Fisher to Edward Levin."

103. Mossberg, "Blue-Collar Town Fears Urban Renewal Perils Its Way of Life," A2.

104. Bonastia, *Knocking on the Door* (2008), 105–8.

105. Bonastia, *Knocking on the Door* (2008), 107.

106. Quoted in Bonastia, *Knocking on the Door* (2008), 109.

107. "Romney and Mitchell Discuss Rights Riff."

108. Strout, "Romney Ready to Quit Cabinet."

109. Romney, "Memo to President Richard M. Nixon."

110. Clawson, "Top Nixon Aides Urged Housing Shift."

111. Ehrlichman, "Strategy for Metropolitan Open Communities."

112. "Administrative Law"; "Racial Impact of Federal Urban Development."

113. Jansen, "Integration Held Housing Aid Goal."

114. Braestrup, "'Open Communities' Is Goal of HUD."

115. Kelley, *Race Rebels*, 39.

116. Hager, "Housing Officials Await Ruling on Referendum," 20.

117. Cavin, "Right to Housing in the Suburbs."

118. Sobel, *New York and the Urban Dilemma*, 44.

119. "436 F2d 108 Kennedy Park Homes Association v. City of Lackawanna New York"; "Rule City Did Discriminate"; "City Appeals Decision on Bias," 40.

120. Carnegie, "Romney Housing Plans Come Tumbling Down."

121. Garment, "Forced Integration Memo to John Ehrlichman."

122. Garment, "Forced Integration Memo to John Ehrlichman."

123. Garment, "Forced Integration Memo to John Ehrlichman," 2.

124. "Richard Nixon: The President's News Conference."

125. "Richard Nixon: Statement about Federal Policies Relative to Equal Housing Opportunity."

126. "Richard Nixon: Statement about Federal Policies Relative to Equal Housing Opportunity."

127. "Richard Nixon: Statement about Federal Policies Relative to Equal Housing Opportunity."

128. "Richard Nixon: Statement about Federal Policies Relative to Equal Housing Opportunity" (emphasis added).

129. "Richard Nixon: Statement about Federal Policies Relative to Equal Housing Opportunity."

130. "Richard Nixon: Statement about Federal Policies Relative to Equal Housing Opportunity."

131. U.S. Commission on Civil Rights, *Federal Civil Rights Enforcement Effort: Seven Months Later*, 6.

132. U.S. Commission on Civil Rights, *Federal Civil Rights Enforcement Effort: Seven Months Later*, 6.

133. Glickstein, "Letter to Romney."

134. Nolan, "Plain-Talking Daley and Housing Sham."

135. "Justice Department Files Six More Housing Suits."

136. Kotlowski, *Nixon's Civil Rights*, 59; "Open Housing Activists Draw Romney's Warning."

137. "Open Housing Activists Draw Romney's Warning."

138. "HUD Ask U.S. Suit on Zoning Bias"; Clawson, "U.S. Files Housing Bias Suit."

139. Bonastia, *Knocking on the Door* (2008), 118–20; Kotlowski, *Nixon's Civil Rights*, 63–64.

140. Herbers, "Rights Panel Says U.S. Housing Plan Aids Segregation."

141. U.S. Commission on Civil Rights, *Home Ownership for Lower Income Families*, 1.

142. U.S. Commission on Civil Rights, *Federal Civil Rights Enforcement Effort* (1971), 157–60.

143. Rubinowitz and Trosman, "Affirmative Action and the American Dream," 507.

144. Lawson, *Above Property Rights*, 13.

CHAPTER 4

1. U.S. Commission on Civil Rights, *Home Ownership for Lower Income Families*, 38.

2. U.S. Congress, House, Committee on Banking and Currency, *Investigation and Hearing of Abuses*, 81.

3. U.S. Congress, House, Committee on Banking and Currency, *Investigation and Hearing of Abuses*, 81–82.

4. U.S. Congress, House, Committee on Banking and Currency, *Investigation and Hearing of Abuses*, 11.

5. "Crisis in Chicago."

6. "Crisis in Chicago."

7. U.S. Congress, House, Committee on Banking and Currency, *Investigation and Hearing of Abuses*, 18.

8. "New Look of the Federal Housing Administration."

9. "Remarks of Philip J. Maloney," 4; "FHA'ers Told Act or Resign."

10. "Remarks of Philip J. Maloney," 2.

11. "Remarks of Philip J. Maloney," 4.

12. Semple, "F.H.A. Asks Aides to Get Housing for Minorities"; "Remarks of Philip J. Maloney," 10–11.

13. "Remarks of Philip J. Maloney," 19.

14. "Remarks of Philip J. Maloney," 19.

15. U.S. Department of Housing and Urban Development, Office of Audit, *Audit Review of Section 235 Single Family Housing*, 6.

16. "Behind HUD's Reorganization."

17. Bratt, "Federal Homeownership Policy and Home Finance," 144.

18. Kempster, "Romney Asks More Housing for the Poor."

19. U.S. Congress, Senate, Select Committee on Equal Educational Opportunity, *Equal Educational Opportunity*, 2796.

20. U.S. Congress, Senate, Select Committee on Equal Educational Opportunity, *Equal Educational Opportunity*, 2758–60.

21. U.S. Congress, Senate, Select Committee on Equal Educational Opportunity, *Equal Educational Opportunity*, 2759.

22. U.S. Congress, House, Committee on Banking and Currency, *Investigation and Hearing of Abuses*, 1.

23. U.S. Commission on Civil Rights, *Home Ownership for Lower Income Families*, 9.

24. Downie, *Mortgage on America*, 51; see also Hyman, *Borrow*, 186–92.

25. "Typical FHA New Home Hiked $995 from 1968." The cost of the housing was increasing, reducing how much could be purchased with the varying levels of appropriations. Homes purchased in 1968 cost $19,568, but by 1969, this had jumped by 5 percent to $20,563. For existing housing, the cost of a single-family home was $16,814, which was 4 percent higher than the cost of existing housing in 1968.

26. "Typical FHA New Home Hiked $995 from 1968."

27. U.S. Commission on Civil Rights, *Home Ownership for Lower Income Families*, 23; DiPentima, "Abuses in the Low Income Homeownership Programs," 463–65.

28. Quoted in U.S. Commission on Civil Rights, *Home Ownership for Lower Income Families*, 5.

29. U.S. Commission on Civil Rights, *Home Ownership for Lower Income Families*, 6.

30. Downie, *Mortgage on America*, 3. Profitopolis is described as "a promised land of windfall profits, capital gains, mortgage interest and tax benefits. Too often when these people gain, others stand to lose."

31. U.S. Congress, House, Committee on Banking and Currency, *Investigation and Hearing of Abuses*, 4.

32. U.S. Congress, House, Committee on Banking and Currency, *Investigation and Hearing of Abuses*, 1.

33. U.S. Congress, House, Committee on Banking and Currency, *Investigation and Hearing of Abuses*, 11.

34. U.S. Congress, House, Committee on Banking and Currency, *Investigation and Hearing of Abuses*, 96.

35. Clancy, "Basement Still Leaking as FHA Investigation Continues."

36. Clancy, "Basement Still Leaking as FHA Investigation Continues."

37. Clancy, "Basement Still Leaking as FHA Investigation Continues."

38. Clancy, "Basement Still Leaking as FHA Investigation Continues."

39. Clancy, "Basement Still Leaking as FHA Investigation Continues."

40. U.S. Congress, House, Committee on Banking and Currency, *Investigation and Hearing of Abuses*, 136.

41. U.S. Congress, House, Committee on Banking and Currency, *Investigation and Hearing of Abuses*, 137.

42. U.S. Congress, House, Committee on Banking and Currency, *Investigation and Hearing of Abuses*, 139.

43. U.S. Congress, House, Committee on Banking and Currency, *Investigation and Hearing of Abuses*, 141.

44. U.S. Congress, House, Committee on Banking and Currency, *Investigation and Hearing of Abuses*, 138.

45. U.S. Congress, House, Committee on Banking and Currency, "Compilation of the Housing and Urban Development Act of 1968," 11.

46. Adams, "1000 Pct. Markups Revealed in Housing"; "High Profit in Poor Housing."

47. U.S. Department of Housing and Urban Development, *Homeownership for Lower Income Families (Section 235)*, 8.

48. U.S. Congress, House, Committee on Banking and Currency, *Investigation and Hearing of Abuses*, 5.

49. "Panic Sellers Play Fear against Fear—Skirt Law."

50. "Panic Sellers Play Fear against Fear—Skirt Law."

51. U.S. Congress, House, Committee on Banking and Currency, *Investigation and Hearing of Abuses*, 86.

52. U.S. Department of Housing and Urban Development, *Homeownership for Lower Income Families (Section 235)*, 38.

53. U.S. Department of Housing and Urban Development, *Homeownership for Lower Income Families (Section 235)*, 59.

54. U.S. Commission on Civil Rights, *Home Ownership for Lower Income Families*, 59.

55. "US Confirms Abuse, Halts Housing Plan."

56. "US Confirms Abuse, Halts Housing Plan."

57. U.S. Department of Housing and Urban Development, Office of Audit, *Audit Review of Section 235 Single Family Housing*, 2–3.

58. U.S. Department of Housing and Urban Development, Office of Audit, *Audit Review of Section 235 Single Family Housing*, 71.

59. U.S. Department of Housing and Urban Development, Office of Audit, *Audit Review of Section 235 Single Family Housing*, 67.

60. U.S. Department of Housing and Urban Development, Office of Audit, *Audit Review of Section 235 Single Family Housing*, 4.

61. U.S. Congress, House, Committee on Banking and Currency, *Interim Report*, 16–17.

62. Quoting A. E. Reinman of the Society of Real Estate Appraisers, in Bradford, *Redlining and Disinvestment*, 161.

63. Quoting Dexter McBride, in Bradford, *Redlining and Disinvestment*, 30.

64. U.S. Congress, House, Ad Hoc Subcommittee on Home Financing Practices and Procedures, *Financing of Inner-City Housing*, 22–24.

65. According to Rubinowitz and Trosman, "Affirmative Action and the American Dream," 508:

> United States v. American Inst. of Real Estate Appraisers (AIREA), 442 F. Supp. 1072 (N.D. Ill. 1977). In *AIREA*, the district court approved and ordered the entry of an agreement between AIREA and the Justice Department, settling a suit which charged that the appraisers' standard appraisal technique, treating race and national origin as factors that lower the overall valuation of a property, violated the Fair Housing Act. The settlement agreement provided in pertinent part: (1) It is improper to base a conclusion or opinion of value upon the premise that the racial, ethnic, or religious homogeneity of the inhabitants of an area or a property is necessary for maximum value. (2) Racial, religious or ethnic factors are deemed unreliable predictors of value trends or price variance. (3) It is improper to base a conclusion or opinion of value, or a conclusion with respect to neighborhood trends, upon stereotyped or biased presumptions relating to race, color, religion, sex or national origin or upon unsupported presumptions relating to the effective age or remaining life of the property being appraised or the life expectancy of the neighborhood in which it is located.

66. Rubinowitz and Trosman, "Affirmative Action and the American Dream," 442.

67. Quoting a student guide of AIREA, in Bradford, *Redlining and Disinvestment*, 41.

68. Mitchell, *Dynamics of Neighborhood Change*, 20.

69. Quoted in Bradford, *Redlining and Disinvestment*, 42.

70. U.S. Congress, House, Committee on Banking and Currency, *Investigation and Hearing of Abuses*, 5–8.

71. U.S. Congress, House, Committee on Banking and Currency, *Investigation and Hearing of Abuses*, 5.

72. U.S. Department of Housing and Urban Development, *Homeownership for Lower Income Families (Section 235)*, 7.

73. Wilson, "Exploiting the Home-Buying Poor"; U.S. Congress, Senate, Committee on Banking and Currency, Subcommittee on Housing and Urban Affairs, *Analysis of the Section 235 and 236 Programs*, 11–13; U.S. Congress, House, Committee on Banking and Currency, *Investigation and Hearing of Abuses*, 5–8.

74. U.S. Congress, House, Committee on Banking and Currency, *Investigation and Hearing of Abuses*, 100: "Unfortunately the liberalized FHA procedure applied in these [central-city] cases has all too often resulted in issuance of mortgages the physical security for which is far below the stated objectives of the FHA Minimum Property Standards.... In addition there is some evidence that the liberalized policy applicable to blighted areas has generated laxness with respect to appraisal inspections in the case of properties located elsewhere."

75. Braestrup, "HUD Jobs to Be Cut by 7.5%," A1; "Romney Job Cuts May Reach 50."

76. Braestrup, "HUD Jobs to Be Cut by 7.5%," A2.

77. U.S. Department of Housing and Urban Development, Office of Audit, *Audit Review of Section 235 Single Family Housing*, 20.

78. U.S. Department of Housing and Urban Development, Office of Audit, *Audit Review of Section 235 Single Family Housing*, 9.

79. Barlett and Steele, "Appraisers Jack Up Value on Many Poor Homes Here."

80. Barlett and Steele, "Appraisers Jack Up Value on Many Poor Homes Here."

81. U.S. Department of Housing and Urban Development, Office of Audit, *Audit Review of Section 235 Single Family Housing*, 28.

82. See, for extensive detail on the corruption of FHA appraisers, Boyer, *Cities Destroyed for Cash*.

83. Barlett and Steele, "160 Housing Appraisers Suspended in FHA Case."

84. "Area Chief Orders Probe of Patman Scandal Charge," 21.

85. For a discussion of the mortgage point system and FHA lending, see Feins, "Urban Housing Disinvestment and Neighborhood Decline," 230–34, 273–75; Wilson, "Exploiting the Home-Buying Poor," 548–51; Boyer, *Cities Destroyed for Cash*; Northwestern University, Urban-Suburban Investment Study Group, and Illinois Housing Development Authority, *Role of Mortgage Lending Practices in Older Urban Neighborhoods*, 151–59.

86. Northwestern University, Urban-Suburban Investment Study Group, and Illinois Housing Development Authority, *Role of Mortgage Lending Practices in Older Urban Neighborhoods*, 159.

87. Bradford, "Financing Home Ownership," 327–28.

88. Feins, "Urban Housing Disinvestment and Neighborhood Decline," 73.

89. Dombrowski, "Hike in Mortgage Rate Ceiling Is Viewed as Tactical Blunder"; "Mortgage Rate Hike Denounced."

90. Jones, "Battle Looms on Housing Policy"; "Bankers View."

91. Bratt, Stone, and Hartman, *Right to Housing*, 85–86; "Officials See More Mortgage Money—More Housing."

92. Porter, "Budget Gloomy on 'Initiatives' in Next 5 Years"; Oliphant, "Ginny & Fannie Shore Up Housing Slump."

93. Van Dusen, "Civil Rights and Housing."

94. Quoted in U.S. Department of Housing and Urban Development, *Homeownership for Lower Income Families (Section 235)*, 59.

95. U.S. Department of Housing and Urban Development, *Homeownership for Lower Income Families (Section 235)*, 47.

96. Quoted from an interview with Philadelphia FHA office on July 14, 1970, in U.S. Commission on Civil Rights, *Home Ownership for Lower Income Families*, 81.

97. U.S. Department of Housing and Urban Development, Office of Audit, *Audit Review of Section 235 Single Family Housing*, 6.

98. U.S. Commission on Civil Rights, *Home Ownership for Lower Income Families*, 47.

99. "Letter from George Romney to Wright Patman," September 3, 1970, in U.S. Congress, House, Committee on Banking and Currency, *Investigation and Hearing of Abuses*, 109.

100. U.S. Congress, House, Committee on Appropriations, Subcommittee on HUD, Space, Science, and Veterans Appropriations, *HUD, Space, Science and Veterans Appropriations for 1973*, 1320.

101. U.S. Congress, House, Committee on Banking and Currency, *Investigation and Hearing of Abuses*, 4–5.

102. "Civil Rights Commission Gives Administration Mixed Progress Rating."

103. Braestrup, "Rights Commission Hits U.S. on Bias"; U.S. Commission on Civil Rights, *Federal Civil Rights Enforcement Effort* (1970), 424–66.

104. U.S. Commission on Civil Rights, *Federal Civil Rights Enforcement Effort* (1970), 6; "Civil Rights Commission Gives Administration Mixed Progress Rating."

105. Viorst, "Blacks Who Work for Nixon."

106. U.S. Commission on Civil Rights, *Federal Civil Rights Enforcement Effort* (1970), 147.

107. U.S. Commission on Civil Rights, *Equal Opportunity in Suburbia*, 23.

108. U.S. Commission on Civil Rights, *Equal Opportunity in Suburbia*, 21.

109. "Racist Ruling on HUD Hailed."

110. "Racist Ruling on HUD Hailed"; "HUD Discriminates, New Study Finds."

111. "Black HUD Employees Hold Racial Injustices Meeting."

112. "Black HUD Employees Hold Racial Injustices Meeting."

113. Booker, "Washington Notebook," 26.

114. "Black HUD Employees Hold Racial Injustices Meeting"; Booker, "Washington Notebook."

115. Ward and Whitaker, "100 at Rally Protest U.S. Bias"; Delaney, "HUD Is Charged with Racial Bias."

116. McCombs, "Black HEW Employees Charge Agency Biased."

117. Ward, "Employee Protests Heard by Romney."

118. "HUD's Romney Runs Away from Anti-Bias Petition."

119. Whitaker, "HUD Gives Promotions to 42 Aides."

120. Meyer, "160 Black HUD Employees Face Suspension for Protesting."

121. Delaney, "HUD Is Charged with Racial Bias."

122. "HUD Discriminates, New Study Finds."

123. "HUD Discriminates, New Study Finds."

124. "HUD Discriminates, New Study Finds."

125. Delaney, "HUD Is Charged with Racial Bias."

126. "HUD Discriminates, New Study Finds."

127. Herbers, "Rights Panel Says U.S. Housing Plan Aids Segregation."

128. Braestrup, "HUD Perpetuates Bias, Rights Report Charges."

129. Meyer, "Home Ownership Nightmare in NW."

130. Braestrup, "HUD Perpetuates Bias, Rights Report Charges"; U.S. Department of Housing and Urban Development, *Homeownership for Lower Income Families (Section 235)*, 90.

131. "Civil Rights Unit Says Housing Bias Study Shows HUD Has Failed to Change Pattern"; Testimony of George Romney, in U.S. Commission on Civil Rights, *Hearing before the United States Commission on Civil Rights*, 245.

132. U.S. Commission on Civil Rights, *Hearing before the United States Commission on Civil Rights*, 245–46.

133. U.S. Commission on Civil Rights, *Hearing before the United States Commission on Civil Rights*, 248:

Mr. Glickstein: But, nevertheless, I would guess that most of the housing market consists of existing housing. Secretary Romney: You mean that we are supplying or is being sold?

Mr. Glickstein: That people are moving into. They are moving into existing housing in the suburbs and existing housing in the cities, and I take it that your affirmative marketing circular doesn't cover existing housing? Secretary Romney: I think that's right. It applies to subsidized and FHA-insured. Mr. Glickstein: But not existing housing. Secretary Romney: FHA-insured. Mr. Glickstein: Existing housing? Secretary Romney: No, not existing. Mr. Glickstein: Just the new starts. Secretary Romney: That's right. Mr. Glickstein: So as I understand the way . . . Secretary Romney: Look, we are not ducking this question that you're raising. Now what you are really talking about is the dual housing market that exists in this country and the fact that most minority citizens when they go into a real estate office are shown the book for blacks instead of the book for whites.

134. U.S. Commission on Civil Rights, *Hearing before the United States Commission on Civil Rights*, 256.

CHAPTER 5

1. U.S. Congress, House, Committee on Banking and Currency, "Compilation of the Housing and Urban Development Act of 1968," 10–11.

2. Nadasen, *Welfare Warriors*, 29.

3. "FHA Policy Aids Minority Buyers—and Panic Sellers."

4. See Williams, *Politics of Public Housing*, and Williams, "'We're Tired of Being Treated Like Dogs,'" 31–32. Williams looks at the activism of Black women as public housing residents, but the discussion of poor women's social activism pertains here as well. See also Kornbluh, *Battle for Welfare Rights*, 114–35, and Nadasen, *Welfare Warriors*.

5. U.S. Congress, House, Committee on Appropriations, Subcommittee on HUD, Space, Science, and Veterans Appropriations, *HUD, Space, Science and Veterans Appropriations for 1973*, 62.

6. "Housing Probe."

7. U.S. Congress, House, Committee on Banking and Currency, Subcommittee on Housing, *Real Estate Settlement Costs*, 34–35.

8. U.S. Congress, House, Committee on Banking and Currency, Subcommittee on Housing, *Real Estate Settlement Costs*, 73–75.

9. "Housing Probe."

10. Whitbeck memo in full on p. 264 of U.S. Congress, Joint Economic Committee, Subcommittee on Priorities and Economy in Government, *Housing Subsidies and Housing Policies: Hearings*; "Romney Aide Scores Inner-City Program."

11. Sparkman, "Defaults and Foreclosures."

12. Holifield, "Defaults on FHA-Insured Home Mortgages, Detroit, Michigan," 3.

13. Ball, "Foreclosures Costing FHA Millions."

14. Boyer, "HUD Scandal Profited All but Taxpayer."

15. Ball, "Foreclosures Costing FHA Millions."

16. Barlett and Steele, "Anatomy of Failure."

17. Barber, "Patman's Probe May Have Missed Biggest Housing Program Scandal."

18. U.S. Congress, House, Committee on Appropriations, Subcommittee on HUD, Space, Science, and Veterans Appropriations, *HUD, Space, Science and Veterans Appropriations for 1973*, 1323.

19. Freeman, "Reform of FHA Set."

20. Phillips and Zekman, "Judge Calls HUD a Slumlord."

21. Bliss and Neubauer, "FHA Wastes $4 Billion and Creates City Slums"; Barlett and Steele, "Phila Is Leader among Large Cities in FHA Mortgage Foreclosure Rate"; Associated Press, "Report Says Poor Bilked during FHA Program"; Ricke, "Stories of Hope, Broken Vows, and a Lot of FHA Money," 18.

22. U.S. Congress, House, Committee on Government Operations, Subcommittee on Legal and Monetary Affairs, *Defaults on FHA-Insured Mortgages (Detroit)*, pt. 2, 304.

23. U.S. Congress, Joint Economic Committee, Subcommittee on Priorities and Economy in Government, *Housing Subsidies and Housing Policies: Hearings*, 10: "In our investigating, 41 matters were identified as prima facie violations of section 1010, title 18, U.S. Code, false statements to FHA. We referred these 41 Cases to the Federal Bureau of Investigation. Furthermore, as a result of our central office-technical review we also referred to the FBI 45 additional matters involving alleged false statements and certifications concerning required repairs, mortgagor investment, ownership of properties, forged certifications and possible fraudulent appraisal reports."

24. Kohler-Hausmann, *Getting Tough*; Chappell, *War on Welfare*.

25. Karmin, "Restoring Cities after the Scandals" (emphasis added).

26. Karmin, "Restoring Cities after the Scandals."

27. *Social and Economic Status of the Black Population in the United States*, 29–30.

28. U.S. Congress, House, Committee on Banking and Currency, *Investigation and Hearing of Abuses*, 160.

29. Kahrl, "Capitalizing on the Urban Fiscal Crisis."

30. "FHA Policy Aids Minority Buyers—and Panic Sellers" (ellipsis in original).

31. Karp, "St. Louis Rent Strike of 1969"; Yonah Freemark, "Myth #5: Public Housing Ended in Failure during the 1970s," in Bloom, Umbach, and Vale, *Public Housing Myths*, 121–28; Nicholas Dagen Bloom, "Myth #4: High-Rise Public Housing Is Unmanageable," in Bloom, Umbach, and Vale, *Public Housing Myths*, 91–118; Goetz, *New Deal Ruins*, 49–52.

32. U.S. Congress, Joint Economic Committee, Subcommittee on Priorities and Economy in Government, *Housing Subsidies and Housing Policies: Hearings*, 258–59, testimony from Walter L. Smart, executive director of the National Federation of Settlements and Neighborhood Centers. NFS has 200 member agencies that operate 419 centers in 80 cities and 30 states. Seventeen metropolitan or regional federations of neighborhood centers also are affiliated with the national federation.

33. U.S. Commission on Civil Rights, *Home Ownership for Lower Income Families*, 37–38.

34. "Ads Page."

35. Barlett and Steele, "Phila Is Leader among Large Cities in FHA Mortgage Foreclosure Rate," 1.

36. Barlett and Steele, "Phila Is Leader among Large Cities in FHA Mortgage Foreclosure Rate," 10.

37. U.S. Congress, House, Committee on Banking and Currency, *Interim Report*, 5.

38. Boyer, "HUD Scandal Profited All but Taxpayer."

39. U.S. Commission on Civil Rights, *Home Ownership for Lower Income Families*, 69, quoted from an interview with the Community Relations Office, Philadelphia County Board of Assistance.

40. Barlett and Steele, "Anatomy of Failure."

41. Nadasen, *Welfare Warriors*, 16.

42. "Circular Letter Number 181," 166.

43. U.S. Commission on Civil Rights, *Home Ownership for Lower Income Families*, 46.

44. U.S. Department of Housing and Urban Development, *Homeownership for Lower Income Families (Section 235)*, 47; Wilson, "Exploiting the Home-Buying Poor," 537.

45. U.S. Commission on Civil Rights, *Home Ownership for Lower Income Families*, 69.

46. Wilson, "Exploiting the Home-Buying Poor."

47. Wilson, "Exploiting the Home-Buying Poor," 537.

48. Wilson, "Exploiting the Home-Buying Poor," 525–71, information based on "interview with confidential source, a real estate broker who participates in the FHA market in Saint Louis, March 1972."

49. U.S. Department of Housing and Urban Development, "Report of Staff Investigation of the Country Ridge Housing Development (Baltimore)."

50. U.S. Congress, House, Committee on Government Operations, Subcommittee on Legal and Monetary Affairs, *Defaults on FHA-Insured Mortgages (Detroit)*, pt. 2, 141.

51. "Save the HUD Program."

52. Boyer, "Probers Hear Success Stories to Counter City's FHA Woes"; Holmes, "Agents Deny Profiteering."

53. Boyer, "HUD Scandal Profited All but Taxpayer."

54. Ricke, "Stories of Hope, Broken Vows, and a Lot of FHA Money," 18.

55. Ricke, "Stories of Hope, Broken Vows, and a Lot of FHA Money," 18.

56. Ricke, "Stories of Hope, Broken Vows, and a Lot of FHA Money," 19.

57. Ricke, "Stories of Hope, Broken Vows, and a Lot of FHA Money," 19.

58. Ricke, "Stories of Hope, Broken Vows, and a Lot of FHA Money," 20.

59. Ricke, "Stories of Hope, Broken Vows, and a Lot of FHA Money," 21.

60. Boyer, "ADC Defaults Soar in FHA Program"; Ricke and Benjamison, "ADC Housing Plan Is Stopped."

61. Boyer, "ADC Defaults Soar in FHA Program."

62. Boyer, "ADC Defaults Soar in FHA Program"; U.S. Congress, House, Committee on Government Operations, Subcommittee on Legal and Monetary Affairs, *Defaults on FHA-Insured Mortgages (Detroit)*, 180.

63. Holmes, "Agents Deny Profiteering."

64. Boyer, "Probers Hear Success Stories to Counter City's FHA Woes."

65. Holmes, "Agents Deny Profiteering."

66. Kohler-Hausmann, *Getting Tough*; Chappell, *War on Welfare*.

67. U.S. Congress, House, Committee on Government Operations, Subcommittee on Legal and Monetary Affairs, *Defaults on FHA-Insured Mortgages (Detroit)*, pt. 2, 152.

68. Testimony of Lawrence Katz, in U.S. Congress, House, Committee on Government Operations, Subcommittee on Legal and Monetary Affairs, *Defaults on FHA-Insured Mortgages (Detroit)*, pt. 2, 143.

69. Katz memo to president of Mortgage Bankers Association, in U.S. Congress, House, Committee on Government Operations, Subcommittee on Legal and Monetary Affairs, *Defaults on FHA-Insured Mortgages (Detroit)*, pt. 2, 169; Gray, "Counseling Key to Success of Section 235," 3.

70. Trbovich, "U.S. Curbs Profits of FHA Sales."

71. U.S. Congress, House, Committee on Government Operations, Subcommittee on Legal and Monetary Affairs, *Defaults on FHA-Insured Mortgages (Detroit)*, pt. 2, 145: "The prudent buyer is frequently not present in the inner city."

72. U.S. Congress, House, Committee on Government Operations, Subcommittee on Legal and Monetary Affairs, *Defaults on FHA-Insured Mortgages (Detroit)*, pt. 2, 145.

73. Official Testimony of Lawrence Katz, in U.S. Congress, House, Committee on Government Operations, Subcommittee on Legal and Monetary Affairs, *Defaults on FHA-Insured Mortgages (Detroit)*, pt. 2, 165.

74. Katz Testimony, in U.S. Congress, House, Committee on Government Operations, Subcommittee on Legal and Monetary Affairs, *Defaults on FHA-Insured Mortgages (Detroit)*, pt. 2, 147; Gray, "Counseling Key to Success of Section 235," 6.

75. Letter from Lawrence Katz to James Grootemaat, President, Mortgage Bankers Association, Milwaukee, Wisconsin, in U.S. Congress, House, Committee on Government Operations, Subcommittee on Legal and Monetary Affairs, *Defaults on FHA-Insured Mortgages (Detroit)*, pt. 2, 170–71.

76. Katz Testimony, in U.S. Congress, House, Committee on Government Operations, Subcommittee on Legal and Monetary Affairs, *Defaults on FHA-Insured Mortgages (Detroit)*, pt. 2, 147.

77. Theoharis and Woodard, *Groundwork*, 259–79; for more on the Commandos, see Jones, *Selma of the North*.

78. Katz Testimony, in U.S. Congress, House, Committee on Government Operations, Subcommittee on Legal and Monetary Affairs, *Defaults on FHA-Insured Mortgages (Detroit)*, pt. 2, 152.

79. Katz Testimony, in U.S. Congress, House, Committee on Government Operations, Subcommittee on Legal and Monetary Affairs, *Defaults on FHA-Insured Mortgages (Detroit)*, pt. 2, 151.

80. Gray, "Counseling Key to Success of Section 235," 1; U.S. Congress, House, Committee on Government Operations, Subcommittee on Legal and Monetary Affairs, *Defaults on FHA-Insured Mortgages (Detroit)*, pt. 2, 170, Katz memo to MBA.

81. Katz Testimony, in U.S. Congress, House, Committee on Government Operations, Subcommittee on Legal and Monetary Affairs, *Defaults on FHA-Insured Mortgages (Detroit)*, pt. 2, 146.

82. Katz Testimony, in U.S. Congress, House, Committee on Government Operations, Subcommittee on Legal and Monetary Affairs, *Defaults on FHA-Insured Mortgages (Detroit)*, pt. 2, 147.

83. Katz Testimony, in U.S. Congress, House, Committee on Government Operations, Subcommittee on Legal and Monetary Affairs, *Defaults on FHA-Insured Mortgages (Detroit)*, pt. 2, 151.

84. Boyer, "Probers Hear Success Stories to Counter City's FHA Woes."

85. Gray, "Counseling Key to Success of Section 235."

86. Katz Testimony, in U.S. Congress, House, Committee on Government Operations, Subcommittee on Legal and Monetary Affairs, *Defaults on FHA-Insured Mortgages (Detroit)*, pt. 2, 146.

87. U.S. Congress, Joint Economic Committee, Subcommittee on Priorities and Economy in Government, *Housing Subsidies and Housing Policies: Hearings*, 223–25.

88. Testimony of Margaret Lancaster, in U.S. Commission on Civil Rights, *Hearing before the United States Commission on Civil Rights*, 87–88.

89. U.S. Congress, Joint Economic Committee, Subcommittee on Priorities and Economy in Government, *Housing Subsidies and Housing Policies: Hearings*, 226.

90. Katz written statement, in U.S. Congress, House, Committee on Government Operations, Subcommittee on Legal and Monetary Affairs, *Defaults on FHA-Insured Mortgages (Detroit)*, pt. 2, 168.

91. Letter from Lawrence Katz to James Grootemaat, President, Mortgage Bankers Association, Milwaukee, Wisconsin, May 24, 1968, in U.S. Congress, House, Committee on Government Operations, Subcommittee on Legal and Monetary Affairs, *Defaults on FHA-Insured Mortgages (Detroit)*, pt. 2, 168–69.

92. Organization and Bach, *Study of the Effectiveness of Voluntary Counseling Programs for Lower-Income Home Ownership*, 115–16.

93. Trbovich, "U.S. Curbs Profits of FHA Sales."

94. U.S. Congress, Joint Economic Committee, Subcommittee on Priorities and Economy in Government, *Housing Subsidies and Housing Policy: Report*, 15; Organization and Bach, *Study of the Effectiveness of Voluntary Counseling Programs for Lower-Income Home Ownership*, 26.

95. See McClaughry, "Troubled Dream," 19, for an extensive discussion on counseling and homeownership.

96. Statement of National Federation of Housing Counselors, Inc., April 18, 1977, in U.S. Congress, House, Committee on Appropriations, Subcommittee on HUD—Independent Agencies, *Department of Housing and Urban Development—Independent Agencies Appropriations for 1978*, 1287.

97. "Save the HUD Program."

98. Quoted in Organization and Bach, *Study of the Effectiveness of Voluntary Counseling Programs for Lower-Income Home Ownership*, 49.

99. Organization and Bach, *Study of the Effectiveness of Voluntary Counseling Programs for Lower-Income Home Ownership*, 4.

100. Wilson, "Exploiting the Home-Buying Poor," 539.

101. Wilson, "Exploiting the Home-Buying Poor," 537–38.

102. Wilson, "Exploiting the Home-Buying Poor," 541.

103. Wilson, "Exploiting the Home-Buying Poor," 541, interview by Wilson with Ernie Gross, HUD public information officer, in Washington, D.C., Feb. 24, 1972.

104. U.S. Congress, House, Committee on Banking and Currency, *Investigation and Hearing of Abuses*, 4.

105. U.S. Congress, House, Committee on Banking and Currency, *Investigation and Hearing of Abuses*, 165.

106. U.S. Congress, House, Committee on Banking and Currency, *Investigation and Hearing of Abuses*, 167.

107. U.S. Congress, House, Committee on Banking and Currency, *Investigation and Hearing of Abuses*, 168.

108. "Mortgage Banking," 10.

109. *Simplified Housekeeping Directions for Homemakers*.

110. U.S. Congress, House, Committee on Banking and Currency, *Investigation and Hearing of Abuses*, 8.

111. Steele, "HUD Confirms Violations by FHA Unit Here."

112. Steele, "HUD Confirms Violations by FHA Unit Here."

113. U.S. Congress, House, Committee on Banking and Currency, Subcommittee on Housing, *Real Estate Settlement Costs*, 280.

114. Lear, "FHA-235 Program 'A Fraud and Outrage' Homeowners Insist."

115. "A Mother Speaks from Experience," in U.S. Community Services Administration, *"Right to a Decent Home,"* 17.

116. Herbers, "F.H.A. Overhaul Urged by Percy"; Paprino, "Mrs. Chisholm Hits Housing Program."

117. Breckenfeld, "Housing Subsidies Are a Grand Delusion."

118. U.S. House of Representatives, Congressional Black Caucus, "Position on Housing," 16.

119. Herbers, "Federal Housing Reform Unlikely."

120. U.S. Congress, House, Committee on Government Operations, Subcommittee on Legal and Monetary Affairs, *Defaults on FHA-Insured Mortgages (Detroit)*, pt. 2, 333. There were 1,805 investigations in 1971 and 2,254 investigations from January 1972 to October 1972.

121. U.S. Congress, House, Committee on Government Operations, Subcommittee on Legal and Monetary Affairs, *Defaults on FHA-Insured Mortgages (Detroit)*, 478.

122. Boyer, *Cities Destroyed for Cash*.

123. "Office of the Audit Report," sent to George Romney on December 10, 1971, p. 38 of report, in U.S. Congress, House, Committee on Banking and Currency, Subcommittee on Housing, *Real Estate Settlement Costs*, 116.

124. Chapman, "FHA Scandal Spreads across Nation."

125. Chapman, "FHA Scandal Spreads across Nation."

126. Chapman, "FHA Scandal Spreads across Nation."

127. Asbury, "Dun & Bradstreet among 50 Named in Housing Fraud."

128. "40 Charged in $200 Million FHA Bribery Scandal in N.Y."; Asbury, "Dun & Bradstreet among 50 Named in Housing Fraud."

129. Asbury, "Dun and Bradstreet among 50 Named in Housing Fraud"; Asbury, "FHA Aide Pleads Guilty to Fraud."

130. Barlett and Steele, "Real Estate Brokers Sail South," 16.

131. Barlett and Steele, "Real Estate Brokers Sail South," 17.

132. Barlett and Steele, "Shapp Cabinet Member Was on Broker's Cruise," December 19, 1971, 1.

133. Barlett and Steele, "Shapp Cabinet Member Was on Broker's Cruise," December 19, 1971, 1.

134. Barlett and Steele, "Shapp Cabinet Member Was on Broker's Cruise," December 19, 1971, 17.

135. "Court Rules HUD, Director Guilty of Discrimination."

136. "Court Rules HUD, Director Guilty of Discrimination."

137. "Bribery Indictments Hold Four Detroit FHA Workers"; Davis, "4 FHA Officials, 9 Others Named in Bribery Scheme," 1; Chapman, "FHA Scandal Spreads across Nation."

138. "HUD Suspends Firms, Brokers," A3.

139. "Bribery Indictments Hold Four Detroit FHA Workers."

140. Gallagher, "Department of Housing and Urban Development."

141. "Bribery Indictments Hold Four Detroit FHA Workers."

142. U.S. Congress, House, Committee on Government Operations, Subcommittee on Legal and Monetary Affairs, *Defaults on FHA-Insured Mortgages (Detroit)*, 476.

143. "Three Plead Not Guilty in Case Involving Senator Gurney."

144. "Sen. Gurney Indicted in Builder Kickbacks."

145. Kneeland, "McGovern Assails Nixon Administration as 'Scandal-Ridden.'"

146. Letter from Attorney Robert Bergstrom to Andrew Hess of the FHA, Seattle, Washington, August 4, 1970, in U.S. Congress, House, Committee on Banking and Currency, *Investigation and Hearing of Abuses*, 18–19.

147. Letter from Attorney Robert Bergstrom to Andrew Hess of the FHA, Seattle, Washington, August 4, 1970, in U.S. Congress, House, Committee on Banking and Currency, *Investigation and Hearing of Abuses*, 19.

148. Quoted from text of legal complaint filed in lawsuit of *Liza M. Perry et al. v. HUD, George Romney et al., United States et al.*, in U.S. Congress, House, Committee on Banking and Currency, *Investigation and Hearing of Abuses*, 23.

149. U.S. Congress, House, Committee on Banking and Currency, *Investigation and Hearing of Abuses*, 19–20; U.S. Congress, House, Committee on Banking and Currency, "Compilation of the Housing and Urban Development Act of 1968," 126.

150. U.S. Congress, House, Committee on Banking and Currency, *Investigation and Hearing of Abuses*, 18–30.

151. Letter from Stephen Idema, Attorney, The Wyandotte Legal Aid Society, to Committee of Banking and Currency, Washington, D.C., December 3, 1970, in U.S. Congress, House, Committee on Banking and Currency, *Investigation and Hearing of Abuses*, 72–73.

152. Letter from James Kushner, Attorney, to House Banking and Currency Committee, November 17, 1970, in U.S. Congress, House, Committee on Banking and Currency, *Investigation and Hearing of Abuses*, 75–76.

153. Gould, "G'twn Attorney Testifies before Congress on Housing Plight of Black Philadelphians."

154. U.S. Congress, Senate, Committee on Banking and Currency, Subcommittee on Housing and Urban Affairs, *Housing and Urban Development Legislation of 1970*, pt. 2, 1537–38.

155. Barlett and Steele, "Law Cites Homeowner Aid."

156. Barlett and Steele, "Law Cites Homeowner Aid."

157. Barlett and Steele, "Law Cites Homeowner Aid," 8.

158. Lear, "Homeowners Picket FHA Officials over Broken-Down Homes, Unkept Promises."

159. Chapman, "FHA Scandal Spreads across Nation."

160. Lear, "FHA-235 Program 'A Fraud and Outrage' Homeowners Insist."

161. Lear, "FHA-235 Program 'A Fraud and Outrage' Homeowners Insist."

162. "Is FHA Providing Good Housing for Poor People?"

163. Carmel McCrudden Testimony, in U.S. Congress, House, Committee on Government Operations, Subcommittee on Legal and Monetary Affairs, *Defaults on FHA-Insured Mortgages (Detroit)*, pt. 2, 393–95; McCrudden Testimony, in U.S. Congress, Senate, Committee on Banking, Housing, and Urban Affairs, Subcommittee on Housing and Urban Affairs, *Oversight on Housing and Urban Development Programs*, pt. 1, Pub. L. No. HRG-1973-BHU-0026, 435–37.

164. Lear, "Homewners Picket FHA Officials over Broken-Down Homes, Unkept Promises."

165. Interview with George Gould.

166. Barlett and Steele, "Low-Cost Housing Sales Frozen in FHA Drive."

167. Barlett and Steele, "Low-Cost Housing Sales Frozen in FHA Drive," 6.

168. Phillips and Zekman, "Judge Calls HUD a Slumlord."

169. "Brown v. Lynn, 385 F. Supp. 986 (N.D. Ill. 1974)."

170. "Brown v. Lynn, 385 F. Supp. 986 (N.D. Ill. 1974)."

171. U.S. Congress, Senate, Committee on Banking, Housing, and Urban Affairs, Subcommittee on Housing and Urban Affairs, *Abandonment Disaster Demonstration Relief Act of 1975*, 44 (quote from McGraw-Hill Newsstory reprint).

172. U.S. Congress, Senate, Committee on Banking, Housing, and Urban Affairs, Subcommittee on Housing and Urban Affairs, *Abandonment Disaster Demonstration Relief Act of 1975*, 44.

173. Rhonda Y. Williams, "Something's Wrong Down Here: Poor Black Women and Urban Struggles for Democracy," in Kusmer and Trotter, *African American Urban History since World War II*, 318.

174. Camp, *Incarcerating the Crisis*, 10–12.

CHAPTER 6

1. "Richard Nixon: Radio Address."

2. Taylor, *From #BlackLivesMatter to Black Liberation*, chap. 3, "Black Faces in High Places."

3. Weaver, "Urban Crisis"; Pritchett, "Which Urban Crisis?"

4. Oliphant, "Romney to Leave HUD Job, Cites Difficulty of Reform," 31.

5. "Housing and Urban Affairs Daily: HUD Budget Slashed in 'Reform.'"

6. "Housing and Urban Affairs Daily: Freeze Imposed on Major HUD Programs."

7. "White House Said to Plan Freeze on Public Housing."

8. Moritz, "Romney's Leaving, but U.S. Housing Problems Hang On."

9. Herbers, "Tragedy of the Decaying Cities"; Herbers, "Federal Agencies Press Inquiry on Housing Frauds in Big Cities"; Herbers, "Abandonment of Federal Housing Blights Inner Cities."

10. Samuelson, "Romney."

11. "White House Said to Plan Freeze on Public Housing," 12.

12. Quoted in Bonastia, *Knocking on the Door* (2006), 137.

13. "Housing and Urban Affairs Daily: Freeze Imposed on Major HUD Programs," 16.

14. "Housing and Urban Affairs Daily: HUD Budget Slashed in 'Reform.'"

15. Darrow, "HUD's 'Goldberg' Housing Breakthrough."

16. "New Nixon Action to Affect Blacks."

17. "New Nixon Action to Affect Blacks."

18. "New Nixon Action to Affect Blacks."

19. Foldessy and Schellhard, "Backing Off."

20. Foldessy and Schellhard, "Backing Off."

21. "Housing and Urban Affairs Daily: HUD Budget Slashed in 'Reform,'" 69.

22. U.S. Congress, Joint Economic Committee, Subcommittee on Priorities and Economy in Government, *Housing Subsidies and Housing Policy: Report*, 4.

23. Salpukas, "Moratorium on Housing Subsidy Spells Hardship for Thousands."

24. McBee, "Subsidized Housing Frozen before Justification by HUD."

25. Salpukas, "Moratorium on Housing Subsidy Spells Hardship for Thousands."

26. Rippeteau, "Mortgage Defaults Increase Number of Homes U.S. Owns."

27. Walker, "Housing Freeze Evil or Good?"

28. Jacobs, "Subsidies Moratorium Dismal News for Builders."

29. Parks, "Revisiting Shibboleths of Race and Urban Economy," 113.

30. Causey, "Rundown on Nixon's 1974 Budget."

31. U.S. Congress, Senate, Committee on Banking and Currency, Subcommittee on Housing and Urban Affairs, *Housing and Urban Development Legislation of 1968.*

32. Darrow, "Money for Poor Ebbs."

33. Darrow, "Money for Poor Ebbs."

34. Goldberg and Griffey, *Black Power at Work*, 134–60.

35. "Blacks Hurt by Housing Ban for Families of Low Income."

36. Associated Press, "NAACP Chief Raps Nixon Leadership."

37. Stanley, "United Black Mortgage Bankers Assail Nixon."

38. Jensen, "Romney Discloses Halt in Subsidies for New Housing."

39. McBee, "Joblessness Feared in HUD Cuts"; Jensen, "Romney Discloses Halt in Subsidies for New Housing."

40. Statement of Gail Cincotta, West Side Coalition, in U.S. Congress, Senate, Committee on Banking, Housing, and Urban Affairs, Subcommittee on Housing and Urban Affairs, *Oversight on Housing and Urban Development Programs—Chicago*, 26.

41. McCrudden Testimony, in U.S. Congress, Senate, Committee on Banking, Housing, and Urban Affairs, Subcommittee on Housing and Urban Affairs, *Oversight on Housing and Urban Development Programs, Washington, D.C.*, 437.

42. Quoted in U.S. Congress, Senate, Committee on Banking, Housing, and Urban Affairs, Subcommittee on Housing and Urban Affairs, *Oversight on Housing and Urban Development Programs, Washington, D.C.*, 440.

43. "Richard Nixon: Radio Address."

44. "Richard Nixon: Radio Address."

45. "Richard Nixon: Radio Address."

46. "White House Said to Plan Freeze on Public Housing," 51.

47. Legates and Morgan, "Perils of Special Revenue Sharing for Community Development," 256–58.

48. Kovach, "Mayors Oppose Nixon Fund Plan."

49. "Administration Housing Moratorium Comes Under Fire."

50. "Administration Housing Moratorium Comes Under Fire."

51. U.S. Commission on Civil Rights, *Home Ownership for Lower Income Families*, 16.

52. "Richard Nixon: Special Message to the Congress."

53. From the written statement of George Romney, in U.S. Congress, House, Committee on Government Operations, Subcommittee on Legal and Monetary Affairs, *Defaults on FHA-Insured Mortgages (Detroit)*, pt. 2, 332.

54. Written statement of George Romney, in U.S. Congress, House, Committee on Government Operations, Subcommittee on Legal and Monetary Affairs, *Defaults on FHA-Insured Mortgages (Detroit)*, pt. 2, 332.

55. Written statement of George Romney, in U.S. Congress, House, Committee on Government Operations, Subcommittee on Legal and Monetary Affairs, *Defaults on FHA-Insured Mortgages (Detroit)*, pt. 2, 332.

56. Romney Testimony, in U.S. Congress, House, Committee on Banking and Currency, Subcommittee on Housing, *Real Estate Settlement Costs*, 49; "Romney: HUD Can't Solve City Housing Problems." This became a theme in talks Romney gave throughout the spring, generating this kind of headline.

57. Desmond, *Evicted*, 299–300.

58. U.S. Commission on Civil Rights, *Home Ownership for Lower Income Families*; U.S. Commission on Civil Rights, *Federal Civil Rights Enforcement Effort* (1971); U.S. Commission on Civil Rights, *Hearing before the United States Commission on Civil Rights*; U.S. Commission on Civil Rights, *Federal Civil Rights Enforcement Effort: Seven Months Later*; U.S. Commission on Civil Rights, *Understanding Fair Housing*.

59. Yudis, "Both Critics, Experts Have Second Thoughts."

60. "FHA Homes Rot as Paperwork Shuffles across Country," 1.

61. Commission on the Cities in the '70's, *State of the Cities*, 70.

62. Commission on the Cities in the '70's, *State of the Cities*; Metzger, "Planned Abandonment."

63. Romney Testimony, in U.S. Congress, House, Committee on Banking and Currency, Subcommittee on Housing, *Real Estate Settlement Costs*, 47; Romney Testimony, in U.S. Congress, House, Committee on Government Operations, Subcommittee on Legal and Monetary Affairs, *Defaults on FHA-Insured Mortgages (Detroit)*, pt. 2, 305.

64. "Draft Copy of George Romney Address to Detroit Economic Club."

65. "Draft Copy of George Romney Address to Detroit Economic Club."

66. Angelo, "Deep Social Changes at Work."

67. "Remarks Prepared for Delivery by George Romney."

68. See Bloom, Umbach, and Vale, *Public Housing Myths*.

69. Goetz, *New Deal Ruins*, 40–44; Karp, "St. Louis Rent Strike of 1969"; Williams, *Politics of Public Housing*.

70. *Papers Submitted to Subcommittee on Housing Panels*, 491.

71. Freidrichs, *Pruitt-Igoe Myth*.

72. Ira S. Lowry, "Housing Assistance for Low-Income Urban Families: A Fresh Approach," in *Papers Submitted to Subcommittee on Housing Panels*, 497.

73. Goetz, *New Deal Ruins*, 38–40.

74. "Remarks Prepared for Delivery by George Romney."

75. "Remarks Prepared for Delivery by George Romney."

76. Alsop, "Road to Hell."

77. Alsop, "Road to Hell."

78. "Remarks Prepared for Delivery by George Romney."

79. "Remarks Prepared for Delivery by George Romney."

80. "Remarks Prepared for Delivery by George Romney."

81. Smith, *Uneven Development*.

82. Camp, *Incarcerating the Crisis*, 9–10.

83. Katz, *Undeserving Poor*, 206.

84. See Spitzer, "Toward a Marxian Theory of Deviance," and Parenti, *Lockdown America*, 46.

85. Banfield quoted in Parks, "Making It over the Race Barrier."

86. "American Underclass"; Chappell, *War on Welfare*, 141–43.

87. Kohler-Hausmann, *Getting Tough*; Schram, Fording, and Soss, "Neo-Liberal Poverty Governance"; Kohler-Hausmann, "Guns and Butter"; Chappell, *War on Welfare*, 106–25.

88. Harvey, *Brief History of Neoliberalism*; Hackworth, *Neoliberal City*; McNally, *Global Slump*; Soss, Fording, and Schram, *Disciplining the Poor*; Chappell, *War on Welfare*, 143–48.

89. "Remarks Prepared for Delivery by George Romney."

90. For more on public sector workers, see Taylor, *From #BlackLivesMatter to Black Liberation*, 55–61; Honey, *Going Down Jericho Road*, 7–127; and Brenner, Brenner, and Winslow, *Rebel Rank and File*.

91. Sugrue, *Sweet Land of Liberty*, 505.

92. See chap. 2, "From Civil Rights to Colorblind," in Taylor, *From #BlackLivesMatter to Black Liberation*, 53–60, and Bonilla-Silva, *Racism without Racists*, 49–52, 54–60.

93. Murakawa, *First Civil Right*, 7.

94. Perlstein, "Exclusive."

95. Klein, *Shock Doctrine*, 7: "For more than three decades, Friedman and his powerful followers had been perfecting this very strategy: waiting for a major crisis, then selling off pieces of the state to private players while citizens were still reeling from the shock, then quickly making the reforms permanent."

96. Friedman, "What Is Killing the City?"

97. Friedman, *Capitalism and Freedom*, xvi.

98. Article reprinted within *Congressional Record*, "Nixon's New Budget: What It Means to Black Americans," *Congressional Record*, vol. 119, 16615.

99. "Richard Nixon: Labor Day Message": "We are faced this year with the choice between the 'work ethic' that built this Nation's character and the new 'welfare ethic' that could cause that American character to weaken."

100. See Kohler-Hausmann, *Getting Tough*.

101. "Richard Nixon: Labor Day Message."

102. "Congress Must Dig Deep into HUD's Failures."

103. Bowsher, "1973"; Reed, "One Hundred Years of Price Change."

104. Matusow, *Nixon's Economy*, 228.

105. Mort, "Boycott Slices Meat Prices at 1 Chain," 155; Phillips-Fein, *Invisible Hands*, 155.

106. Matusow, *Nixon's Economy*, 229; Maize, "Food Inflation."

107. "Richard Nixon: Address to the Nation."

108. Matusow, *Nixon's Economy*, 231.

109. Cowie, *Stayin' Alive*, 91.

110. Quoted in Matusow, *Nixon's Economy*, 240.

111. Delaney, "Brimmer of Federal Reserve Finds Black Job Gains in 1973," 34.

112. "Black Unemployment Remained High in April."

113. Johnson, "Urban League Finds 25.4% of Blacks Are Still Jobless"; Hill, "Illusion of Progress."

114. "Options Ahead for the Debt Economy"; Cowie, *Stayin' Alive*, 363–64. Also see Smith, *Subterranean Fire*.

115. Quoted in Cowie, *Stayin' Alive*, 225.

116. Smith, *Subterranean Fire*, 249.

117. U.S. Congress, Senate, Committee on Banking, Housing, and Urban Affairs, Subcommittee on Housing and Urban Affairs, *Oversight on Housing and Urban Development Programs*, pt. 1, Pub. L. No. HRG-1973-BHU-0026, 71.

118. U.S. Congress, Senate, Committee on Banking, Housing, and Urban Affairs, Subcommittee on Housing and Urban Affairs, *Oversight on Housing and Urban Development Programs*, pt. 1, Pub. L. No. HRG-1973-BHU-0026, 71.

119. "Lynn of HUD Critical of Senate Housing Bill."

120. Karmin, "Pros and Cons."

121. "Interview with HUD Secretary James T. Lynn."

122. "Interview with HUD Secretary James T. Lynn."

123. Johnson, "Housing Policy at the Crossroads," 20.

124. Johnson, "Housing Policy at the Crossroads," 20.

125. Johnson, "Housing Policy at the Crossroads," 20.

126. Johnson, "Housing Policy at the Crossroads," 19.

127. Lubin, "Black Firms' Blues."

128. Rubinowitz and Trosman, "Affirmative Action and the American Dream," 491.

129. Quoted in Hays, *Federal Government and Urban Housing* (1995), 188.

130. See Rooks, *Cutting School*; Lassiter, *Silent Majority*, chap. 6, "The Fight for 'Freedom of Association': School Desegregation and White Withdrawal"; Kruse, *White Flight*, 161; and Bonastia, *Southern Stalemate*.

131. Bonastia, "Low-Hanging Fruit," 552; Lassiter, *Silent Majority*, 133.

132. Lassiter, *Silent Majority*. See Bonastia, *Knocking on the Door* (2006).

133. Harney, "Even Subsidies Possible."

134. "Milliken v. Bradley"; Riddle, "Race and Reaction in Warren, Michigan."

135. "Jones v. Alfred H. Mayer Co., 392 U.S. 409 (1968)."

136. Gill, "Moving to Integration?," 669.

137. Connolly, "New Housing Law Gets Mixed Reviews"; Lamb, *Housing Segregation in Suburban America since 1960*; von Hoffman, *House by House, Block by Block*.

138. "Gerald R. Ford: Statement on the Housing and Community Development Act of 1974."

139. "Gerald R. Ford: Statement on the Housing and Community Development Act of 1974."

140. Witcover, "President OKs Revenue Sharing at Independence Hall Ceremony."

141. Kushner, "Community Planning and Development under the Housing and Community Development Act of 1974," 665.

142. Marshall and Swinton, "Federal Government Policy in Black Community Revitalization."

143. Kushner, "Community Planning and Development under the Housing and Community Development Act of 1974," 664; Mollenkopf, *Contested City*, 134–35; Logan and Molotch, *Urban Fortunes*, 173; Hays, *Federal Government and Urban Housing* (1995), 190.

144. Mollenkopf, *Contested City*, 135.

145. Morris, "HUD to Revive Low-Income Home Ownership Subsidy"; Jones, "Industry Unimpressed by Nixon Housing Plan"; Curry, "Housing Plan Aims to Aid Workers Making under $11,000"; "Executive Summary on Restoring Section 235."

146. Kushner, "Community Planning and Development under the Housing and Community Development Act of 1974," 673.

147. Kushner, "Community Planning and Development under the Housing and Community Development Act of 1974," 665; Hays, *Federal Government and Urban Housing* (2012), 207–9.

148. Hays, *Federal Government and Urban Housing* (2012), 157–62; Harney, "HUD on the Spot with 'Section 8.'"

149. Hays, *Federal Government and Urban Housing* (2012), 148–51.

150. Gill, "Moving to Integration?," 670.

151. Hays, *Federal Government and Urban Housing* (1995), 159.

152. Hays, *Federal Government and Urban Housing* (1995), 146–47; Logan and Molotch, *Urban Fortunes*, 173.

153. Gill, "Moving to Integration?," 671.

154. "Gerald R. Ford: Statement on the Housing and Community Development Act of 1974."

155. "Ethnic Treasure."

156. Mollenkopf, *Contested City*, 134.

CONCLUSION

1. U.S. President's Commission on Housing, *Report of the President's Commission on Housing*, xvii–viii.

2. Lydon, "Carter Defends All-White Areas."

3. U.S. Commission on Civil Rights, *Understanding Fair Housing*, 1.

4. "Black Homeownership and the American Dream."

5. Perry, Rothwell, and Harshbarger, *Devaluation of Assets in Black Neighborhoods*, 2.

6. Reed, "Black Home Ownership Now American Nightmare."

BIBLIOGRAPHY

"40 Charged in $200 Million FHA Bribery Scandal in N.Y.: Dun, Bradstreet Accused of False Credit Claims." *Los Angeles Times*, March 30, 1972, E14.

"436 F2d 108 Kennedy Park Homes Association v. City of Lackawanna New York." OpenJurist, http://openjurist.org/436/f2d/108/kennedy-park-homes-association-v-city-of-lackawanna -new-york-1-t-d-1-d-j. Accessed February 17, 2017.

Abrams, Charles. *Forbidden Neighbors: A Study of Prejudice in Housing.* New York: Harper, 1955.

———. *Home Ownership for the Poor: A Program for Philadelphia.* New York: Praeger, 1970, https//catalog.hathitrust.org/Record/000955460.

Adams, Jim. "1000 Pct. Markups Revealed in Housing." *Atlanta Constitution*, January 6, 1971, 5.

"Administration Housing Moratorium Comes Under Fire." *CQ Almanac 1973*, 29th ed., 428–32. Washington, D.C.: Congressional Quarterly, 1974, http://library.cqpress.com/cqalmanac /cqa173–1228677.

"Administrative Law. Urban Renewal. HUD Has Affirmative Duty to Consider Low Income Housing's Impact upon Racial Concentration. Shannon v. HUD, 436 F. 2d 809 (3d Cir. 1970)." *Harvard Law Review* 85, no. 4 (1972): 870–80, https://doi.org/10.2307/1339996.

Administrator of HHFA. "Assistance to Members of Minority Groups." Annual Report of the Voluntary Home Mortgage Credit Program. Housing and Home Finance Agency, April 1, 1958.

"Ads Page." *Detroit Free Press*, June 23, 1971, 10B.

Alexander, Michelle. *The New Jim Crow: Mass Incarceration in the Age of Colorblindness.* New York: New Press, 2013.

Allen, Robert L. *Black Awakening in Capitalist America: An Analytic History.* Garden City, N.Y.: Doubleday, 1969.

———. *A Guide to Black Power in America: A Historical Analysis.* London: Victor Gollancz, Ltd., 1969.

Alsop, Stewart. "Road to Hell." *Boston Globe*, March 6, 1972, 23.

American Life Convention and Life Insurance Association of America. "$1 Billion Urban Investment Program of the Life Insurance Business," March 1969. "Employment, investment in urban areas by life insurance companies, and United Nations in NAACP correspondence." Papers of the NAACP, Part 28: Special Subject Files, 1966–1970, Group IV, series A, Administrative File, General Office File, Manuscript Division, Library of Congress.

"The American Underclass." *Time*, August 29, 1977, 18.

Angel, Dan. *Romney: A Political Biography.* New York: Exposition Press, 1967.

Angelo, Frank. "Deep Social Changes at Work: Romney Touches Cities Tender Spot." *Detroit Free Press*, March 31, 1972, 9.

"Annual Message to the Congress on the State of the Union," January 12, 1966. The American Presidency Project, https://www.presidency.ucsb.edu/documents/annual-message-the -congress-the-state-the-union-27.

"Area Chief Orders Probe of Patman Scandal Charge." *Philadelphia Inquirer*, August 1, 1970, 21.

Asbury, Edith Evans. "Dun & Bradstreet among 50 Named in Housing Fraud: F.H.A. Mortgage Insurance Obtained through False Data." *New York Times*, March 30, 1972, 1.

———. "FHA Aide Pleads Guilty to Fraud: Multimillion-Dollar Scheme Involved Mortgages." *New York Times*, September 13, 1972, 17.

Associated Press. "NAACP Chief Raps Nixon Leadership." *Boston Globe*, January 9, 1973, 28.

———. "Report Says Poor Bilked during FHA Program." *Boston Globe*, January 6, 1971, 4.

Babcock, Frederick M. *The Appraisal of Real Estate*. New York: Macmillan, 1927.

Ball, Don. "Foreclosures Costing FHA Millions: Safeguards Started." *Washington Post*, December 12, 1971, G1.

"Bankers View: Divert Funds to Save Homes, HUD Urged." *Detroit Free Press*, December 9, 1970, 7A.

"Bank of America Hit for 35th Time: Guardsmen Alerted on California Rallies." *Washington Post, Times Herald*, May 2, 1971, A3.

Baradaran, Mehrsa. *The Color of Money: Black Banks and the Racial Wealth Gap*. Cambridge, Mass.: Belknap Press of Harvard University Press, 2017.

Barber, Richard J. "Patman's Probe May Have Missed Biggest Housing Program Scandal." *Philadelphia Inquirer*, August 22, 1971, 17.

Barlett, Donald L., and James B. Steele. "160 Housing Appraisers Suspended in FHA Case." *Philadelphia Inquirer*, August 27, 1971, morning ed., 1

———. "An Anatomy of Failure: The Poor as Homeowners." *Washington Post, Times Herald*, February 27, 1972, 1.

———. "Appraisers Jack Up Value on Many Poor Homes Here." *Philadelphia Inquirer*, October 6, 1971, final city ed., 1.

———. "Law Cites Homeowner Aid: 159 Ask, 0 Aided." *Philadelphia Inquirer*, October 31, 1971, 2.

———. "Low-Cost Housing Sales Frozen in FHA Drive—Sellers, Lenders Now Liable under New Ruling by FHA." *Philadelphia Inquirer*, October 2, 1971, sec. A.

———. "Phila Is Leader among Large Cities in FHA Mortgage Foreclosure Rate." *Philadelphia Inquirer*, August 29, 1971, sec. A.

———. "Real Estate Brokers Sail South: 'Poor' Home Buyers Pay the Tab." *Philadelphia Inquirer*, December 12, 1971, A16–A17.

———. "Shapp Cabinet Member Was on Broker's Cruise," *Philadelphia Inquirer*, December 19, 1971, final city ed., sec. A.

"Behind HUD's Reorganization." *Boston Globe*, November 16, 1969, 47.

"The Big Questions We Should Have Asked before Spending So Many Billions," n.d. Box 7, folder Correspondence, HUD, Administrative Correspondence, Record Group 207, National Archives and Records Administration, College Park, Md.

Biles, Roger. *The Fate of Cities: Urban America and the Federal Government, 1945–2000*. Lawrence: University Press of Kansas, 2011.

"Billion-Dollar Slum Fund Hailed by LBJ." *Philadelphia Tribune*, September 23, 1967, 15.

Biondi, Martha. *To Stand and Fight: The Struggle for Civil Rights in Postwar New York City*. Cambridge, Mass.: Harvard University Press, 2003.

"Black Homeownership and the American Dream: An Expert Dialogue." How Housing Matters, https://howhousingmatters.org/articles/black-homeownership-american-dream -expert-dialogue/. Accessed November 24, 2018.

"Black HUD Employees Hold Racial Injustices Meeting." *Baltimore Afro-American*, October 17, 1970, 19.

"Blacks Hurt by Housing Ban for Families of Low Income." *Jet*, January 25, 1973, 20.

"Black Unemployment Remained High in April." *Atlanta Daily World*, May 16, 1975, 5.

Bliss, George, and Chuck Neubauer. "FHA Wastes $4 Billion and Creates City Slums: Thousands Abandon, Lose Homes." *Chicago Tribune*, June 24, 1975, 1.

Bloom, Nicholas Dagen, Fritz Umbach, and Lawrence J. Vale. *Public Housing Myths: Perception, Reality, and Social Policy*. Ithaca, N.Y.: Cornell University Press, 2015.

Boggs, James, and Grace Lee Boggs. "The City Is the Black Man's Land." *Monthly Review*, April 4, 1966, 35–46, https://doi.org/10.14452/MR-017-11-1966-04_4.

"Bombs Found in 8 U.S. Banks." *Washington Post, Times Herald*, January 8, 1972, A1.

Bonastia, Christopher. *Knocking on the Door: The Federal Government's Attempt to Desegregate the Suburbs*. Princeton, N.J.: Princeton University Press, 2006.

———. *Knocking on the Door: The Federal Government's Attempt to Desegregate the Suburbs*. Princeton, N.J.: Princeton University Press, 2008.

———. "Low-Hanging Fruit: The Impoverished History of Housing and School Desegregation." *Sociological Forum* 30 (June 1, 2015): 549–70, https://doi.org/10.1111/socf.12177.

———. *Southern Stalemate: Five Years without Public Education in Prince Edward County, Virginia*. Chicago: University Of Chicago Press, 2011.

Bonilla-Silva, Eduardo. *Racism without Racists: Color-Blind Racism and the Persistence of Racial Inequality in America*. Lanham, Md.: Rowman & Littlefield, 2018.

Booker, Simeon. "Washington Notebook." *Ebony*, March 1974, 26.

Bowsher, Norman N. "1973: A Year on Inflation." *Federal Reserve Bank of St. Louis Review*, December 1973.

Boyer, Brian D. "ADC Defaults Soar in FHA Program." *Detroit Free Press*, February 24, 1972, 1.

———. *Cities Destroyed for Cash: The FHA Scandal at HUD*. Chicago: Follett, 1973.

———. "HUD Scandal Profited All but Taxpayer." *Detroit Free Press*, March 19, 1972, A3.

———. "Probers Hear Success Stories to Counter City's FHA Woes." *Detroit Free Press*, February 25, 1972, 8.

Bradford, Calvin. "Financing Home Ownership: The Federal Role in Neighborhood Decline." *Urban Affairs Quarterly* 14, no. 3 (March 1, 1979): 313–35, https://doi.org/10.1177/107808747901400303.

———. *Redlining and Disinvestment as a Discriminatory Practice in Residential Mortgage Loans*. Washington D.C.: Dept. of Housing and Urban Development, Office of Assistant Secretary for Fair Housing and Equal Opportunity, 1977.

Braestrup, Peter. "HUD Halts Building at Mich. Site." *Washington Post, Times Herald*, February 9, 1971, A2.

———. "HUD Jobs to Be Cut by 7.5%; Deeper Slashes under Study." *Washington Post, Times Herald*, October 12, 1971, A1–A2.

———. "HUD Perpetuates Bias, Rights Report Charges." *Washington Post, Times Herald*, April 18, 1971, A1.

———. "HUD's Biggest Housing Effort Runs into Trouble in Michigan." *Washington Post, Times Herald*, February 16, 1971, A3.

———. "'Open Communities' Is Goal of HUD." *Washington Post, Times Herald*, July 27, 1970, A6.

———. "Rights Commission Hits U.S. on Bias." *Washington Post, Times Herald*, September 15, 1970, A3.

Bratt, Rachel G. "Federal Homeownership Policy and Home Finance: A Study in Program Operations and Impacts on the Consumer." Ph.D. diss., Massachusetts Institute of Technology, 1976.

Bratt, Rachel G., Michael E. Stone, and Chester W. Hartman. *A Right to Housing: Foundation for a New Social Agenda*. Philadelphia: Temple University Press, 2006.

Brauer, Carl M. "Kennedy, Johnson, and the War on Poverty." *Journal of American History* 69, no. 1 (June 1, 1982): 98–119, https://doi.org/10.2307/1887754.

Breckenfeld, Gurney. "Housing Subsidies Are a Grand Delusion." *Fortune* 85, no. 2 (February 1972): 166.

Brenner, Aaron, Robert Brenner, and Calvin Winslow. *Rebel Rank and File: Labor Militancy and Revolt from Below during the Long 1970s*. New York: Verso, 2010.

Breslin, Jimmy. "The Rats Come Every Night . . . Takes Off Shoe." *Washington Post, Times Herald*, July 25, 1967, A4.

"Bribery Indictments Hold Four Detroit FHA Workers." *Baltimore Afro-American*, December 9, 1972, 20.

Brownstein, Philip N. Oral History Interview, November 22, 1968. Interviewer, David G. McComb, University of Texas Oral History Project. In *Oral Histories of the Johnson Administration, 1963–1969*, pt. 1, *The White House and Executive Departments*. Accessed through ProQuest History Vault.

"Brown v. Lynn, 385 F. Supp. 986 (N.D. Ill. 1974)." Justia Law, http://law.justia.com/cases/federal/district-courts/FSupp/385/986/1429412/. Accessed July 14, 2017.

Burstein, Joseph. "A Lawyer's View of Operation Breakthrough." *Urban Lawyer* 2, no. 2 (1970): 137–45.

Business and the Urban Crisis, February 1, 1968. Box 24, President's Committee on Urban Housing, LBJ Presidential Library, Austin, Tex.

"A Businessman's Call to Action in the Cities: The Urban Crisis." *Newsday*, Nassau ed., January 29, 1968, 26.

"By Lyndon B. Johnson: War on Poverty and the 1964 Campaign." *New York Times*, October 19, 1971, sec. Archives, https://www.nytimes.com/1971/10/19/archives/by-lyndon-b-johnson-war-on-poverty-and-the-1964-campaign-a.html.

Calhoun, Lillian S. "Metropolitan Prexy Denies NAACP Charges." *Chicago Daily Defender*, May 13, 1965, 6.

Califano, Joseph A. "The Public Interest Partnership." *New Leader*, December 18, 1967.

Camp, Jordan T. *Incarcerating the Crisis: Freedom Struggles and the Rise of the Neoliberal*

State. Oakland: University of California Press, 2016, http://www.jstor.org/stable/10.1525
/j.ctt1b3t8fn.

"Can't Sleep in 'Rat-Infested Slum,' Says Mother of Three." *Chicago Defender*, July 17, 1965, 31.

Carmichael, Stokely, and Charles V. Hamilton. *Black Power: The Politics of Liberation in America*. New York: Vintage, 1992.

Carnegie, Christa. "Romney Housing Plans Come Tumbling Down." *Christian Science Monitor*, June 12, 1971, 1.

Causey, Mike. "Rundown on Nixon's 1974 Budget." *Washington Post, Times Herald*, January 30, 1973, B13.

Cavin, Aaron. "A Right to Housing in the Suburbs: James v. Valtierra and the Campaign against Economic Discrimination." *Journal of Urban History* 45, no. 3 (June 10, 2017): 427–51, https://doi.org/10.1177/0096144217712928.

Chapman, William. "FHA Scandal Spreads across Nation." *Washington Post*, March 10, 1974, 12.

Chappell, Marisa. *The War on Welfare: Family, Poverty, and Politics in Modern America*. Philadelphia: University of Pennsylvania Press, 2010.

"Charge Rats Killed Baby Disputed." *Washington Post, Times Herald*, February 12, 1966, sec. A.

"Chi NAACP to Picket Metropolitan Life." *Chicago Daily Defender*, April 22, 1965, 5.

"Circular Letter Number 181, 'From the Desk of Lawrence S. Katz, Director,' Federal Housing Administrator, Milwaukee, Wisconsin." April 22, 1968. In U.S. Congress, House, Committee on Government Operations, Subcommittee on Legal and Monetary Affairs, *Defaults on FHA-Insured Mortgages*, pt. 2, *February 24; May 2, 3, 4, 1972*. Washington, D.C.: U.S. Government Printing Office, 1972.

"The City: Detroit's Ditto." *Time*, June 13, 1969, 24.

"A City Appeals Decision on Bias: Lackawanna Denies Court's Finding It Is Antiblack." *New York Times*, August 23, 1970, 40.

"The Civil Rights Bill of 1866." U.S. House of Representatives History, Art & Archives, https://history.house.gov/Historical-Highlights/1851-1900/The-Civil-Rights-Bill-of-1866/. Accessed May 15, 2018.

"Civil Rights Commission Gives Administration Mixed Progress Rating: HUD Is Criticized as the Agency That Has 'Regressed' Furthest in Its Enforcement Stance." *Wall Street Journal*, May 11, 1971, 14.

"Civil Rights Unit Says Housing Bias Study Shows HUD Has Failed to Change Pattern." *Wall Street Journal*, June 11, 1971, 1.

Clancy, John. "Basement Still Leaking as FHA Investigation Continues." *Philadelphia Inquirer*, August 1, 1970, 1.

Clawson, Ken. "Top Nixon Aides Urged Housing Shift." *Washington Post*, June 12, 1971, sec. A.

———. "U.S. Files Housing Bias Suit: Missouri City Sued; Zoned to Bar Project." *Washington Post*, June 15, 1971, 1.

Clearinghouse on Corporate Social Responsibility (U.S.) and Life Insurance Joint Committee on Urban Problems. *A Report on the $2 Billion Urban Investment Program of the Life Insurance Business, 1967–1972*. New York: Clearinghouse on Corporate Social Responsibility, 1973.

Clearinghouse Review. Chicago: National Clearinghouse for Legal Services, 1970.

Clifton, Donna R. "'Freedom Town' Snob Zoning Snubs Moderate-Income People: Principle Approved, Plan Rejected." *Christian Science Monitor*, September 24, 1970, 9.

Cloward, Richard A., and Frances Fox Piven. *Ghetto Redevelopment: Corporate Imperialism for the Poor*. Ann Arbor, Mich.: Radical Education Project and Students for a Democratic Society, 1963.

Coates, Ta-Nehisi. "The Case for Reparations." *Atlantic*, June 2014, http://www.theatlantic .com/magazine/archive/2014/06/the-case-for-reparations/361631/.

Cohen, Lizabeth. *A Consumers' Republic: The Politics of Mass Consumption in Postwar America*. New York: Vintage, 2003.

Commission on the Cities in the '70's. *The State of the Cities: Report*. Foreword by Sol M. Linowitz. New York: Praeger, 1972.

Congressional Record: Proceedings and Debates of the . . . Congress. Vol. 119. Washington, D.C.: U.S. Government Printing Office, 1973.

"Congress Must Dig Deep into HUD's Failures." *Detroit Free Press*, March 1, 1972, sec. A.

Conley, Dalton. *Being Black, Living in the Red: Race, Wealth, and Social Policy in America*. Berkeley: University of California Press, 1999, http://search.ebscohost.com/login.aspx?direct =true&scope=site&db=nlebk&db=nlabk&AN=42137.

Connolly, N. D. B. *A World More Concrete: Real Estate and the Remaking of Jim Crow South Florida*. Chicago: University of Chicago Press, 2014.

Connolly, William G. "New Housing Law Gets Mixed Reviews: U.S. Outlays for Subsidized Housing." *New York Times*, September 8, 1974, sec. Real Estate.

Countryman, Matthew J. *Up South*. Philadelphia: University of Pennsylvania Press, 2006.

"Court Rules HUD, Director Guilty of Discrimination." *New Pittsburgh Courier*, September 18, 1971, 1.

Cowie, Jefferson. *Stayin' Alive: The 1970s and the Last Days of the Working Class*. New York: New Press, 2010.

"Crisis in Chicago: Fear, Greed Used by Panic Peddlers." *Chicago Tribune*, August 8, 1971, 1.

"Crisis in the Cities: Does Business Hold the Key?" *Dun's Review*, November 1967.

Curry, Leonard. "Housing Plan Aims to Aid Workers Making under $11,000." *Washington Post*, October 25, 1975, C34.

Danielson, Lisa A. "Installment Land Contracts: The Illinois Experience and the Difficulties of Incremental Judicial Reform." *University of Illinois Law Review* 1986 (1986): 91.

Danielson, Michael N. *The Politics of Exclusion*. New York: Columbia University Press, 1976.

Darrow, Joy. "HUD's 'Goldberg' Housing Breakthrough." *Chicago Daily Defender*, January 25, 1973, 9.

———. "Money for Poor Ebbs." *Chicago Daily Defender*, January 27, 1973, 4.

Davis, Robert. "4 FHA Officials, 9 Others Named in Bribery Scheme." *Chicago Tribune*, July 28, 1972, 1.

Davis, Saville R., Donald M. Kendall, and Maurice H. Stans. "Private Enterprise and the Urban Crisis." *The Creative Interface, American University, Center for the Study of Private Enterprise* 3 (1971).

"Davis v. Romney, 355 F. Supp. 29 (E.D. Pa. 1973)." Justia Law, https://law.justia.com/cases /federal/district-courts/FSupp/355/29/1447928/. Accessed November 27, 2018.

Delaney, Paul. "Brimmer of Federal Reserve Finds Black Job Gains in 1973." *New York Times*, February 8, 1974, 34.

———. "HUD Is Charged with Racial Bias: U.S. Aide Finds It Guilty of Discrimination in Jobs." *New York Times*, October 22, 1971, 11.

Deppe, Martin L. *Operation Breadbasket: An Untold Story of Civil Rights in Chicago, 1966–1971*. Athens: University of Georgia Press, 2017.

Desmond, Matthew. *Evicted: Poverty and Profit in the American City*. New York: Penguin Random House, 2017.

Dickinson, W. B. "Changing Housing Climate." *Editorial Research Reports*. Washington D.C.: Congressional Quarterly, 1963, http://library.cqpress.com/cqresearcher/cqresrre1963041000.

———. "Urban Renewal Under Fire." *Editorial Research Reports*. Washington D.C.: CQ Press, August 21, 1963, http://library.cqpress.com/cqresearcher/cqresrre1963082100.

"A Different Kind of Choice: Educational Inequality and the Continuing Significance of Racial Segregation." Economic Policy Institute, http://www.epi.org/publication/educational-inequality-racial-segregation-significance/. Accessed December 5, 2012.

Dim, Stuart. "Metropolitan Agrees to Rent to Nonwhites." *Newsday*, Nassau ed., August 12, 1963.

DiPentima, Vincent. "Abuses in the Low Income Homeownership Programs: The Need for a Consumer Protection Response by the FHA." *Temple Law Quarterly* 45 (1971–72): 461–83.

"Discrimination against Minorities in the Federal Housing Programs." *Indiana Law Journal* 31 (1955–56): 501–15.

Dombrowski, Louis. "Hike in Mortgage Rate Ceiling Is Viewed as Tactical Blunder." *Chicago Tribune*, January 7, 1970, 10.

Donnell, Laurence G. "Can Romney's Approach Work at HUD?" *Wall Street Journal*, January 22, 1969, 18.

Downie, Leonard. *Mortgage on America*. New York: Praeger, 1974.

"Draft Copy of George Romney Address to Detroit Economic Club," April 1972. Box 5, folder Detroit Housing, George Romney Post-Gubernatorial Papers, 1969–1973, Bentley Historical Library, University of Michigan, Ann Arbor.

Driscoll, Theodore. "HUD Outlines Conditions for Federal Assistance." *Hartford Courant*, March 26, 1970, 50.

Drummond, Roscoe. "Standard Doctrine . . . : Business Changes Views on Policy." *Washington Post, Times Herald*, April 16, 1965, A22.

Dudziak, Mary L. *Cold War Civil Rights: Race and the Image of American Democracy*. Princeton, N.J.: Princeton University Press, 2000.

Duneier, Mitchell. *Ghetto: The Invention of a Place, the History of an Idea*. New York: Farrar, Straus and Giroux, 2017.

"Dwight D. Eisenhower: Special Message to the Congress on Housing," http://www.presidency.ucsb.edu/ws/index.php?pid=9952. Accessed October 21, 2017.

Edito, Tom Walker. "Builders Urge Credit Controls." *Atlanta Constitution*, August 24, 1969, 13H.

Ehrlichman, John. "Strategy for Metropolitan Open Communities," August 12, 1969. Box 2, folder Cabinet Meeting, George Romney Post-Gubernatorial Papers, 1969–1973, Bentley Historical Library, University of Michigan, Ann Arbor.

"Ethnic Treasure." *New York Times*, April 18, 1976, 128.

"Excerpts from President Johnson Speech at Syracuse, New York, August 19, 1966," n.d. Papers of Lyndon Johnson, LBJ Presidential Library, Austin, Tex.

"Executive Summary on Restoring Section 235," n.d. Box 15, GAO Lawsuit for Impounded Funds, Carla A. Hills Papers, Hoover Institution for War and Peace, Stanford, Calif.

Feins, Judith D. "Urban Housing Disinvestment and Neighborhood Decline: A Study of Public Policy Outcomes." Ph.D. diss., University of Chicago, 1977.

Ferguson, Karen. *Top Down: The Ford Foundation, Black Power, and the Reinvention of Racial Liberalism*. Philadelphia: University of Pennsylvania Press, 2013.

"FHA Developments in Analysis of Risk: Adapted from Speech by Assistant FHA Administrator Frederick Babcock." *Insured Mortgage Portfolio*, September 1939.

"FHA'ers Told Act or Resign." *Baltimore Afro-American*, December 9, 1967, 20.

"FHA Homes Rot as Paperwork Shuffles across Country." *Chicago Tribune*, June 27, 1975, 1.

"FHA Policy Aids Minority Buyers—and Panic Sellers." *Chicago Tribune*, August 12, 1971, 1.

Filson, Susan. "Woman, Children Face Loss of Rat-Ridden Home." *Washington Post, Times Herald*, November 2, 1965, B2.

Fine, Sidney. *Expanding the Frontiers of Civil Rights: Michigan, 1948–1968*. Detroit: Wayne State University Press, 2000.

Finger, Harold. *HUD, Space, and Science Appropriations for 1972*, pt. 2. Department of Housing and Urban Development, Pub. L. No. Y4.Ap6/1:H81/2/pt. 2. 1971.

Finney, John W. "G.O.P. Urban Plank Asks Industry Aid in 'Crisis of Slums.'" *New York Times*, August 3, 1968, 1.

Foldessy, Edward, and Timothy Schellhard. "Backing Off: Lenders Sharply Cut Writing of FHA Loans as Red Tape Mounts." *Wall Street Journal*, May 14, 1973, 1.

Foley, Thomas J. "Romney Asks Attack on Problems of the Cities: Governor Says Tighter Law Enforcement Alone Is Not Answer to Crime, Violence." *Los Angeles Times*, January 12, 1968, 5.

"Form Housing Unit to Spur Black Enterprise in Field." *Chicago Daily Defender*, May 3, 1969, 13.

Fowler, Glenn. "Operation Breakthrough Passes a Milestone." *New York Times*, November 8, 1970, https://www.nytimes.com/1970/11/08/archives/operation-breakthrough-passes-a-milestone.html.

Freeman, Saul. "Reform of FHA Set." *Philadelphia Inquirer*, February 23, 1972, 3.

Freidrichs, Chad. *The Pruitt-Igoe Myth*. Documentary film, 2015, http://kanopystreaming.com/node/126058.

Freund, David M. P. *Colored Property: State Policy and White Racial Politics in Suburban America*. Chicago: University of Chicago Press, 2007.

Fried, Joseph P. "City Charges Bias at Three Projects: Booth Says the Metropolitan Bars Minorities in Housing." *New York Times*, May 25, 1968, 27.

Friedman, Milton. *Capitalism and Freedom*. 40th anniversary ed. Chicago: University of Chicago Press, 2009.

———. "What Is Killing the City?" *Newsweek Magazine*, March 20, 1972, 96.

Fusfeld, Daniel R. "The Rise of the Corporate State in America." *Journal of Economic Issues* 6, no. 1 (March 1, 1972): 1–22, https://doi.org/10.2307/4224117.

Gallagher, Thomas. "Department of Housing and Urban Development, Federal Housing Administration, Circular Letter No. 149, 'All Approved Mortgagees and Interested Parties: FHA Procedures,'" April 21, 1970. Urban Archives, folder HUD News II, Housing Activism of the Delaware Valley, Temple University, Philadelphia, Pa.

Gans, Herbert J. "The Failure of Urban Renewal." *Commentary*, April 1, 1965, https://www.commentarymagazine.com/articles/the-failure-of-urban-renewal/.

Garment, Len. "Forced Integration Memo to John Ehrlichman," March 15, 1971. Box 13, folder

President-Ehrlichman 1971, George Romney Post-Gubernatorial Papers, 1969–1973, Bentley Historical Library, University of Michigan, Ann Arbor.

Gelfand, Mark I. *A Nation of Cities: The Federal Government and Urban America, 1933–1965*. New York: Oxford University Press, 1975.

"Gerald R. Ford: Statement on the Housing and Community Development Act of 1974," http://www.presidency.ucsb.edu/ws/?pid=4632. Accessed June 1, 2013.

"Ghetto Housing Program Announced." *Crisis*, September 1968.

Gilbert, Cromwell. "Insurance Boycott Ready." *Chatham Weekly*, May 12, 1965. Papers of the NAACP, Part 5: Campaign against Residential Segregation, 1914–1955, Supplement: Residential Segregation, General Office Files, 1956–1965, Group III, series A, Administrative File, General Office File—Housing, Manuscript Division, Library of Congress.

Gill, Andrea M. K. "Moving to Integration? The Origins of Chicago's Gautreaux Program and the Limits of Voucher-Based Housing Mobility." *Journal of Urban History* 38, no. 4 (July 1, 2012): 662–86, https://doi.org/10.1177/0096144211428771.

"Gil Scott-Heron—Whitey on the Moon." Genius, https://genius.com/Gil-scott-heron-whitey -on-the-moon-annotated. Accessed November 15, 2018.

Gimlin, H. "Private Housing Squeeze." *Editorial Research Reports 1969*, vol. 3. Washington, D.C.: Congressional Quarterly Press, 1969, http://library.cqpress.com.ezproxy.princeton. edu/cqresearcher/cqresrre1969070900.

Ginzberg, Eli. *The Negro Challenge to the Business Community*. New York: McGraw-Hill, 1964.

Glass, Andrew J. "75 Invade Capitol Hill for Rat Bill." *Washington Post, Times Herald*, August 8, 1967, A1.

Glazer, Nathan, and Davis McEntire. *Studies in Housing and Minority Groups*. Berkeley: University of California Press, 1960.

Glickstein, Howard. "Letter to Romney," n.d. Box 4, folder HUD's Civil Rights Policy, George Romney Post-Gubernatorial Papers, 1969–1973, Bentley Historical Library, University of Michigan, Ann Arbor.

Goetz, Edward G. *New Deal Ruins: Race, Economic Justice, and Public Housing Policy*. Ithaca, N.Y.: Cornell University Press, 2013.

Goldberg, David A., and Trevor Griffey. *Black Power at Work: Community Control, Affirmative Action, and the Construction Industry*. Ithaca, N.Y.: ILR Press/Cornell University Press, 2010, http://site.ebrary.com/id/10467992.

Goldston, Eli. "New Prospects for American Business." *Daedalus* 98, no. 1 (January 1, 1969): 78–112, https://doi.org/10.2307/20023865.

Gotham, Kevin Fox. *Race, Real Estate, and Uneven Development: The Kansas City Experience, 1900–2000*. Albany: SUNY Press, 2002.

———. *Race, Real Estate, and Uneven Development: The Kansas City Experience, 1900–2010*. Albany: SUNY Press, 2014.

Gould, George. "G'twn Attorney Testifies before Congress on Housing Plight of Black Philadelphians." *Philadelphia Tribune*, October 12, 1971, 4.

"Government Moves to End Suburban 'Snob-Zoning.'" *Cleveland Call and Post*, February 12, 1972, 1B.

Gray, Robert L. "Counseling Key to Success of Section 235." *Washington Post, Times Herald*, June 24, 1972, sec. Real Estate.

Hackworth, Jason R. *The Neoliberal City: Governance, Ideology, and Development in American Urbanism*. Ithaca, N.Y.: Cornell University Press, 2007.

Hager, Philip. "Housing Officials Await Ruling on Referendum: Test Pending on California Law Requiring Voter Approval of Public Low-Rent Units." *Los Angeles Times*, August 3, 1970, 20.

Haintze, Bill Van, and Edward G. Smith. "Nab 3 in Bombing of LI Negro's Home." *Newsday*, Nassau ed., December 7, 1967, 1.

Hanson, Royce. *The Evolution of National Urban Policy, 1970–1980: Lessons from the Past*. Washington, D.C.: National Academy Press, 1982.

Harney, Kenneth. "Even Subsidies Possible: Plans to Aid Beleaguered Housing May Involve Some Subsidy Programs." *Washington Post*, January 12, 1974, D1.

———. "HUD on the Spot with 'Section 8.'" *Washington Post*, May 17, 1975, E1.

Harris, Cheryl I. "Whiteness as Property." In *Critical Race Theory: The Key Writings That Formed the Movement*, edited by Kimberlé Crenshaw, Neil Gotanda, Gary Peller, and Kendall Thomas. New York: New Press, 1995.

"Harry S. Truman: Statement by the President upon Signing the Housing Act of 1949," http://www.presidency.ucsb.edu/ws/?pid=13246. Accessed May 19, 2013.

Hartman, Chester W. "The Politics of Housing." *Dissent*, December 1967, 701–14.

Harvey, David. *A Brief History of Neoliberalism*. New York: Oxford University Press, 2005.

Harvey, Joseph. "Court Says State Can Overrule 'Snob Zoning' Laws in Suburbs." *Boston Globe*, March 23, 1973, 1.

Hays, R. Allen. *The Federal Government and Urban Housing*. Albany: SUNY Press, 2012.

———. *The Federal Government and Urban Housing: Ideology and Change in Public Policy*. Albany: SUNY Press, 1995.

Hayward, Clarissa Rile. *How Americans Make Race: Stories, Institutions, Spaces*. New York: Cambridge University Press, 2013.

Helper, Rose. *Racial Policies and Practices of Real Estate Brokers*. Minneapolis: University of Minnesota Press, 1969.

Henderson, Scott A. *Housing and the Democratic Ideal: The Life and Thought of Charles Abrams*. New York: Columbia University Press, 2000.

Henson, Ray D. "Installment Land Contracts in Illinois: A Suggested Approach to Forfeiture." *DePaul Law Review* 7, no.1 (Fall–Winter 1957): 1–15.

Herbers, John. "Abandonment of Federal Housing Blights Inner Cities." *New York Times*, January 13, 1972, 1.

———. "Federal Agencies Press Inquiry on Housing Frauds in Big Cities." *New York Times*, May 8, 1972, 28.

———. "F.H.A. Overhaul Urged by Percy: Building Manufacturers Unit Is Told Consumer Suffers." *New York Times*, April 25, 1972, 47.

———. "Federal Housing Reform Unlikely: Congress Is Unlikely to Reform Housing Laws Despite Scandals." *New York Times*, September 20, 1972, 97.

———. "Rights Panel Says U.S. Housing Plan Aids Segregation." *New York Times*, June 11, 1971, 1.

———. "Romney Asks Ban on Rules Curbing Housing for Poor: Federal Law Would Prohibit the Use of Local Codes to Prevent Construction." *New York Times*, June 3, 1970, 1.

————. "Romney Making His Greatest Impact outside Government by Challenging U.S. Institutions." *New York Times*, May 15, 1969, 32.

————. "Suburbs Accept Poor in Ohio Housing Plan." *New York Times*, December 21, 1970, 1.

————. "Tragedy of the Decaying Cities: Housing." *New York Times*, April 2, 1972, E1.

"High Profit in Poor Housing." *Newsday*, January 6, 1971, 64.

Highsmith, Andrew R. *Demolition Means Progress: Flint, Michigan, and the Fate of the American Metropolis*. Chicago: University of Chicago Press, 2015.

Hill, Laura Warren, and Julia Rabig. *The Business of Black Power: Community Development, Capitalism, and Corporate Responsibility in Postwar America*. Rochester, N.Y.: University of Rochester Press, 2012.

Hill, Robert. "The Illusion of Black Progress." *Black Scholar* 10, no. 2 (October 1978): 20–22, https://jstor.org/stable/41163664.

Hirsch, Arnold R. "'The Last and Most Difficult Barrier': Segregation and Federal Housing Policy in the Eisenhower Administration, 1953–1960." Poverty and Race Research Council, March 22, 2005, https://www.prrac.org/pdf/hirsch.pdf.

————. *Making the Second Ghetto: Race and Housing in Chicago, 1940–1960*. Chicago: University of Chicago Press, 1998.

————. "Searching for a 'Sound Negro Policy': A Racial Agenda for the Housing Acts of 1949 and 1954." *Housing Policy Debate* 11, no. 2 (January 1, 2000): 393–441, https://doi.org/10.1080/10511482.2000.9521372.

Hirsch, Arnold R., and Raymond A. Mohl. *Urban Policy in Twentieth-Century America*. New Brunswick, N.J.: Rutgers University Press, 1993.

Hoffman, David. "Johnson Signs Housing Bill." *Washington Post, Times Herald*, August 2, 1968, J2.

Holifield, Chester. "Defaults on FHA-Insured Home Mortgages, Detroit, Michigan." June 20, 1972. In U.S. Congress, House, Committee on Government Operations, Subcommittee on Legal and Monetary Affairs, *Defaults on FHA-Insured Mortgages (Detroit). Hearings before a Subcommittee of the Committee on Government Operations, House of Representatives, Ninety-Second Congress, First [and Second] Session[s]*. Washington, D.C.: U.S. Government Printing Office, 1972.

Holmes, Susan. "Agents Deny Profiteering: Housing Deals Strap Moms." *Detroit Free Press*, January 8, 1971, 1.

Honey, Michael K. *Going Down Jericho Road: The Memphis Strike, Martin Luther King's Last Campaign*. New York: Norton, 2007.

Horne, Gerald. *Fire This Time: The Watts Uprising and the 1960s*. Boston: Da Capo Press, 1997.

"Housing and Urban Affairs Daily: Freeze Imposed on Major HUD Programs," January 9, 1973. Urban Archives, Housing Association of Delaware Valley, box 37, Temple University, Philadelphia, Pa.

"Housing and Urban Affairs Daily: HUD Budget Slashed in 'Reform,'" January 31, 1973. Urban Archives, Housing Association of Delaware Valley, box 37, Temple University, Philadelphia, Pa.

"Housing Probe." *Congressional Quarterly*. 28th ed. Washington D.C.: CQ Almanac, 1973, http://library.cqpress.com.ezproxy.princeton.edu/cqalmanac/cqal72-1249770.

"Housing Segregation Is Noted in 3 More Cities." *Chicago Defender*, February 4, 1967.

"HUD Ask U.S. Suit on Zoning Bias." *Chicago Tribune*, November 1, 1970, sec. C.

"HUD Decentralized to 23 Area Cities." *Atlanta Daily World*, November 5, 1970, 3.

"HUD Discloses Plan for the Renovation of Rundown Housing." *Wall Street Journal*, July 21, 1970, 34.

"HUD Discriminates, New Study Finds." *New York Amsterdam News*, October 30, 1971, B6.

"HUD Pressuring Suburbs to House Poor Families." *Cleveland Call and Post*, June 20, 1970, 18A.

Hudson, Joseph L. *The Urban Crisis: A Call for Corporate Action*. Ann Arbor: Graduate School of Business Administration, University of Michigan, 1968.

"HUD's Romney Runs Away from Anti-Bias Petition." *Afro-American*, October 17, 1970, 1.

"HUD Suspends Firms, Brokers." *Washington Post, Times Herald*, October 29, 1972, A3.

Hughes, Emmet John. "The Negro's New Economic Life." *Fortune* 54, no. 3 (September 1956): 126–28.

Humphrey, Hubert H. *Private Enterprise and the City*. Washington, D.C.: U.S. Dept. of Housing and Urban Development, 1967.

Hunter, Marcus Anthony, Mary Pattillo, Zandria F. Robinson, and Keeanga-Yamahtta Taylor. "Black Placemaking: Celebration, Play, and Poetry." *Theory, Culture, and Society* 33, no. 7–8 (December 1, 2016): 31–56, https://doi.org/10.1177/0263276416635259.

Hyman, Louis. *Borrow: The American Way of Debt*. New York: Vintage, 2012.

———. "The House That George Romney Built." *New York Times*, January 31, 2012, sec. Opinion, http://www.nytimes.com/2012/02/01/opinion/the-house-that-george-romney -built.html.

Institute of Life Insurance. "Institute of Life Insurance." *Ebony*, June 1968, 199.

———. "When You Invest a Billion Dollars to Help the Cities, You Learn Some Things." *Ebony*, July 1969, 59.

"Insurance Firms Continue Programs to Help Inner Cities." *Afro-American*, January 29, 1972, 22.

"Insurance Firms Will Aid Ghettos: $1-Billion Mortgage Investment." *Newsday*, Nassau ed., September 14, 1967, 1.

"Insured Financing for Low-Cost Homes." *Insured Mortgage Portfolio*, Fall 1954.

Interview with George Gould by author, August 18, 2017.

"Interview with George Romney in *Building Materials Merchandiser*," June 1969. Box 11, folder Publicity and Press Clippings Romney, George Romney Post-Gubernatorial Papers, 1969–1973, Bentley Historical Library, University of Michigan, Ann Arbor.

"An Interview with HUD Secretary James T. Lynn." *Black Enterprise*, February 1974, 25–26.

Isaacs, Arnold R. "Romney: Caught between the 'Backbone' and the White House's Lack of One." *Baltimore Sun*, September 27, 1970.

"Is a Breakthrough Near in Housing?" *BusinessWeek*, September 13, 1969, 80–110.

"Is FHA Providing Good Housing for Poor People?" *Philadelphia Tribune*, May 2, 1972, 3.

Jackson, Kenneth T. *Crabgrass Frontier: The Suburbanization of America*. New York: Oxford University Press, 1985.

———. "Race, Ethnicity, and Real Estate Appraisal: The Home Owners Loan Corporation and the Federal Housing Administration." *Journal of Urban History* 6, no. 4 (August 1, 1980): 419–52, https://doi.org/10.1177/009614428000600404.

Jackson, Mandi Isaacs. "Harlem's Rent Strike and Rat War: Representation, Housing Access, and Tenant Resistance in New York, 1958–1964." *American Studies* 47, no. 1 (April 1, 2006): 53–79.

Jacobs, Barry. "Subsidies Moratorium Dismal News for Builders." *Courier-Journal & Times*, January 14, 1973, 1.

Jansen, Donald. "Integration Held Housing Aid Goal: Federal Court Tells Agency to Determine if Projects Will Widen Imbalance." *New York Times*, January 5, 1971, 1.

Jensen, Michael C. "Romney Discloses Halt in Subsidies for New Housing." *New York Times*, January 9, 1973, 1.

"John F. Kennedy: News Release on Conference on Urban Affairs, from the Democratic National Committee Publicity Division, Washington, DC," October 20, 1960, http://www.presidency.ucsb.edu/ws/?pid=74130. Accessed December 25, 2016.

Johnson, Herschel. "Housing Policy at the Crossroads." *Black Enterprise*, February 1974, 19–20.

Johnson, Jeremy B. "Beyond Retrenchment: The Political and Ideological Foundations of the New American Welfare State, 1970–2000." Ph.D. diss., Brown University, 2010, http://search.proquest.com.turing.library.northwestern.edu/dissertations/docview/763491219/abstract/13CDFD3899F73AB76C/28?accountid=12861.

Johnson, Thomas A. "Urban League Finds 25.4% of Blacks Are Still Jobless." *New York Times*, August 8, 1976, 22.

Jones, Carleton. "Battle Looms on Housing Policy." *Baltimore Sun*, October 3, 1971, E1.

Jones, Daniel Stedman. *Masters of the Universe: Hayek, Friedman, and the Birth of Neoliberal Politics*. Princeton, N.J.: Princeton University Press, 2017, http://dx.doi.org/10.23943/princeton/9780691161013.001.0001.

Jones, John A. "Industry Unimpressed by Nixon Housing Plan." *Los Angeles Times*, May 13, 1974, C11.

Jones, Patrick D. *The Selma of the North: Civil Rights Insurgency in Milwaukee*. Cambridge, Mass.: Harvard University Press, 2009.

"Jones v. Alfred H. Mayer Co., 392 U.S. 409 (1968)." Justia Law, https://supreme.justia.com/cases/federal/us/392/409/case.html. Accessed January 3, 2018.

"Justice Department Files Six More Housing Suits." *Washington Post*, June 6, 1971, 2.

Kahrl, Andrew W. "Capitalizing on the Urban Fiscal Crisis: Predatory Tax Buyers in 1970s Chicago." *Journal of Urban History*, May 28, 2015, https://doi.org/10.1177/0096144215586385.

Karmin, Monroe W. "Pros and Cons: Nixon's Moratorium on Subsidized Housing Stirs Debate among Its Critics, Advocates." *Wall Street Journal*, March 16, 1973, 34.

———. "Restoring Cities after the Scandals." *Wall Street Journal*, July 5, 1972, 1.

Karp, Michael. "The St. Louis Rent Strike of 1969: Transforming Black Activism and American Low-Income Housing." *Journal of Urban History* 40, no. 4 (July 1, 2014): 648–70, https://doi.org/10.1177/0096144213516082.

Katz, Michael B. *The Undeserving Poor: America's Enduring Confrontation with Poverty*. Oxford: Oxford University Press, 2013, http://site.ebrary.com/id/10763275.

Kelley, Robin D. G. *Race Rebels: Culture, Politics, and the Black Working Class*. New York: Free Press, 1996.

Kempster, Norman. "Romney Asks More Housing for the Poor." *Hartford Courant*, December 7, 1969, 3.

Kennedy, John F. Executive Order 11063, Equal Opportunity in Housing. November 20, 1962.

Klein, Naomi. *The Shock Doctrine: The Rise of Disaster Capitalism*. New York: Macmillan, 2010.

Kneeland, Douglas E. "McGovern Assails Nixon Administration as 'Scandal-Ridden.'" *New York Times*, October 1, 1972, 46.

Kohler-Hausmann, Julilly. *Getting Tough: Welfare and Imprisonment in 1970s America*. Princeton, N.J.: Princeton University Press, 2017.

———. "Guns and Butter: The Welfare State, the Carceral State, and the Politics of Exclusion in the Postwar United States." *Journal of American History* 102, no. 1 (June 1, 2015): 87–99, https://doi.org/10.1093/jahist/jav239.

Kornbluh, Felicia Ann. *The Battle for Welfare Rights: Politics and Poverty in Modern America*. Philadelphia: University of Pennsylvania Press, 2007.

Kotlowski, Dean J. *Nixon's Civil Rights: Politics, Principle, and Policy*. Cambridge, Mass.: Harvard University Press, 2001.

Kovach, Bill. "Mayors Oppose Nixon Fund Plan." *New York Times*, June 21, 1973, 34.

Krippner, Greta R. *Capitalizing on Crisis: The Political Origins of the Rise of Finance*. Cambridge, Mass.: Harvard University Press, 2012.

Kruse, Kevin M. *White Flight: Atlanta and the Making of Modern Conservatism*. Princeton, N.J.: Princeton University Press, 2007.

———, ed. *The New Suburban History*. Chicago: University of Chicago Press, 2007.

Kushner, James A. "Community Planning and Development under the Housing and Community Development Act of 1974." *Clearinghouse Review* 8 (January 1975): 665.

Kusmer, Kenneth L., and Joe William Trotter. *African American Urban History since World War II*. Chicago: University of Chicago Press, 2009.

Kwak, Nancy H. *A World of Homeowners: American Power and the Politics of Housing Aid*. Chicago: University of Chicago Press, 2015.

Lacy, Karyn R. *Blue-Chip Black: Race, Class, and Status in the New Black Middle Class*. Berkeley: University of California Press, 2007.

Lamb, Charles M. *Housing Segregation in Suburban America since 1960: Presidential and Judicial Politics*. New York: Cambridge University Press, 2005.

Lassiter, Matthew D. *The Silent Majority: Suburban Politics in the Sunbelt South*. Princeton, N.J.: Princeton University Press, 2007.

Lawson, Simpson F. *Above Property Rights*. Washington, D.C.: U.S. Commission on Civil Rights, 1973.

League of Women Voters of Illinois. "Minority Group Housing: The Problem," n.d. Box 235, folder 2134, Martin Bickham Papers, Current Agenda for 1965–1967, Richard J. Daley Library, University of Illinois at Chicago.

Lear, Len. "FHA-235 Program 'A Fraud and Outrage' Homeowners Insist." *Philadelphia Tribune*, May 16, 1972, 5.

———. "Homeowners Picket FHA Officials over Broken-Down Homes, Unkept Promises." *Philadelphia Tribune*, June 24, 1972.

Legates, Richard T., and Mary C. Morgan. "The Perils of Special Revenue Sharing for Community Development." *Journal of the American Institute of Planners* 39, no. 4 (July 1, 1973): 254–64, https://doi.org/10.1080/01944367308977866.

Leighninger, Robert D. *Building Louisiana: The Legacy of the Public Works Administration*. Jackson: University Press of Mississippi, 2007.

Leiken, Earl M. "Preferential Treatment in the Skilled Building Trades: An Analysis of the Philadelphia Plan." *Cornell Law Review* 56 (November 1970): 84.

Leimert, Walter. "Teamwork Solves the Small-Home Puzzle." *Insured Mortgage Portfolio*, January 1940.

"Lessons of Leadership Investing in People's Future: Equitable Life's James F. Oates Jr. Talks about Loneliness of Decision Making, Needs of Cities, and Boldness in Capital Financing." *Nation's Business*, June 1968, 98–101.

"Let Others Join Romney in Seeking Urban Answers." *Detroit Free Press*, October 10, 1967, 6.

"Letter from B. T. McGraw (Assistant to the Secretary) to Mr. Marvin Caplan, Director, Washington Office, Leadership Conference on Civil Rights," October 31, 1967. Civil Rights Movement and the Federal Government: Records of the U.S. Commission on Civil Rights, Special Projects, 1960–1970. Record Group 453, Records of the U.S. Commission on Civil Rights, National Archives and Records Administration, College Park, Md.

"Letter from Youth and College Council Members of the NAACP to Metropolitan Life Insurance Company," July 11, 1963. Papers of the NAACP, Part 5: Campaign against Residential Segregation, 1914–1955, Supplement: Residential Segregation, General Office Files, 1956–1965, Group III, series A, Administrative File, General Office File—Housing, folder Housing, Metropolitan Life Insurance Company, Manuscript Division, Library of Congress.

Lineberry, Robert L., and Robert E. Welch. "Who Gets What: Measuring the Distribution of Urban Public Services." *Social Science Quarterly* 54, no. 4 (1974): 700–712.

Logan, John R., and Harvey L. Molotch. *Urban Fortunes: The Political Economy of Place*. Berkeley: University of California Press, 1987.

Looker, Benjamin. *A Nation of Neighborhoods: Imagining Cities, Communities, and Democracy in Postwar America*. Chicago: University of Chicago Press, 2015.

Lovett, Laura L. *Conceiving the Future: Pronatalism, Reproduction, and the Family in the United States, 1890–1938*. Chapel Hill: University of North Carolina Press, 2007.

Lubin, Joann S. "Black Firms' Blues: Recession Hits Minority-Owned Companies Hard." *Wall Street Journal*, April 1, 1975, 1.

Lydon, Christopher. "Carter Defends All-White Areas." *New York Times*, April 7, 1976, 1, https://www.nytimes.com/1976/04/07/archives/carter-defends-allwhite-areas-says -government-shouldnt-try-to-end.html.

"Lyndon B. Johnson: Excerpts from Remarks at a Meeting with Insurance Executives to Discuss Their Plans for Participation in Urban Programs," September 13, 1967, http://www .presidency.ucsb.edu/ws/index.php?pid=28428.

"Lyndon B. Johnson: Remarks to the Members of the U.S. Chamber of Commerce," http:// www.presidency.ucsb.edu/ws/?pid=26193#axzz2h3amo72U. Accessed October 7, 2013.

"Lyndon B. Johnson: Statement by the President upon Appointing the President's Committee on Urban Housing," http://www.presidency.ucsb.edu/ws/index.php?pid=28286. Accessed November 1, 2017.

"Lynn of HUD Critical of Senate Housing Bill." *Chicago Tribune*, March 30, 1974, N16.

Lyons, John. "As New Rights Tactic, Negroes Wouldn't Pay Insurance Premiums: Metropolitan, Other Insurers and Financial Firms Accused of Bias in Mortgage Policies." *Wall Street Journal*, February 11, 1965.

MacLean, Nancy. *Freedom Is Not Enough: The Opening of the American Workplace*. Cambridge, Mass.: Harvard University Press, 2006.

Magnuson, Warren. "How the Ghetto Gets Gypped." *Ebony*, September 1968.

Maize, K. P. "Food Inflation." *Editorial Research Reports 2*. Washington, D.C.: CQ Press, 1978.

Marshall, Sue, and David H. Swinton. "Federal Government Policy in Black Community Revitalization." *Review of Black Political Economy* 10, no. 1 (Fall 1979): 11–29.

Mason, David L. *From Building and Loans to Bail-Outs: A History of the American Savings and Loan Industry, 1831–1989*. New York: Cambridge University Press, 2004, http://site.ebrary .com/id/10131647.

Massey, Douglas S., and Nancy A. Denton. *American Apartheid: Segregation and the Making of the Underclass*. Cambridge, Mass.: Harvard University Press, 1993.

Matlin, Daniel. *On the Corner: African American Intellectuals and the Urban Crisis*. Cambridge, Mass.: Harvard University Press, 2013, https://login.proxy.bib.uottawa.ca/login?url =http://dx.doi.org/10.4159/harvard.9780674726109.

Matusow, Allen J. *Nixon's Economy: Booms, Busts, Dollars, and Votes*. Lawrence: University Press of Kansas, 1998.

McBee, Susanna. "Joblessness Feared in HUD Cuts." *Washington Post, Times Herald*, January 10, 1973, 12.

———. "Subsidized Housing Frozen before Justification by HUD." *Washington Post, Times Herald*, December 3, 1973, A1.

McClaughry, John. "The Troubled Dream: The Life and Times of Section 235 of the National Housing Act." *Loyola University Chicago Law Journal* 6, no. 1 (Winter 1975): 1–45.

McCombs, Philip A. "Black HEW Employees Charge Agency Biased." *Washington Post, Times Herald*, November 26, 1970, C4.

McEntire, Davis. *Residence and Race*. Berkeley: University of California Press, 1960.

McGuire, Joseph William. *The Changing Nature of Business Responsibilities*. Stillwater: Oklahoma State University, College of Business Administration, 1978.

McKnight, John L. "Possible Agenda Items for the Meeting with Officers of the National Association of Real Estate Brokers," February 13, 1968. Civil Rights Movement and the Federal Government: Records of the U.S. Commission on Civil Rights, Special Projects, 1960–1970. Record Group 453, Records of the U.S. Commission on Civil Rights, National Archives and Records Administration, College Park, Md.

McLaughlin, Malcolm. "The Pied Piper of the Ghetto: Lyndon Johnson, Environmental Justice, and the Politics of Rat Control." *Journal of Urban History* 37, no. 4 (July 1, 2011): 541–61, https://doi.org/10.1177/0096144211403085.

McNally, David. *Global Slump: The Economics and Politics of Crisis and Resistance*. Oakland, Calif.: PM Press, 2010.

"Memo from Francis Fisher to Edward Levin on Strategies for Administering HUD Program," April 16, 1970. Box 10, folder Open Communities, HUD, Papers of Under Secretary Richard C. Van Dusen, 1969–72, Record Group 207, National Archives and Records Administration, College Park, Md.

"Memo on Housing Production," 1969. Box 2, folder Budget Miscellaneous, George Romney Post-Gubernatorial Papers, 1969–1973, Bentley Historical Library, University of Michigan, Ann Arbor.

Mendenhall, Ruby. "The Political Economy of Black Housing: From the Housing Crisis of the

Great Migrations to the Subprime Mortgage Crisis." *Black Scholar* 40, no. 1 (March 1, 2010): 20–37, https://doi.org/10.1080/00064246.2010.11413507.

"Metropolitan Life Denies Bias on Loans." *Chicago Sun-Times*, May 13, 1965. Papers of the NAACP, Part 5: Campaign against Residential Segregation, 1914–1955, Supplement: Residential Segregation, General Office Files, 1956–1965, Group III, series A, Administrative File, General Office File—Housing, Manuscript Division, Library of Congress.

"Metropolitan Life Housing Open to Non-White Tenants." *Baltimore Sun*, August 12, 1963, 1.

Metzger, John T. "Planned Abandonment: The Neighborhood Life-Cycle Theory and National Urban Policy." *Housing Policy Debate* 11, no. 1 (2000): 7–40, http://www.tandfonline.com /doi/abs/10.1080/10511482.2000.9521359. Accessed August 18, 2017.

Meyer, Eugene L. "160 Black HUD Employees Face Suspension for Protesting." *Washington Post, Times-Herald*, May 27, 1971, 5.

———. "A Home Ownership Nightmare in NW." *Washington Post, Times Herald*, July 15, 1972, B1.

———. "Slum Properties Eyed for Housing Renewal: Renewal Housing Project May Buy 4 Buildings Owned by Slum Landlord." *Washington Post, Times Herald*, April 23, 1971, C1.

Meyer, Stephen Grant. *As Long as They Don't Move Next Door: Segregation and Racial Conflict in American Neighborhoods*. Lanham, Md.: Rowman & Littlefield, 2000.

Milkis, Sidney M., ed. *The Great Society and the High Tide of Liberalism*. Amherst: University of Massachusetts Press, 2005.

"Milliken v. Bradley." Legal Information Institute, https://www.law.cornell.edu/supreme court/text/433/267. Accessed November 23, 2018.

"Minutes: Meeting of the Indiana State Advisory Committee to the U.S. Commission on Civil Rights," January 26, 1968. "Life Insurance Companies Financing of Urban Improvement Programs, 1967–1968." Civil Rights Movement and the Federal Government: Records of the U.S. Commission on Civil Rights, Special Projects, 1960–1970. Record Group 453, Records of the U.S. Commission on Civil Rights, National Archives and Records Administration, College Park, Md.

Mitchell, James. *The Dynamics of Neighborhood Change*. Washington, D.C.: Office of Policy Development and Research of the U.S. Department of Housing and Urban Development, 1975.

Mixon, John. "Installment Land Contracts: A Study of Low Income Transactions, with Proposals for Reform and a New Program to Provide Home Ownership in the Inner City." *Houston Law Review* 7 (May 1970): 523.

Moeller, Charles. "Economic Implications of the Life Insurance Industry's Investment Program in the Central Cities: Abstract." *Journal of Risk and Insurance* 36, no. 1 (March 1969): 93–101.

Mollenkopf, John H. *The Contested City*. Princeton, N.J.: Princeton University Press, 1983.

Moritz, Owen. "Romney's Leaving, but U.S. Housing Problems Hang On." *Detroit Free Press*, August 28, 1972, 5.

Morris, Hugh. "HUD to Revive Low-Income Home Ownership Subsidy." *Boston Globe*, November 2, 1975, B2.

Mort, Robert. "Boycott Slices Meat Prices at 1 Chain." *Washington Post*, April 6, 1973, sec. C.

"Mortgage Banking." *Mortgage Banker* 32 (January 1972): 10.

"Mortgage Rate Hike Denounced." *Hartford Courant*, January 1, 1970, 26.

Mossberg, Walter S. "A Blue-Collar Town Fears Urban Renewal Perils Its Way of Life." *Wall Street Journal*, November 2, 1970, A1–A2.

Moynihan, Daniel Patrick. *Toward a National Urban Policy*. New York: Basic Books, 1970.

Murakawa, Naomi. *The First Civil Right: How Liberals Built Prison America*. New York: Oxford University Press, 2014.

Myrdal, Gunnar. *An American Dilemma: The Negro Problem and Modern Democracy*. New York: Harper & Row, 1962.

"NAACP and Metropolitan Life Insurance Company Agree on Mortgage Loan Policy," September 28, 1965. Papers of the NAACP, Part 5: Campaign against Residential Segregation, 1914–1955, Supplement: Residential Segregation, General Office Files, 1956–1965, Group III, series A, Administrative File, General Office File—Housing, folder Housing, Metropolitan Life Insurance Company, Manuscript Division, Library of Congress.

Nadasen, Premilla. *Welfare Warriors: The Welfare Rights Movement in the United States*. Hoboken, N.J.: Taylor & Francis, 2004.

"NAREB Encourages Negro Housing: Real Estate Board Survey Finds Race Good Business Risk." *Pittsburgh Courier*, November 18, 1944, 1–2.

"National Association of Home Builders Report," 1969. Box 2, folder NAHB, Romney Papers, George Romney Post-Gubernatorial Papers, 1969–1973, Bentley Historical Library, University of Michigan, Ann Arbor.

National Commission on Urban Problems. *Building the American City: Report of the National Commission on Urban Problems to the Congress and to the President of the United States*. Washington, D.C.: U.S. Government Printing Office, 1969.

The Negro and the City. New York: Time-Life Books, 1968.

"Negro House Need Told by NAREB: 600 Realty Boards in 46 States to Study Home Outlook of Colored Population." *Hartford Courant*, June 11, 1944, B2.

"Negro Men Get Housing Lift." *New Pittsburgh Courier*, January 4, 1969, 3.

Nelson, Grant S., and Dale A. Whitman. "The Installment Land Contract—A National Viewpoint." *Brigham Young University Law Review* 1977 (1977): 541.

Neubeck, Kenneth J., and Noel A. Cazenave. *Welfare Racism: Playing the Race Card against America's Poor*. Hoboken, N.J.: Taylor & Francis, 2004.

Newfield, Jack. "Kennedy's Search for a New Target." *Life*, April 12, 1968, 35.

"The New Look of the Federal Housing Administration, Philip Brownstein." *Congressional Record—House*, October 27, 1967, 30351.

"New Nixon Action to Affect Blacks." *Chicago Daily Defender*, January 10, 1973, 6.

"New York Slumlords Told to Fix Tenements: Law Now Requires Repair of Buildings Described by Official as 'Horror Houses.'" *Los Angeles Times*, January 23, 1967, 17.

Nixon, Richard M. *New Federalism*, ca. 1969. Box 77, folder Presidential Statements 1968–72, HUD, Papers of Under Secretary Richard C. Van Dusen, 1969–72, Record Group 207, National Archives Records and Administration, College Park, Md.

Nolan, Martin. "Plain-Talking Daley and Housing Sham." *Boston Globe*, June 15, 1971, 14, http://search.proquest.com.turing.library.northwestern.edu/docview/375440947/abstract/13E77221C7060C568F1/5?accountid=12861.

———. "Urban Council Sets Course." *Boston Globe*, January 24, 1969, 1.

Northwestern University (Evanston, Ill.), Urban-Suburban Investment Study Group, and

Illinois Housing Development Authority. *The Role of Mortgage Lending Practices in Older Urban Neighborhoods: Institutional Lenders, Regulatory Agencies and Their Community Impacts: A Report*. Evanston, Ill.: Center for Urban Affairs, Northwestern University, 1975.

Nuccio, Sal. "Insurers Facing a Negro Boycott: Discrimination Is Charged in Mortgage Lending." *New York Times*, February 14, 1965, 70.

O'Connor, Alice. *Poverty Knowledge: Social Science, Social Policy, and the Poor in Twentieth-Century U.S. History*. Princeton, N.J.: Princeton University Press, 2009.

———. "The Privatized City, the Manhattan Institute, the Urban Crisis, and the Conservative Counterrevolution in New York." *Journal of Urban History* 34, no. 2 (January 1, 2008): 333–53, https://doi.org/10.1177/0096144207308672.

"Officials See More Mortgage Money—More Housing." *Hartford Courant*, November 1, 1970, 2.

Oliphant, Thomas. "Ginny & Fannie Shore Up Housing Slump." *Boston Globe*, February 8, 1970, B1.

———. "Romney to Leave HUD Job, Cites Difficulty of Reform." *Boston Globe*, November 28, 1972, 31.

"Open Housing Activists Draw Romney's Warning." *Hartford Courant*, June 16, 1971, 15.

"The Options Ahead for the Debt Economy." *BusinessWeek*, October 12, 1974, 120–21.

Organization for Social and Technical Innovation and Victor Bach. *A Study of the Effectiveness of Voluntary Counseling Programs for Lower-Income Home Ownership*. Newton, Mass: Department of Housing and Urban Development, 1974.

Orren, Karen. *Corporate Power and Social Change: The Politics of the Life Insurance Industry*. Baltimore: Johns Hopkins University Press, 1974.

"Out of Slums into Instant Homes in 48 Hours." *Life*, May 12, 1967, 57.

"Panic Sellers Play Fear against Fear—Skirt Law: How Fear Merchants Skirt Housing Laws." *Chicago Tribune*, August 10, 1971, 1.

Papers Submitted to Subcommittee on Housing Panels on Housing Production, Housing Demand, and Developing a Suitable Living Environment. Washington, D.C.: U.S. Government Printing Office, 1971, http://congressional.proquest.com/congcomp/getdoc?CRDC-ID =CMP-1971-BCU-0008.

Paprino, Elissa. "Mrs. Chisholm Hits Housing Program." *Lowell Sun*, April 22, 1972, 1.

Parenti, Christian. *Lockdown America: Police and Prisons in the Age of Crisis*. New York: Verso, 2001.

Parks, Henry G. "Making It over the Race Barrier." *BusinessWeek*, April 4, 1970, 8–9.

Parks, Virginia. "Revisiting Shibboleths of Race and Urban Economy: Black Employment in Manufacturing and the Public Sector Compared, Chicago 1950–2000." *International Journal of Urban and Regional Research* 35, no. 1 (January 1, 2011): 110–29, https://doi.org /10.1111/j.1468-2427.2010.00942.x.

Pattillo, Mary. *Black on the Block: The Politics of Race and Class in the City*. Chicago: University of Chicago Press, 2010.

Percy, Charles. "A New Dawn for Our Cities—A Homeownership Achievement Plan." *Congressional Record—Senate*, June 29, 1967, 18035.

Perlstein, Rick. "Exclusive: Lee Atwater's Infamous 1981 Interview on the Southern Strategy." *Nation*, November 13, 2012, http://www.thenation.com/article/170841/exclusive-lee -atwaters-infamous-1981-interview-southern-strategy.

———. *Nixonland: The Rise of a President and the Fracturing of America*. New York: Scribner, 2008.

Perry, Andre, Jonathan Rothwell, and David Harshbarger. *The Devaluation of Assets in Black Neighborhoods: The Case of Residential Property*. Metropolitan Policy Program at Brookings Institution, 2018, https://www.brookings.edu/wp-content/uploads/2018/11/2018.11 _Brookings-Metro_Devaluation-Assets-Black-Neighborhoods_final.pdf. Accessed June 3, 2019.

Phillips, Richard, and Pamela Zekman. "Judge Calls HUD a Slumlord, Rips 'Forced' Foreclosures." *Chicago Tribune*, October 24, 1974, 11.

Phillips-Fein, Kim. *Invisible Hands: The Businessmen's Crusade against the New Deal*. New York: Norton, 2010.

Philpot, Tasha S. *Conservative but Not Republican: The Paradox of Party Identification and Ideology among African Americans*. Cambridge: Cambridge University Press, 2017.

Pietila, Antero. *Not in My Neighborhood: How Bigotry Shaped a Great American City*. Chicago: Ivan R. Dee, 2010.

Pilisuk, Marc. *How We Lost the War on Poverty*. New Brunswick, N.J.: Transaction Books, 1973.

Poinsett, Alex. "The Economics of Liberation." *Ebony*, August 1969.

Polikoff, Alexander. *Waiting for Gautreaux: A Story of Segregation, Housing, and the Black Ghetto*. Evanston, Ill.: Northwestern University Press, 2006.

Porter, Frank C. "Budget Gloomy on 'Initiatives' in Next 5 Years: Nixon Sees Cuts Curbing Price Spiral." *Washington Post, Times Herald*, February 3, 1970, A1.

President's Committee on Urban Housing. *A Decent Home: The Report of the President's Committee on Urban Housing*. Washington, D.C.: U.S. Government Printing Office, 1969.

Pritchett, Wendell E. *Robert Clifton Weaver and the American City: The Life and Times of an Urban Reformer*. Chicago: University of Chicago Press, 2010.

———. "Which Urban Crisis? Regionalism, Race, and Urban Policy, 1960–1974." *Journal of Urban History* 34, no. 2 (January 1, 2008): 266–86, https://doi.org/10.1177/0096144207 08678.

"Private Enterprise Called Key for Cities." *Baltimore Sun*, February 25, 1968, F5.

"Progress Report on Federal Housing and Urban Development Programs: Description of Each of the Federal Programs on Housing and Urban Development (Including Mass Transportation) and the Progress of These Programs." *Congressional Report*. Washington D.C.: US Congress, 1970.

"'Project Rehab' to Rebuild Slums on Large Scale: Romney's Program to Help Cities Aid on Big Scale Quietly Started in First 10 Cities." *Norfolk New Journal and Guide*, August 1, 1970, B22.

Pynoos, Jon, Robert Schafer, and Chester W. Hartman. *Housing Urban America*. New York: AldineTransaction, 1980.

Quadagno, Jill. *The Color of Welfare: How Racism Undermined the War on Poverty*. New York: Oxford University Press, 1996.

Quinn, Sarah Lehman. "Government Policy, Housing, and the Origins of Securitization, 1780–1968." Ph.D. diss., University of California, Berkeley, 2010, http://search.proquest .com.turing.library.northwestern.edu/docview/861338626/abstract/13AB9E1BBD829 D12B84/1?accountid=12861.

"Racial Impact of Federal Urban Development." The Public Interest Law Center, https://www
.pubintlaw.org/cases-and-projects/shannon-v-hud/. Accessed November 14, 2017.

"Racist Ruling on HUD Hailed." *New Pittsburgh Courier*, December 25, 1971, 28.

Radford, Gail. *Modern Housing for America: Policy Struggles in the New Deal Era*. Chicago:
University of Chicago Press, 2008.

Rankin, Deborah. "Insurance Firms' Aid to Ghetto: Good, Bad?" *Austin Statesman*, May 30,
1973.

"Real Estate Boards Urged . . . Improve Negro Housing: NAREB Suggests Methods to Meet
Serious Problem." *Pittsburgh Courier*, June 17, 1944.

Reed, Stephen. "One Hundred Years of Price Change: The Consumer Price Index and the American Inflation Experience: Monthly Labor Review: U.S. Bureau of Labor Statistics," https://
www.bls.gov/opub/mlr/2014/article/one-hundred-years-of-price-change-the-consumer
-price-index-and-the-american-inflation-experience.htm. Accessed November 23, 2018.

Reed, William. "Black Home Ownership Now American Nightmare." *Philadelphia Tribune*,
July 31, 2012, http://www.phillytrib.com/commentaryarticles/item/5128-black-home
-ownership-now-american-nightmare.html. Accessed January 3, 2013.

Reichley, A. James. "George Romney Is Running Hard at HUD." *Fortune* 82, no. 6 (December
1, 1970): 100.

"Release by National Association for the Advancement of Colored People and Metropolitan
Life Insurance Company," July 30, 1963. Papers of the NAACP, Part 5: Campaign against
Residential Segregation, 1914–1955, Supplement: Residential Segregation, General Office
Files, 1956–1965, Group III, series A, Administrative File, General Office File—Housing,
folder Housing, Metropolitan Life Insurance Company, Manuscript Division, Library of
Congress.

"Remarks of Philip J. Maloney, Deputy Assistant Secretary-Deputy FHA Commissioner to
the Washington Conference of FHA Directors and Chief Underwriters," October 25, 1967.
HUD Civil Rights Activities and Programs, Focusing on Housing Discrimination and
Urban Areas, pp. 1–29, 1965–1968. Civil Rights Movement and the Federal Government:
Records of the U.S. Commission on Civil Rights, Special Projects, 1960–1970. Record
Group 453, Records of the U.S. Commission on Civil Rights, National Archives and Records
Administration, College Park, Md.

"Remarks Prepared for Delivery by George Romney, Secretary of the Department of Housing
and Urban Development at the 41st Convention, National Housing Conference at Statler
Hilton Hotel, Washington D.C.," March 6, 1972. Box 5, folder Detroit Housing, George
Romney Post-Gubernatorial Papers, 1969–1973, Bentley Historical Library, University of
Michigan, Ann Arbor.

"Rent Strike in Harlem: Fed Up Tenants Declare War on Slum Landlords and Rats." *Ebony*,
April 1964, 113–14.

"A Response to the Urban Crisis: A Report on the Urban Investment Program of the Life
Insurance Business," December 1969. Records of the Southern Christian Leadership Con-
ference, 1954–1970. Part 2: Records of the Executive Director and Treasurer, subgroup II,
Executive Director, series IV, Andrew Young [subseries 1, Correspondence], Martin Luther
King Jr. Center for Nonviolent Social Change, Atlanta, Ga.

Reston, James. "Gardner Will Head Private Campaign on Urban Poverty." *New York Times*,
February 14, 1968, A1.

Reuschling, Thomas L. "The Business Institution: A Redefinition of Social Role." *Business and Society* 9, no. 1 (Autumn 1968): 28.

"Richard Nixon: Address Accepting the Presidential Nomination at the Republican National Convention in Miami Beach, Florida," http://www.presidency.ucsb.edu/ws/?pid=25968. Accessed June 4, 2013.

"Richard Nixon: Address to the Nation on the Post-Freeze Economic Stabilization Program: 'The Continuing Fight against Inflation.'" http://www.presidency.ucsb.edu/ws/?pid=3183. Accessed August 21, 2018.

"Richard Nixon: Labor Day Message," http://www.presidency.ucsb.edu/ws/index.php?pid =3557. Accessed August 15, 2018.

"Richard Nixon: The President's News Conference," http://www.presidency.ucsb.edu/ws /index.php?pid=2840. Accessed November 14, 2017.

"Richard Nixon: Radio Address about the State of the Union Message on Community Development," March 4, 1973, http://www.presidency.ucsb.edu/ws/?pid=4128.

"Richard Nixon: Special Message to the Congress Proposing Legislation and Outlining Administration Actions to Deal with Federal Housing Policy," http://www.presidency.ucsb .edu/ws/index.php?pid=3968. Accessed August 17, 2018.

"Richard Nixon: Statement about Federal Policies Relative to Equal Housing Opportunity," http://www.presidency.ucsb.edu/ws/?pid=3042. Accessed April 10, 2013.

"Richard Nixon: Statement on the Life Insurance Industry's Pledge of Additional Investment Capital for Urban Core Areas," http://www.presidency.ucsb.edu/ws/index.php?pid=2000. Accessed October 17, 2017.

Ricke, Tom. "Stories of Hope, Broken Vows, and a Lot of FHA Money: How Two Black Families Got Taken in the Home Scandal." *Detroit Free Press*, June 18, 1972, 18–21.

Ricke, Tom, and Peter Benjamison. "ADC Housing Plan Is Stopped: HUD Blames Small Maintenance Grant." *Detroit Free Press*, January 4, 1972, 3.

Riddle, David. "Race and Reaction in Warren, Michigan, 1971 to 1974: 'Bradley v. Milliken' and the Cross-District Busing Controversy." *Michigan Historical Review* 26, no. 2 (October 1, 2000): 1–49, https://doi.org/10.2307/20173858.

Rippeteau, Jane. "Mortgage Defaults Increase Number of Homes U.S. Owns: Number of Foreclosures by U.S. Rises." *Washington Post*, December 29, 1974, D1.

Robbins, William. "Manpower Held Housing Problem: Mortgage and 'Snob' Zoning Also Seen as Obstacles." *New York Times*, January 13, 1969, 76.

———. "Negro Housing Producers Seek to Widen Market Share." *New York Times*, May 18, 1969, 1.

Roberts, Steven V. "Slum Role Seen for Private Enterprise." *New York Times*, September 7, 1967, 34.

"Robert Weaver, Secretary of HUD, UPI Interview Program, 'From the People,' Washington, June 10, 1967." *Congressional Record—Senate*, June 29, 1967, 18037.

"Robert Weaver, Unpublished Narrative History of the Department of Housing and Urban Development, Chapter Three," March 5, 1966. Presidential Papers of Lyndon Baines Johnson, vol. 1, box 1, folder FG170, President's Committee on Urban Housing, LBJ Presidential Library, Austin, Tex.

Romney, George W. "Memo to All Regional Administrators," n.d. Box 1, HUD, Office of the

Assistant Secretary for Housing Management, Subject Files of G. Richard Dunells, 1970–73, Record Group 207, National Archives Records and Administration, College Park, Md.

———. "Memo to President Richard M. Nixon on the Current Housing Picture," n.d. Box 77, folder Presidential Statements, Office of the Under Secretary Richard C. Van Dusen, 1969–72, Record Group 207, National Archives Records and Administration, College Park, Md.

"Romney: HUD Can't Solve City Housing Problems." *St. Louis Post Dispatch*, April 26, 1972, 49.

"Romney Aide Scores Inner-City Program, Warning of Massive Mortgage Defaults." *Wall Street Journal*, November 22, 1972, 1.

"Romney and Mitchell Discuss Rights Riff." *St. Louis Post Dispatch*, November 27, 1970, Special Dispatch, *Chicago Sun-Times* edition, 2.

"Romney Bids U.S. Put Housing First: Urges Top Priority after War and Inflation End." *New York Times*, July 23, 1969, http://search.proquest.com.turing.library.northwestern.edu /docview/118574253/abstract/13F82DB533F15081B42/5?accountid=12861.

"Romney Job Cuts May Reach 50." *Newsday*, Nassau ed., October 12, 1971, 9.

"Romney Opens $20 Million Test Program for Volume Output of Lower-Cost Homes." *Wall Street Journal*, May 9, 1969, 6.

"Romney Suspends All Housing Action." *New York Times*, February 8, 1969, 14.

"Romney Urges Law Support at Flint Rally." *Los Angeles Times*, August 21, 1967, pt. 1.

Rooks, Noliwe. *Cutting School: Privatization, Segregation, and the End of Public Education.* New York: New Press, 2017.

Roth, Arthur. "A Lender Looks at Title I Homes." *Insured Mortgage Portfolio*, February 1940, 5–7, 13.

Rothstein, Richard. *The Color of Law: A Forgotten History of How Our Government Segregated America.* 1st ed. New York: Liveright, 2017.

———. *The Color of Law: A Forgotten History of How Our Government Segregated America.* New York: Liveright, 2018.

Rubinowitz, Leonard S., and Elizabeth Trosman. "Affirmative Action and the American Dream: Implementing Fair Housing Policies in Federal Homeownership Programs." *Northwestern University Law Review* 74, no. 4 (November 1979): 491–616.

"Rule City Did Discriminate." *Chicago Daily Defender*, April 6, 1971, 5.

Sagalyn, Lynne Beyer. "Mortgage Lending in Older Urban Neighborhoods: Lessons from Past Experience." *Annals of the American Academy of Political and Social Science* 465 (January 1, 1983): 98–108.

Salpukas, Agis. "Moratorium on Housing Subsidy Spells Hardship for Thousands." *New York Times*, April 16, 1973, 30.

Samuelson, Robert J. "Romney: Subsidized Housing in Trouble." *Washington Post, Times Herald*, January 8, 1972, D1.

Sanders, Charles. "Industry Gives New Hope to the Negro." *Ebony*, June 1968, 194.

Satter, Beryl. *Family Properties: Race, Real Estate, and the Exploitation of Black Urban America.* New York: St. Martin's Press, 2009.

"Save the HUD Program." *Detroit Free Press*, January 18, 1971, 6.

Schanber, Sydney H. "Police in Chicago Clash with Whites after 3 Marches." *New York Times*, August 15, 1966, 1.

Schram, Sanford F., Richard C. Fording, and Joe Soss. "Neo-Liberal Poverty Governance: Race,

Place, and the Punitive Turn in US Welfare Policy." *Cambridge Journal of Regions, Economy and Society* 1, no. 1 (April 1, 2008): 17–36, https://doi.org/10.1093/cjres/rsm001.

"Scientists Analyze Philly Riot; Advise Change." *Los Angeles Sentinel*, March 3, 1966, sec. B.

Scott, Stanley. "Nation's Ghettoes Teeming with Discontent: Undercover Reporter Poses as Drifter in Riot Cities." *Chicago Daily Defender*, September 12, 1966.

Seligman, Amanda. *Block by Block: Neighborhoods and Public Policy on Chicago's West Side.* Chicago: University of Chicago Press, 2005.

Semple, Robert, Jr. "F.H.A. Asks Aides to Get Housing for Minorities: Warns That Greater Effort Is Needed—Says Negroes Lag under U.S. Program." *New York Times*, November 21, 1967, 30.

"Sen. Gurney Indicted in Builder Kickbacks." *Los Angeles Times*, July 11, 1974, A1.

"Shelley v. Kraemer, 334 U.S. 1, 68 S. Ct. 836, 92 L. Ed. 2d 1161, 1948 U.S. LEXIS 2764—CourtListener.Com." CourtListener, https://www.courtlistener.com/opinion/104545 /shelley-v-kraemer/. Accessed September 7, 2018.

Simplified Housekeeping Directions for Homemakers. Department of Housing and Urban Development, 1967. Urban Archives, Housing Association of Delaware Valley, box 37, Temple University, Philadelphia, Pa.

Singh, Nikhil Pal. *Black Is a Country: Race and the Unfinished Struggle for Democracy.* Cambridge, Mass.: Harvard University Press, 2004.

"Single House Becomes More Elusive in U.S." *Washington Post, Times Herald*, June 28, 1969, D33.

"Slum Rats Chew Out Baby's Eye; Baby Dies." *Jet*, February 24, 1966, 46.

"Slum Rehabilitation Put into Operation." *Los Angeles Times*, July 22, 1970, 4.

"Slums, Suburbs, and 'Snob-Zoning.'" *Jewish Advocate*, August 14, 1969, A2.

Smith, Neil. *Uneven Development: Nature, Capital, and the Production of Space.* Athens: University of Georgia Press, 2010.

Smith, Preston H. *Racial Democracy and the Black Metropolis: Housing Policy in Postwar Chicago.* Minneapolis: University of Minnesota Press, 2012.

Smith, Sharon. *Subterranean Fire: A History of Working-Class Radicalism in the United States.* Chicago: Haymarket Books, 2006, http://www.loc.gov/catdir/toc/ecip068/2006005731.html.

Sobel, Lester A. *New York and the Urban Dilemma.* New York: Facts on File, 1976.

The Social and Economic Status of the Black Population in the United States, 1971. Washington, D.C.: U.S. Government Printing Office, 1972.

Soss, Joe, Richard C. Fording, and Sanford F. Schram. *Disciplining the Poor: Neoliberal Paternalism and the Persistent Power of Race.* Chicago: University of Chicago Press, 2011.

Sparkman, John, Chairman, Senate Subcommittee on Housing and Urban Affairs. "Defaults and Foreclosures." *Congressional Record—Senate*, February 8, 1972, 3121.

"Special Message to the Congress on Urban Problems: 'The Crisis of the Cities.'" The American Presidency Project, https://www.presidency.ucsb.edu/documents/special-message-the -congress-urban-problems-the-crisis-the-cities. Accessed November 16, 2018.

Spitzer, Steven. "Toward a Marxian Theory of Deviance." *Social Problems* 22, no. 5 (June 1, 1975): 638–51, https://doi.org/10.2307/799696.

Squires, Gregory D. *Capital and Communities in Black and White: The Intersections of Race, Class, and Uneven Development.* Albany: State University of New York Press, 1994.

———, ed. *Unequal Partnerships: The Political Economy of Urban Redevelopment in Postwar America*. New Brunswick, N.J.: Rutgers University Press, 1989.

Stanley, Frank. "United Black Mortgage Bankers Assail Nixon." *Chicago Daily Defender*, March 10, 1973, 6.

"Statement to the President, Francis Ferguson, Chairman of the Joint Committee on Urban Problems, of the American Life Convention and the Life Insurance Association of America and President of the Northwestern Mutual Life Insurance Company," April 15, 1969. Papers of the NAACP, Part 28: Special Subject Files, 1966–1970, Group IV, series A, Administrative File, General Office File, Manuscript Division, Library of Congress.

Steele, James B. "HUD Confirms Violations by FHA Unit Here: Patman Upheld on Laxity by FHA in Phila." *Philadelphia Inquirer*, May 2, 1971, 16.

Strout, Richard L. "Romney Ready to Quit Cabinet." *Christian Science Monitor*, August 17, 1972, 4.

Sugrue, Thomas J. *The Origins of the Urban Crisis: Race and Inequality in Postwar Detroit*. Princeton: Princeton University Press, 2005.

———. *Sweet Land of Liberty: The Forgotten Struggle for Civil Rights in the North*. New York: Random House, 2008.

Tabb, William K. *The Political Economy of the Black Ghetto*. New York: Norton, 1970.

Taylor, Henry Louis. *Race and the City: Work, Community, and Protest in Cincinnati, 1820–1970*. Urbana: University of Illinois Press, 1993.

Taylor, Henry Louis, and Walter Hill. *Historical Roots of the Urban Crisis: African Americans in the Industrial City, 1900–1950*. New York: Garland, 2000.

Taylor, Keeanga-Yamahtta. "Back Story to the Neoliberal Moment." *Souls* 14, no. 3–4 (July 1, 2012): 185–206, https://doi.org/10.1080/10999949.2012.764836.

———. *From #BlackLivesMatter to Black Liberation*. Chicago: Haymarket Books, 2016.

"Testimony of Secretary of the Department of Housing and Urban Development, Robert Weaver," July 17, 1965. Box 5, Presidential Commission on Urban Housing, Charles Percy folder, LBJ Presidential Library, Austin, Tex.

Theoharis, Jeanne, and Komozi Woodard. *Groundwork: Local Black Freedom Movements in America*. New York: NYU Press, 2005.

Thomas, June Manning, and Marsha Ritzdorf. *Urban Planning and the African American Community: In the Shadows*. Thousand Oaks, Calif.: Sage, 1997.

"Three Plead Not Guilty in Case Involving Senator Gurney." *New York Times*, July 30, 1974, 67.

Thurston, Chloe N. *At the Boundaries of Homeownership: Credit, Discrimination, and the American State*. Cambridge: Cambridge University Press, 2018.

"Transcript of Kenneth M. Wright Testimony before Kerner Commission." In *Official Transcript Proceedings Before the National Advisory Commission on Civil Disorders, October 23, 1967*, 2670. Civil Rights during the Johnson Administration, 1963–1969, Part V: Records of the National Advisory Commission on Civil Disorders (Kerner Commission).

Travis, Dempsey. *An Autobiography of Black Chicago*. Chicago: Urban Research Institute, 1981.

Trbovich, Marco. "U.S. Curbs Profits of FHA Sales." *Detroit Free Press*, March 16, 1972, 1.

Turpin, Dick. "Housing Act 'Not Cure-All.'" *Los Angeles Times*, August 11, 1968, J2.

Tuskegee Institute. Dept. of Records and Research. *Negro Year Book: A Review of Events*

Affecting Negro Life, 1952. Tuskegee, Ala.: Negro Year Book Pub. Co., ca. 1952, http://archive
.org/details/negroyearbook52tuskrich.

"Typical FHA New Home Hiked $995 from 1968." *Chicago Daily Defender*, May 30, 1970, 32.

"Union Loans Negroes Over $7½ Million." *Philadelphia Tribune*, August 7, 1965, 3.

United States. *Recommendations on Government Housing Policies and Programs, a Report.*
Washington, D.C.: U.S. Government Printing Office, 1953.

U.S. Commission on Civil Rights. *Equal Opportunity in Suburbia: A Report of the United
States Commission on Civil Rights*. Washington: The Commission, 1974, http://books.
google.com/books?id=7XRAAAAAIAAJ.

———. *Federal Civil Rights Enforcement Effort: A Report of the United States Commission on
Civil Rights*. Washington, D.C.: U.S. Government Printing Office, 1970.

———. *Federal Civil Rights Enforcement Effort: A Report of the United States Commission on
Civil Rights*. Washington, D.C.: U.S. Government Printing Office, 1971.

———. *Federal Civil Rights Enforcement Effort: Seven Months Later, a Report*. Washington,
D.C.: U.S. Government Printing Office, 1971.

———. *Hearing before the United States Commission on Civil Rights. Hearing Held in Washington, D.C., June 14–17, 1971*. Washington, D.C.: U.S. Government Printing Office, 1972,
http://archive.org/details/hearingbeforejune1972unit.

———. *Home Ownership for Lower Income Families: A Report on the Racial and Ethnic Impact
of the Section 235 Program*. Washington, D.C.: U.S. Government Printing Office, 1971.

———. *Housing: 1961 Commission on Civil Rights Reports, Book 4*. Washington, D.C.: U.S.
Government Printing Office, 1961.

———. *A Sheltered Crisis: The State of Fair Housing in the Eighties: Presentations at a Consulta-
tion Sponsored by the United States Commission on Civil Rights, Washington, D.C., September 26–27, 1983*. Washington, D.C.: U.S. Commission on Civil Rights, 1985.

———. *Understanding Fair Housing*. Washington, D.C.: U.S. Government Printing Office,
1973, http://catalog.hathitrust.org/api/volumes/oclc/615201.html.

U.S. Community Services Administration. *"A Right to a Decent Home . . .": Housing Improvement Initiatives for Public Welfare Agencies*. Washington, D.C.: U.S. Dept. of Health, Education, and Welfare, Community Services Administration, 1977.

"US Confirms Abuse, Halts Housing Plan." *Boston Globe*, January 15, 1971, 1.

U.S. Congress. House. Ad Hoc Subcommittee on Home Financing Practices and Procedures.
*Financing of Inner-City Housing: Hearings before the Ad Hoc Subcommittee on Home Financ-
ing Practices and Procedures of the Committee on Banking and Currency, House of Representatives, Ninety-First Congress, First Session, on Financing of Inner-City Housing*. Washington,
D.C.: U.S. Government Printing Office, 1969.

U.S. Congress. House. Committee on Appropriations. Subcommittee on HUD, Space, Science, and Veterans Appropriations. *HUD, Space, Science and Veterans Appropriations for
1973*. Pt 3. Washington, D.C.: U.S. Government Printing Office, 1972.

U.S. Congress. House. Committee on Appropriations. Subcommittee on HUD—Independent
Agencies. *Department of Housing and Urban Development—Independent Agencies Appropriations for 1978: Hearings Before a Subcommittee of the Committee on Appropriations, House
of Representatives, Ninety-Fifth Congress, First Session*. Washington, D.C.: U.S. Government
Printing Office, 1977.

U.S. Congress. House. Committee on Banking and Currency. "Compilation of the Housing and Urban Development Act of 1968. P.L. 90-448, with Related Documents." August 1, 1968.

———. *Housing and Urban Development Act of 1969*, http://congressional.proquest.com/cong comp/getdoc?CRDC-ID=CMP-1969-BCU-0002.

———. *Interim Report on HUD Investigation of Low- and Moderate-Income Housing Programs, Hearing before . . . , 92-1 . . . , March 31, 1971*. Washington, D.C.: U.S. Government Printing Office, 1971.

———. *Investigation and Hearing of Abuses in Federal Low- and Moderate-Income Housing Programs: Staff Report and Recommendations*. Washington, D.C.: U.S. Government Printing Office, 1970.

U.S. Congress. House. Committee on Banking and Currency. Subcommittee on Housing. *Housing Act of 1960*. Section-by-Section Summary, http://congressional.proquest.com /congcomp/getdoc?CRDC-ID=CMP-1960-BCU-0005.

U.S. Congress. House. Committee on Banking and Currency. Subcommittee on Housing, and U.S. Department of Housing and Urban Development. *Real Estate Settlement Costs, FHA Mortgage Foreclosures, Housing Abandonment, and Site Selection Policies. Hearings, Ninety-Second Congress, Second Session, on H.R. 13337 . . . February 22 and 24, 1972*. Washington, D.C.: U.S. Government Printing Office, 1972, http://congressional.proquest.com /congcomp/getdoc?HEARING-ID=HRG-1972-BCU-0001.

U.S. Congress. House. Committee on Government Operations. *Operations of the Federal Housing Administration of the Department of Housing and Urban Development, Hearing before the Subcommittee of . . . , 92-1, October 13 and 14, 1971*. Washington, D.C.: U.S. Government Printing Office, 1971.

U.S. Congress. House. Committee on Government Operations. Subcommittee on Legal and Monetary Affairs. *Defaults on FHA-Insured Mortgages (Detroit). Hearings before a Subcommittee of the Committee on Government Operations, House of Representatives, Ninety-Second Congress, First [and Second] Session[s]*. Washington, D.C.: U.S. Government Printing Office, 1972.

———. *Defaults on FHA-Insured Mortgages*. Pt. 2, *February 24, May 2, 3, 4, 1972*. Washington, D.C.: U.S. Government Printing Office, 1972.

U.S. Congress. House. Committee on the Judiciary. *Civil Rights: Hearings before Subcommittee No. 5 on H.R. 140 [and Other] Miscellaneous Bills Regarding the Civil Rights of Persons within the Jurisdiction of the United States . . . .* Washington, D.C.: U.S. Government Printing Office, 1957.

U.S. Congress. Joint Economic Committee. Subcommittee on Priorities and Economy in Government. *Housing Subsidies and Housing Policies: Hearings before the Subcommittee on Priorities and Economy in Government of the Joint Economic Committee, Congress of the United States, Ninety-Second Congress, Second Session, December 4, 5, and 7, 1972*. Washington, D.C.: U.S. Government Printing Office, 1973.

———. *Housing Subsidies and Housing Policy: Report of the Subcommittee on Priorities and Economy in Government of the Joint Economic Committee, Congress of the United States, Together with Minority Notes, March 5, 1973*. Washington, D.C.: U.S. Government Printing Office, 1973.

U.S. Congress. Senate. Committee on Banking and Currency. *Nomination of George W. Romney. Hearing before the Committee on Banking and Currency, United States Senate,*

Ninety-First Congress, First Session, on the Nomination of George W. Romney to Be Secretary of the Department of Housing and Urban Affairs. January 16, 1969. Washington, D.C.: U.S. Government Printing Office, 1969.

U.S. Congress. Senate. Committee on Banking and Currency. Subcommittee on Financial Institutions. *Financial Institutions and the Urban Crisis: Hearings before the United States Senate Committee on Banking and Currency, Subcommittee on Financial Institutions, Ninetieth Congress, Second Session, on Sept. 30, Oct. 1–4, 1968.* Washington, D.C.: U.S. Government Printing Office, 1968, http://congressional.proquest.com/congcomp/getdoc ?HEARING-ID=HRG-1968-BCS-0026.

U.S. Congress. Senate. Committee on Banking and Currency. Subcommittee on Housing and Urban Affairs. *An Analysis of the Section 235 and 236 Programs. Prepared for the Subcommittee on Housing and Urban Affairs of the Committee on Banking, Housing and Urban Affairs, U.S. Senate.* Washington, D.C.: U.S. Government Printing Office, 1973.

———. *Fair Housing Act of 1967: Hearings before the Subcommittee on Housing and Urban Affairs, Ninetieth Congress, First Session, on S. 1358, S. 2114, and S. 2280, Relating to Civil Rights and Housing, August 21, 22, and 23, 1967.* Washington, D.C.: U.S. Government Printing Office, 1967.

———. *FHA Mortgage Foreclosures: Hearings before the United States Senate Committee on Banking and Currency, Subcommittee on Housing, Eighty-Eighth Congress, Second Session, on Jan. 27, 28, 1964.* Washington, D.C.: U.S. Government Printing Office, 1964, http:// congressional.proquest.com/congcomp/getdoc?HEARING-ID=HRG-1964-BCS-0012.

———. *Housing and Urban Development Legislation of 1968: Hearings before the Subcommittee on Housing and Urban Affairs of the Committee on Banking and Currency, Ninetieth Congress, Second Session, on Proposed Housing Legislation for 1968.* Washington, D.C.: U.S. Government Printing Office, 1968.

———. *Housing and Urban Development Legislation of 1970.* Washington, D.C.: U.S. Government Printing Office, 1970.

U.S. Congress. Senate. Committee on Banking, Housing, and Urban Affairs. Subcommittee on Housing and Urban Affairs. *Abandonment Disaster Demonstration Relief Act of 1975.* Washington, D.C.: U.S. Government Printing Office, 1975.

———. *Oversight on Housing and Urban Development Programs.* Pt. 1. Pub. L. No. Y4.B22/3: H81/67/pt. 1. 1973.

———. *Oversight on Housing and Urban Development Programs.* Pt 1. Pub. L. No. HRG-1973-BHU-0026. 1973.

———. *Oversight on Housing and Urban Development Programs—Chicago, Illinois, Hearings before the Subcommittee on Housing and Urban Affairs . . . , 93-1 . . . , March 30 and 31, 1973.* Pub. L. N. HRG-1973-BHU-0024. 1973.

———. *Oversight on Housing and Urban Development Programs, Washington, D.C.: Hearings before the Subcommittee on Housing and Urban Affairs of the Committee on Banking, Housing and Urban Affairs, United States Senate; Ninety-Third Congress, First Session,* 1973, http:// heinonline.org/HOL/Page?handle=hein.cbhear/osihudprio0001&id=1&size=3&collection =congrec.

U.S. Congress. Senate. Committee on Government Operations. Subcommittee on Executive Reorganization. *Urban Crisis in America: The Remarkable Ribicoff Hearings.* Washington, D.C.: Washington National Press, 1969.

U.S. Congress. Senate. Select Committee on Equal Educational Opportunity. *Equal Educational Opportunity. Hearings, Ninety-First Congress, Second Session [and Ninety-Second Congress, First Session]*. Washington, D.C.: U.S. Government Printing Office, 1970.

U.S. Department of Housing and Urban Development. *Homeownership for Lower Income Families (Section 235)*. Washington, D.C.: U.S. Dept. of Housing and Urban Development, 1971.

———. "Report of Staff Investigation of the Country Ridge Housing Development (Baltimore)." December 30, 1971. In U.S. Congress, House, Committee on Government Operations, Subcommittee on Legal and Monetary Affairs, *Defaults on FHA-Insured Mortgages*, pt. 2, *February 24; May 2, 3, 4, 1972*. Washington, D.C.: U.S. Government Printing Office, 1972.

U.S. Department of Housing and Urban Development. Office of Audit. *Audit Review of Section 235 Single Family Housing*. Washington, D.C.: U.S. Dept. of Housing and Urban Development, 1971.

U.S. Federal Housing Administration. *Underwriting Manual: Underwriting Analysis under Title II, Section 203 of the National Housing Act*. Washington, D.C.: U.S. Government Printing Office, 1938.

———. "A New Small-Home Ownership Program." *Insured Mortgage Portfolio*, February 1940.

U.S. Federal Trade Commission. *Economic Report on Installment Credit and Retail Sales Practices of District of Columbia Retailers*. Washington, D.C.: U.S. Government Printing Office, 1968.

U.S. House of Representatives. Congressional Black Caucus. "A Position on Housing." April 2, 1972. Urban Archives, Housing Association of Delaware Valley, box 38, Position Paper of Congressional Black Caucus, Temple University, Philadelphia, Pa.

U.S. National Advisory Commission on Civil Disorders. *Report of the National Advisory Commission on Civil Disorders*. Washington, D.C.: U.S. Government Printing Office, 1968.

U.S. President's Commission on Housing. *The Report of the President's Commission on Housing*. Washington, D.C.: President's Commission on Housing, 1982, http://catalog.hathitrust.org /api/volumes/oclc/8493725.html.

U.S. President's Task Force on Low Income Housing. *Toward Better Housing for Low Income Families: The Report of the President's Task Force on Low Income Housing*. Washington, D.C.: U.S. Government Printing Office, 1970.

Vale, Lawrence J., and Yonah Freemark. "From Public Housing to Public-Private Housing." *Journal of the American Planning Association* 78, no. 4 (September 1, 2012): 379–402, https:// doi.org/10.1080/01944363.2012.737985.

Van Dusen, Richard C. "Civil Rights and Housing." *Urban Lawyer* 5 (1973): 576.

Viorst, Milton. "The Blacks Who Work for Nixon." *New York Times*, November 29, 1970, 260.

Voluntary Home Mortgage Credit Program. "First Annual Report of the Administrator," Washington, D.C.: Administrator, Housing and Home Finance Agency, 1955, https://babel .hathitrust.org/cgi/pt?id=mdp.39015076028250;view=1up;seq=1.

Von Eschen, Penny M. *Race against Empire: Black Americans and Anticolonialism, 1937–1957*. Ithaca, N.Y.: Cornell University Press, 1997.

von Hoffman, Alexander. "Calling upon the Genius of Private Enterprise: The Housing and Urban Development Act of 1968 and the Liberal Turn to Public-Private Partnerships." *Studies in American Political Development* 27, no. 2 (2013): 165–94, https://doi.org/10.1017 /S0898588X13000102.

———. *Enter the Housing Industry, Stage Right: A Working Paper on the History of Housing Policy.* Cambridge, Mass.: Joint Center for Housing Studies, Harvard University, 2008.

———. "High Ambitions: The Past and Future of American Low-Income Housing Policy." *Housing Policy Debate* 7, no. 3 (1996): 423–46, https://doi.org/10.1080/10511482.1996.9521228.

———. *House by House, Block by Block: The Rebirth of American Urban Neighborhoods.* New York: Oxford University Press, 2004.

———. *Let Us Continue: Housing Policy in the Great Society.* Pt. 1. Cambridge, Mass.: Joint Center for Housing Studies, Harvard University, 2009.

Walker, Tom. "Housing Freeze Evil or Good?" *Atlanta Constitution*, February 4, 1973, 6.

Ward, Alex. "Employee Protests Heard by Romney." *Washington Post*, October 13, 1970, 1.

Ward, Alex, and Joseph Whitaker. "100 at Rally Protest U.S. Bias," *Washington Post*, November 3, 1970, 2.

Warden, Philip. "Negroes Pay Color Tax—King." *Chicago Tribune*, December 16, 1966, sec. A.

Washington, Betty. "Every Morning, a War on Rats: At 6:30, the Day Begins Drearily in Westside Flat." *Chicago Defender*, March 1, 1966, 1.

Waters, Enoch P. "Urban League Says Chicagoans Paid Huge 'Color Tax.'" *Atlanta Daily World*, May 25, 1961.

Weaver, Robert. "Departmental Policy Governing Equal Opportunity in HUD Operations and Programs," January 23, 1967. Papers of the NAACP, Part 28: Special Subject Files, 1966–1970, Group IV, series A, Administrative File, General Office File, Manuscript Division, Library of Congress.

Weaver, Robert Clifton. *The Urban Complex: Human Values in Urban Life.* New York: Doubleday, 1964.

Weaver, Timothy. "Urban Crisis: The Genealogy of a Concept." *Urban Studies* 54, no. 9 (July 1, 2017): 2039–55, https://doi.org/10.1177/0042098016640487.

Welless, Benjamin. "Romney Appoints 2 Negroes to Fill Major Positions: Assistant Secretaries Picked for Equal Opportunity and Metropolitan Programs." *New York Times*, January 26, 1969, 1.

Whitaker, Joseph D. "HUD Gives Promotions to 42 Aides." *Washington Post, Times Herald*, October 29, 1970, B5.

"The White House Press Conference with Daniel Patrick Moynihan," April 8, 1969. Box 78, folder State of the Union, 1970–1972, HUD, Office of the Under Secretary Richard C. Van Dusen, 1969–72, Record Group 207, National Archives and Records Administration, College Park, Md.

"White House Said to Plan Freeze on Public Housing: Moratorium on Public Housing Reported Administration Plan." *New York Times*, December 23, 1972.

Wiese, Andrew. *Places of Their Own: African American Suburbanization in the Twentieth Century.* Chicago: University of Chicago Press, 2009.

Williams, Bob. "Seek Hate Combine in Heights Bombing: Community Pledges Fair Housing Aid." *Cleveland Call and Post*, July 2, 1966, 1A.

Williams, Rhonda Y. *The Politics of Public Housing: Black Women's Struggles against Urban Inequality.* New York: Oxford University Press, 2004.

———. "'We're Tired of Being Treated Like Dogs': Poor Women and Power Politics in Black Baltimore." *Black Scholar* 31, no. 3/4 (Fall/Winter 2001): 31–41, https://jstor.org/stable /41069812. Accessed September 11, 2018.

Wilson, Harry B., Jr. "Exploiting the Home-Buying Poor: A Case Study of Abuse of the National Housing Act." *Saint Louis University Law Journal* 17, no. 4 (Summer 1973): 525–71.

Wilson, Warren. "Why We Did It: Looters." *Chicago Daily Defender*, August 23, 1965, 1.

"Winners Assembled for Breakthrough." *BusinessWeek*, February 28, 1970, 35.

Witcover, Jules. "President OKs Revenue Sharing at Independence Hall Ceremony: Revenue Sharing." *Los Angeles Times*, October 21, 1972, A1.

"Women Are Poverty War Force: Johnson." *Chicago Tribune*, June 29, 1966, sec. B.

Wood, Robert E. "B of A Acts to Show Students 'The Establishment' Also Cares." *Los Angeles Times*, May 12, 1970, C7.

Woods, L. L. "The Federal Home Loan Bank Board, Redlining, and the National Proliferation of Racial Lending Discrimination, 1921–1950." *Journal of Urban History* 38, no. 6 (April 9, 2012): 1036–59, https://doi.org/10.1177/0096144211435126.

"Words of the Week." *Jet*, March 8, 1973.

Wright, Richard. *Native Son.* New York: Perennial, 2003.

Wright Rigueur, Leah. *The Loneliness of the Black Republican: Pragmatic Politics and the Pursuit of Power.* Princeton: Princeton University Press, 2017, http://dx.doi.org/10.23943/princeton/9780691159010.001.0001.

Yinger, John. "An Analysis of Discrimination by Real Estate Brokers," February 1975, https://eric.ed.gov/?id=ED106410.

Yudis, Anthony. "Both Critics, Experts Have Second Thoughts: Not Housing So Much as Environment." *Boston Globe*, May 14, 1972, 5.

Zelizer, Julian E. *The Fierce Urgency of Now: Lyndon Johnson, Congress, and the Battle for the Great Society.* Reprint. New York: Penguin, 2015.

INDEX

Page numbers in italics refer to illustrations.